Westminster Pelican Commentaries
Edited by D. E. Nineham

*Revelation*

# *Revelation*

J. P. M. SWEET

The Westminster Press
PHILADELPHIA

The Bible text in this publication is from the *Revised Standard Version* of the Bible, copyright 1946 and 1952 by the Division of Christian Education, National Council of Churches, and used by permission.

Published by The Westminster Press®
Philadelphia, Pennsylvania

PRINTED IN THE UNITED STATES OF AMERICA

9 8 7 6 5 4 3 2 1

Library of Congress Cataloging in Publication Data

Sweet, John Philip McMurdo.
   Revelation.

   (Westminster Pelican commentaries)
   Bibliography: p.
   Includes indexes.
   1. Bible. N.T. Revelation—Commentaries.
I. Bible. N.T. Revelation. English. Revised standard.
1979. II. Title. III. Series.
BS2825.3.S93      228'.07'7      78-26383
ISBN 0-664-21375-8
ISBN 0-664-24262-6 pbk.

# Contents

Editorial Foreword     ix

Acknowledgments     x

References, Abbreviations and Technical Terms     xi

Bibliography     xiv

Map     xvi

INTRODUCTION     1

1. Apocalyptic     1
2. Synopsis     5
3. Interpretation     13
   (a) Hebrew imagery     13
   (b) Daniel and the Lord's Apocalypse     17
4. Date     21
   (a) The historical argument     22
   (b) The psychological argument     24
5. Situation     27
   (a) Christians and Jews     28
   (b) Compromise with pagan society     31
   (c) John's view     34
6. Authorship and composition     35
   (a) Unity     35
   (b) John in tradition     36
      (i) John the apostle     36
      (ii) Pseudonymity     37
      (iii) Another John     38

(c) Internal evidence 38
  (i) Asia 38
  (ii) Old Testament 39
  (iii) New Testament 40
  (iv) Liturgy 41
  (v) The mind of the author 42
(d) Structure 44

7. Place in the New Testament 47
(a) How it got there 47
(b) Is it Christian? 48
  (i) Hope deferred 48
  (ii) Vengeance 49
  (iii) The wrath of the Lamb 50

Outline 52

COMMENTARY

1 Prologue 55
  1.1–3      Title 57
  1.4–11     John's letter 60
  1.12–20    The vision of the Son of man 69

2–3  The Letters to the Seven Churches 75
  2.1–7      To the church in Ephesus 78
  2.8–11     To the church in Smyrna 83
  2.12–17    To the church in Pergamum 87
  2.18–29    To the church in Thyatira 91
  3.1–6      To the church in Sardis 97
  3.7–13     To the church in Philadelphia 101
  3.14–22    To the church in Laodicea 105

4–5  The Heavenly Liturgy 111
  4.1–11     The heavenly temple 114
  5.1–14     The enthronement of the Lamb 121

# CONTENTS

6–7   The Seven Seals Opened     133

    6.1–8     The four horsemen     136

    6.9–11     The fifth seal: the cry of the martyrs   141

    6.12–17     The sixth seal: the wrath of the Lamb   143

    7.1–8     The sealing of God's servants   146

    7.9–17     Beyond the great tribulation   149

8–14   The Seven Trumpets     155

    8.1–5     The prayers of the saints   158

    8.6–13     The first four trumpets   161

    9.1–12     The fifth trumpet and the first woe – locusts   165

    9.13–21     The sixth trumpet and the second woe – cavalry   170

10.1–11.14   The Little Scroll and the Two Witnesses   175

    10.1–11     The little scroll   175

    11.1–14     The two witnesses   180

11.15–13.18   The Seventh Trumpet and the Third Woe   190

    11.15–19     Heavenly liturgy   191

    12.1–6     The woman and the dragon   193

    12.7–12     The expulsion of the dragon   198

    12.13–17     The woman and the dragon – continued   202

    13.1–10     The beast from the sea   206

    13.11–18     The beast from the earth   213

14   The Triumph of the Gospel     220

    14.1–5     The followers of the Lamb   220

    14.6–12     The gospel   223

    14.13–20     The Son of man: harvest and vintage   228

# CONTENTS

15.1–22.5  The Seven Bowls: The Harlot and the
           Bride                                        235
  15.1–8      The song of Moses and of the Lamb         238
  16.1–9      The first four bowls                      242
  16.10–21    The last three bowls                      245
  17.1–6      The great harlot                          252
  17.7–11     The harlot and the beast                  255
  17.12–18    The harlot, the beast and ten kings       260

18.1–24   The Lament over Babylon                       264
  18.1–8      The judgment of Babylon (1)               264
  18.9–19     The lament for Babylon                    270
  18.20–24    The judgment of Babylon (2)               273

  19.1–10     The vindication of the saints             276
  19.11–16    The coming of Christ                      281
  19.17–21    The defeat of the beasts                  284
  20.1–6      The millennium                            286
  20.7–10     The rebellion of Gog                      290
  20.11–15    The last judgment                         293
  21.1–8      A new heaven and a new earth              295
  21.9–21     The new Jerusalem                         300
  21.22–22.5  The healing of the nations: paradise
              regained                                  307

  22.6–21     Come, Lord Jesus!                         313

Index of References
Index of Authors
Index of Subjects

# Editorial Foreword

Biblical commentaries are of various kinds. Some are intended solely for the specialist; others are devotional commentaries meant simply to help the Christian believer in his prayer and meditation. The commentaries in this series belong to neither class. Though they are based on full scholarly study and deal with technical points wherever necessary, the aim throughout has been to bring out the meaning the evangelists intended to convey to their original readers. Since that meaning was religious, it is hoped that the commentaries, while being of interest to readers of any religious persuasion or none, and giving a fair indication of the current position in gospel study, will help Christian readers to a deeper and more informed appreciation of the gospels.

Technical terms have been avoided wherever possible; where used they have been fully explained in the Introductions, and readers are advised to read the Introduction to each volume before beginning on the commentary proper. The extended introduction to the volume on Mark is in some degree intended as an introduction to the series as a whole.

# *Acknowledgments*

I would like to thank the General Editor of the SCM Pelican Commentaries, Dennis Nineham, Warden of Keble College, Oxford, for his invitation to write this commentary, and for his stimulating teaching, patient encouragement and constructive criticism over many years: Audrey Brooks, who typed it; Andrew Lake, who made the indexes; Jean Cunningham, who prepared it for the press; my daughter Alison, who made the map; and many colleagues and pupils for help and advice, especially Richard Bauckham, Colin Hemer, Vivian Nutton, Stephen Pattison and Christopher Rowland.

I owe much to the late R. H. Lightfoot, who left me his copy of Lohmeyer's commentary on Revelation, and to the late Alan Richardson and the members of his seminar at Nottingham University, 1956–57, who kindled my interest in Revelation. I owe most of all to my wife.

*Cambridge*                                                                                    J.P.M.S.
*November 1978*

# References, Abbreviations and Technical Terms

The biblical text used is the *Revised Standard Version*.

The titles of the books of the Bible receive their customary abbreviations. Biblical references are given by chapter and verse, and where necessary also by section of verse; thus Heb. 1.3a means the first half of verse 3 of chapter 1 of the Epistle to the Hebrews.

Articles in periodicals are cited by the abbreviated title of the periodical, followed by the volume number and its date, then the page number. Standard collections of documents are referred to by the editor's name or an abbreviated title, followed by volume and/or page numbers.

Commentaries and books listed in the bibliography are usually referred to by the author's name only (except where there are two by the same author).

| | |
|---|---|
| Apocrypha | The fourteen books, or parts of books, found in LXX but not the Hebrew Bible. The word means 'hidden', and refers to books which are spurious, or of unknown date and origin, or suitable for the initiated only. |
| *AP* | R. H. Charles, *Apocrypha and Pseudepigrapha of the Old Testament* I–II, Clarendon Press 1913. |
| *c.* | *circa*, about |
| *ECW* | *Early Christian Writings*, translated by M. Staniforth, Penguin Books, 1968 |
| ET | English translation |
| *ExpT* | *Expository Times*, Edinburgh |
| Gk. | Greek |
| gloss | explanatory comment |
| Heb. | Hebrew |

| | |
|---|---|
| Ibid. | In the same work |
| *JBL* | *Journal of Biblical Literature*, Philadelphia |
| *JTS* | *Journal of Theological Studies*, Oxford |
| LXX | The Greek version of the Old Testament, the Septuagint, so called because it was believed to be the work of seventy-two translators working independently, and by a miracle producing an identical version in seventy-two days. It differs considerably from the Hebrew text on which our English translations are based. |
| MS (S) | manuscript(s) – the NT books, like all early writings, were copied by hand. This could lead to mistakes of eye or ear, and to conscious or unconscious alterations by copyists to improve style or sense. But in addition to the Greek MSS, we have the 'versions' (translations into other ancient languages like Latin and Syriac) and citations from early Christian writers (the 'Fathers'): all these, referred to as 'ancient authorities' by RSV in its footnotes, enable us to establish the original text with considerable confidence. When MSS differ we talk of 'variant readings'; the few cases where it is not easy to be sure which of the 'variants' is the 'true reading' are discussed in the commentary. |
| NEB | New English Bible (1970) |
| *NovT* (Suppl.) | *Novum Testamentum* (Supplements), Leiden |
| NT | New Testament |
| *NTS* | *New Testament Studies*, Cambridge |
| op. cit. | work already cited |
| OT | Old Testament |
| par. | parallel – in a reference to the synoptic gospels; e.g. 'Matt. 24 par.' indicates reference to the parallel passages in Mark and Luke as well |
| RSV | Revised Standard Version of the Bible (1952) |
| RV | Revised Version of the Bible (1885) |
| S–B | H. P. Strack and P. Billerbeck, *Kommentar zum Neuen Testament aus Talmud und Midrasch*, Munich, 1922–28. |

| | |
|---|---|
| Stevenson | J. Stevenson (ed.), *A New Eusebius*, SPCK and Macmillan, New York, 1957. |
| variant | see under MS(S) |
| Vermes | G. Vermes, *The Dead Sea Scrolls in English*, Penguin Books, 1962 |
| *ZNW* | *Zeitschrift für die neutestamentliche Wissenschaft*, Berlin |

# Bibliography

COMMENTARIES

Detailed and scholarly:

Swete, H. B., *The Apocalypse of St. John*, Macmillan, 1906.

Beckwith, I., *The Apocalypse of John*, Macmillan, New York, 1919.

Charles, R. H., *Revelation* I–II (International Critical Commentary), T. & T. Clark and Scribner's, 1920.

Lohmeyer, E., *Die Offenbarung des Johannes* (Handbuch zum Neuen Testament 16), 2nd ed., ed. G. Bornkamm, J. C. B. Mohr, Tübingen, 1953.

Kraft, H., *Die Offenbarung des Johannes* (Handbuch zum Neuen Testament 16a), J. C. B. Mohr, Tübingen, 1974. This has the most complete and up-to-date bibliography.

For the reader without ancient languages:

Preston, R. H. and Hanson, A. T., *The Revelation of St John the Divine* (Torch Bible Commentaries), SCM Press and Macmillan, New York, 1949.

Farrer, A. M., *The Revelation of St John the Divine*, Clarendon Press, 1964.

Caird, G. B., *The Revelation of St John the Divine* (New Testament Commentaries), A. & C. Black and Harper & Row, 1966.

Morris, L., *Revelation*, Tyndale Press and Eerdmans, 1969.

Beasley-Murray, G. R., *The Book of Revelation* (New Century Bible), Oliphants, 1974.

STUDIES

Ramsay, Sir William, *The Letters to the Seven Churches of Asia*, Hodder & Stoughton and Armstrong, 1904.

Carrington, P., *The Meaning of Revelation*, SPCK, 1931.

Scott, E. F., *The Book of Revelation*, SCM Press, 1939, Scribner's, 1940.

Stauffer, E., *Christ and the Caesars*, ET SCM Press, 1952, Westminster Press, 1955, ch. XI.

Niles, D. T., *As Seeing the Invisible*, Harper & Row, 1961, SCM Press, 1962.

Daniélou, J., *Primitive Christian Symbols*, ET Helicon Press (Compass Books) and Burns & Oates, 1964.

Prigent, P., *Apocalypse et Liturgie*, Delachaux et Niestlé, 1964.

Feuillet, A., *The Apocalypse*, ET Alba House, New York, 1965.

Rissi, M., *Time and History*, ET John Knox Press, Richmond, Va, 1966.

— *The Future of the World*, ET (Studies in Biblical Theology, 2.23), SCM Press and Allenson, 1972.

Minear, P. S., *I Saw a New Earth*, Corpus Books, Washington, 1968.

Wilcox, M., *I saw Heaven Opened*, Inter-Varsity Press, 1975.

## ON APOCALYPTIC

Charles, R. H., *The Apocrypha and Pseudepigrapha of the Old Testament* I–II, Clarendon Press, 1913 (cited as *AP*).

Rowley, H. H., *The Relevance of Apocalyptic* (1944), 3rd ed., Lutterworth Press, 1963, Association Press, 1964.

Russell, D. S., *Between the Testaments*, SCM Press and Muhlenberg Press, 1960.

— *The Method and Message of Jewish Apocalyptic*, SCM Press and West- minster Press, 1964.

Hennecke, E., *New Testament Apocrypha* II, ET Lutterworth Press, 1965, Westminster Press, 1966, reissued SCM Press, 1974, pp. 579ff.

Morris, L., *Apocalyptic*, Inter-Varsity Press, 1973.

To all these and many more the present commentary is indebted, particularly to Farrer, Caird and Minear, and to C. J. Hemer, whose Ph.D. dissertation on 'The Letters to the Seven Churches of Asia' Manchester University, 1969, awaits publication.

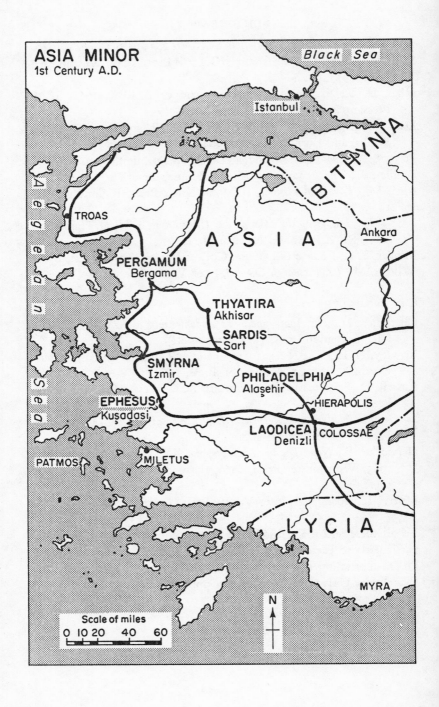

ASIA MINOR
1st Century A.D.

Black Sea

BITHYNIA

Istanbul

TROAS

Aegean Sea

ASIA

Ankara

PERGAMUM
Bergama

THYATIRA
Akhisar

SARDIS
Sart

SMYRNA
Izmir

PHILADELPHIA
Alaşehir

HIERAPOLIS

EPHESUS
Kuşadasi

LAODICEA
Denizli

COLOSSAE

PATMOS

MILETUS

LYCIA

MYRA

Scale of miles
0  10 20    40    60

N

# Introduction

Reading through Revelation for the first time is, for many people, like visiting a famous but remote tropical island. They have seen photographs of its scenery – some of haunting beauty, some bizarre, some savagely ugly – but before they begin their exploration they need a large-scale map, to show where they are going and how it all fits together. This Introduction tries to meet that need with an interpretative account of the contents of the book and of the thought-world from which it sprang. The first principle of good interpretation, as of good exploring, is to accept the strangeness of the terrain and try to see it on its own terms, not blinkered by inherited assumptions. However, the reader who wants to start exploring straight away may skip much, or all, of this Introduction; there are references back to it in the commentary and in the indexes.

## I. APOCALYPTIC

The book announces itself as *the revelation of Jesus Christ*. 'Revelation' (=unveiling) is the Latin equivalent of the Greek 'apocalypse' (=uncovering). It could refer to the disclosure of a specific fact or of a comprehensive picture of things hidden – past, present and future. Such revelations had become an influential literary and theological genre in Judaism, called 'apocalyptic', of which the book of Daniel is the archetype.[a] There are a number of recurring characteristics. First and foremost is the conviction that the present is the final age of world history, and that the end is imminent, but the author writes under the guise of a prophet or hero of the past, like Enoch, who is

a On Daniel see pp. 17–19; see also Wisd. 10–19 and II Esdras in the Apocrypha, and the texts translated and annotated in R. H. Charles, *AP* II. For further reading on apocalyptic, see the section in the Bibliography (above).

I

conducted in vision round heaven and hell by an interpreting angel, and is told the fate of his people up to the end of history (that is, the author's own day), for their encouragement in a world which *seems* to be out of God's control. Linked with this pessimistic view of the present is a dualistic and deterministic theology, which sees this world as given over to Satan and his angels until God and his angels finally intervene, and universal judgment ushers in the world to come. There is luxuriant elaboration of OT prophecies and motifs, particularly the idea that 'the end will be as the beginning', with cosmic catastrophes and Paradise restored. There is cryptic reference to current affairs in bizarre allegories and symbols, sometimes decoded, but for the most part obvious enough to the original audience, like our political cartoons. Some acquaintance with apocalyptic is indispensable for the serious explorer.

But if Revelation was based on the assumption – evidently wrong – that the world was about to end, of what further importance can it be? The question concerns the teaching of Jesus too: Revelation can be seen as an updating of his apocalypse, given on the Mount of Olives (see pp. 19–21). The question may be easier to answer if we consider first the nature of biblical prophecy.

A prophet in the biblical sense is not simply one who predicts the future, but one who sees into the realities that lie behind the appearances of this world and sets them out, with the consequences he sees, so that people may act accordingly. What matters is the truth of his vision of God's nature and will, and of the world in that light. Lacking this, even successful predictions will soon be forgotten; given this, the prophet's words may still be of value to future generations, even if his exact predictions prove wrong. In a world which was accepting a deified state under a deified head as the source of all salvation, and in a church which was accepting this valuation at the expense of its proper witness to the rule of God, Revelation uncovered the missing dimension, so that Christians should act according to the will of the God they could not see, rather than of the Caesar they could – so that at whatever cost, they should put eternal destiny before apparent security and prosperity in the present.

If such an apocalypse or 'uncovering' asserts that the time when the real will break through the appearances is very close, and the breakthrough does not happen as and when predicted, the analysis may still have continuing value. Illusions cannot reign for ever; the sooner men come to terms with reality the better, and as Marxists know, to expect the breakthrough is to help it to come. There is an analogy with the biblical apocalypses in the writings of modern ecologists who examine current assumptions and practices in the light of the realities of population growth, pollution, wastage of natural resources, increasing political violence etc. The pictures they paint may be lurid, because of the intensity both of their own apprehension of these unrecognized facts and of their desire to wake us up before it is too late. Their specific predictions of disaster may fail to come off, but their basic perceptions about exploitation, irresponsibility and complacency may still be sound, so that the longer they are ignored the greater the ultimate disaster.

We may note further analogies with modern concern for the future of the world. First, much of the writing is scientific and fully intelligible only to those with scientific training, because the authors are appealing to those who, as scientists, have the knowledge to shape the world's future. Those who read their writings without scientific training may misunderstand and misapply them. By the same token, Revelation was written for people versed in the Jewish scriptures who had been entrusted (they believed) with God's truth for the world's salvation. Readers not so versed are likely to misunderstand and misapply Revelation.

On the other hand, much of the reaction against the exploitative tendencies of the Western world is more aesthetic and ethical than scientific. William Blake and D. H. Lawrence (whose last work *Apocalypse*[b] was devoted to Revelation) have been the focus of a growing revolt against the life-diminishing inhumanity of modern industrial society, and the 'counter-culture', whose making has been charted by Theodore Roszak,[c] appeals to the apocalyptic tradition (often explicitly to Revelation) and echoes its symbolism in protest against the tyranny of what men take to be objective fact. By the same token, the biblical symbolism of Revelation, often bizarre and

[b] D. H. Lawrence, *Apocalypse*, Heinemann 1931, Penguin Books 1974.
[c] Theodore Roszak, *The Making of a Counter Culture*, Doubleday 1969, Faber & Faber 1970, especially the last two chapters.

repulsive, is integral to its protest against the Graeco-Roman vision of the world.

In this movement there is the conviction that exposure of the false assumptions on which modern society is based must be backed up by the witness of an alternative style of living; truth of belief and quality of life are inseparable. By the same token Revelation attacks idolatry and immorality within the church ($2^{14,\ 20}$), while witness to the truth and purity of life are the positive themes of the sections structured by the seven trumpets (8–14) and the seven bowls (15–22). Christians inherited from the Jews the belief that failure to acknowledge God as Creator leads to idolatry, and that idolatry leads to corruption of mind and body, and of the whole creation; likewise they believed that true acknowledgment of God, on the pattern of Jesus' response to his Father, was the secret of salvation for the whole world.

There is a further parallel in that ecologists' predictions of doom and calls for repentance are rejected by many who are equally informed and equally sincere: doom is *not* imminent; man through science and technology has learnt to control his environment and can cope with any crisis that lies ahead. Sackcloth (cf. Rev. $11^3$) is a symbol of lack of faith and loss of nerve. Ever-increasing economic growth will lead to ever-increasing prosperity (salvation) for the whole world. By the same token there would have been many sincere Christians, especially those from a Greek background, who rejected the Jewish-Christian expectation of imminent divine intervention, which had already several times been raised to fever-pitch with disastrous results. They would have soft-pedalled final resurrection in favour of spiritual rebirth now, and seen Christ's promise of coming on the clouds as fulfilled in his spiritual presence in the church. They would have seen the empire as God's ordering of the world (cf. Rom. $13^{1-7}$) and the apocalyptic attitude as false and subversive; Antichrist was not the emperor but a demonic power threatening the ordered world and kept at bay by the empire itself (cf. II Thess. $2^{3-7}$).

It is possible, then, that in spite of its time-bound imagery and unfulfilled promises of Christ's return Revelation may still be saying things which are of timeless relevance for the world's health. Many will regard its vision as false and injurious; historically, apocalyptic has encouraged both passive detachment from the world and active

4

subversion, and the example of the 'counter-culture' warns us of the need to see things also from the point of view of the governing classes and of those who try to work with the present order. But the validity and value of a protest can only be assessed in terms of the situation in which it was uttered. This we will try to elucidate later, so far as Revelation is concerned (pp. 27–35), but first it may be helpful to those unfamiliar with the terrain to give a synopsis of Revelation (from the point of view we are adopting) and some guides to interpretation.

## 2. SYNOPSIS

### Chapter 1

The first thing to notice about this apocalypse is that it is not an esoteric treatise but in the form of a letter (1⁴), to be read aloud to the congregations in seven cities of the Roman province of Asia (what is now western Turkey), and that it purports to be written not by Enoch or Elijah but by someone who calls himself simply God's *servant, John.* He was on the island of Patmos, not far from Ephesus, the chief city of Asia and a great Christian centre: Paul worked at Ephesus, and according to later tradition so did the apostle John, who was widely held to have written both the Gospel and the Revelation. But the book itself gives no hint of this (see pp. 36–8).

It begins with this John's vision on the Lord's day of *one like a son of man* (a Christian title for Jesus as judge of the universe, drawn from Dan. 7), who walks among the *seven golden lamps*, which symbolize the *seven churches*. To the *angel* of each church, taken as personifying the members of each congregation, John is commanded to write the words of this 'son of man', in which he takes stock of their position, with encouragement and warning, to prepare them for his coming.

### Chapters 2 and 3

The letters are full of biblical symbolism and local reference. The first, to Ephesus, warns of *false apostles* and of *Nicolaitans*, who in the third and fourth letters, to Pergamum and Thyatira, are linked with idolatry and fornication by reference to the biblical villains Balaam, Balak and Jezebel, who tried to introduce heathen religion and morals into Israel. The second and sixth letters, to Smyrna and Philadelphia, speak of opposition from *false Jews*, who bear the name of God's people but do Satan's work: they attack the church's faith, while the Nicolaitans adulterate it. The fifth church, Sardis, is asleep (*dead*); the seventh, Laodicea, is complacent (*lukewarm*). Christ calls the churches to repent, to be faithful unto death and to reproduce his witness to his Father, with promises for *him who conquers* and the demand for ears to *hear what the Spirit is saying* – the messages, like the gospel parables, would not have been altogether comfortable for their original hearers.

### Chapters 4 and 5

The letters set the scene on earth and show that the church's chief dangers are internal: complacency, somnolence and compromise with worldly values. But there is also real danger of external attack, and the scene now shifts to *heaven*, where John is shown things which would have served to strengthen Christians in the face of Jewish slander and against all the dangers, natural and supernatural, of their world. First he sees all the creatures of the universe ranged in ceaseless worship round the *throne* of the heavenly temple, on which is seated one whose description evokes Isaiah's and Ezekiel's visions of the divine glory. He is the Creator, and he holds a *scroll, sealed with seven seals*, which can only be opened by a *Lamb*, who has won the right to open it by his sacrificial death, the marks of which he still bears. His victory is celebrated in a *new song* – throughout the book the heavenly hymns serve to interpret the visions: here the point is that his death, like that of the Passover lamb in Egypt, has ransomed out of slavery a people for God's service. The themes of Genesis and Exodus, of creation and redemption, dominate the book.

### Chapter 6

The Lamb now *opens the seals* of the scroll or book, which symbolizes the scriptures, as containing God's whole will for the world. At the first four unsealings *horses* of different colours, evoking the visions of Zechariah, come forth: their riders, the notorious four horsemen, are armed with weapons of conquest – *sword, famine* and *pestilence* – which refer both to Jesus' prophecy on the Mount of

Olives (Mark 13³⁻⁸ par.) and, probably, to catastrophic events of John's own day. The opening of the fifth seal reveals the souls of *martyrs* under the heavenly altar, calling to God for vengeance on *those who dwell upon the earth*, and the opening of the sixth shows what they have prayed for: the demolition of the earth's fabric, leaving the earth-dwellers cowering before the face of the Enthroned One and *the wrath of the Lamb*.

## Chapter 7

Before the seventh *seal* is opened, there is an interlude while the servants of God are *sealed* as a sign of divine protection (such word-plays and such delays in the unfolding of the drama are characteristic), for preservation against supernatural attack. Their number is given as *a hundred and forty-four thousand*, the square of the *twelve* tribes or thousands of Israel (the church, in spite of Jewish slander, *is* the Israel of God, ransomed to serve him). Then John sees a *countless multitude* joining the worship of all the creatures round the throne, and is told that they have *come out of the great tribulation*, having *washed their clothes in the blood of the Lamb*, and are now for ever in the presence of God – not a different group from the hundred and forty-four thousand but the Israel of God seen in its ultimate inclusiveness and fulfilment.

We may sum up the message of the seals section (4–7) as 'assurance': the churches are to know that they have an inalienable status and ultimate security as God's people, and that the dangers and sufferings which threaten them are pre-ordained, part of the working out of Christ's victory, in which they share.

## Chapters 8 and 9

We might seem to have reached journey's end, but when the *seventh seal* is opened, there is *silence* in heaven for *half an hour*, followed by a heavenly incense-liturgy and *seven angels* blowing *trumpets*. Like the unsealings, the trumpet blasts bring disasters for the earth, but whereas those were natural these are supernatural; they are modelled on the ten plagues of Egypt, which led up to the exodus. As with the unsealings, the first four trumpet visions form a group, and the symbolism suggests that the disasters, the scorching of the earth and the poisoning of the waters, represent the recoil of men's arrogance and idolatry upon themselves and their world.

The last three trumpet visions are even more clearly defined as a group by the triple scream of *Woe!* from *an eagle flying in midheaven*. But though the first two *woes*, at the fifth and sixth trumpet blasts, step up the supernatural horrors with an invasion of demonic *locusts* from the *abyss* and of innumerable *cavalry* on *lion-headed horses* from the *river Euphrates* (the point of danger for both the Jews of the Old Testament and the eastern provinces of the Roman empire), and though men refuse to repent of their idolatries and immoralities, again the end is delayed.

### Chapters 10 and 11

Before the seventh trumpet blast and the *third woe* come a series of symbolic scenes. An angel comes down from heaven and gives John, who is now on earth, a *little scroll* which (like the prophet Ezekiel) he is to *eat*; he is then to *prophesy* (like Jeremiah) about many peoples and nations. This melts into the prophesying of the Lord's *two witnesses* for *three and a half years*, which in Daniel represents a limited period of tyranny and suffering for the faithful in Israel before final vindication. Their activity is introduced by an acted symbol: John is told to *measure the temple of God and its worshippers*, but to give the *court outside to be trampled by the nations for forty-two months* (= three and a half years), probably signifying inward protection for the church, the spiritual temple, in its witness-bearing, in the face of outward rejection and defeat. The two witnesses are a *torment* to the earth-dwellers but are finally killed by the *beast* which ascends from the abyss, and their corpses lie in *the street of the great city* which is *spiritually called Sodom and Egypt*, where their Lord *was crucified* ($11^8$ – a key verse for interpreting all John's geography). But like their Lord they are raised up and ascend to heaven; an earthquake shatters the city, and the survivors *give glory to God*. The seventh angel blows his trumpet, and heavenly hymns celebrate the reign of God and of his Christ and the destruction of the destroyers of the earth.

### Chapters 12 and 13

But again the end is not yet. The *third woe* has still to come, and it is introduced by a portent in the sky: a pregnant *woman*, arrayed with the lights of heaven, is faced by a *great red dragon*, which waits to devour her child. But her son, who is to rule the nations with a rod of iron (Ps. 2⁹), is caught up to God's throne (a reference to Jesus' exaltation – no mention here of his life and death, through which he triumphs)ᵈ and the woman *flees into the wilderness*, where she is to be preserved – again for three and a half years. She seems to represent a gallery of figures: Eve, the mother of all living; Israel, the mother of the Messiah (= Christ); Mary, the mother of Jesus; the church, mother of Christians – with overtones of pagan myths as well.

Now there is *war in heaven*: Michael, the champion of God's people, and his angels drive out the dragon and his angels, and the dragon, the *ancient serpent* of Gen. 3, who is also called the Devil and Satan, the *deceiver* and *accuser* of men, is thrown down to earth. A voice calls for rejoicing in *heaven*, where his accusations have been stilled by the blood of the Lamb, but '*woe to the earth*': this is the *third woe*, the descent of the devil who summons from the sea (or abyss) a *beast*, which mirrors his attributes as the Son mirrors the Father's, and which parodies the Son's death and resurrection as the devil parodies God; it can therefore appropriately be called Antichrist, which implies not just opposition to Christ but the claim to *be* Christ, as Satan claims to be God. This beast is a composite of the four beasts of Dan. 7, which represent world empires, and is to make war on the woman's *seed* or offspring, in fulfilment of God's words to the serpent (Gen. 3¹⁵), 'I will put enmity between your seed and her seed; he shall bruise your head and you shall bruise his heel.'

Taught by another *beast* (the third person of the satanic trinity, which counterfeits the powers of the Holy Spirit), the whole world accepts the first beast's divine claims with enthusiam; all who refuse to worship its *image* or be branded with its *mark* are destroyed. This second beast may represent the imperial priesthood, which propagated the emperor cult in Asia; the first beast is identified by the number of its name, *666*. Most probably this was not mysterious to John's

---

d Some scholars see here prediction of a birth and a battle in the future, but we take the reference to be to the birth and death of Jesus which set in motion the events leading up to the 'third woe'. John's vision contains elements of past and present as well as future.

hearers, as it has been to their successors, and stood for Nero – the personification of the Roman empire as a blasphemous totalitarian power, arrogating to itself divinity, engineering the adulation of its subjects and liquidating dissidents. This, which the world takes to be its supreme blessing, is the *third woe*, the final disaster.

### Chapter 14

The trumpet series is rounded off by further symbolic scenes: the Lamb with his one hundred and forty-four thousand, who have his *name*, not the mark of the beast, on their foreheads, stands inviolate on Mount Zion; an angel flying in midheaven balances the eagle's screams of 'Woe' with an *eternal gospel*; other angels declare the fall of *Babylon*, symbol of arrogance and enmity to God's people, and the *eternal torment* of those who worship the beast; one like *a son of man* appears, seated on a cloud, and more angels, who set in motion the reaping of the earth's *harvest* and the gathering of its *vintage*, which is trampled in the *wine press* of the wrath of God (figures taken from Joel 3 and Isa. 63). Again we might seem to have reached the end, but another series of disasters is to come.

Looking back over the trumpets section (8–14), we can see a kind of counterpoint. Men's idolatrous arrogance brings disasters which only harden them in their idolatry, and leads to eternal torment: Christian witness to God brings men temporal torment, but leads to repentance. God's Son and his saints defeat Satan in heaven: Satan's beasts defeat the Son and his saints on earth. Christians are called to take sides and choose between earthly and heavenly salvation (13$^{9f.}$, 14$^{12f.}$).

### Chapters 15 and 16

Now another series of angels, carrying *bowls* full of the final plagues of God's wrath, pour out another series of disasters, which again echo the plagues of Egypt. They seem merely to recapitulate the trumpet plagues, and like them they harden men in their blasphemies, but they are directed specifically against the beast's worshippers, its throne and its city, *Babylon*, which is made finally to drain the *cup of God's wrath*. Her nature and destruction are set out in the next two chapters.

## Chapters 17 and 18

One of the seven bowl-angels shows 'Babylon' to John as the *great harlot*, arrayed in purple and scarlet and jewels (a parody of the glorious woman of ch. 12) and seated on the *seven-headed beast*. She carries a *cup* to intoxicate the earth-dwellers with the *wine of her fornication*, and is herself *drunk with the blood of the saints* (a reference to Nero's massacre of Christians in AD 65). But the beast, whose seven heads are interpreted as a series of emperors which has nearly run its course, turns on the harlot in the person of one of the seven, who *ascends from the abyss* – a reference to the belief that Nero would return from the dead with armies from the east to take vengeance on Rome, which had turned against him.

Chapter 18 describes the harlot's destruction as the ruin of a great mercantile city, in language largely taken from Ezekiel's dirge over Tyre (the city of Jezebel, who contributes to the picture of the harlot as she had done already to that of the Christian prophetess of Thyatira in ch. 2).

Chapters 13–18 might seem to be simply a paean of hate against the Roman empire and its rulers, but they are interspersed with enigmatic warnings to Christians (13[9f.,] [18], 14[12f.], 16[15], 17[9], 18[4]) which confirm what the letters have already indicated, that John's main concern is to wake up the churches which are slipping into conformity with their world, at the expense of their witness to it. They must be shown its true nature and destiny under its glamour and power – the deadliness of compromise in spite of its apparent rewards, and the real rewards of witness to the truth in spite of its apparently suicidal folly.

## Chapters 19[1] – 22[5]

Heavenly hymns now celebrate Babylon's fall and *the marriage of the Lamb*, whose *bride*, the true City of God, replaces the harlot. Heaven is opened, and a horseman, who is identified by his attributes as the Son of man of the opening vision, appears with his saints as the conquering *Word of God*. The *two beasts* join battle against him but are thrown into *the lake of fire and brimstone*, and their armies are killed by *the sword which issues from his mouth*.

The *dragon*, however, is still not destroyed. He is *bound for a thousand years* in the abyss, while those who had not worshipped the beast rise from the dead and *reign with Christ for a thousand years*: this is the origin of the 'millennium' (= thousand-year period) which has dominated later speculation, although it occupies only a tiny part of John's canvas. At the end of it Satan is released and marches with a countless host against *the beloved city*, but *fire from heaven* consumes them, and Satan joins the two beasts in the *lake of fire*.

Now all the dead are gathered before the *great white throne* and judged according to two *books*: the register of their deeds, and the Lamb's register of the living. Earth and sky have fled away, and John sees *a new heaven and a new earth*, and the *holy city, new Jerusalem*, coming down from heaven, like a *bride* adorned for her husband. Her clothing has already been identified with the righteous deeds of the saints (19⁸), and her jewellery contrasts pointedly with the harlot's adornment, which symbolizes the luxury and immorality of the Roman world; the foundations of the true city are even now being laid on earth in the fidelity and purity of God's people. In fulfilment of the prophecies of Isaiah *the nations* and their *kings* bring in their glory. *The tree of life* grows in the city's street; its leaves are *for the healing of the nations*, and the curse of Gen. 3 is no more. The promises made in the letters to *him who conquers* are honoured, and all men find their eternal fulfilment in the worship of God and of the Lamb. It is deeply significant that John is shown the bride (21⁹) by one of the angels who carried the bowls of God's wrath and showed him the judgment of the harlot (17.1): divine vengeance and destruction go hand in hand with cleansing and re-creation.

### Chapter 22⁶⁻²⁰

The book is brought to a close by a series of personal admonitions and liturgical phrases (not unlike those found at the end of some of the Pauline letters), which pick up themes from the seven letters and from 1¹⁻³. This little prologue, which was perhaps added in the light of the book as a whole, indicates that it is to be *read aloud*, presumably (like Paul's letters) at the churches' Sunday gatherings, when they 'show forth the Lord's death till he comes' (I Cor. 11²⁶). '*Surely I am coming soon*'. Amen, Come, Lord Jesus! (22²⁰).

## 3. INTERPRETATION

### (a) Hebrew imagery

If the whole book was read aloud at one sitting (which would take about an hour and a half), it would have made its impact on its first hearers *as a whole*, like a poetic drama or an opera; indeed one should perhaps regard it as more like music than rational discourse. In that case the repetitions, delays and changes of key can be seen to contribute to a total effect which is emotional as much as rational, and the proportions of the whole are more important than the individual scenes. We must notice, then, that the visions of destruction are bracketed by the overarching vision of God the Creator and Redeemer (4, 5), who makes all things new (21, 22); carnage and chaos make way for the fulfilment of all men's dreams. But the fashioning of this new order is not just a divine fiat; it is bound up with the faithfulness of God's people now: the whole drama is itself bracketed by the message of Christ to those people, which is set out in 1–3 and 22⁶–end. The more we can learn of them and their situation, the better our understanding of the apocalyptic drama in its original impact.

If the broad sweep of the composition is what matters, it might be thought that minute attention to details is misplaced. There is some truth in this. The original hearers would not have had time to reflect on the details. The numbers and colours, the scriptural allusions, the heavenly hymns – all these things build up a cumulative impression; 'the medium is (almost) the message'. But even if the book was in the first instance read aloud as a whole, we can be sure that like Paul's letters it was subsequently pored over in detail, and we find, as in St John's Gospel, a texture of cross-references and allusions which is not accidental and repays close study, such as is attempted in the commentary. On the other hand, when Revelation came to be regarded as scripture, it was studied as a mine of literal information about the heavenly world and future events, which it was never intended to convey; and modern commentators, who are aware of its symbolic nature, may let their ingenuity in elucidating symbols and allusions take them beyond what the writer could have intended and what the hearers could have taken in. As a balance against over-attention to detail we should be sensitive to the general effect Revelation's imagery would have conveyed.

Broadly speaking, Hebrew imagery appealed to the ear rather than to the eye and created a dynamic psychological impression without necessarily evoking a picture in the mind.[e] Indeed much of it, if visualized, is merely bizarre, like the figure with a sword issuing from his mouth ($1^{16}$) or the composite beast with seven heads and ten horns ($13^1$), and the images are often kaleidoscopic, as with the heavenly woman of ch. 12, one meaning merging into another. The jewels in the description of the new Jerusalem ($21^{11-21}$) give by their very sound an impression of radiant beauty, in contrast with the abominations (*bdelugmata*) of the harlot ($17^{4f.}$).

The *numbers* which keep appearing contribute to the overall impression both by repetition and by their symbolic significance. For us such significance is residual; we say 'third time lucky' and thirteen means bad luck. But in the ancient world both letters and numbers were sacred – not merely conventional signs but structural elements of the cosmos, with magical power. The use of numbers in Revelation is not directly magical, but against this background it contributes to the general effect, heightened by parody and innuendo.

The meanings conveyed by specific numbers may be indicated as follows:

*Two* is the number of witness ($11^3$; cf. Deut. $19^{15}$).

✳ *Three* is the number of God ($1^{4f.}$); it is parodied at $16^{13}$.

✳ *Four* is the number of the universe ($7^1$). There are four seasons, winds, corners of the earth.

*Five*, the fingers of one hand, is a natural round number.

✳ *Six* is the number of Antichrist, seven minus one, the number of imperfection, penultimacy and evil. Its fundamental inadequacy is expressed in its intensification, *six hundred and sixty-six, the number of the beast* ($13^{18}$).

✳ *Seven* is four plus three, signifying completeness. There are seven

e See T. Boman, *Hebrew Thought Compared with Greek*, ET SCM Press and Westminster Press 1960, ch. 2, and our comment on $1^{12-20}$; also p. 125 below on seeing and hearing.

planets, days of the week, colours of the rainbow. It is parodied by Antichrist ($12^3$, $13^1$); the beast has *seven heads*, representing the deified emperoros of Rome, an overwhelmingly impressive appearance of unity, which is mocked by the inadequacy of 666. Antichrist's number is also three and a half ($11^9$, $13^5$; cf. Dan. $7^{25}$).

✷ *Eight* is the number of Jesus,[f] seven plus one, the first of a new series or 'week' – again parodied by Antichrist ($17^{11}$).

*Ten*, the fingers of both hands, is a natural round number, but lacks the symbolic richness of seven and twelve: *the ten horns which are ten kings* ($17^{12-14}$) are an undifferentiated collection rather than an integrated whole like the seven churches or twelve tribes.

✗ *Twelve* is four times three, like seven signifying wholeness, unity in diversity. There are twelve months, signs of the Zodiac, tribes of Israel, apostles of the Lamb ($21^{12-14}$).

Multiplication intensifies – retribution may be sevenfold (Gen. $4^{15, 24}$, Lev. $26^{18-27}$; contrast Matt. $18^{22}$). A square is a perfect figure – even more so a cube ($21^{16}$). 144,000 ($7^4$) is the square of the tribes of Israel, multiplied by a thousand.

These significances are not exhaustive, but may help to give the modern reader the feel.

The geography likewise is symbolical (see on $11^8$).[g] Like Guernica and Hiroshima for us, Sodom, Egypt, Babylon and Jerusalem were heavy with meaning. The 'great city', in whose street the witnesses lie, cannot any more than Vanity Fair be limited to one place and time. 'Those who dwell upon the earth' are all whose horizons are in practice bounded by this earth – the 'worldly', as we say – whether outside the church or in it. Likewise 'heaven-dwellers' ($12^{12}$, $13^6$)

[f] Numbers in both Greek and Hebrew were represented by letters of the alphabet – a = 1, b = 2 etc. (they did not have Arabic numerals) – and so any word or name could be given a numerical value by adding up its letters, a procedure called *isopsēphia* or *gēmatria*. Nero Caesar in Hebrew letters gave 666; Jesus in Greek letters gave 888 (see below on $13^{18}$).

For further discussion of the significance of numbers, see the commentaries of Swete, pp. cxxx–cxxxiii, and Beckwith, pp. 250–55; D. T. Niles, *As Seeing the Invisible*, pp. 29–31; D. H. Lawrence, *Apocalypse*, pp. 100–13.

[g] See P. S. Minear, 'The Cosmology of the Apocalypse', *Current Issues in NT Interpretation*, ed. W. Klassen and G. F. Snyder, SCM Press and Harper & Row 1962, pp. 23–37.

are not necessarily angels but those whose centre or treasure is in heaven, that is, with God.

Heaven and earth are in fact correlative terms – with the 'new earth' goes a 'new heaven' also ($21^1$). Heaven represents not a different world so much as the inward and spiritual behind the outward and physical, and comprehends paradoxically the abyss (see on $4^6$, $9^1$) which we think of as hell: heaven contains the spiritual powers behind all things in our world, both evil and good. Heavenly events are seen sometimes as determining earthly realities (angels expelled from heaven seduce men on earth – see on $8^{8-11}$), sometimes as determined by earthly realities (Christ's victory on the cross and Christian witness lie behind Satan's expulsion from heaven – see on $12^{7-12}$). See p. 113. Angels and demons likewise are the correlates of earthly authorities. People certainly believed in their literal existence, but the realities they represent are what matter.[h]

The Greek style of the book also plays its part: it is idiosyncratic and does frequent violence to grammar and syntax – not out of ignorance but (it seems) deliberately, to create a 'biblical' effect on the hearer.

The probability is that the writer, thinking in Hebrew or Aramaic, consciously or unconsciously carried over Semitic idioms into his Greek, and that his 'howlers' are deliberate attempts to reproduce the grammar of classical Hebrew at certain points – at other places he uses the same construction correctly and for the most part he keeps the rules; his command of tenses is better than that of other NT writers. The Greek translations of the Hebrew scriptures in the LXX strove for closeness to the original so much that the effect was often bizarre. John perhaps sought a similar effect, to establish the solidarity of his writings with the scriptures, which were regarded as the words of God – cf. the curse at $22^{18, 19}$, which perhaps inhibited the normal tendency of later scribes to tidy up the Greek.[i] Though in places bizarre, his style is usually clear, often powerful, sometimes poetical.

---

*h* See G. B. Caird, *Principalities and Powers*, Clarendon Press 1956.

*i* See Charles, *Revelation* I, pp. cxvii–clix, 'A Short Grammar of the Apocalypse'; C. G. Ozanne, 'The Language of the Apocalypse', *Tyndale House Bulletin* 16, 1965, pp. 3–9; G. Mussies, *The Morphology of Koine Greek as used in the Apocalypse* (*NovT* Suppl. 27), 1971 – an exhaustive examination of Rev. in comparison with non-literary Koine ('common') Greek.

Its effect is thus conveyed better by AV than by modern translations.

There is a logic, then, but it is more auditory than visual. There are constant echoes and evocations of biblical scenes heavy with theological meaning: the garden of Eden, the serpent and the tree; the plagues of Egypt, the exodus and Mount Sinai; Babel-Babylon; Elijah and Jezebel. What John sees is again and again interpreted by what he hears; for example, the meaning of *the lamb standing, as though it had been slain,* is given by the new song of the living creatures and elders ($5^{6-10}$). The refrain of the letters to the churches is *He who has an ear, let him hear.* 'Hearing' opens up the whole realm of scripture, the words of God which demand man's obedient response. 'Blessed is he who reads aloud the words of the prophecy, and blessed are those who hear, and who keep what is written therein; for the time is near' ($1^3$).

## (b) Daniel and the Lord's Apocalypse

'For the time is near': the theme is taken up in the epilogue ($22^{10}$), in clear allusion to Dan. 12. Among the many differences between John's world and ours, one of the sharpest is the conviction that the last chapter of world history, which had been set in motion by Christ's coming, was very soon to be completed by his parousia or return and the resurrection of the dead for final judgment.

To enter into this 'eschatological' way of thinking we may start with the book of Daniel,[j] which from both the literary and the theological point of view is indispensable for understanding Revelation. In the first six chapters the anonymous author uses stories of Jewish exiles in Babylon in the sixth century BC who stood firm under pressure to give up their faith, in order to encourage his compatriots to stand firm at the time of the Maccabean revolt against Antiochus IV Epiphanes, king of Syria (175–164 BC), who was trying to proscribe Judaism and secure the conformity of the Jews to state policy and religion – with the assistance of a considerable party within Israel. These stories are frequently alluded to in Revelation, especially that of

j See H. H. Rowley, *The Relevance of Apocalyptic,* ch. I; E. W. Heaton, *The Book of Daniel* (Torch Commentary), SCM Press and Macmillan, New York, 1956.

the furnace into which were thrown the Jews who refused to worship Nebuchadnezzar's image (Dan. 3).

In ch. 7 the book passes over to the visions of one of these Babylonian heroes, Daniel, who sees rising out of the primeval sea a series of beasts which represent world empires, culminating in that of Alexander the Great; on the head of this fourth beast sprouts 'a little horn' with 'a mouth speaking great things', which is Antiochus Epiphanes (= 'God manifest'). Then one who is 'ancient of days' holds court; the beasts lose their sovereignty; 'one like a son of man' comes with the clouds of heaven and appears before him, to be invested with everlasting sovereignty. He represents 'the saints', God's faithful people who on earth are being worn out by the little horn, and signifies their heavenly vindication in and through their earthly sufferings.

The visions continue with symbolic reference to Antiochus' desecration of the temple at Jerusalem by putting in it a statue of Zeus, 'the abomination of desolation', i.e., the sacrilege which brings ruin ($8^{13}$, $9^{27}$, $11^{31}$, $12^{11}$). The archangel Gabriel comes to instruct and encourage Daniel for the benefit of a future generation; he reveals that the archangel Michael, Israel's heavenly champion or prince, is his ally against the angel or prince of Persia, and will later help him against the prince of Greece ($10^{13-21}$). A symbolic account of events from the Persian period up to the writer's own day (c. 164 BC) follows, under the guise of Gabriel showing Daniel what is written in the heavenly 'book of truth' ($11^{1-39}$); it includes comment on the Maccabean crisis from a loyalist point of view: some will be seduced by flattery; those who know God will stand firm and act; some will fall, to purify the people and make them white ($11^{30-35}$).

At $11^{40f.}$ this veiled history evidently passes over into genuine (but unsuccessful) prediction, for it describes the fate of Antiochus 'at the time of the end' in terms which bear no relation to what actually happened. (It became a regular practice in apocalyptic writing for the author to preface his forecast of the immediate future with a résumé of recent events put into the mouth of some seer or revealer in the past: the correctness of the résumé lent authority to the forecast.) At that time, Daniel is told in the final chapter, there will be unparalleled trouble for the Jews, but those whose names are 'written in the book' will be delivered. There will be a resurrection of the dead, some to everlasting life, some to everlasting disgrace. The length of the ordeal is specified in cryptic arithmetic ('a time, two times, and half a time' – the three and a half days or years of Revelation); fidelity under it will bring the new age.

From this crisis arose the Jewish theology of martyrdom. Those who bear witness (Greek *marturia*) to God's truth in word and life represent true humanity (the 'son of man') against the idolatrous arrogance which ruins the earth (the beasts). Their suffering and death is not pointless folly, or a sign of God's impotence, but is expiatory: it purifies the people and turns away God's wrath; it guarantees far worse punishment for their persecutors in the age to come, and a glorious resurrection for the martyrs. The imminent recrudescence of evil and chastening of God's people are part of his preordained plan; they are the birth-pangs of the new age.

The book of Daniel, reflecting this crisis and this theology, was a powerful influence in the following centuries. Its veiled references to the Greeks and their collaborators and its cryptic chronology allowed it to be reapplied to the Romans in their occupation of Judaea. It gave form and colour to the genre of writing we call 'apocalyptic', which gave expression to the contrast felt between the world as men had made it and God's original hidden purpose, and to the ardent expectation of his coming to put it right, along with the conviction that the present generation was the last.

For Christians this expectation of imminent divine intervention, the coming of the kingdom of God, had been partially realized in Jesus' ministry and resurrection, and their belief that it would soon be completed by his return was rooted in his own prophecy, given to his disciples before his arrest, as recorded in the synoptic gospels (Mark 13; Matthew 24; Luke 21; it is often referred to as the Synoptic Apocalypse). It is not clear how much of Mark 13 actually goes back to Jesus himself, but there would have been no doubt of its genuineness and authority when John wrote (probably *c*. AD 95, but see pp. 21–7), though there may well have been differences of opinion as to how it was to be understood. Matthew and Luke have each reshaped their Marcan model for their own situation, and John's apocalypse can be seen as an updating of his Lord's, an elaboration of its themes for his own time, much as his Lord had updated the themes of Daniel.

The Synoptic Apocalypse begins with warnings against deceivers (elaborated by John in the letters to the churches). Before the end there must be wars and rumours of wars, earthquakes and famines: these are 'the beginning of birth-pangs' (they appear in Revelation under the guise of the Four Horsemen, $6^{1-8}$). Christians will be brought before Jewish and pagan courts for his sake, and will bear witness – the gospel must be proclaimed to all the nations before the end. This period of catastrophe, persecution and witness will be brought to a close by 'the abomination of desolation' (Mark $13^{14}$), which will inaugurate a time of unparalleled affliction; Daniel's symbol is reapplied to contemporary Judaea where Roman arrogance and Jewish rebelliousness were already colliding, with obvious danger to Jerusalem and the temple, long before the Jewish war of AD 66–70. But the chief danger will be spiritual: 'false Christs and false prophets' (we know of several such messianic claimants from Josephus e.g. *Ant.* XX. 97f., 169–72; cf. Acts $21^{38}$) 'who will do signs and miracles to deceive even the elect' (Mark $13^{21-23}$).

In Revelation all this is rephrased in terms of the two witnesses and the two beasts, which form the climax of the trumpet plagues. In John's time the danger was not that Christians might see God's presence in a messianic pretender, a 'false Christ', and leave their role of faithful witness to Jesus for armed rebellion, but that they might join the world in finding God in Caesar, who is 'Antichrist', something much more subtle and dangerous. The danger now was not of Rome desecrating the temple at Jerusalem – it had already been destroyed – but of the Roman world desecrating the spiritual temple, the church, in the person of Christian fellow-travellers.

After this affliction (Mark $13^{24}$), sun and moon will be darkened and the stars will fall; then they will see the Son of man coming on the clouds, and he will send the angels to gather his elect. At his trial before the high priest Jesus used the Son of man prophecy to assert his own imminent vindication (Mark $14^{62}$); in Mark 13 it is referred to his return in glory to vindicate his followers. His Apocalypse has little to say about this final stage of the drama, and goes on to warnings about preparedness: it will all happen within this generation, but no one except God knows the precise day, so keep awake (Mark 13²⁸-end). In Revelation, however, the gathering of the faithful is richly expanded in terms of the adorning of a bride and the building of a city, images which Isaiah had used in prophesying the return of the exiles from Babylon (49¹⁶⁻¹⁹, 54¹¹⁻¹⁴), and this reconstitution of God's people the far side of suffering and defeat is balanced against the destruction of the beast's kingdom, the stripping of the harlot, the demolition of the great city: these are the themes of the bowls section (15–22), with the coming of the Son of man at the centre (19¹¹ff.). John too ends with calls to preparedness – 'Behold I am coming soon' (22⁷, ¹², ²⁰).

## 4. DATE

We have assumed so far that the book was written well after the fall of Jerusalem in AD 70, but the evidence is far from conclusive. At first sight Revelation itself tells us at least under which emperor it was written, in the decoding of the seven-headed beast as a series of emperors, of whom five have fallen (17¹⁰). But as we shall see below (pp. 255–8), various solutions are possible, and on our view it was not the author's concern to say which emperor was reigning – he was not writing for posterity but for his contemporaries, and they did not need to be told.

The earliest external evidence, which is accepted by most scholars, is that of Irenaeus (c. AD 180), who came from Asia and had known Polycarp, (c. AD 70–156), the bishop of Smyrna, and others of his generation; he says that the Apocalypse 'was seen no long time ago, but almost in our own day, towards the end of Domitian's reign' (Adversus Haer. V. 30.3). Domitian reigned AD 81–96. This is the practically unanimous view of the earliest Christian tradition, and most scholars accept a date c. AD 95, but Irenaeus could have been mistaken, as he seems to have been over the identification of John (see p. 36). There are later but still ancient traditions that it was written under Trajan (AD 98–117), or under Nero (AD 54–68). This latter belief could have arisen from the obvious references to Nero's notorious persecution of Christians, but a date c. AD 68 has been supported by excellent

NT scholars and Roman historians, most recently by J. A. T. Robinson in *Redating the NT* (SCM Press 1976).

Robinson allows that the external evidence on its own points decisively to *c.* AD 95, but thinks that the internal evidence from the book itself outweighs it. His main arguments for the earlier date are (*a*) historical: the links in Rev. 11, 17 and 18 with events in Jerusalem and Rome in AD 64–70; (*b*) psychological: the vindictive intensity of the passages about Babylon drunk with the blood of Jesus' witnesses – only intelligible, he maintains, under the immediate impact of Nero's *pogrom*. But as we shall see, while both points are consistent with the earlier date, neither in fact requires it.

## (*a*) The historical argument

In AD 64 there was a great fire in Rome, which according to rumour Nero had engineered to make room for his architectural plans. Unable to scotch the rumour, he had the blame put on the Christians; the incendiary language of their writings perhaps helped the charge to stick (cf. Luke 12$^{49}$, 3$^{17}$, 9$^{54}$). Large numbers were executed, probably in early 65, with tortures which sickened even the Romans. Tacitus' account, written about fifty years later, is worth quoting in full:

> But all human efforts, all the lavish gifts of the emperor and propitiations of the gods, did not banish the sinister belief that the conflagration was the result of an order. Consequently, to get rid of the report, Nero fastened the guilt and inflicted the most exquisite tortures on a class hated for their abominations, called Christians by the populace. Christus, from whom the name had its origin, suffered the extreme penalty during the reign of Tiberius at the hands of one of our procurators, Pontius Pilatus, and a deadly superstition, thus checked for the moment, again broke out not only in Judaea, the first source of the evil, but also in the City, where all things hideous and shameful from every part of the world meet and become popular. Accordingly, an arrest was first made of all who confessed; then, upon their information, an immense multitude was convicted, not so much of the crime of arson as of hatred of the human race. Mockery of every sort was added to their

deaths. Covered with the skins of beasts, they were torn by dogs and perished, or were nailed to crosses, or were doomed to the flames and burnt, to serve as a nightly illumination when daylight had expired. Nero had offered his gardens for the spectacle, and put on a show in the Circus, mingling with the people in the dress of a charioteer or standing up in a chariot. Hence, even for criminals who deserved extreme and exemplary punishment, there arose a feeling of compassion, for it was not, as it seemed, for the public good, but to glut one man's cruelty, that they were being destroyed.[k]

According to later tradition Peter and Paul were among those put to death. This was the first official move against Christians as such, and left an indelible scar on the Christian imagination.

A year later began the Jewish revolt against Rome, with initial successes. Nero gave the command to Flavius Vespasianus, an experienced general, who reduced Galilee in 67, but the final reckoning with Jerusalem was delayed until 70 by the events of the 'year of four emperors'. In June 68, after revolts in Gaul and Spain, Nero was deposed in favour of Galba and stabbed himself. Early in 69 Galba was killed and succeeded by Otho, who three months later was defeated by Vitellius and committed suicide. In December Vitellius was himself defeated and killed, after rioting and arson in Rome, by the forces of Vespasian, who had been proclaimed emperor by the eastern legions. He took firm control, assisted by his sons Titus and Domitian (the Flavian dynasty), and Jerusalem was destroyed in 70 by Titus after a terrible siege.

These cataclysmic events must, for Jews and Christians, have presaged the end of the world. It is easy to see Rev. $11^{1-13}$ as an oracle from the period 68 to early 70, when Jerusalem was threatened by siege but the temple had not yet fallen, and to see the pictures of 'Babylon', the victim of civil war ($17^{12-17}$) and destroyed by fire ($17^{16}$, $18^{8f.}$), as inspired by the events of 64 and 68–9. The return of the beast with the mortal wound that was healed ($13^{3,\ 12,\ 14}$, $17^{8-11}$) clearly refers to the belief, which was current very soon after Nero's suicide, that he was not dead and would return (*Nero redivivus*) with

*k* Tacitus, *Annals XV*. 44, quoted from Stevenson, *A New Eusebius*, pp. 2f. (altered).

armies from the East, where Parthia had been a threat to the Roman imagination since the defeat of Crassus in 53 BC.[1]

But even if these passages were composed 'in AD 68–70, they could have been re-used later with symbolic reference. Revelation is full of 'historical' allusions – to events in the OT, in the story of Jesus and in the contemporary world. There are references which can plausibly be seen as referring to events later than AD 70, e.g. the eruption of Vesuvius in AD 79, when white hot ashes buried Pompeii and Herculaneum and stones fell like hail on the villages around, hiding the sun, and further catastrophes, earthquake, fire and plague, betokened the wrath of the gods and the end of the world ($6^{12-17}$; cf. 8, 9 and 17). But such allusions cannot tell us the date of the book, only the date before which it could not have been written – unless there is reason to tie it closely to the events alluded to. This brings us to Robinson's second point, which is at first sight much stronger.

### (b) The psychological argument

. . . The Apocalypse, unless the product of a perfervid and psychotic imagination, was written out of an intense experience of the Christian suffering at the hands of the imperial authorities, represented by the 'beast of Babylon' – see $6^{9-11}$, $17^6$, $18^{20, 24}$, $19^2$, $20^4$ – '. . . if something quite traumatic had not already occurred in Rome which was psychologically still very vivid, the vindictive reaction, portraying a blood-bath of universal proportions ($14^{20}$), is scarcely credible. The sole question is what terrible events are here being evoked (Robinson, pp. 230f.).

Robinson is clearly right that there was nothing like this under Domitian or any other of the possible emperors. A Domitianic persecution has been widely accepted by NT scholars (not by Roman historians), but the only evidence for it is from Christian writers who, from Melito of Sardis (mid-second century) on, held Domitian to have been the next great persecutor after Nero – he was regarded by the Roman aristocracy as a second Nero (e.g. Juvenal IV. 37ff.) and

[1] The kingdom of the Parthians covered much of the old Persian empire, whose western domains, now ruled by the Romans, they were eager to recover. Their mounted archers were famous – hence the 'Parthian shot'.

this may have affected later beliefs.[m] But to the Asian provincials of his own day he was a popular figure, a good administrator and generous benefactor, like the other Flavians. The Jews hated them as the destroyers of Jerusalem (cf. II Esd. 12$^{22-28}$), but the Christians saw its fall as divine punishment of the Jews, and would have appreciated Domitian's efforts to protect the lower classes against the rapacity of provincial governors and local magnates.[n] There is no evidence whatever for large-scale or widespread persecution of Christians.

Another ill-founded idea, which goes hand in hand with that of the 'Domitianic persecution', is that Christians were required by Domitian to participate in the emperor cult. In the East rulers had long been regarded as divine and the source of well-being ('salvation') for their people; their cult was a focus of patriotism. Gratitude to Augustus for bringing peace after decades of civil war made his cult inevitable. (Technically it was not the emperor who was worshipped, but in his lifetime his 'genius' or spirit. At his death he became god, *divus*; the ruling emperor was 'son of god', *divi filius*, with many other titles like 'saviour'.) Most of the earlier emperors deprecated divine honours at home (cf. Vespasian's death-bed remark, 'I rather think I am becoming a god'), but encouraged the cult in association with the local cults in the provinces, as can be seen from inscriptions and the coinage, as a necessity of state. Nero and Domitian did affect divinity; Domitian indeed required to be addressed as 'Lord and God'. (The titles given to Christ both in Revelation and in other NT writings may be in conscious opposition to such imperial pretensions.) But in actual practice the emperor cult, as opposed to general acceptance of the divinity of

*m* Rev. itself may have helped: since in the second century it was held to have been written under Domitian, its allusions to the murder of prophets and saints may have been assumed to refer to events in his reign. He executed or banished a few aristocrats who may or may not have been Christians, but there was no general move against Christians as such (but see p. 30 below on the 'Jewish tax'). See Stevenson, pp. 8–10; W. H. C. Frend, *Martyrdom and Persecution in the Early Church*, Blackwell and Doubleday 1965, pp. 211–17.

*n* See D. Magie, *Roman Rule in Asia Minor*, Princeton 1950, Oxford University Press 1951, pp. 576–82; his evidence is amplified by H. W. Pleket, 'Domitian, the Senate and the Provinces', *Mnemosyne* 14, 1961, pp. 296–315.

Rome and the emperor, was the preserve of the local aristocracy; the average provincial had no direct part.[o]

The reference in 17[6] etc. must be to Nero's persecution. But, first, the passages mentioned also owe much to OT fulminations, against Nineveh, Babylon and Tyre (e.g. Nahum 3[1-4], Jer. 51, Ezek. 26, 27), and to Jesus' denunciation of scribes and Pharisees and of Jerusalem which murders the prophets (Matt. 23[29-38]). There is a 'stock' element in John's most highly coloured writing, as in other apocalyptic books, and 'Babylon' is far more than simply Rome (see on 11[8]). Secondly, though Nero's action has certainly added vital colour, it could have been evoked later even by a sane imagination (can we be sure that John's was *not* vindictive or psychotic, by our standards?), if the situation demanded it. Such a situation might be provided not by general experience of persecution (there was none), but by general avoidance of persecution. The letters to the churches suggest that persecution was occasional and selective, and that the chief dangers were complacency and compromise.[p] On our view Revelation was written at a time when some Christians were disposed to forget what John took to be the true character of the 'great city'; they needed reminding of her inherent idolatrousness, and of what she had done to God's people, whether under Pharaoh, Jezebel or Antiochus, or in the guise of Sodom, Nineveh, Babylon, Jerusalem or finally Rome. The more magnificent and divinely approved Rome might seem (we must remember there had been a pro-Roman party among the Jews, as there had been a pro-Greek party at the time of Antiochus), the more violent the denunciation required.[q] If it were established by

o For the beginnings of the emperor cult under Augustus, see L. R. Taylor, *The Divinity of the Roman Emperor*, Middletown, Conn., 1931. On the persecutions see F. Millar, 'The Imperial Cult and the Persecutions', *Le Culte des Souverains dans l'Empire Romain*, Fondation Hardt, Entretiens XIX, 1973, pp. 145–75, and, with particular reference to Domitian, the three articles by P. Prigent, 'Au Temps de l'Apocalypse', *Revue d'Histoire et de Philosophie Religieuses* 54, 55, 1974–75.

p 'Christianity was not *religio licita* [authorized religion] and if it drew attention to itself its members were liable to punishment. Otherwise sleeping dogs would be allowed to lie' (Frend, p. 220).

q The enthusiastic propagation of the emperor cult in union with local cults under Domitian branded Rome, for a strict Jewish Christian, as the 'mother of earth's abominations' (17[5]); cf. Frend, pp. 103f.

other means that Revelation was written in AD 68–70, our view would still stand: it would then have been composed to warn complacent Christians in Asia that what had just happened in Rome was their story too. But Domitian's reign, when there was more apparent justification for the imperial titles of Saviour and Benefactor and Roman claims to eternity, provides from this point of view a more plausible setting. The only hard information provided by 17$^{8-11}$ is that at the time of writing the beast 'is not'; i.e., the 'head' or emperor now reigning lacks the overt marks of the beast.

The intensity of the language could be due also to the vividness of the author's own experience – he may have been involved in the events of AD 64–70 and himself have suffered under Domitian – as well as to the complacency of the majority of Christians who were prospering under Domitian and forgetting Nero. To invent a modern analogy, if after Hitler's death Germany had pulled through and his Thousand-Year *Reich* had triumphed, more beneficent but still totalitarian, with Russia but a vague menace to the east, and if in the prosperous 1970s the churches were coming to terms with the régime, forgetting past horrors and coming judgment, then a Polish prophet, imprisoned for his Christian witness, might evoke with similar intensity the horrors of Treblinka, of the Warsaw revolt and of the German débâcle of 1945, and predict coming vengeance under the image of Hitler *redivivus*. Whether his imagination was to be judged psychotic would depend on the view taken of the régime which imprisoned him, and of the Bible which inspired him.

To sum up, the earlier date *may* be right, but the internal evidence is not sufficient to outweigh the firm tradition stemming from Irenaeus.

## 5. SITUATION

If a date at the end of Domitian's reign is accepted, it is important to recognize that Revelation was written at a time of comparative peace for the Christians, when they were coming to terms with the delay of Christ's return, which must have seemed excitingly imminent in the upheavals of AD 66–70, and with the world they had to continue living in. There was persecution, of which Antipas (2$^{13}$) and John himself were probably victims, but it was local and selective rather than systematic,[r] the result of overt witness-bearing and non-conformity, and could be avoided by not attracting attention. The situation was no doubt complex and varied from place to place, but we can isolate two main factors: Jewish-Christian relations, and compromise with pagan society.

## (a) Christians and Jews

In Roman law any religion was 'illicit' or unauthorized outside its country of origin, though punitive action was not normally taken unless there was anti-social behaviour.[s] The Jews, who had communities in almost every city of the empire, were the exception: they were allowed to practise their national religion outside Palestine, and for a time Christians were able to shelter under this umbrella, as a Jewish sect. Two things removed this cover: Nero's action after the fire of AD 64, perhaps influenced by his wife's Jewish favourites, action which was directed against the Christians as such and formed a deadly precedent; and the Jewish War of AD 66–70, in which the Christians avoided identification with the Jews. Judaism after the war closed its ranks and took steps to exclude all heretics from the synagogue, especially the Christians, who for their part took the destruction of the temple as God's judgment for the murder of Jesus, and regarded themselves as the true Israel, from which the Jews so-called had cut themselves off.

Outside Palestine the synagogue had long attracted Gentile adherents, but then Christianity began to steal them with the offer of what must have seemed to the Jews cut-price salvation, without the obligation to be circumcised and keep the law of Moses. Their jealousy took the form of 'slander' (Rev. 2⁹, 3⁹), in particular legal accusation by informers (as implied by the letter to Smyrna) and theological polemic (as implied by that to Philadelphia).[t] Christians would be tempted to avoid legal harassment by adopting a 'low

r See the next section. The beast who 'makes war on the saints' is absent (17⁸⁻¹¹).

s See Frend, ch. 4.

t Some scholars see here reference not to Jews but to Judaizing Christians – see on 2⁹.

profile', following a Jewish life-style and not being too active in their 'witness'; at the same time theological attack would undermine the faith by which active witness could alone be sustained. Christians were not sought out by the authorities but they had a bad official reputation (cf. pp. 22 and 31). Those accused as Christians by informers (who were notoriously active under Domitian – see p. 30) could be executed if they refused to recant, as appears from Pliny's procedure as governor of Bithynia (the northern part of modern Turkey) c. AD 113, which he described in his letter to the Emperor Trajan.[u]

Many of those named by informers denied ever having been Christians; others said they had given up 'some three years ago, some several years, a few even twenty years ago' (i.e., c. AD 93) – presumably under pressure. Similar pressures no doubt operated in the province of Asia. Pliny's strategy was to encourage apostasy by letting off those who recanted; at his direction they then 'recited a prayer to the gods, made supplication with incense and wine to your statue, which I had ordered to be brought into court for the purpose together with the images of the gods, and moreover cursed Christ...'. Trajan confirmed that Christians were not to be 'sought out', but that they were to be punished if accused and convicted.

The correspondence shows that there was no existing legislation of Senate or emperor against the Christians, and the main motive for their persecution was probably not legal or political, but religious: the people of the empire resented, and the governors were predisposed to punish, any attack on the established religions, such as was implicit in the Christian 'witness'. 'The religious sentiments of the pagan world, if of a different type, were no less real and powerful than those of the Christians', T. D. Barnes, 'Legislation against the Christians', *Journal of Roman Studies* 58, 1968, p. 49. See also G. E. M. de Ste Croix, 'Why Were the Early Christians Persecuted?', *Past and Present* 26, 1963, pp. 6–38, and his 'Rejoinder' to A. N. Sherwin-White's 'Amendment', *Past and Present* 27, 1964, pp. 23–33.

u *Letters*, X.96, 97; see A. N. Sherwin-White, *The Letters of Pliny*, Clarendon Press 1966, pp. 691–712, 772–87; Stevenson, pp. 13–16, gives translation and notes.

It is in such a context that Jesus is presented as the one who died and came to life and as giver of the crown of life, and the Jews as not Jews (= God's people) at all but a 'synagogue of Satan' ($2^{8-10}$): as at the death of Jesus they are in league with the Roman power; their attacks would have no cutting edge but for the Roman sword – Pergamum, the provincial capital, is Satan's throne ($2^{13}$). But Jesus is lord of the 'second death' in the world to come ($2^{11}$).

It would be tempting, then, where the Jews were strong, to adopt an outwardly Jewish way of life, and this might in fact be done out of theological persuasion. Many Gentiles were impressed by the antiquity of the Jewish religion and scriptures; those who became Christians were set under these same scriptures as the inspired word of God – there was no 'New Testament' yet – and might be led by them towards what we would call an Old Testament ethos (as many Christians have been since), seeing Christ as part of Judaism instead of as sovereign over both Judaism and its scriptures. Ignatius of Antioch, on his way through Asia to martyrdom at Rome, warned the Magnesians and Philadelphians of this (c. AD 115). It is in such a context that Jesus is presented as holder of the key of David in the letter to Philadelphia ($3^7$), as Root of David and opener of the sealed book ($5^5$, $22^{16}$).

Another factor, working in the opposite direction, was the encouragement under Domitian of informers in connection with the 'Jewish tax': the half-shekel paid by all adult male Jews to the temple in Jerusalem (cf. Ex. $30^{11-16}$), which Vespasian directed in AD 70 to the treasury of Jupiter Capitolinus. Under Domitian it was ruthlessly exacted even of Jews who had ceased to practise, and of non-Jews who followed a Jewish way of life (Suetonius, *Domitian* 12.2; Christians, who claimed to be the true Israel, could be caught on either or both counts), and the activities of informers made such an impression that his successor, Nerva, issued coins with the legend FISCI JUDAICI CALUMNIA SUBLATA ('false accusation relating to the Jewish tax having been removed') as a manifesto of the new régime. 'Domitian may have become a persecutor *malgré lui* through the arbitary outworking of a policy.'[v] There must have been pressure here on Christians to cut

v C. J. Hemer, 'The Edfu Ostraka and the Jewish Tax', *Palestinian Exploration Quarterly* 105, 1973, p. 11; cf. Frend, pp. 212f.

loose from their Jewish heritage, and this would have reinforced the steady intellectual pressure to drop the whole of the OT with its savage God and barbarous law, which came to a head with Marcion in the second century, and to abandon the primitive Jewish-Christian hope of Christ's imminent return. It was difficult, while attacking the Jews, to maintain the church's Jewish roots (as Paul had also found – Rom. 11$^{13-24}$), and it is in such a context that we may see Revelation's very Jewish, or rather scriptural, presentation of Jesus, and the repeated 'I am coming soon'.

## (b) Compromise with pagan society

The ordinary provincial, as we have said, had no necessary part in the emperor cult as such, but religion was woven into his political and social life. He lived in an atmosphere permeated by the symbols of the old fertility cults and of the deified state and emperor, which were propagated by the temples and public buildings, by the law courts, by the theatres and gladiatorial games, above all by the coinage. To the ordinary man it may not have meant very much: it was the age-old patriotic idiom, like singing the national anthem in a football stadium or taking the oath on the Bible in court. But to some Christians brought up on the Jewish scriptures it was blasphemy, and connivance was like the idolatry of the Israelites when they reached the promised land; they must take a stand like Elijah before Jezebel.

Such a stand did not endear them to their neighbours who, even if they did not take their religion seriously, resented its being insulted or ignored – and many did take it seriously; cf. Acts 19$^{34}$ and p. 29 above. Christian aloofness gave rise to charges of atheism and hatred of the human race: public religion, as opposed to private belief, was part of the fabric of human life and abstention brought danger to society; earthquake, famine, plague – any natural disaster was interpreted as the wrath of the gods, and could be blamed on the 'atheists'. Some Christians from a Greek background would have rejected Jewish-Christian intransigence, and have wished to take a positive part in the social life of their cities, finding freedom to do so in the interpretation of Christianity from a 'gnostic' point of view which I Corinthians shows to have been already current in the fifties.

By 'gnosticism',[w] as opposed to the developed gnostic systems of the second century, we mean a climate of thought which was widespread in the first century AD, among Jews as well as Greeks. Its main features were concern for individual salvation through spiritual knowledge (*gnōsis*), and depreciation of the material world. Man is an immortal soul 'fallen' into a material body, from which he will be released at death. 'Sin' is estrangement from God not by disobedience in daily life, but by blind involvement in material concerns: 'salvation' therefore lies in escape from the domination of matter and in *gnōsis*, which may be achieved here and now by initiation into philosophical mysteries and sacramental rites. Christianity provided just such an initiation and *gnōsis*, accompanied by exciting spiritual manifestations, and an 'existential' interpretation of the primitive faith soon developed which had little interest in the historical life and death of Jesus, or in his future return and men's bodily resurrection for final judgment. On this view, his importance had been as revealer of divine truth, which continues to be revealed by prophets in the present; the divine Spirit left his body before his death, which was merely a hollow victory for the powers of this world and of no continuing significance; resurrection, judgment and salvation happen now, in turning from worldly darkness to spiritual light; the body is a temporary lodging, and bodily actions are 'things indifferent', without importance for eternal life. This attitude could lead to asceticism ('severity to the body', Col. $2^{20-23}$), or more often to moral indifference which might issue in licentiousness (I Cor. $6^{12-19}$). Religion is a matter of spiritual experience rather than moral obedience, of seeing rather than hearing and doing.

Such an attitude probably lies behind the 'teaching of the Nicolaitans',[x] who encouraged Christians to 'eat food sacrificed to idols and commit fornication' ($2^{6, \ 14f., \ 20}$) – or from their point of view, to share in the social and religious life of their city. One problem was

---

[w] See R. Bultman, *Primitive Christianity in its Contemporary Setting*, ET Thames & Hudson and Longmans, Toronto, 1956, pp. 162–71; E. Lohse, *The New Testament Environment*, ET Abingdon and SCM Press 1976, pp. 253–77.

[x] The later fathers connected them with gnosticism, but we know only what can be deduced from $2^{14f.}$ (see commentary).

over pagan dinner-parties. These were often held in a temple; even if not, the meat served was likely to have come from animals slaughtered for the temple sacrifices (only part was burnt, and the rest was sold in the market). Could a Christian take part without being involved in idolatry? In Corinth some took the line that 'an idol is nothing'; Christian 'knowledge' set them free from Jewish tabus, which were observed only by the 'weak in faith' (I Cor. 8$^{1-10}$; cf. Rom. 14$^{1ff.}$). Paul in his reply had begun by agreeing with the 'strong' as far as he could, before warning them of the dangers in their position (I Cor. 10$^{14-22}$), and had ended by saying 'Eat anything sold in the market without quibbles of conscience' – unless someone else's conscience was at risk (I Cor. 10$^{25-29}$). Paul's permission may have become a precedent, without Paul's qualifications.

As for 'fornication', it is a regular metaphor for idolatry in the OT, but pagan religion and sexual promiscuity were still linked as in the time of Balaam (see on 2$^{14, 20}$); prostitution, male and female, was a regular part of the fertility cults. To some Corinthian Christians sexual intercourse was simply a natural function like eating (I Cor. 6$^{13}$). The two issues of meat sacrificed to idols and fornication are treated side by side in I Corinthians and in the apostolic decrees of Acts 15, which sought to regulate Gentile converts in their relations with Jewish Christians. The precise scope and meaning of these decrees is now far from clear, but it looks as if John was recalling Christians to the old apostolic standard of abstention from practices in which some of them saw no harm (see on 2$^{24-25}$).

A particular problem would have been posed by trade-guilds, which we know from inscriptions to have been numerous at Thyatira. Membership involved religious ceremonies which were no doubt merely conventional to most members, including 'strong' Christians (cf. Freemasonry today). Must Christians opt out? How could they withdraw from all aspects of city life which were touched by pagan religion without committing social and economic suicide, and foregoing all chance of influence and success? Jesus had said, 'Render to Caesar what is Caesar's' when shown the Roman coin with which tribute was paid (Mark 12$^{17}$). Peter and Paul had regarded the state as ordained by God and had ordered Christians to obey the authorities and pray for them (I Peter 2$^{13-17}$, Rom. 13$^{1ff.}$; cf. I Tim. 2$^{1f.}$,

Titus 3¹). Was it necessary to take a rigid stand, with all the disquali-fications and dangers it involved? What value was there in provoking martyrdom? The issue was not so much actual idolatry or emperor-worship as the relations of church and world, which have been a perennial problem to Christians and admit of no simple universal answer.

## (c) John's view

To John, however, in his time and place, the issue was black and white. The true line lay not with the 'strong' who 'knew' that an idol has no real existence' (I Cor. 8⁴), but with the spiritual descendants of Elijah and the Hasidim, the loyal Jews who let themselves be tortured and killed rather than compromise under Antiochus; in his eyes, just as Israel, called to be God's witness to the nations in their idolatry, had prostituted herself in commerce with the Phoenician cities, so the church, which was now God's Israel, the sevenfold lamp of witness, was giving herself over to fornication in the Asian cities; behind the idolatry and materialism of pagan society lay the baleful influence of deified Rome, 'the great harlot', which the provincials regarded as the eternal source of their blessings and the proper object of grateful worship; through his servant, Christ was seeking to open the churches' eyes and ears, to prepare them for the final crisis, which would herald his coming in judgment. A recent parallel might be the attempts of Bonhoeffer and others to alert the 'German Christians' of the 1930s to the true nature of Hitler's *Reich*, at a time when men were dazzled by his achievements and he was widely regarded as civilization's bulwark against Bolshevism; treason was the truest loyalty.

What then is Revelation's message for such a situation? Practically, it demands separation from the 'world', not in physical but in moral terms: the 'wilderness' in which the woman is nourished (12¹³) is no Qumran-like monastery but a symbol of the spiritual preservation of the church, while physically Christians are maintaining 'the testimony of Jesus' and validating it with their lives in 'the street of the great city' (12¹³⁻¹⁷, 11⁸). Theologically, it provides the undergirding for such suicidal folly. If Christians were on the one hand being told by Jews that Jesus was no Messiah and they no Israel, and on the other were under pressure to give up their Jewish heritage, in favour of a gnostic understanding of Christianity which found salvation in present spiritual experience, made no moral demands and regarded Jesus as only one revealer among many, then Revelation can be seen as setting out Jesus as the unique and all-sufficient Son of God, who by his death and resurrection had fulfilled the whole Jewish dispensation and set in motion the judgment of the world, which he would soon return to complete. At the same time it showed the churches their crucial role as God's Israel, and the final destiny which men prepared for themselves in taking the mark of the beast or in following the Lamb.

The two poles of the book are the death of the Lamb, and the promise 'I am coming soon', the aspects of past and future which gnostic existentialism neglected. Likewise Paul had had to remind the Corinthians that in the eucharist, the sacrament of present salvation, 'you show forth the Lord's death till he come' (I Cor. 11$^{26}$). To those in danger for their faith John revealed the eternal victory of Jesus' death and of theirs (if it should be required); those too sure of their present salvation he warned that the fulness of what they were enjoying was only for the conqueror, who 'keeps my works until the end' (2$^{26}$).

## 6. AUTHORSHIP AND COMPOSITION

### (a) Unity

Tantalizingly little can be discovered about the author, and it is not even clear that the book is the unified work of one man: many scholars have argued for revisions, interpolations and dislocations of the text. On a first reading it does seem impossibly disordered and incoherent, and it is quite possible that, like many of the books of the Bible, it went through a process of editing and re-editing before our present text was fixed. On the other hand, a glance at other apocalyptic books shows that the genre is in its nature incoherent, with bewildering changes of scene and speaker, interjections, repetitions and inconsistencies. It works with pictures and symbols rather than a logically constructed argument. Further, a proposed emendation or rearrangement of a passage which we find unintelligible may give a clear sense, but before we can accept it as the original text we must be able to explain how what was originally clear and sensible was later reduced to nonsense: editors and copyists try to improve the sense, not destroy it. It is a primary canon of textual critics that, where the MSS provide more than one form of words, 'the harder reading is to be preferred', assuming there has been no obvious mechanical error in transcription.

Often the 'harder reading' seems impossibly difficult, but we must beware of rewriting a text from another culture according to our canons of consistency. The first principle of good interpretation is to accept the strangeness of the text – to try and follow the sense of what is given rather than read in our own sense, to tolerate loose ends and admit that understanding may at the moment be beyond us. It is only in this way that our perceptions can be enlarged – as with unfamiliar forms of art and music. On our view, allowing for the looseness of the genre, Revelation is an impressively coherent whole, and can be taken as substantially the work of one mind.

### (b) John in tradition

There are three possibilities: that Revelation was written by John the apostle; that it purports to be written by John the apostle, i.e., that it is pseudonymous; or that it was written by another John.[y]

### (i) John the apostle

This was the belief of Irenaeus (c. AD 180), who had known people who had known John the apostle; it was shared by Melito of Sardis and Justin Martyr (mid-second century) and most later writers. Irenaeus also believed that this same John wrote the Fourth Gospel and the Johannine Epistles, and that he was released from Patmos and lived on into Trajan's reign (98–117). This view was widely held in the early church, but the differences in language, style and thought make it hard to believe that Revelation and the Fourth Gospel were the work of the same man, as Dionysius of Alexandria perceived (c. AD 250); and if he was one of Jesus' first disciples, John could hardly have been less than ninety when Revelation was written. This is not impossible, but a Neronian date would fit much better with

---

y The theory of J. M. Ford (*Revelation*, Anchor Bible 38, Doubleday 1975) that the author was John the Baptist has not attracted support.

apostolic authorship. Most modern scholars hold, with Dionysius, that the author could not have written the Gospel and Epistles as well.

### (ii) Pseudonymity[2]

Another possibility is that Revelation, like Daniel and the other apocalyptic books, *purports* to be written by a hero of the past. James and John, nicknamed 'sons of thunder' (Mark 3[17]), an appropriate title for the author of Revelation, formed with Peter the inner ring of the twelve (later John was one of the 'pillars' of the Jerusalem church, Gal. 2.9) and had been told that they would drink Jesus' cup of suffering (Mark 10[38]). James was martyred *c.* AD 44 (Acts 12[2]) and there are some hints in ancient tradition that John may have been martyred too. If so, his name might have been chosen to lend authority to a later call to martyrdom – many scholars hold that the epistles to Timothy and Titus, and II Peter (if not other epistles) were similarly attributed to Paul and Peter after their deaths. If Revelation was later accepted as having been composed by John about AD 95 (when it was published), that could account for the view of Irenaeus, which became universally accepted, that John lived to a ripe old age in Ephesus.

This view, if right, could provide a neat solution to the puzzle of the seven-headed beast (see on 17.8–11, pp. 256f.), and the allusions to events of AD 64–70 (see pp. 22–4) could be seen as recreating the atmosphere of the supposed time of writing. But it is not universally agreed that pseudonymous authorship was an accepted practice in Christian circles at this time, and there are difficulties in this particular suggestion: the letters to the churches seem to present actual situations, contemporary with the book's publication, rather than the supposed situations of a generation earlier; the evidence for John's martyrdom is tenuous; above all, no capital is made of the fictitious attribution. The author is simply 'a servant of God' (1[1]), 'I, John, your brother' (1[9]). So far from claiming that he is John the apostle he refers to 'the twelve apostles of the Lamb' (21[14]) without hint that he is one of them.

z See the essays by K. Aland and D. S. Guthrie in *The Authorship and Integrity of the NT*, SPCK Theological Collections 4, 1965; D. S. Russell, *The Method and Message of Jewish Apocalyptic*, pp. 127–39.

The only status the author claims is, by implication, that of 'prophet' ($1^3$, $22^9$), a term widely used in early Christian writings for inspired persons who received revelations and exercised leadership in the congregation.[a] The author is clearly a leader, but his authority, so far from being accepted as that of one of the twelve, is challenged at Thyatira by the 'prophetess' he calls Jezebel.

### (iii) Another John

The third possibility is that there was another John, who in later tradition was confused with the apostle. This was the view of Dionysius of Alexandria, on the basis of a traveller's report of two tombs of John in Ephesus. Papias, bishop of Hierapolis near Laodicea c. AD 150, referred to the Elder (*presbuteros*) John alongside the apostle, and many have supposed this was the author of Revelation.[b] This is perhaps the solution with the least difficulties, but it does not tell us anything about the author. The writer of II and III John refers to himself as 'the Elder' (I John is anonymous), and Jung makes play with the possibility that the same man wrote Revelation and the Johannine Epistles (see pp. 42–4), but in language and thought they are as far apart as Revelation and the Fourth Gospel.

To sum up, it seems wisest to admit that we cannot know more about the author than his book tells us; indeed he himself claims only to be a reporter – it is the message that matters ($22^{6-9,\ 18-20}$).

### (c) Internal evidence

### (i) Asia

Whoever the author was, Sir William Ramsay[c] showed that he had an intimate knowledge of the Asian cities, to which the seven letters were addressed, in their past history and present circumstances.

a See D. Hill, 'Prophecy and Prophets in the Revelation of St John', *NTS* 18, 1972, pp. 401–18; the author claims a very special commission which sets him above or at least apart from his brethren (p. 410).

b For Dionysius' views see Stevenson, pp. 271–74; for Papias, see Stevenson, pp. 50–52, and D. G. Deeks, 'Papias Revisited', *ExpT* 88, 1977, pp. 296–301, 324–9.

c In *The Letters to the Seven Churches*, published in 1904, based on pioneering archaeological and literary studies.

Ramsay's work has been confirmed and amplified by the first-hand investigations of C. J. Hemer.[d] Some scholars have supposed that he also knew Rome, from the references to 'Babylon' in Rev. 17 and 18, but these could all have come from the OT or from common knowledge.[e] It is clear from his symbolism that he breathed the intellectual and spiritual atmosphere of his world; we may note the hints of astrology and magic, by which both Jews and Greeks were deeply influenced. The changes and chances of this fleeting world were held to be governed by the predictable movements of the stars, which were seen as angels or spiritual powers; these, and the powers of nature, could be controlled by knowledge (*gnōsis*), through rituals and formulas. A. M. Farrer worked out a fascinating, if hardly convincing, astrological structure for the book in terms of zodiacal symbolism. But the symbolism is there, even if we are no longer able to follow it as the first readers could, and John uses it to express Christ's control of even these cosmic powers, to which man feels himself subject (cf. Rom. 8[37-39]).[f]

## (ii) Old Testament

However much a citizen of Asia, he was even more clearly a Jew, and one who received his formation within the Hebraic rather than the Hellenistic orbit. He had an astonishing grasp of the Jewish scriptures, which he used with creative freedom. He never quotes a passage verbatim, but paraphrases, alludes and weaves together motifs in such a way that to follow up each allusion usually brings out further dimensions of meaning. A study of the references to Ezekiel has shown that he had a creative grasp of that diffuse and obscure

*d* Hemer's Manchester Ph.D thesis, 'A Study of the Letters to the Seven Churches of Asia, with Special Reference to their Local Background', 1969, awaits publication.

*e* Tertullian said that the apostle John was brought before Domitian in Rome and, 'after suffering no hurt from being plunged in boiling oil, was remitted to his island exile' (*De Praescriptione Haereticorum* 36; Stevenson, p. 175), but later traditions about John in Rome, when not manifestly legendary, could have been deduced from the book itself.

*f* See Lohse, *NT Environment*, pp. 226ff.; Bultmann, *Primitive Christianity*, pp. 146-55; A. M. Farrer, *A Rebirth of Images*, Dacre Press 1949, chs. 7 and 8, and his Commentary passim. Acts 18[19] mentions magic in Ephesus.

book: he has clarified and concentrated its message, and enlarged its vision.[g] It appears that he normally had in mind the Hebrew text rather than the Greek translation called the Septuagint (LXX), but he shows knowledge of both the Greek interpretation of the Hebrew represented by the LXX and the Aramaic interpretation used in the synagogue, found in the expanded paraphrases called Targums.[h] He may also have known the Wisdom of Solomon and most of II Esdras in the Apocrypha; these and the books of Enoch and Baruch, the Testaments of the Twelve Patriarchs and the Sibylline Oracles are interesting for comparison.[i] In fact Revelation can be seen as a Christian re-reading of the whole Jewish scriptural heritage, from the stories of the Beginning to the visions of the End.

## (iii) New Testament

It can be questioned how far he has moved beyond the spirit of the OT (see p. 48), but there are echoes of most of the NT, especially the gospels and Pauline epistles. His practice of alluding rather than quoting makes for uncertainty in detecting references to NT books, and the relationship of Revelation to the other Johannine writings is a particular puzzle.[j] Though the differences in language and thought are such as to make common authorship improbable, the affinities are so deep and pervasive that a number of scholars hold to it nevertheless. There are deep links with Pauline thought, especially in I Corinthians, which was written from Ephesus, Ephesians, Colossians (Colossae was close to Laodicea) and II Thessalonians. There is,

g A. Vanhoye, 'L'Utilization du Livre d'Ézéchiel dans l'Apocalypse', *Biblica* 43, 1962, pp. 436–76.

h See M. McNamara, *The New Testament and the Palestinian Targum to the Pentateuch*, Pontifical Biblical Institute, Rome, 1966, pp. 97–125, 189–237.

i See p. 1 note a above. The echoes of the Jewish Wisdom tradition (Enoch, Daniel and Ezra were men of wisdom) are particularly interesting. Like the Fourth Gospel, Colossians and Ephesians, Revelation presents Christ as the Wisdom of God in person – see on 3[14]. For the roots of apocalyptic in the Wisdom tradition, see G. von Rad, *The Message of the Prophets*, ET SCM Press 1968, Harper & Row 1972, pp. 271–4, and *Wisdom in Israel*, ET SCM Press and Abingdon Press 1972, pp. 263–83.

j See E. S. Fiorenza, 'The Quest for the Johannine School: the Apocalypse and the Fourth Gospel', *NTS* 23, 1977, pp. 402–27.

however, no clear literary dependence on either John or Paul, and the structural importance for Revelation of the Synoptic Apocalypse (see pp. 19–21) suggests that if 'John' is to be 'placed' in early Christianity it is in the prophetic-apocalyptic school or strand which also influenced Paul. Ephesus was the centre of both the Pauline and the Johannine traditions, and an Asian Christian at the end of the century could have been steeped in both without slavish dependence on either.

## (iv) Liturgy

All the NT writings (except perhaps Acts) were probably from the start read aloud in meetings for worship, and contain much liturgical material – fragments of hymns, acclamations, blessings, prayers and homilies. Revelation is particularly rich in these, and it is tempting to suppose that they echo the actual worship of John's day. This cannot be substantiated, since the only evidence is from later liturgies which are themselves influenced by the NT writings. But we are on firmer ground with the worship of the synagogue, in which John and many other Christians would have first heard the scriptures read and expounded. The texts of the liturgies, though only written down much later, are thought to give substantially the form known in the first century AD, and Pierre Prigent has shown the striking parallels between the *Yotser* liturgy, celebrating creation, redemption from Egypt and the giving of the law, and Rev. 4 and 5.[k]

He has also argued persuasively that the literary structure of the Seven Letters is drawn from the formal 'scrutiny', or examination of the worshippers, which preceded the eucharist – a theme taken up in ch. 22 – and that much of the symbolism of these chapters is drawn from that of baptism and eucharist.[l] It seems that the themes of the

[k] Prigent, *Apocalypse et Liturgie*, pp. 46–76. The ancient Near Eastern 'myth and ritual' pattern, which probably influenced the worship of Solomon's temple, may still have influenced men's minds in NT times; see below on Rev. 4 and 12, and S. H. Hooke's essay, 'The Myth and Ritual Pattern in Jewish and Christian Apocalyptic', in *The Labyrinth*, SPCK and Macmillan, New York, 1935, pp. 213–33, which he edited.

[l] Prigent, pp. 37–45; cf. G. Bornkamm, *Early Christian Experience*, ET SCM Press 1969, Harper & Row 1970, pp. 161–76. Prigent's suggestions chime in with the researches of J. Daniélou, *Primitive Christian Symbols*.

Jewish pilgrim feasts, especially Passover and Tabernacles, also contribute to the structure of Revelation, as to that of the Fourth Gospel.

According to Prigent, Revelation is evoking the message of Christian worship, i.e., that the final coming of Christ and the blessedness of the heavenly banquet are anticipated here and now in his eucharistic presence; but this is transposed into the idiom of apocalyptic, with stress on the ambivalence of this presence and its danger, as a foretaste of final judgment, for the unprepared.

## (v) The mind of the author

The ancient notion of a prophet as a mouthpiece for revelations from outside himself, a pen moved by the Holy Spirit, has given way for us to less mechanical, more personal, ideas of inspiration. The accounts in Revelation of things seen and heard are so full of allusions to the scriptures and to contemporary circumstances that some see the book as a meditation on current events in the light of the church's liturgy and scriptures, a literary exercise cast in visionary form. But how far was the conscious mind in control? Deep meditation on the scriptures could itself lead to ecstatic experience (in Jewish tradition the first chapter of Ezekiel, the 'chariot vision' which lies behind Rev. 4, was notorious in this respect; it has been suggested that Paul was reading it on the Damascus road!), and current events can take control of an artist, as the bombing of Guernica took hold of Picasso.[m] Modern psychology has illuminated the depths out of which visions and auditions emerge, and it is not enough to see Revelation as simply a literary exercise. Thinking of the Cargo Cults of the Pacific, or the paintings of Hieronymus Bosch and the literature of the Protestant underworld of the Reformation,[n] we should be alert to recognize the welling up of the unconscious mind, whether of the individual or his group.

In this part of the terrain there are no firm landmarks but the prospective explorer should know of C. G. Jung's analysis in *Answer to*

m See Farrer, pp. 23–9; J. Lindblom, *Gesichte und Offenbarungen*, C. W. K. Gleerup, Lund, 1968, ch. 10.

n See the references to 'apocalyptic' in the index of E. G. Rupp, *Patterns of Reformation*, Epworth Press and Fortress Press 1969. Thomas Müntzer (p. 303) saw himself as another Elijah, as John did (pp. 34 and 92).

*Job.*[o] He assumes that 'John' is the 'son of thunder', and that he wrote I John, in which he talks so certainly of sinlessness and perfect love that he 'runs the risk of a dissociation. Under these circumstances a counter position is bound to arise in the unconscious, which can then irrupt into consciousness in the form of a revelation' (p. 121). The Christ of the opening vision is a figure of fear, not love, and sends a series of threatening letters to the churches. 'This apocalyptic "Christ" behaves rather like a bad-tempered, power-conscious "boss" who very much resembles the "shadow" of a love-preaching bishop' (p. 123). In chs. 5 and 6 there is nothing of 'the meek Lamb who lets himself be led unresistingly to the slaughter; there is only the aggressive and irascible ram whose rage can at last be vented. In all this I see less a metaphysical mystery than the outburst of long pent-up negative feelings such as can frequently be observed in people who strive for perfection. . . . A veritable orgy of hatred, wrath, vindictiveness, and blind destructive fury that revels in fantastic images of terror breaks out . . .' (pp. 124f.).

Even if 'John', as most scholars think, was not the author of I John, this could still be a true picture of his state of mind, except that Jung fails to recognize that these images, which are so fantastic and horrific to us, were to John and his audience largely conventional, and that John may be rephrasing and recombining apocalyptic clichés, in the light of the remembered life and death of Jesus, to achieve what might be called a 'rebirth of images'.[p] The 'wrath of the Lamb' (6$^{16}$) may still represent a 'metaphysical mystery', even if the book springs from negative feelings. An idea is not dissolved by explanation of its genesis; a work of art must be considered for what it is, apart from the composer's state of mind.

But Jung's purpose is not to make fun of John: it was not, he says, merely a question of an outburst of ill-humour from his personal unconscious, but of 'visions which came up from a far greater and more comprehensive depth, namely from the collective unconscious' (p. 134). He was both responding to what Jung calls the dark side of

---

*o* C. G. Jung, *Answer to Job*, ET Routledge & Kegan Paul 1954, reissued Hodder & Stoughton 1965, pp. 121ff. (also in *Collected Works*, vol. 11, Routledge & Kegan Paul and Pantheon Books 1958).

*p* See pp. 50f. below, and the commentary on 5$^6$.

God, which is usually suppressed – 'God is light, and in him is no darkness at all' (I John $1^{5}$) – and expressing the resolution of the two aspects, the 'embrace of opposites', e.g., in the vision of the heavenly woman and man child in ch. 12. Jung draws in the mythological and astrological echoes in Revelation, linking them with the speculations of the medieval alchemists. But here we cannot pretend to guide the explorer, except by pointing to important and fascinating ground to be explored.

### (*d*) *Structure*

Though we must reckon with an element of incoherence and with the building up of impressions after the manner of music rather than logical argument, on our view the author was in general control of his materials, and a loose structure can be discerned: a prologue (ch. 1) balanced by an epilogue ($22^{6}$–end), with the four 'septets' of letters, seals, trumpets and bowls in between. But what is the relation of the letters to the visionary part, and the relation of seals, trumpets and bowls to each other? As to the latter, some scholars see just recapitulation: each series covers the same ground, carrying through to a vision of the End; the bowls repeat the motifs of the trumpets, and both draw on the plagues of Egypt. But there is also development: each series centres on a different moment of the Synoptic Apocalypse (see pp. 20f.), bringing us nearer to the End, which is sketched in an anticipatory way at the close of the seals and the trumpets. At the same time, what is presented as a story, one stage succeeding another, is in another sense already happening – see notes on the mysterious 'three and a half' years or days (pp. 182f.). The Jews used stories about the end, as about the beginning of things, to illuminate the present.

As for the relation of the letters to the rest, Farrer pointed out a a linkage between the themes of each of the first four letters and the themes of the corresponding septet.[q]

The *first* letter, to Ephesus, is concerned with false apostles and

*q* Farrer, pp. 83–6; each septet divides 4:3, and the last three letters back up the themes of the first four: the fifth and sixth are linked with the first and second by the titles of Christ in the opening verse of each, and the seventh letter has special links with the third and fourth.

Nicolaitans, and the church's need to repent: the central concern of the letters as a whole is complacency and compromise, propagated by influential leaders, and the need to repent.

The *second* letter, to Smyrna, supported by the sixth, to Philadelphia, is concerned with Jewish slander and diabolical testing for the church: the seals section (4–7) is concerned with the church as the true Israel, bought from among all nations by Christ's death and sealed against demonic tribulations.

The *third* letter, to Pergamum, is concerned with the church's witness under the shadow of Satan's throne, and the danger of being seduced into idolatry as Israel was by Balak and Balaam: the trumpets section (8–14) sets out the plagues which idolatry brings down on the world, with the apotheosis of idolatry in the beast and false prophet (13), which correspond to Balak and Balaam; woven in is the theme of witness, its earthly defeat and heavenly victory (10–12).

The *fourth* letter, to Thyatira, is concerned with fornication, the moral aspect of idolatry (Jezebel); the seventh, to Laodicea, with the church's complacent affluence (the sleeping bride, $3^{20}$): the bowls section ($15^1$–$22^5$) centres on the stripping of the harlot Babylon (Jezebel) in her complacent affluence, and the adornment of the Bride, the new Jerusalem.

Admittedly this linkage is not explicitly pointed out, and Revelation can be read well enough without it, but there is enough to suggest that it was in John's mind, and to justify using it as a principle of interpretation in the commentary.

Other more detailed structures have been discerned – e.g., Revelation has been seen as a drama, with Prologue, Epilogue and seven Acts[r] – and there may well be subsidiary patterns, scriptural, liturgical and astrological, but for a general plan we can be content with the pattern of the four septets, based on the Synoptic Apocalypse – see the Outline, pp. 52–4.

One alternative reading should, however, be mentioned, which

---

[r] J. W. Bowman, 'The Revelation to John: its Dramatic Structure and Message', *Interpretation* 9, 1955, pp. 436–53; cf. R. R. Brewer, 'The Influence of Greek Drama on the Apocalypse of John', *Anglican Theological Review* 18, 1936, pp. 74–92.

gives a rather different picture from ours.[s] There seems to be a natural break at the end of ch. 11 which makes the book (apart from prologue and epilogue) fall into two roughly equal parts: 4–11 is thoroughly Jewish in tone and ends with the destruction of Jerusalem; 12–20 centres on the beast (= the emperor) and Babylon (= Rome). Part I, on this view, ('The Church and the Jews') sets out God's judgment on Israel: the imagery of seals and trumpets picks up the OT prophecies against disobedient Israel; the 144,000 are the faithful remnant of the old Israel, set under God's seal of preservation; and ch. 11 describes a final prophetic ministry to the Jews in Jerusalem, which ends in their conversion. Part II ('The Church and the World') sets out God's judgment on all who take the mark of the beast rather than follow the Lamb, and leads into the vision of all things made new and the nations bringing their glory into the new Jerusalem. Revelation can be seen as giving imaginative shape to the Pauline conviction that God has not cast off his ancient people the Jews, and that their conversion must precede the final salvation of the world (Rom. 11).

But on our view there is no structural break at the end of ch. 11. $12^{12}-13^{18}$ sets out the 'third woe', the climax of the trumpet series, and the references to 'three and a half' bind 11–13 together ($11^{2f.}$, 9, 11, $12^6$, 14, $13^5$). It is impossibly strained to see the disasters of chs. 6, 8 and 9 as directed only against Israel; the prophets' strictures against Israel for its idolatry have been redirected against the world, the 'earth-dwellers'; but not simply the outside world – rather the world as penetrating the church, the true Israel. The Jerusalem of ch. 11 is not simply the literal Jerusalem, any more than Babylon is simply Rome: it is the 'great city', which is also Sodom and Egypt ($11^8$). The old distinction between ethnic Israel and the Gentile world has been torn down (cf. Mark $15^{38-39}$, Acts $10^{15}$); the 'real Jew' is he who is one 'inwardly' (Rom. $2^{28-29}$); the 144,000 are those who 'follow the Lamb' (Rev. $14^4$). The Jewish themes of 4–11 are better explained in terms of the need to give Christians theological reassurance, in face of Jewish polemic, that Jesus *is* God's Messiah and

s Cf. A. Feuillet, 'Essai d'Interprétation du ch. 11 de l'Apocalypse', *NTS* 3, 1957, pp. 183–200, and *The Apocalypse*, pp. 54–62; W. J. Harrington, *The Apocalypse of St John*, Chapman 1969, pp. 28–40.

that they *are* God's people, and to remind them that as God's people they have a testimony to maintain before the world.[t]

Within the four septets pattern there is one feature, already mentioned on p. 13, which is crucial for the right understanding of the book. The visions of destruction (6–20) are bracketed by the over-arching vision of God the Creator and Redeemer (4–5), who makes all things new ($21^1$–$22^5$): carnage and chaos are within the divine plan and lead through into the fulfilment of man's destiny in final union with God.

## 7. PLACE IN THE NEW TESTAMENT

Revelation is unlike any other book in the NT: why is it there, and does it deserve its place?

### (a) How it got there

The church's 'canon', or list of authoritative writings, was not finally settled until the fourth century. One of the criteria was apostolic authorship, and as we have seen (pp. 36–8), this was early and widely accepted for Revelation. But it would not have been upheld if Revelation had not been felt to be apostolic also in content – that is, in harmony with the pattern of Christian truth in the other apostolic writings. If Alexandrian Christians rejected it in the third century, it was not primarily on literary grounds but because of the crudely physical millennial expectations which their contemporaries drew from it; it was part of their overall rejection of apocalyptic Christianity. But though its apocalyptic character would have been obnoxious to many in the first century too, it would have been no general disqualification either in the third century or in the first.

Revelation did not, then, spring from the lunatic fringe (even if it has since been exploited there). It represents the Danielic version of

---

*t* This is not 'anti-Semitism', though Rev. has no doubt fed anti-Semitism. For John the world is divided now not into Gentiles and Jews but earth-dwellers and heaven-dwellers (see pp. 15f.), those who take the mark of the beast and those who follow the Lamb. The Jews are from his point of view false Jews, 'a synagogue of Satan', not essentially but functionally – in so far as at Smyrna and Philadelphia ($2^9$, $3^9$) they actively take Satan's part.

Christianity, stressing Christ's sacrificial death and imminent return, which stamps the synoptic gospels and most of the epistles. It may have been a minority view in the province of Asia at the end of the first century, if the view is right that John was attacking an influential 'gnostic' version of Christianity at a time of comparative affluence and success, when Christ's return seemed remote and martyrs were few. But as the attitude of the authorities hardened against Christianity and conformity with the world became less viable, the stern apocalyptic version regained ground. Revelation became the encouragement and solace of martyrs in growing numbers;[u] its spirit and its imagery sustained the church in its sometimes almost suicidal resistance to persecution. It has sustained and strengthened countless Christians since.

Certainly Revelation is not the whole of early Christianity; it is only one aspect, and must be read alongside the other early Christian writings, especially those more sympathetic to the gnostic idiom like the Fourth Gospel, I John, Colossians and Ephesians. But it does represent what was historically a vital aspect, without which there might have been no Christianity, and no New Testament, today. Yet it may still be felt by a sensitive reader that if it secured the survival of Christianity it was at the expense of Christ's spirit.

### (b) Is it Christian?

In one sense, undoubtedly. If to be Christian is to call Christ God and put his death at the centre of the universe, then there is no more Christian book in the Bible. The Lamb stands in the middle of the throne, bearing the marks of slaughter; he is Alpha and Omega – he shares God's titles and God's worship.

It is Christian, then, according to the letter, but what of the spirit? In spirit it may seem unchristian, even anti-christian – D. H. Lawrence called it the Judas of the NT.

### (i) Hope deferred

Authentic Christianity holds that though salvation is to be consummated hereafter it is already present and tangible now: 'if anyone

---

*u* It encouraged also the obstinate courting of martyrdom which annoyed Roman magistrates, and no doubt the Nicolaitans.

is in Christ, there is a new creation' (II Cor. 5[17]); 'if then you have been raised with Christ, seek the things that are above' (Col. 3[1]). In Revelation, however, salvation and victory may seem to lie in the future, to be earned by human effort and self-denial; in fact the book seems intoxicated with the future – intoxicated with reigning in glory hereafter, as Lawrence saw it, to compensate the frustrated desire to reign now.

But in our view Revelation was written for Christians who were intoxicated with the present, like the Corinthians whom Paul sarcastically congratulated on having already come into their fortune and entered their kingdom – and left him out (I Cor. 4[8]). The victorious Christ is present now among the churches (2[1]), and Christians already share in his victory as 'heaven-dwellers' (12[10-12]) and follow the Lamb wherever he goes (14[4]). But they may lose their crowns, unless they hold fast (3[11]); like Israel in the desert they may fall on their way to the promised land, through idolatry and fornication (2[14, 20], 12[17]–13[18]; cf. I Cor. 10[1-13]).

This is not to deny that Revelation (like I Cor.) does concentrate on the future, and may stimulate fantasies of future grandeur and revenge among the deprived, as apparently it did in the miners' chapels of Lawrence's youth. It is rather to insist that Revelation, like Paul's letters, was written to a particular situation, outside which it may be misunderstood,[v] and that the belief that the goal of human life is only fully realized beyond 'this world' is central to the NT.

## (ii) Vengeance

There is a vindictive harping in chs. 6–20 on the torture and destruction of enemies: the saints cry for vengeance (6[10]), and are told to rejoice over fallen Babylon (18[20]); for those who worship the beast 'the smoke of their torment goes up for ever and ever' (14[11]); the blood from the winepress of God's wrath floods the earth (14[20]); the birds are summoned to 'the great supper of God', to gorge on the flesh of great and small (19[17-21]).

It may be said that the vindictiveness is directed against abstractions – Babylon, the beasts, the dragon – and that equally violent

*v* Cf. C. F. D. Moule, 'The Influence of Circumstances on the Use of Eschatological Terms', *JTS* XV, 1964, pp. 1–15.

language is used today about Fascism, Communism and other -isms. It may be said that the language is part of the conventional idiom of apocalyptic and that the images are drawn from the Jewish scriptures, which were a formative influence on John and his contemporaries. Tyrannical rulers, torture and execution were part of daily life and figure in Jesus' parables. There is terrible severity in his denunciations of scribes and Pharisees, and of those who make little ones stumble, and in Paul's curses against his opponents.

But when all has been said it must be admitted that there is a spirit in Revelation which is at home in the Old Testament but hardly in the New; what can be found in small deposits elsewhere in the NT crops up here in lethal concentration. These excesses might be excused as the product of the author's personal situation and psychology – an outburst of negative feelings, as Jung put it (see pp. 42–4), in one striving for perfection. But the picture of God in Revelation cannot so easily be excused if it endorses and propagates such a spirit.

## (iii) *The wrath of the Lamb*

Lawrence pointed out that the titles of God and of Christ in Revelation are always titles of power, never of love. For him there were two kinds of Christianity, one focused on Jesus and the command to love one another, the Christianity of tenderness, the other focused on the Apocalypse, the sanctification of the undying will-to-power in man; the devil, ostensibly shut out, has slipped into the NT at the last moment in apocalyptic disguise: 'just as inevitably as Jesus had to have Judas Iscariot among his disciples, so did there have to be a Revelation in the New Testament' (*Apocalypse*, pp. 14f.).

If Revelation in its picture of God reflects ideas of kingship current in the OT and in the contemporary world, instead of transforming them in the light of Jesus (cf. Mark 10$^{42-45}$), then it hardly belongs in the NT. But just such a transformation is signalled, in the eyes of some scholars, in the master-image of the slain Lamb: John is told that the Lion of the tribe of Judah has conquererd, but sees 'in the very middle of the throne' a Lamb with the marks of sacrificial slaughter upon him, signifying the power of redemptive love (5$^{5f.}$; see pp. 124–8). Others, however, can see only a 'Maccabean' understanding of Christ's death (see pp. 19, 126), as procuring salvation for the elect and vengeance for the persecutors. For Lawrence the Lamb is but 'a lion in sheep's clothing'; 'we never see it slain, we only see it slaying mankind by the million' (*Apocalypse*, pp. 58f.).

Who is right? On our view, Lawrence misses the thrust of the symbolism. The second beast, which looks like a lamb but speaks like a dragon (13$^{11}$), which uses trickery and violence to make men worship the beast – this is indeed a dragon in sheep's clothing. It is a deliberate parody of the spirit of the Lamb, whose only power is that of the sword which issues from his mouth (1$^{16}$, 2$^{12, 16}$, 19$^{15}$) – his words, which pierce men's souls (cf. Heb. 4$^{12}$). Is this 'slaughter' simply punitive, leading to eternal torment? Or does it represent the impact of truth on illusion – the only possibility of true healing?

> The wounded surgeon plies the steel
> That questions the distempered part;
> Beneath the bleeding hands we feel
> The sharp compassion of the healer's art ...[w]

As we have seen (pp. 13 and 47), the structure of the book does make the severity of 6–20 subordinate to the pictures of Creation and Redemption in 4 and 5, and of healing and fulfilment in 21$^1$–22$^5$.[x]

To sum up, our conclusion is that Revelation, though different from the other books of the NT, does belong, indeed that in its reinterpretation of the scriptures it draws together the themes of both Testaments and deserves its place as last book of the Bible. Work on this commentary has brought awareness of a deep community of thinking and feeling between John and the other NT writers.[y]

This is not to say that his vision and attitudes ought to be accepted,

---

[w] T. S. Eliot, 'East Coker' IV, from *Four Quartets*, in *Collected Poems 1909–62*, Faber & Faber and Harcourt Brace Jovanovich, Inc. 1963, p. 201.

[x] In a similar way Paul's argument in Rom. 9–11 comes to a climax: 'God has consigned all men to disobedience [and its consequences], that he may have mercy upon all' (Rom. 11$^{32}$).

[y] Cf. Farrer p. 4: 'No other New Testament writing presents such embarrassing pictures ... yet to a large extent Revelation merely colours in what was everywhere taken for granted ... And as for divine vengeance, no New Testament Christian felt any qualms about it. God's mercy was outpoured to save as many as would repent; but the triumph of his power over irreconcilable hostility was to have all the splendour of a victory.'

by Christians or anyone else. To return to the analogy of visiting a tropical island or an art gallery, if the visitor is revolted by what he sees and hears it is no immediate help to tell him he might feel differently if he had lived all his life there, to suggest that his own vision is defective. He cannot deny his repugnance or meekly agree to call ugly beautiful. But he can be asked to be patient, and to be willing to open himself to an unfamiliar context and to new ways of seeing and hearing. He may not in the end be changed, but unless he is *willing* to be changed there is no possibility of real communication and enrichment.

For perhaps Revelation's greatest value for our day lies in its symbolic richness. As Farrer says (p. 4):

> We cannot appropriate all St John's visionary parables, as they stand, to our own use; it is vain to tell a man to imagine in a way that he finds unimaginable. But, suffering as our religion manifestly does from imaginative starvation, it can find much to feed upon in the Apocalypse, if we make the initial effort of sympathy, and yield ourselves to the movement of St John's mind.

## OUTLINE

with parallel verses from Matt. 24 in right hand column

| | | |
|---|---|---|
| 1.1–11 | Opening address | |
| 12–end | Vision of Son of man | |
| | | |
| 2, 3 | THE SEVEN LETTERS | |
| *Ephesus* | State of churches: deception, lawlessness | (4–5, 9–12) |
| *Sardis* | | |
| 2.1–7 | Ephesus: false apostles, Nicolaitans | |
| 8–11 | Smyrna: false Jews, tribulation | |
| 12–17 | Pergamum: witness, idolatry | |
| 18–29 | Thyatira: Jezebel, fornication | |
| 3.1–6 | Sardis: sleep, soiled garments | |
| 7–13 | Philadelphia: false and true Jews | |
| 14–22 | Laodicea: affluence, nakedness | |

| | | |
|---|---|---|
| 4.1–8.1 | THE SEVEN SEALS | |
| *Smyrna* | Assurance and endurance | (13) |
| *Philadelphia* | | |
| 4 | God the Creator – rainbow and sea | |
| 5 | God the Redeemer – Lamb's conquest unseals book | |
| 6.1–8 | Four horsemen = beginning of birth-pangs | (6–8) |
| 1–2 | First seal – conquest (the gospel?) | |
| 3–4 | Second seal – war | |
| 5–6 | Third seal – famine | |
| 7–8 | Fourth seal – death (pestilence) | |
| 6.9–11 | Fifth seal – comfort for martyrs | (13–14) |
| 12–17 | Sixth seal – cosmic demolition ('wrath of Lamb') | (29–30) |
| 7.1–8 | Sealing of true Israel (144,000) | |
| 9–17 | Final ingathering from all nations | (31) |
| 8.1 | Seventh seal – silence (birth of New Age?) | |
| | | |
| 8.2–14.20 | THE SEVEN TRUMPETS (THREE WOES) | |
| *Pergamum* | Idolatry and witness | (14–15) |
| *Laodicea* | | |
| 8.2–5 | Heavenly altar of incense | |
| 6–12 | First four trumpets: destruction of nature | (29) |
| 13 | Eagle – three woes | |
| 9.1–12 | Fifth trumpet = first woe: locust-scorpions | |
| 13–21 | Sixth trumpet = second woe: lion-cavalry self-destruction of idolatry; impenitence | |
| 10 | Little scroll (= the gospel) | |
| 11.1–13 | Measuring of temple, two witnesses | (14) |
| | Church's witness; penitence | (Mark 13.9–13) |
| 11.14–13.18 | Seventh trumpet = third woe (12.12) | |
| 15–19 | Heavenly worship | |
| 12.1–12 | Defeat of dragon in heaven leads to | |
| 13–17 | Flight of woman (= church) | (16–20) |
| 13 | Kingdom of beasts on earth | (15) |
| 1–10 | Sea beast: war on saints | (21–22) |
| 11–18 | Land beast: deception | (23–26) |

| | | |
|---|---|---|
| 14.1–5 | 144,000 – first fruits | |
| 6–11 | Eternal gospel; consequence of refusal | |
| 12–20 | Coming of Son of man | (30–31) |
| | Final ingathering: harvest and vintage | |
| | | |
| 15.1–22.5 | THE SEVEN BOWLS | |
| *Thyatira* | Fornication and purity: Bridegroom comes | (30) |
| *Laodicea* | | |
| 15.1–4 | Song of Moses and Lamb | |
| 5–8 | Heavenly temple | |
| 16.1–9 | First four bowls of wrath: cf. trumpets | |
| 10–11 | Fifth bowl: beast's kingdom darkened | (29) |
| 12–16 | Sixth bowl: Armageddon | |
| 17–22 | Seventh bowl: beast's city destroyed | |
| 17 | Harlot destroyed by beast | |
| 18 | Doom of harlot = Babylon = Rome | (37–40) |
| 19.1–10 | Marriage supper of Lamb | (25.1–13) |
| 11–16 | Coming of Son of man, as Word of God | (30) |
| 17–21 | Destruction of beasts | |
| 20.1–6 | Binding of Satan, rule of saints – thousand years (millennium) | |
| 7–10 | Release and final destruction of Satan | |
| 11–15 | Last judgment | |
| 21.1–8 | New Creation, expounded as | |
| 9–21 | Adornment of bride – holy city | |
| 21.22–22.5 | Ingathering of nations | |
| | Tree of life – paradise restored | |
| | | |
| 22.6–end | Final attestation | |

# Revelation 1^1-20

# *Prologue*

The work is described as a *revelation*, but takes the form of a letter *to the seven churches that are in Asia* (the Roman province, covering the western sea-board of modern Turkey). As in the Pauline letters, the opening and closing verses repay detailed study since their purpose is to introduce and underscore the author's primary concerns. The greetings and observations at beginning and end of Revelation serve to 'place' the contents of the book with respect to the historical situation and the divine plan, and in the setting of the church's worship.

I$^{1-3}$                      **TITLE**

*¹The revelation of Jesus Christ, which God gave him to show to his servants what must soon take place; and he made it known by sending his angel to his servant John, ²who bore witness to the word of God and to the testimony of Jesus Christ, even to all that he saw. ³Blessed is he who reads aloud the words of the prophecy, and blessed are those who hear, and who keep what is written therein; for the time is near.*

Before the normal epistolary opening (1$^{4ff.}$) comes a title reminiscent of OT prophetic books, a description of the work as a whole after it has been completed (cf. Isa. 1$^1$), based on 22$^{6-9}$. The Greek word for *revelation* (*apokalupsis*) means 'unveiling', the disclosure of what is hidden from human minds because it belongs to the heavenly sphere, and it gives its name to the Jewish literary genre called 'apocalyptic' (see pp. 1ff., 17ff.). These heavenly things will usually belong to the future, but the prophet may equally be required to disclose the significance of things past and present: in heaven past, present and future are in being together (see on 1$^{19}$).

The revelation is Jesus Christ's and the chain of communication

(God–Jesus–angel–John–churches) reflects the current assumption of God's remoteness from the world of men, an assumption which is, however, shattered throughout the book by the direct intervention of Jesus or God himself (as at I$^8$). While Christians expressed themselves in the thought-forms and literary conventions of their time, and were deeply influenced by them, nevertheless the immediacy of their experience of God in Christ was constantly breaking in (what they called 'the Holy Spirit'). Like the OT prophets, John claims that God is speaking directly through him to the present situation.

The purpose of the revelation is that Jesus may show his servants *what must soon take place*: the imminent fulfilment of the divine plan, of which Jesus had given advance warning, according to the synoptic gospels, on the Mount of Olives (Matt. 24 and parallels; see pp. 19–21). But the scenes and events which John goes on to describe are repetitive and jump back and forth in time; as they stand they cannot be made to fit a linear time-scale. He presents not a detailed forecast of events like a political commentator, but the invisible relentless self-assertion of God's justice and its implications for his people, in a series of symbolic tableaux and dramatic scenes, which may, however, contain much historical reference and political perception.

Did John expect the imminent end of the world? It depends whether we mean the end of the physical universe, or the end of the present world-order. The OT prophets predicted the latter in the language of the former: the sun darkened and the stars falling – demolition of the old structures to make way for a new order on *earth*. In NT times the physical language was often taken literally, but the concern was still social rather than physical; cf. II Peter 3$^{11-13}$. For Christians the end of the world in this social sense had already begun with the resurrection of Jesus and would be consummated, after various signs had happened, in his universal recognition (see on I$^7$). It was this that John believed was imminent, in contrast (we suspect) with many of his hearers who assumed from Jesus' own apocalypse that the end was not yet; cf. Luke's version (21$^{9, 12}$). He tells them that the expected signs have already been set in motion by the Lamb's victory (ch. 6), and the climax in the 'desolating sacrilege' (ch. 13; the 'abomination of desolation' of Daniel) and the coming of the Son of man (19$^{11ff.}$) is at hand. But it is clear from the epilogue

(22$^{6ff.}$) that his expectation centres on the person from whom the final events devolve. His coming must mean the end of the world which rejects him – in which the churches are in danger of being included. It is the dismantling of this human world which, as in the OT prophets, the cosmic darkenings and demolitions represent. The end of the universe is another matter: according to ch. 20 the Son of man's coming is followed by a thousand-year reign on earth.

※※

1

*his servants:* lit. slaves; in the OT 'the king's servants' were his cabinet, and the term was applied to the prophets who 'stood in God's council' (Amos 3$^7$, Jer. 23$^{18}$). Some think it refers to Christian prophets here (cf. 10$^7$ and perhaps 11$^{18}$; see D. Hill's article mentioned on p. 38, note *a*), but as at 22$^6$ it surely refers to all Christians: John writes as their colleague and brother (v. 9) having the same *Lord* (= master).

*his angel:* lit. messenger, part of the machinery of apocalyptic; see on 19$^{9f.}$, 22$^{8f.}$: he too is a fellow *servant*.

2

*the word of God:* *word* has its OT sense of a thought or purpose and the communication which makes it effective; cf. Isa. 55$^{10f.}$. In this book John *bore witness* to the whole divine plan and the testimony to it which Jesus gave, in so far as he had been enabled to see it. *Bore witness* hints already at possible unwillingness to accept it – see on 22$^{18, 20}$.

*the testimony of Jesus:* a key phrase. As at 1$^9$, 19$^{10}$, 20$^4$, it could mean testimony *to* or *about* Jesus (objective genitive), but the subjective genitive, 'Jesus' testimony', is established by the parallel *word of God*. The legal sense of the word had already acquired religious overtones in the OT, where God was represented as arraigning the nations, with Israel as his witnesses (e.g. Isa. 43$^{8-12}$): they knew his dealings at first hand. To Christians Jesus was the true Israel, God's 'son'. He was the *faithful witness* (v. 5) who gave his testimony before Pontius Pilate (John 18$^{37}$, I Tim. 6$^{13}$).

3

*Blessed is he:* the first of seven 'beatitudes'. The expression is common in the OT (e.g. Ps. 1¹ᶠ·), and for Christians had renewed force from Jesus' use of it (Matt. 5³⁻¹¹). To the woman who exclaimed 'Blessed is the womb that bore you', he replied, 'Blessed rather are those who hear the word of God and keep it' (Luke 11²⁷ᶠ·). There is an implicit warning in the expression (see on 16¹⁵), as in *bore witness*.

*he who reads aloud:* reading in antiquity was generally aloud (cf. the Ethiopian eunuch, Acts 8³⁰). Here the reference is to liturgical reading, which took place at the Christian meeting (I Tim. 4¹³) as in the synagogue (Acts 13¹⁵). Revelation should be *heard* as well as read – the effect intended being perhaps more akin to that of music than of intellectual discourse. 'The medium is' in some sense 'the message' (see pp. 13–17).

*who keep:* another keyword (*terein*), connoting both meditation (Luke 2⁵¹) and action (Rev. 12¹⁷); see on 3³. The message is far more than the medium – it is a *prophecy*, i.e. not simply a prediction but a communication from God, which contains commands as well as information. Revelation contains much prediction but is essentially exhortation; note esp. 22¹⁸ᶠ·.

*the time is near:* cf. 22¹⁰. How near? See on 17¹⁰ᶠ·, and the Danielic 'half week', pp. 182f.

$\mathrm{I}^{4-11}$          JOHN'S LETTER

⁴*John to the seven churches that are in Asia:*

*Grace to you and peace from him who is and who was and who is to come, and from the seven spirits who are before his throne,* ⁵*and from Jesus Christ the faithful witness, the first-born of the dead, and the ruler of kings on earth.*

*To him who loves us and has freed us from our sins by his blood* ⁶*and made us a kingdom, priests to his God and Father, to him be glory and dominion for ever and ever. Amen.* ⁷*Behold, he is coming with the clouds, and every eye will see him, every one who pierced him; and all tribes of the earth will wail on account of him. Even so. Amen.*

⁸*'I am the Alpha and the Omega,' says the Lord God, who is and who was and who is to come, the Almighty.*

⁹*I John, your brother, who share with you in Jesus the tribulation and the kingdom and the patient endurance, was on the island called Patmos on account of the word of God and the testimony of Jesus.* ¹⁰*I was in the Spirit*

*on the Lord's day, and I heard behind me a loud voice like a trumpet* <sup></sup>$^{11}$*saying, 'Write what you see in a book and send it to the seven churches, to Ephesus and to Smyrna and to Pergamum and to Thyatira and to Sardis and to Philadelphia and to Laodicea.'*

A secular letter began 'A to B, greeting' (Acts 23$^{26}$) and might continue with thanksgiving to the gods and prayer for the recipient before the message proper. In the NT this conventionally religious form is enriched or replaced by Christian themes, selected to prepare for the main ideas of the letter. Here 'greeting' is replaced as in Paul's letters by the Christian keywords *grace* and *peace*, and their source is described in three threefold statements. *Grace and peace* are not simply from 'God our Father and the Lord Jesus Christ', Paul's usual formula, but

(1) *from him who is and was and is to come*, proclaiming God's active everlastingness, over against the *aeternitas* claimed on Rome's coinage; cf. his self-disclosure to Moses in Egypt (Ex. 3$^{14}$);

(2) *from the seven spirits who are before the throne*, representing God's active presence, which is (or should be) embodied in the churches;

(3) *from Jesus Christ* (= Messiah, anointed), who is himself given a triple title, based verbally on the messianic Psalm 89:

(*a*) *the faithful witness* (see on v. 2), whose witness is (or should be) reproduced in his church;

(*b*) *the first-born of the dead*, who by his resurrection has inaugurated a new order and guaranteed the resurrection of all;

(*c*) *the ruler of kings on earth*, who is already reigning over those who condemned him.

This description of Christ in himself is followed by a corresponding description of him in his effect on believers:

(*a*) *who loves us*, – the manward aspect of his 'faithful witness' to God (cf. John 13$^{1}$);

(*b*) *has freed us from our sins by his blood*, as God rescued Israel from Egyptian bondage by the blood of the Passover lamb; his resurrection can promise us life only because his death has made us at one with God;

(*c*) *made us a kingdom, priests to his God and Father*, as God made Israel (Ex. 19$^{4-6}$). Christ's rule over earthly kings is in and through his people.

The exodus echoes recur throughout, with constant allusions to Isa. 40–66 and the second exodus from Babylon, which Isaiah saw as a new act of creation. *Grace and peace* are from the exodus God, who has already rescued his people by Christ's death on the cross, but, as we shall see, much can go wrong in their journey through the wilderness, before they reach the promised land, where many of them think they already are.

The little ascription of praise (vv. 5f.) itself announces a theme which recurs throughout the book – the giving (or refusing) of glory to God. Worship is the true creaturely response of man to God and in itself the defeat of the rebellious powers which were operative in Egypt and Babylon, and now Rome. 'Meet more often to give thanks and glory to God', wrote Ignatius[a] on his way to martyrdom in Rome, 'for when you meet frequently Satan's powers are thrown down' (*Eph.* 13; *ECW*, p. 79). Revelation constantly echoes the themes and phraseology of Christian worship.

Verse 7 raises questions crucial for the right understanding of all that follows. *Even so. Amen* marks its significance – in the language of worship, not literal prediction. It is echoed at the end: 'Even so; I am coming soon.' 'Amen; Come, Lord Jesus.'

The verse runs together two OT passages which were highly significant for the first Christians. First, Dan. $7^{13}$:

> Behold, with the clouds of heaven
> there came one like a son of man,
> and he came to the Ancient of Days
> and was presented before him.
> And to him was given dominion . . .

Daniel saw the vindication in heaven of a human figure, representing

---

*a* Ignatius was bishop of Antioch early in the second century. He was taken under arrest to Rome overland through Asia Minor, and wrote seven letters – four from Smyrna, to the churches in Ephesus, Magnesia and Tralles, and to the Romans; three from Troas, to the churches in Philadelphia and Smyrna which had entertained him, and to Polycarp the bishop of Smyrna. His letters can be read in the translation by M. Staniforth, *Early Christian Writings*, Penguin Classics 1968 (referred to as *ECW*). Though he wrote to three of the churches addressed by John about fifteen years later, there is no sign that he knew Rev. – but see note *f* on $3^{12}$ below.

Israel suffering on earth for its faith, over against a series of beasts, representing heathen empires – men reduced to the level of beasts by idolatrous arrogance as Nebuchadnezzar was (Dan. 4). The words had been quoted according to tradition by Jesus at his trial, in reply to the High Priest's question, 'Are you the Messiah?', and earlier in his own apocalypse (Matt. 24³⁰), where the 'Son of man's coming' signified not his vindication before God but his universal recognition by men, as it does here.

This fits in with the second passage, Zech. 12¹⁰ff. (also woven in at Matt. 24³⁰): 'I will pour out on the house of David and the inhabitants of Jerusalem a spirit of compassion and supplication, so that when they look on him whom they have pierced, they shall mourn for him, as for an only child . . . a first-born' (cf. Rev. 1⁵). But what is the sense of 'mourn'? Zechariah goes on to describe the mourning of all the tribes of the land (the word in Hebrew and Greek could also mean *earth*) and the opening of a fountain for cleansing from sin and uncleanness (cf. Rev. 22¹⁻³), coupled with the removal of idols, false prophets and the unclean spirit (cf. 16¹³, 19²⁰).

But such a picture of Christ's coming attended by penitence and purification seems clean counter to the carnage of the coming described at 19¹⁷⁻²¹; cf. the wine press full of blood (14²⁰) and the fire from heaven (20⁹). Many, therefore, take the *mourning* to be vain remorse, and assume that Zechariah is being quoted without respect to context, as seems to be the case at Matt. 24³⁰.[b] On the other hand, John's use of scripture usually shows marked awareness of context, and Daniel and Zechariah are two of his chief sources. Universal penitence and cleansing is nowhere described in Revelation but it is adumbrated at 11¹³ and assumed at 21²⁴⁻22³, where the nations bring their glory into the new Jerusalem, the leaves of the tree of life are for their healing, and there is no more curse.

---

[b] 'Then will appear the sign of the Son of man in heaven, and then all the tribes of the earth will mourn.' The 'sign' is probably the cross, as at *Didache* 16⁶ read in the light of the *Letter of Barnabas* 12²⁻⁴ (both in *ECW*); its appearance proclaims Christ's triumph, to the dismay of all but the elect. John no doubt shared the same expectation, but may have seen wider and deeper significance in the cross: the Son of man who comes is the 'Lamb with the marks of slaughter upon him' (see on 5⁶).

It is vital for understanding Revelation to recognize that John thinks in symbolic pictures, which may be formally contradictory, and that in seeking a synthesis we should let the framework interpret the apocalyptic visions and not vice versa (see p. 13). If we do, the carnage is not the last word but represents the destruction of falsehood and all who follow it, leading to redemption and a new order; and we shall see that the pictures of carnage carry hints of Christ's sacrificial death. His final coming is not something separate from his first coming which ended on the cross, but its consummation: those who pierced him will be pierced by his 'sword' (19¹⁵; cf. John 19³⁴⁻³⁷; see p. 51). John, like Paul, shares the OT hope that God will gather in all nations – through the death of his Son and the witness of his royal and priestly people (v. 6). It is their witness, or the lack of it, which is John's main concern, as the letters to the *seven churches* will show.

Like Paul writing to his own churches, *John* needs no introduction to them (though we would dearly like to know who he was; see p. 38), only a reminder of what they *share in Jesus*, a sovereignty based on suffering and validated by endurance – a different kind of *kingdom* from what some Christians had in mind (cf. I Cor. 4⁸). *Patmos* was 65 miles from Ephesus. There is no contemporary evidence that it was used as a penal settlement, but *relegatio ad insulam* (committal to an island) was a means sometimes used by provincial governors, normally against *honestiores* (men of high rank – was John one?[c]) to keep them out of mischief.

Verse 10 gives the dramatic setting of the revelation as a whole (its constituent parts may come from various times and places). *In the Spirit* means under the control of God's Spirit, like the OT Prophets, and the *Lord's day* is probably Sunday, the first day of the week, when Jesus rose from the dead and when the church met to celebrate the Lord's Supper. Some take it to mean the OT 'Day of the Lord', when God will come in judgment, to which John has been transported by the Spirit, but as early Christians understood the Lord's Supper, the final coming of Christ was anticipated in it, for good or ill

[c] Cf. J. N. Sanders, 'St John on Patmos', *NTS* 9, 1963, pp. 75–85; for Tertullian's reference to his being exiled by Domitian, see the Introduction, p. 39, note *e*.

(cf. I Cor. 11²⁶⁻³²). It is therefore a time for self-examination, which is reflected in the structure of the seven letters in chs. 2 and 3, and again in the epilogue.

There were many more congregations in Asia than *seven*. 'The seven churches' are introduced as a known group (see p. 78). Some see John as a local Christian leader who had conventicles in just these seven places, which he was trying to control from his exile, but the seven represent all the churches: *seven* is the number of fulness (see p. 14), and the scope of the book is ecumenical, not sectarian.

**4**

*from him who is...*: the Divine Name I AM at Ex. 3¹⁴ was interpreted by the LXX as 'He who is'. Such triple formulas are found in Greek religion, but the expected 'who will be' is pointedly changed to *who is to come* – lit. *the coming one*. God is dynamic, not static. This is the first example of John's peculiar Greek grammar (see p. 16): instead of genitives after *from* there are nominatives. God is 'always the subject' (Caird, p. 16). But this cannot be pressed, or it must apply to the devil too (20²)!

*the seven spirits*: they signify God active in the world, substantially no different from 'the Holy Spirit', but a different scriptural model – the seven lamps of Zech. 4² (cf. Rev. 4⁵) and the seven eyes of Zech. 4¹⁰, 'which range through the whole earth' (cf. Rev. 5⁶). The author is thinking of the Spirit as the inspirer of the churches (cf. 3¹): *seven* again signifies completeness.

**5**

*the faithful witness*: cf. Ps. 89³⁷ (RSV margin); Isa. 55⁴, referring to David, the model for the Messiah. The title is applied to Antipas (2¹³) and pointedly repeated at the beginning of the letter to Laodicea (3¹⁴), where there is no witness. Again, this and the following phrases are in the nominative instead of genitive.

*the first-born of the dead*: cf. Ps. 89²⁷, and more pertinently Col. 1¹⁸. To Jews the resurrection of the dead was not individual resuscitation but a corporate event at the end of the age. Consequently the first Christians understood Jesus' resurrection as proleptic, the 'first fruits' of the general resurrection (I Cor. 15²⁰) – in Jewish thought the first of a series includes the whole (see on 14⁵). Another phrase from Col. 1¹⁵⁻²⁰ is also used at 3¹⁴: were Christians tending to undervalue Christ over against 'principalities and powers', as at Colossae, Laodicea's neighbour?

*ruler of kings on earth:* cf. Ps. 89²⁷ again, and John 18³⁶: his kingship is not of this world but of the real world 'above'. He is master of the spiritual powers behind the human authorities (Col. 1¹⁶, 2¹⁵), before whom Christians must bear their witness (Mark 13⁹).

*has freed us:* better *freed*; the tense is aorist, in contrast with the present *loves*. His eternal love was revealed in the moment of his death (cf. I John 1⁷⁻²², 4¹⁰). In Jewish thought a martyr death could win atonement for the sins of the people, but the primary reference is to the Passover lamb (cf. John 1²⁹, I Peter 1¹⁸ᶠ·). Many MSS (see p. x) read *washed* for *freed* (*lousanti* for *lusanti*), which gives attractive sense (cf. 7¹⁴, Eph. 5²⁵ᶠ·), but *freed* has stronger MS support and fits better the exodus imagery. *Washed* could have got in through mishearing (texts were copied by dictation), or through misunderstanding of *by his blood*: *by* is lit. *in* (Gk. *en*, which was used in translation from Hebrew to represent *b*, meaning 'by means of' or 'at the cost of').

## 6

*a kingdom, priests:* exodus echoes again (Ex. 19⁶; cf. I Peter 2⁹). *Kingdom* means 'rule' as well as 'realm': Christians state Christ's rule over earthly kings. Their office is priestly: representing God to the world and offering the world's worship to God – the 'priesthood' belongs to the church as a whole, not individuals. See on 2²⁶, 5¹⁰, 20⁴⁻⁶, 21²²⁻²²⁵.

*to him be glory:* ascription of glory was not just formal piety; words effected what they signified. God is recognized and his presence made effective in the world through his people's praises; likewise Satan (13⁴ᶠ·).

## 7

*He is coming with the clouds:* universal recognition of the final victory already won on the cross; see on 5⁵ᶠ·. The unnamed witness of the *piercing* at John 19³⁵ will be expanded to *every eye. All the tribes* is taken from Zech. 12¹²ᶠᶠ·, but prepares for the recurrent formula 'tribe, tongue, people and nation' for those redeemed by the Lamb, deceived by the beast, and finally taken up into the city of the twelve tribes of

Israel. The *wailing* may be self-regarding, *on account of* his vindication and their impending condemnation, but the Greek (*koptesthai epi*) and the context in Zech. 12$^{10}$ both suggest sorrow *for* him, for what they had done to him. The same question – remorse or penitence? – arises at 11$^{13}$.

*Even so. Amen.: Amen* ('so be it') is the human response to the divine *Nai* ('yes'), which prepares for God's declaration in v. 8; cf. 22$^{20}$ and II Cor. 1$^{20}$.

**8**

*the Alpha and the Omega:* the first and last letters of the Greek alphabet, the sum of all things. For possible connection with *Lord*, the Greek paraphrase of the divine name JHVH, which in Greek magic became IAO, see Farrer, p. 63. Playing with letters and numbers was important then, if not to us (see pp. 14f.).

*the Almighty: pantokrator* is the Greek translation of Hebrew *sabaoth*, 'of hosts'. It is a favourite title for God (4$^8$, 11$^{17}$, 15$^3$, 16$^{7, 14}$, 19$^{6, 15}$, 21$^{22}$), and denotes 'not One who can do anything, but One who holds together and controls all things',[d] over against the pretensions of the dragon and the beast (13$^{2ff.}$).

**9**

*Tribulation* and *kingdom* (sovereignty, cf. v. 6) are two sides of one coin, and the tension between them is expressed by *endurance*, a keyword (2$^{2f.,}$ $^{19}$, 3$^{10}$, 13$^{10}$, 14$^{12}$), with a flavour of expectancy, not stoicism.

*the word of God and testimony of Jesus:* see on v. 2. John was on Patmos either to receive the revelation (cf. v. 2), or more likely because of his own witness. For the legend of his being plunged in boiling oil by Domitian before being exiled, see p. 39 note *e*.

**10**

*the Lord's day:* there is no firm evidence that this means Sunday till much later; it may originally have meant Easter Day. But the significance of Easter is enshrined in 'the first day of the week', when Christians met (Acts 20$^7$, I Cor. 16$^2$), through the first day/eighth day

d F. J. A. Hort, *The Apocalypse of St John, I–III*, Macmillan 1908, p. 14.

pattern which is basic to Revelation.[e] This stemmed from the seven 'days' of creation in Gen. 1, taken as each a thousand years (Ps. 90[4]). At the end of the sixth day, which was held to be given over to Satan, God would send his Messiah to usher in the seventh day of rest (the 'millennium'; see on 20[1ff.]), to be followed by the eighth day of the timeless Age to Come. The eighth day is of course the *first* day of the next week, and Christians saw Jesus' resurrection on the first day of the week as inaugurating the Age to Come, and giving them a share in it through his presence in the eucharist. *In the Spirit on the Lord's day* John is immersed in the ultimate timeless reality, on which he reports in a series of quasi-historical pictures.

There is evidence to suggest that in Asia and Egypt the first day of the month, and perhaps one of the days of the week, was called *Sebastē*, Emperor's Day. Christians may have called Sunday (*dies solis*) Lord's Day (*kuriakē*) in reaction. Certainly Revelation presents Christ as true Emperor, in contrast with the Antichrist of ch. 13, and as *sun* (v. 16).[f]

*like a trumpet: like* recurs constantly, as in Ezekiel. Heavenly things can only be communicated by analogy, and the associations of a term are more important than its literal meaning. For *trumpet* see on 8[1-5].

**11**
*write what you see:* see on v. 19. As in the OT prophets, *see* covers words as well as visions: 'the words of Amos . . . which he saw' (Amos 1[1]).

*book:* a scroll, as used for the scriptures in the synagogue or at Qumran. This is to be read in the churches as scripture; cf. 22[18-19].

*churches: ecclēsia* in secular Greek meant an assembly; in the LXX it was used for 'the congregation of the Lord', Israel. Christians saw themselves as God's Israel, and each local church as embodying the whole church. John uses the word only in the local sense, but *the seven* signify the whole church, just as the seven spirits (v. 4) signify the Spirit.

On each of the seven cities, see on chs. 2 and 3.

e See pp. 14f. above on the significance of numbers.

f On 'Emperor's Day' see A. Deissmann, *Bible Studies*, ET T. & T. Clark and Scribner's 1901, pp. 218ff. For the whole question see W. Rordorf, *Sunday*, ET SCM Press and Westminster Press 1968.

THE VISION OF THE SON OF MAN

$^{12}$Then I turned to see the voice that was speaking to me, and on turning I saw seven golden lampstands, $^{13}$and in the midst of the lampstands one like a son of man, clothed with a long robe and with a golden girdle round his breast; $^{14}$his head and his hair were white as white wool, white as snow; his eyes were like a flame of fire, $^{15}$his feet were like burnished bronze, refined as in a furnace, and his voice was like the sound of many waters; $^{16}$in his right hand he held seven stars, from his mouth issued a sharp two-edged sword, and his face was like the sun shining in full strength.

$^{17}$When I saw him, I fell at his feet as though dead. But he laid his right hand upon me, saying, 'Fear not, I am the first and the last, $^{18}$and the living one; I died, and behold I am alive for evermore, and I have the keys of Death and Hades. $^{19}$Now write what you see, what is and what is to take place hereafter. $^{20}$As for the mystery of the seven stars which you saw in my right hand, and the seven golden lampstands, the seven stars are the angels of the seven churches and the seven lampstands are the seven churches.'

The 'son of man' theme has already been announced in the allusion to Dan. 7$^{13}$ at v. 7, and will be taken up at 14$^{14ff.}$ and 19$^{11ff.}$. The details of this vision will serve to introduce each of the seven letters. So the theme is of great structural importance, and the Danielic context of persecution, vindication and judgment should be kept in mind. But it is more than a rehash of Daniel. There, the *one like a son of man* is a symbolic figure (over against the beasts) representing the saints of the Most High. Here he is a real man who *died* and is *alive* (v. 18); but this man is described in terms belonging to the glory of God in Ezekiel's vision, or even to the Ancient of Days himself (*hair like wool*, Dan. 7$^9$); and, though an individual, he retains the inclusiveness of Daniel's human figure: in *the midst of the lampstands* signifies his presence in his churches, the *seven stars in his hand* his hold and control over them (v. 20). In this vision John sees what every eye will see (v. 7) – a sight too much for mortal eyes (v. 17) – but his concern is less with the future coming than with the present demands and promises of the unseen Lord, which are spelt out in the seven letters and backed up in the following visions.

Whatever John actually *saw*, the details of the vision are drawn mainly from Daniel and Ezekiel, and build up an impression which is not visual so much as auditory and dynamic. T. Boman (*Hebrew Thought Compared with Greek*, ch. 2) argues that whereas to the Greeks beauty was visual (harmonious order), the Hebrews were interested not in the photographic appearance of things but in the dynamic impression which description of them conveyed, through ear rather than eye. Descriptions of Noah's ark or Solomon's temple tell how they were made; descriptions of God tell what he is and does. They do not help us to visualize the scene; indeed often the result would be grotesque: e.g. 'the trees of the field shall clap their hands' (Isa. 55$^{12}$), 'my breasts are like towers' (Song of Songs 8$^{10}$), or the *sword issuing from his mouth* (v. 16), which has produced unhappy results in Christian art.$^g$ But taken functionally these images express cosmic joy or virgin inaccessibility, just as the sword expresses the piercing word of God (Heb. 4$^{12}$). Thus the *whiteness* of *head* and *hair* (v. 14) convey antiquity – Jesus too is *first and last* (v. 17), Alpha and Omega (22$^{13}$).

Even colours are dynamic rather than simply visual. 'It was not colours but light and what illuminates which were for the Israelites the ideal of beauty ... God did not surround himself with colours but shrouded himself in *light* as in a mantle (Ps. 104$^2$); ... [his] glory appeared on the top of the mountain like a devouring *fire* (Ex. 24$^{17}$)' (Boman, pp. 88f.). Thus '*white* as snow, eyes like *fire*, feet like *bronze* refined in a *furnace*' all convey the speaker's divine glory; cf. the rainbow and jewels at 4$^3$. As beauty conveys the reality of God, so the ugliness which parodies it in later visions conveys the false reality of Satan (On Hebrew imagery, see also pp. 13–17).

It would be a mistake, however, to consider only the Hebraic background. John wrote in Greek for people living in the cradle of Greek civilization. There are local references in *white wool* and *burnished bronze* which the people of Laodicea and Thyatira might pick up, and the *seven stars* suggest a challenge to the imperial mythology,

g Cf. Jung's comment on the lamb with seven horns and seven eyes, 'Altogether it must have looked pretty awful' (*Answer to Job*, p. 124).

propagated through the coinage (Stauffer, pp. 151f.). When Domitian's son died in 83 he had him proclaimed a god, and coins were struck which showed his mother Domitia as queen of heaven and the child sitting on the globe of heaven, playing with the stars. The seven planets were a symbol of heavenly dominion, and *in his right hand he held seven stars* would be read both as a contemputuous dismissal of imperial pretensions, and as a bold assertion of the cosmic significance of the congregations of humble and persecuted people whom the *seven stars* represent (v. 20). 'It was necessary to provide the church with a make-weight against the power which heathenism exerted over the Asian cities through its abundant use of symbolism in literature and in art' (Swete, p. cxxxiv).

꼬꼬

**12**

*seven golden lampstands:* better *lamps* – the distinction between *stand* and *lamp*, as at Matt. 5$^{15}$, is not in mind. The Greek word is used for the seven-branched candelabrum of the Jewish sanctuary (Ex. 25$^{31}$, Zech. 4$^{2,}$ $^{10}$). This has become *seven lamps*, which are interpreted as the *seven churches* (v. 20). The *lamps* suggest their role of *witness*, which is developed from the imagery of Zech. 4 at 11$^{3ff.}$; cf. 'let your light shine before men' (Matt. 5$^{14-16}$).

**13**

*in the midst of the lampstands:* the Son of man who is to come is already and always present in his churches; the final 'coming' is the unveiling of what already is.

*one like a son of man: son of* in the Bible expresses nature ('sons of thunder'), function ('sons of the bridechamber') or destiny ('son of perdition').

**13–16**

To track down each motif is to 'unweave the rainbow' (Caird, p. 25), but we need to be aware of the knowledge of the OT and of the local background which John shared with his hearers.

**13**

A *long robe* reaching to the feet was worn by the Jewish high priest (Ex. 28$^4$, Wisd. 18$^{24}$); for the *golden girdle* cf. Dan. 10$^5$.

## 14

The *head* comes from the picture of the Ancient of Days (Dan. 7$^9$, I Enoch 46$^1$); for *white wool* see on 3$^{18}$.

The *eyes* come from the angel of Dan. 10$^6$; *flame of fire* suggests spiritual insight; cf. Rev. 4$^5$ and 5$^6$; Isa. 11$^{2f.}$. See also Rev. 2$^{18}$, 19$^{12}$.

## 15

For the *feet* cf. again Dan. 10$^6$, and Ezek. 1$^{4, 7}$: the four living creatures which support God's throne. *Burnished bronze* is a guess: *chalkolibanos* is only found in Greek literature here and at 2$^{18}$, and in dependent passages. It was probably a special product of Thyatira (Hemer, pp. 247-60), but meant to recall Ezekiel's vision of God himself (Ezek. 1$^{27}$, 8$^2$). The *furnace* evokes the story of the three who refused to worship Nebuchadnezzar's great image; cf. Dan. 3, Rev. 13$^{15}$. There is a variant 'as from a fiery furnace' which reflects this. For his *voice* see Ezek. 1$^{24}$, and 43$^2$.

## 16

For the *seven stars* see on v. 20. For the *sword* from his *mouth* cf. Isa. 49$^2$, 'he made my mouth like a sharp sword' and 11$^4$, 'with the breath of his lips he shall slay the wicked'. Eph. 6$^{17}$ speaks of 'the sword of the Spirit, which is the word of God', and Heb. 4$^{12f.}$ brings in the idea of piercing scrutiny which pervades the letters, 'the word of God ... sharper than any two-edged sword, piercing ... and discerning the thoughts of the heart'. The image is taken up in the balancing vision of 19$^{11ff.}$, where Christ is named the Word of God.

Jesus's face shone like the *sun* at the transfiguration (Matt. 17$^2$). The vision was seen on *Sun*day (*dies solis*).

## 17f.

On John *dead* with fear (cf. Dan. 10$^{7ff.}$, Acts 9$^4$) the *living one* lays the *right hand* which held the stars (one must not try to visualize it!). He is *first* and *last*, like God (Isa. 44$^6$, 48$^{12}$), but the emphasis is on his present life. *Living* conveys far more than just being alive: life of the Age to Come (*alive for evermore*); cf. Rom. 5$^{9f.}$.

*I died:* the intellectual atmosphere was conducive to 'docetism', the view that Christ's humanity and suffering were only apparent, a divine charade. Revelation like the other Johannine writings and like Paul stresses the reality of his death; Christians called to face death for their faith needed the assurance of a real death and real resurrection. The words are taken up in the letter to Smyrna, where there was suffering and fear, and docetism may have been in the air, to judge from Ignatius' letter to the Smyrnaeans (*ECW*, pp. 119–23).

*the keys of death and Hades:* according to the rabbis, 'three keys has the Holy One kept in his own power: the key of the womb, the key of rain and the key of the tomb'. *Hades* in Greek mythology was the king and thence the realm of the dead; in the LXX it translates Sheol, the pit. At 6⁸, 20¹⁴ *death and Hades* are powers rather than places, and the keys represent control over death not just as a physical fact but as a spiritual state, and over 'him who has the power of death, that is the devil' (Heb. 2¹⁴; cf. Rev. 9¹, 20¹).

**19**
*what you see:* lit. what you *have seen* – many think it refers to the vision of the Son of man, while *what is* refers to the state of the churches (chs. 2f.) and *what is to take place* to the rest of the book. But chs. 4–22 cannot be regarded simply as a forecast of coming events (see on 1¹⁻³): past, present and future are mixed up together. The phrase is probably an adaptation of the common formula 'what was, is and shall be', expressing the mystery of existence in its totality, which a prophet is privileged to see and declare.[h]

**20**
*mystery:* usually in the NT *mustērion* means 'divine secret' cf. Dan. 2²²⋅²⁷ff., but here and at 17⁷ perhaps no more than 'symbol'.

*the angels of the seven churches: angelos* is literally 'messenger', and can mean 'ruler' (cf. Dan. 10¹³ff.), but to take the angels as couriers, or as the bishops of the churches, is to miss the idiom (see p. 16). Angels are the spiritual counterparts of earthly realities; here they represent the churches seen as spiritual entities. *Stars* are the lamps of heaven; to the Greeks they were gods, to the Jews angels (Farrer, p. 68). The churches spiritually replace the planetary powers, commonly held to control human destiny – see on 2²⁸, and above on imperial pretensions. John

h W. C. van Unnik, 'A Formula Describing Prophecy', *NTS* 9, 1963, pp. 86–94.

may also be drawing on the Targum (see p. 40) of Ex. 39$^{37}$, 40$^4$, where the seven lamps of the candelabrum are taken to represent the planets, and the planets to represent 'the just that shine unto eternity in their righteousness'; cf. Dan. 12$^3$ (McNamara, *Palestinian Targum*, pp. 196–8).

# Revelation 2¹–3²²

These chapters differ so obviously in manner and matter from the rest that many have thought that they were written at a different time. But they are closely linked with ch. 1, from which the titles of Christ at the beginning of each letter are drawn, and with the rest of the book, particularly 19–22, in which the promises at the end of each letter are picked up. We have already noted that the themes of the first four letters relate in turn to the four main divisions of the book (pp. 44f.; cf. pp. 52ff.). If then Revelation is a unity as it stands, it is important to interpret the difference between these chapters and the rest correctly: they are as much part of the overture as ch. 1, giving the key to what follows. The unearthliness of the visions must be held constantly in the light of their down-to-earth concerns.

But how far was John interested in daily life? The seven churches symbolize the church as a whole (p. 65): was he parcelling out a single message artificially, as with the seven seals, trumpets and bowls? Ramsay was able to point to so many motifs which connect with what history and archaeology can tell us about the seven cities,[i] that it is in fact clear that John had intimate pastoral knowledge of each congregation and was dealing with actual situations in each place. Some of Ramsay's instances are far-fetched, as Hemer has shown, but the latter's careful work has abundantly confirmed and amplified his results. In the task of interpretation, therefore, the letters, which deal with real life, provide the key to the visions.

Each letter is composed to a pattern. It is addressed to the 'angel of the church'; begins with a title of the Christ who speaks, drawn

---

i The evidence is often oblique and problematical, and cannot be briefly presented, but W. Barclay, *Letters to the Seven Churches*, SCM Press and Abingdon Press 1957, is a lively and popular account. For Ramsay and Hemer, see Introduction, p. 38 note c and p. 39 note d.

from ch. 1;[j] goes on to a diagnosis of the situation ('I know your works'), followed by praise, censure or warning; and ends with promises (taken up in the final chapters), and the refrain 'He who has an ear, ...'. This pattern may echo the style of imperial edicts (Stauffer, p. 181); also, more significantly, the liturgical pattern of the eucharist, as noted by Bornkamm and Prigent (see the Introduction, p. 41 notes k and l). Announcement of the Lord's coming has a double consequence: promises of grace to some, warning of exclusion (*anathema*) to others. A man must examine himself, to avoid falling under judgment at the Lord's coming (I Cor. 11$^{27-32}$). The theme of the letters is discernment and fidelity; Dan. 1-6, Jesus' Apocalypse and the story of the Last Supper and Gethsemane are very much in mind.

The arrangement of the cities is geographically significant: the seven all lay on a main Roman road and formed a circuit (see map), starting from Ephesus, the nearest to Patmos. From these centres the whole province could be covered[k] – as such they were perhaps an already recognized group (see on 1$^{11}$) and the details of each local situation add up to a unified message for all the churches, which the *seven* symbolize.

$2^{1-7}$      TO THE CHURCH IN EPHESUS

2 *'To the angel of the church in Ephesus write: "The words of him who holds the seven stars in his right hand, who walks among the seven golden lampstands.*

*²I know your works, your toil and your patient endurance, and how you cannot bear evil men but have tested those who call themselves apostles but*

j Farrer gives a brilliant exposition of the relations of the letters to the Son of man vision, and to the four main divisions of the book (pp. 70f., 83–6); see above, pp. 44f.

k Ephesus, Smyrna, Pergamum and Sardis were assize cities; Philadelphia and Thyatira became such later; Laodicea had a strategic position in the south-east of the province.

*are not, and found them to be false;* ³*I know you are enduring patiently and bearing up for my name's sake, and you have not grown weary.* ⁴*But I have this against you, that you have abandoned the love you had at first.* ⁵*Remember then from what you have fallen, repent and do the works you did at first. If not, I will come to you and remove your lampstand from its place, unless you repent.* ⁶*Yet this you have, you hate the works of the Nicolaitans, which I also hate.* ⁷*He who has an ear, let him hear what the Spirit says to the churches. To him who conquers I will grant to eat of the tree of life, which is in the paradise of God."'*

Ephesus was the greatest city of the province of Asia, and vied with Smyrna and Pergamum for the recognition of its primacy. It was a centre not only of the worship of the fertility goddess Artemis (Diana to the Romans), whose temple was one of the seven wonders of the ancient world, but also of the emperor cult and gladiatorial games. There was a strong Jewish community, and much magical practice (Acts 19¹³ᶠᶠ·). It was the base for Paul's work in Asia, Apollos taught there, there was a group of disciples connected with John the Baptist (Acts 18¹⁹–19¹⁰), and in later tradition it was the home of the apostle John to whom both Gospel and Apocalypse were attributed.

As a natural centre for Christian variations and deviations, it demanded of the church a keen nose for heresy (cf. I Tim. 1³ᶠᶠ·, Acts 20²⁸⁻³¹), and the militancy of the devotees of Artemis would make *patient endurance* a standing necessity. In both respects its performance was exemplary (vv. 2f., 6) – but *you have abandoned the love you had at first.* Such loss of love was a mark of the 'great apostasy' expected in the last days – 'False prophets will arise and lead many astray. And because lawlessness is multiplied, most men's love will grow cold' (Matt. 24¹¹ᶠ·) – but here it is linked not with error and lawlessness (as practised by the *Nicolaitans*) but their opposites. If John is taking up an apocalyptic cliché it is in a backhanded way which is important for the interpretation of the book as a whole: 'desolating sacrilege' is found 'in the holy place' (Matt. 24¹⁵), no doubt to the astonishment of its perpetrators. The church has *fallen* (v. 5). John's concern throughout is with truth and falsehood, above all in the church, and 'truth' is far wider than correct belief and action. In the other Johannine writings it is bound up with *love*, as falsehood is with the devil's hatred and murder (John 8$^{31ff.}$, I John 3$^{8-20}$, 4$^{20}$).

Has their orthodoxy become censoriousness? The promise of *the tree of life, in the paradise of God* (v. 7) suggests that the cause of their *fall* is 'that ancient serpent' the source of all falsehood and hatred (John 8$^{44}$), 'the accuser of our brethren' (Rev. 12$^{9f.}$). Censoriousness is the very devil. Revelation is concerned with truth and fidelity, and love is barely mentioned, but this opening letter makes clear, like I Cor. 13, that without love the rest is worthless. Paradise regained is the climax of the book, but orthodoxy on its own is its negation .

The promise is to him who *conquers*, a refrain in the letters and a keyword in Revelation. *Nikan* in the NT is practically confined to the Johannine writings,[1] and to the theme of victory over Satan through apparent defeat (cf. John 16$^{33}$) – victory won by faithful witness to the truth, validated if necessary by death (12$^{11}$, John 18$^{37}$), in contrast with the violence and deceit by which Satan appears to *conquer* (11$^{7}$, 13$^{7}$).

‍‍‍

1

*the angel:* see on 1$^{20}$. The message is to the community as a spiritual entity – each *you* is singular.

*the seven stars . . . lampstands:* the title picks up the end of the Son of man vision (see on 1$^{12-20}$). The speaker is Lord of the churches as spiritual entities, companion of the churches as empirical realities, and *knows* them inside out. *Walks among* perhaps recalls the one like a son of God walking with the three in the furnace (Dan. 3$^{25}$).

2f.

*I know your works:* this is the Lord's day (see on 1$^{10}$), when he brings to light men's hearts and actions (cf. I Cor. 4$^{5}$, 11$^{27-32}$). *Works* was a Jewish and Christian keyword – the performance by which a man stands or falls at the judgment. *Toil* (used by Paul of missionary work) and *patient endurance* (see on 1$^{9}$) are specified as contesting false missionaries (the second *and* is, as often, explanatory), and in v. 3 they are

[1] But note also Rom 12$^{21}$, 'Do not be conquered by evil, but conquer evil with good', which looks like a summary of Jesus' teaching on treatment of enemies.

elaborated with characteristic word-plays: you have *borne* up, though you cannot *bear* evil men; in spite of your toil (*kopos*) you have not grown weary (*kekopiakas*). The commendation may be double-edged, in view of Paul's injunctions to *bear* with erring and difficult brethren (Rom. 15$^1$, Gal. 6$^1$, $^2$, cf. Ignatius to *Polycarp* 1, 2; *ECW*, p. 127).

*call themselves apostles: apostolos* means 'one sent out', a delegate, missionary. In the first century *apostles* were figures of great authority, a wider group than the twelve (21$^{14}$; cf. I Cor. 12$^{28}$, 15$^{5-9}$ – Paul counted himself one) – usually itinerant teachers as in the *Didache*,[m] a manual of church order which may be roughly contemporary with Revelation (*ECW*, pp. 232–7). Since those who *call themselves Jews* in the next letter clearly were Jews in the ordinary sense, presumably these *apostles* did have some authority and their *falseness* lay in their character and teaching, which no doubt bore some relation to that of the *Nicolaitans* (vv. 6, 14) and Jezebel (v. 20). As with Paul's opponents, their outward credentials would have made their falseness harder to discern (cf. II Cor. 11$^{4-15}$). *Testing* was a standard necessity, as in any age of inspiration; cf. Matt. 7$^{15ff}$, I Thess. 5$^{21}$, I John 4$^{1-6}$, *Didache* 11 (*ECW*, pp. 232–4). Deception, even of the elect, was one of the expected signs of the End (Matt. 24$^{24}$, I Tim. 4$^1$, I John 2$^{18ff}$).

**4**

*abandoned the love you had at first:* another mark of the End (Matt. 24$^{12}$). Has brotherly love given way to censoriousness? Cf. Paul's warning (II Thess. 3$^{14f}$, II Tim. 2$^{24-26}$). Ignatius (see p. 62 note *a*), after praising their resistance to false teaching, urged them to pray for all men, and meet their abuse with brotherly forbearance (*Eph.* 10; *ECW*, pp. 78f.).

**5**

*Remember from what you have fallen:* lit. *from where* – not just their previous high standards. The *angel* addressed is a *star* (1$^{20}$): 'How art thou fallen from heaven, O day star, son of the morning!' (Isa. 14$^{12}$); see on 8$^{10}$, 9$^1$, 12$^{4, 9}$. The surprise is in applying this symbolism to the gleaming orthodoxy of Ephesus, but Satan can disguise himself as an angel of light (II Cor. 11$^{14}$). *He who has an ear . . .*

*Remembering* the paradise in which through Christ's death they have

m *Didachē tōn Apostolōn*, 'Teaching of the Apostles', or possibly 'Instruction for Missionaries' (H. Chadwick, *The Early Church*, Penguin Books 1967, p. 46).

already had a share is the road to *repentence* (in biblical Greek not 'feeling sorry' but change of heart and direction). Love begins with God's love to us (I John 4$^{10}$). *The works you did at first* makes a studied contrast with Thyatira (2$^{19}$).

*If not, I will come:* there are several references to *coming* in the letters. At 2$^{16}$, 3$^3$ they are, as here, conditional and cannot therefore (some think) refer to the final coming or parousia – rather to some local intervention. But at 2$^{25}$, 3$^{11}$ no condition is attached and the Greek here – 'If not, I am coming and will . . .' – could well be an example of parataxis, common in biblical Greek, and mean 'when I come, I will . . .'; i.e., what is conditional is not the coming but its effect. In any case for John the parousia is not simply a final future event, as the eucharistic pattern of promise and threat underlying letters and epilogue indicates: in the eucharist parousia and judgment are constantly being anticipated,[n] as they have already been in Christ's death and resurrection; see pp. 35, 41f., and cf. I Cor. 11$^{28-32}$.

*remove your lampstand:* Ramsay saw an allusion to Ephesus' location at the mouth of the Cayster which was always silting up, necessitating physical changes of site, and took it as a threat not of physical destruction but of being made to begin again anew.

6

*the Nicolaitans:* named here in preparation for the assault in the third letter (2$^{14}$). Love does not preclude hating their *works*.

7

*He who has an ear:* John as a prophet presents his message as that of Jesus, who addresses the churches as he once did Israel (Matt. 13$^9$, etc.), but it is equally the Spirit who speaks; see on 5$^6$ and 19$^{10}$; cf. John 16$^{12-14}$. Each message is for all the *churches*. The call for discernment is repeated in each, and recurs in the body of the book (13$^{9f.,}$ $^{18}$, 14$^{12}$, 16$^{15}$, 17$^9$).

*conquers: nikan* has many references – to war, literal and spiritual (6$^2$, 11$^7$, 13$^7$, 17$^{14}$); to the athletic games (cf. the *crown*, 2$^{10}$, 3$^{11}$); to a lawsuit (12$^{10f.}$; cf. Rom. 3$^4$); to Christ's death and resurrection (3$^{21}$, 5$^5$,

[n] See C. F. D. Moule, 'The Judgment Theme in the Sacraments', in W. D. Davies and D. Daube (eds.), *The Background of the New Testament and its Eschatology*, Cambridge University Press 1954, pp. 464–81.

12¹¹) – perhaps also to the *Nicolaitans* by word-play (*Nikolaus* means 'conqueror of the people'); on the human plane theirs was the way of survival and success. It is often held that the reference is not to all Christians, only to martyrs (12¹¹). But at the End there are only two categories, inside and outside (21⁷ᶠ·), and the way in is 'the blood of the Lamb' (7¹⁴; cf. 22¹⁴, where this promise is taken up). A man is constituted *conqueror* (present participle, of continuous action) by his continuing attitude and behaviour, rather than by the circumstances of his physical death – though the coming crisis will indeed demand faithfulness unto death (2¹⁰).

*the tree of life:* Gen. 2⁹. The opening chapters of Genesis, with the exodus story, gave shape to the future hope of Jews and Christians alike – 'the end will be as the beginning'. But for Christians it was not simply that in the future the curse of Genesis 3 would be undone and access granted to paradise again (cf. I Enoch 24⁴ᶠᶠ·, Test. Levi 18); in Christ, the new Adam, it had already been undone. Their hope was for the fulness of what in baptism and eucharist° they already enjoyed. But John's warning is that that is only for *him who conquers*.

2^{8-11}        TO THE CHURCH IN SMYRNA

⁸'*And to the angel of the church in Smyrna write: "The words of the first and the last, who died and came to life.*

⁹*I know your tribulation and your poverty (but you are rich) and the slander of those who say that they are Jews and are not, but are a synagogue of Satan.* ¹⁰*Do not fear what you are about to suffer. Behold, the devil is*

---

*o* For sacramental symbolism see p. 41 and references to Prigent. This by no means excludes other local echoes; cf. Ramsay, pp. 247–9; *paradise* (lit. park or garden) of *God* over against the notorious precinct of Artemis with its rights of asylum; *eat of the tree* over against the forbidden food of the Nicolaitans (2¹⁴). Tree, (*xūlon*) was frequently used for the cross (cf. Gal. 3¹³): did the phrase connote 'gibbet of life', the curse-bearing cross for the repentant in the middle of paradise (the heavenly city, 22²ᶠ·), in contrast with the temporal immunity for criminals in this city's garden of Artemis? So Hemer, following R. Roberts, 'The Tree of Life, Rev. ii. 7'. *ExpT* 25, 1913–14, p. 332.

*about to throw some of you into prison, that you may be tested, and for ten days you will have tribulation. Be faithful unto death, and I will give you the crown of life;* [11]*He who has an ear, let him hear what the Spirit says to the churches. He who conquers shall not be hurt by the second death."* '

Smyrna was a city of great wealth, second only to Pergamum as a centre of the emperor cult, and had a large Jewish community. The letter shows the church to be in imminent danger, from the Roman authorities probably, but at the instigation of the Jews (see pp. 28ff.) – thus reproducing Jesus' suffering under Pontius Pilate, which showed him to be in fact lord of *life*. This real wealth under their poverty is brought out by the title and the promises; not that such closeness to Jesus is easy or can be taken for granted: they are no doubt as afraid, and as much in danger of giving in, as anyone else (v. 10). But the unqualified praise[p] which this church receives in its weakness contrasts with the condemnation of the powerful church in Ephesus, and links it with the church in Philadelphia (the sixth letter), where there is also reference to outward weakness, false Jews, testing and crowns. These letters lie behind the seals passage (4$^1$–8$^1$). Its theme is assurance, of which Christ's death and resurrection is the ground.

৯৩

8

For the title John moves a step back in the Son of man vision to 1$^{17f.}$ (see comment there), 'I am the first and the last . . . I died and behold I am alive for evermore.' Smyrna had *died and come to life*: it was destroyed by the Lydians *c.* 600 BC and refounded *c.* 300. The word means 'myrrh', which was used in the burial of Jesus (John 19$^{39}$).

9

*tribulation:* Christians shared the Jewish concept of the great tribulation which must precede the End (cf. 3$^{10}$, 7$^{14}$, it is depicted in 13), but they believed it had already been anticipated in Jesus' tribulation, as the resurrection of the dead had been in his rising (cf. I Cor. 15$^{20}$). Christians could share in both; see on 1$^9$. Fidelity might lead to mob

*p* Smyrna is the only one of the seven where Christianity never died out.

violence (cf. Heb. $10^{34}$) and loss of livelihood (see p. 33). *Poverty* in the Bible often represents trust not in earthly securities but in God. 'Blessed are the poor in spirit, for theirs is the kingdom of heaven' (Matt. $5^{2}$; contrast the church in Laodicea, $3^{17f.}$).

*slander: blasphēmia.* It could mean simply abuse, of God or man (cf. $13^{6}$), but also defamation. Christians as members of an unauthorized cult were vulnerable to charges of anti-social behaviour. Even if they were false, the magistrate might order them to renounce their Christianity, and refusal would mean execution (see pp. 28–30 cf. I Peter $4^{12-16}$).

*who say that they are Jews:* cf. $3^{9}$; see p. 28.[q] Like the false apostles in Ephesus ($2^{2}$) they claim to serve God, but in fact serve Satan, through their alliance with Rome against Christians, as against Christ under Pilate (cf. John $8^{37, 44}$, $16^{1-4}$, I Cor. $2^{6-8}$). They took a leading part in the martyrdom *c.* AD 150 of Polycarp, bishop of Smyrna, who would have been a young man in 95. The contemporary account of his death (*ECW*, pp. 153–67) gives a vivid picture of the sort of situation John envisaged and of the spirit he encouraged.

10
*Do not fear:* Christ's words at $1^{17}$; cf. Matt. $10^{28-33}$, Luke $12^{4-8}$.

*about to:* Gk. *mellein*, which has overtones of destiny – their suffering and the devil's attack are both within the divine plan.

*the devil: diabolos* means 'slanderer', 'false accuser', and in the LXX translates Hebrew *satan*, which means originally 'adversary', in the legal sense of 'accuser' (Ps. $109^{6}$). In Job 1 and 2 and Zech. 3 'the Satan' appears as a mixture of Public Prosecutor and *agent provocateur* in heaven. By NT times he had become the source of falsehood and deception and the leader of the evil angels or spirits, which oppose God and his people. See on $12^{7-12}$.

*q* Some scholars think that 'those who claim to be Jews' are Judaizing Christians, because the letters of Ignatius to the Magnesians and Philadelphians show that Judaizing was a problem not many years later. But there is no hint that it involved persecution such as the churches at Smyrna and Philadelphia are praised for having endured – see E. S. Fiorenza 'Apocalyptic and Gnosis in the Book of Revelation and Paul', *JBL* 92, 1973, p. 572.

*Some of you: you* is plural down to *tribulation*, then singular again: in earthly reality *some* will suffer (total slaughter figures only in the visions), but as representatives of the *church*; their faithfulness will be derived from it and rewarded in it.

*prison:* not itself punishment, but detention prior to trial and punishment – probably death if they would not deny Christ and worship the emperor. They must therefore go on (*ginou*, present imperative) being *faithful* up to and including *death*.

*tested: peirazein* means both 'test' and 'tempt'. The *tribulation* was Satan's supreme *test* of man's loyalty; if he did not keep awake he might be *tempted* into apostasy (cf. Luke 22²⁸⁻³⁴, ⁴⁰⁻⁴⁶). See also on 3¹⁰. But the time would be limited– *ten days* (cf. Matt. 24²²; Dan. 1¹²⁻¹⁵ may be in mind).

*the crown of life:* cf. 3¹¹ – a Christian commonplace in circumstances of testing (cf. James 1¹²). The *crown* was a wreath of leaves, valuable not in itself but as a symbol: of athletic victory (II Tim. 4⁷ᶠ·; Smyrna was famous for its games); of initiation into a mystery cult (crowning was later a feature of Christian initiation in Syria); of religious celebration, especially at the feast of Tabernacles which anticipated salvation in the messianic age (cf. *Jubilees* 16³⁰). Tabernacles imagery was used by Christians to express the salvation which was theirs in Christ – already through baptism and eucharist, finally in heaven; see on 7⁹ᶠᶠ·, 21, 22. At 3¹¹ the *crown* is a present possession.ʳ

**11**

*hurt:* lit. 'wronged'. *Adikein* is used at 7³ and frequently in 8 and 9 of demonic harm; also at Luke 10¹⁸ᶠ·, a passage which has many links with Revelation and the same conviction that the enemy is already defeated and the *faithful* are already beyond his power. The *second death* is a Jewish phrase for the extinction of the wicked in the Age to Come; see on 20⁶, ¹⁴.

ʳ There are many possible local references: the city was called the 'crown of Asia' and a crown figured in the design of its coins. A crown was awarded to distinguished citizens on their death (Cicero, *pro Flacco*, 31.5, etc.).

¹²'*And to the angel of the church in Pergamum write: "The words of him who has the sharp two-edged sword.*

¹³*I know where you dwell, where Satan's throne is; you hold fast my name and you did not deny my faith even in the days of Antipas my witness, my faithful one, who was killed among you, where Satan dwells.* ¹⁴*But I have a few things against you: you have some there who hold the teaching of Balaam, who taught Balak to put a stumbling block before the sons of Israel, that they might eat food sacrificed to idols and practise immorality.* ¹⁵*So you also have some who hold the teaching of the Nicolaitans.* ¹⁶*Repent then. If not, I will come to you soon and war against them with the sword of my mouth.*

¹⁷*He who has an ear, let him hear what the Spirit says to the churches. To him who conquers I will give some of the hidden manna, and I will give him a white stone, with a new name written on the stone which no one knows except him who receives it."* '

Pergamum was the capital of the old Greek kingdom, and is usually held to have been the Roman provincial capital, though the evidence is not quite clear (Hemer). It was certainly the spiritual capital – the first centre of the cult of Rome and the emperor, and endowed with imposing temples, especially to Zeus and Asclepius the god of healing; both had the title of Saviour and the serpent as symbol. Both politically and religiously it could be called the *throne* of that old serpent *Satan*.ˢ The *sword* (v. 16) evokes the 'power of the sword' (*ius gladii*), the power of capital punishment vested in the provincial governor. Here, where loyalty to Christ was particularly dangerous and Antipas had already suffered for his *witness* (a precedent for the future?), the *church* was faithful but there were some who followed

*s* The cult of Asclepius only blossomed at the end of Domitian's reign, so the primary reference may be to Rome. The temple of Rome and Augustus (29 BC) was the oldest and most famous temple of the imperial cult in Asia. The temples on the Acropolis can still be seen from miles away, dominating the town.

the *teaching of the Nicolaitans*, which probably involved accommodation to pagan society with its quasi-religious banquets and sexual licence (see p. 33), and its adulation of Rome. The *church* is ordered to repent. If not, instead of the Roman sword they have evaded by compromise, its erring members will face the *sword* of Christ's *mouth*. But to the conqueror he will give, instead of earthly securities and satisfactions, final confirmation of the heavenly standing and heavenly bread which through baptism and eucharist he already enjoys.

This letter lies behind the trumpets passage ($8^1$–$14^{20}$), whose themes are idolatry and witness, and has special links with ch. 13.

၏

**12**
*sharp two-edged sword:* another step back in the Son of man vision. The parallels cited at $1^{16}$, especially Heb. $4^{12}$, show that it stands for the word or breath (spirit) of God which exposes and deals with hidden evil. *Sword* is *rhomphaia*, common enough in biblical but very rare in secular Greek – the normal word is *machaira* (as at Rom. $13^4$), which John uses only for the literal sword ($6^4$, $13^{10, 14}$).

**13**
*I know where you dwell:* instead of *your works*. Here the situation is all-important: under the very shadow of Satan whose whole power is deployed through the two beasts to make those who *dwell* on earth ($13^8$, $^{12, 14}$) take his name, i.e. accept his lordship, and to persecute those who *hold fast* Christ's *name* (cf. $13^{16f.}$), which they have owned in baptism (cf. $3^8$).

*my witness, my faithful one:* see on $1^5$, $3^{14}$. For *witness* cf. Acts $1^8$ and $22^{20}$ ('the blood of my witness, Stephen'). *Martus* has almost attained its later technical meaning, 'martyr', which RSV allows it at $17^6$.

*where Satan dwells:* suggesting both his nearness to the church and his implication in the death of Antipas, about whom otherwise nothing is known.

**14**
*a few things:* not that *the teaching of the Nicolaitans* was a trifling matter; $2^6$ suggests it was his chief concern. Presumably it had as yet only a small hold.

*Balaam* is a clue to their *teaching*. He was a prophet, whom *Balak*, king of Moab, tried to hire to curse the invading Israelites (Num. 22¹ff.). According to one tradition he succumbed: it was his advice (31¹⁶) which led to the fornication (metaphorical and actual) described at 25¹⁻⁹: '. . . the people began to play the harlot with the daughters of Moab. These invited the people to the sacrifices of their gods, and the people ate and bowed down to their gods.' He thus became the type of the teacher who leads Israel into infidelity[t] – used by the Jews to refer to Jesus, and linked by Christians with Simon Magus (Acts 8⁹⁻²⁴), the traditional father of gnosticism. Balaam was also linked with the Magi of Persia, and thus with all magic and astrology (see on 2²⁸). But he was also a true prophet of the Messiah (Num. 24¹⁷) – an ambivalent figure, well fitted to embody John's judgment on a position which, as the next letter shows, could claim genuine authority and results.

*Balak* and *Balaam* prefigure the beasts, false king and false prophet, of ch. 13.

*food sacrificed to idols:* see p. 33. Most meat on sale would come from animals sacrificed in temples: what should a Christian do when asked to dinner by a pagan? Paul had given a liberal but cautious answer (I Cor. 8–10). The Apostolic Council at Jerusalem had ordered abstention (Acts 15²⁰, ²⁹).

*practise immorality:* lit. 'commit fornication' – also condemned by the Council (see on 2²⁴ᶠ·) and by Paul (I Cor. 5–6). The term had a long history as a metaphor for religious infidelity, which could well lead to actual fornication, as in the Baal cult; some at Corinth regarded it as morally indifferent. The two phrases indicate some kind of syncretism,[u] probably gnostic, possibly a perversion of Pauline liberalism.

[t] See G. Vermes, *Scripture and Tradition in Judaism*, Brill, Leiden, 1961, pp. 127–77. The rabbinic etymology *bala'-'am*, 'destroy – people', suggests that John saw a similar significance in *Niko-laos*, 'conquer – people'. The references at Jude¹¹ and II Peter 2¹⁵ centre on his venality; they are relevant only as illustrating this typological kind of polemic, and the prevalence of antinomian 'false teaching' (i.e. holding that Christians are absolved from the demands of the moral law).

[u] Syncretism means adopting into a system ideas and practices of diverse origin.

**15**

*the Nicolaitans:* according to Irenaeus they were followers of Nicolaus the proselyte of Antioch, one of the seven appointed to 'serve tables' (Acts 6$^5$), and exponents of the Jewish-Christian gnosticism of Cerinthus, a traditional enemy of the apostle John whom Irenaeus took to be the author of Revelation (*Adversus Haer.* I. 26.3; III. 11.7). But this, and various later views, could have been deduced from the NT.$^v$

**16**

*Repent:* singular – the whole church is involved. For the conditional threat see on 2$^5$. The language is picked up at 19$^{11-15}$: they will be on the wrong side at the final moment of truth, which is constantly being anticipated in present experience.

**17**

*the hidden manna:* God fed Israel in the desert with *manna* (Ex. 16). According to tradition some had been kept in the ark (16$^{32-34}$), and hidden by Jeremiah before the destruction of the first temple; it would be restored in the last days (II Baruch 29$^8$), as part of the blessings of paradise which the desert wanderings prefigured; cf. 2$^7$. For Christians this hope was already fulfilled in Christ's self-giving in the eucharist; cf. I Cor. 10$^3$, John 6$^{31-35}$: again the *conqueror* is promised full and final enjoyment of something he already has in foretaste. There may be a contrast with pagan or gnostic mysteries.

*white stone$^w$:* there are many possible references, perhaps to a ticket of admission, or the juror's vote of acquital. *White* was the fortunate colour, the colour of victory and justification (white robes), the colour of Christ (1$^{14}$, 19$^{11,\ 15}$). He gave the entrée to surer salvation and better mysteries than the Nicolaitans.

*a new name:* cf. 3$^{12}$, 19$^{12}$. Neither there nor here can we expect to know what the name was, since its secrecy is the point: in magic to know someone's name gives power over him; equally, a secret name suggests

*v* See Fiorenza (see note *q* on 29), pp. 567–74; Hemer, *New International Dictionary of NT Theology*, ed. Colin Brown, II, Paternoster Press and Zondervan, 1976, pp. 676–8. For some interesting possibilities see Daniélou, *Symbols*, ch. 7.

*w* The stone of Pergamum and its buildings is dark and rough, unsuitable for *inscriptions*, which were cut on vividly contrasting *white* marble, specially brought (Hemer). This contrast, and the serpent motif, can still be seen.

invulnerability, even in the stronghold of Satan. Change of name also indicates change of character and fortune, as with Jacob (Gen. $32^{28}$); cf. Isa. $62^2$, $65^{15}$, key passages for Rev. 21, 22, referring to Israel released from Babylonian exile. There could again be a reference to baptism – full and final enjoyment of the new character, the *name* of Christ, there received (see on $7^{2f.}$). *New* (*kainos*) means new in quality, belonging to the New Age, which for the Christian is already here (cf. II Cor. $5^{17}$).

$2^{18-29}$         TO THE CHURCH IN THYATIRA

$^{18}$'*And to the angel of the church in Thyatira write: "The words of the Son of God, who has eyes like a flame of fire, and whose feet are like burnished bronze.*

$^{19}$*I know your works, your love and faith and service and patient endurance, and that your latter works exceed the first.* $^{20}$*But I have this against you, that you tolerate the woman Jezebel, who calls herself a prophetess and is teaching and beguiling my servants to practise immorality and to eat food sacrificed to idols.* $^{21}$*I gave her time to repent, but she refuses to repent of her immorality.* $^{22}$*Behold, I will throw her on a sickbed, and those who commit adultery with her I will throw into great tribulation, unless they repent of her doings;* $^{23}$*and I will strike her children dead. And all the churches shall know that I am he who searches mind and heart, and I will give to each of you as your works deserve.* $^{24}$*But to the rest of you in Thyatira, who do not hold this teaching, who have not learned what some call the deep things of Satan, to you I say, I do not lay upon you any other burden;* $^{25}$*only hold fast what you have, until I come.* $^{26}$*He who conquers and who keeps my works until the end, I will give him power over the nations,* $^{27}$*and he shall rule them with a rod of iron, as when earthen pots are broken in pieces, even as I myself have received power from my Father;* $^{28}$*and I will give him the morning star.* $^{29}$*He who has an ear, let him hear what the Spirit says to the churches."* '

Thyatira was the least important of the seven cities, but this is the central letter of the seven, and the longest. Though the Nicolaitans are not mentioned, the letter deals with the same issues as the preceding one ($2^{14,\ 20}$). 'Jezebel' like 'Balaam' is a clue to their nature as well as a value judgment: 'What peace can there be,' said Jehu to Joram, 'so long as the harlotries and sorceries of your mother Jezebel are so many?' (II Kings $9^{22}$); cf. I Kings $16^{31ff.}$ for her encouragement of the worship of Baal, and for the opposition of Elijah, who provides a model for the Christian witness ($11^{5f.}$) – and no doubt for John himself! In other words it is again a question primarily of religious infidelity.

Where the issue was overtly political or religious, discernment (the crux – vv. 21–23) would be easier than at Thyatira where it was perhaps mainly social and economic; see pp. 33f. It was a commercial city[x]; we know of more trade-guilds there than anywhere else. These guilds were religious in origin and vaguely connected, like so much in the ancient world, with idolatry, a formality which few took seriously. Could a Christian belong? Must a convert withdraw? Not to belong would be social and economic suicide – was suicide really necessary? We can imagine appeals to Paul (I Cor. $8^4$), and to Jesus: 'the tree is known by its fruits.' The church had all the practical virtues, in increasing measure, as John acknowledged (v. 19) in deliberate contrast with orthodox Ephesus. Would not an exclusive and rigorist attitude lead to unnecessary loss of influence, unpopularity and danger?

If the position of 'Jezebel' was something like this, we can see why the good Thyatirans should tolerate it, and why John should attack it so violently, aware of the spiritual issues behind the harmless-looking practice (like Paul in I Cor. $10^{14ff.}$). But it was probably not, as Ramsay and others hold, simply a matter of practice. The *deep things of Satan* and the *star* suggest gnosticism and astrology: 'sorceries' as well as 'harlotries' may be in view; *sorcerers* along with fornicators and idolaters are excluded from the city in which the promises of the letters are fulfilled ($21^8$, $22^{15}$). It is difficult for a modern Westerner to appreciate the place of magic and astrology in a world felt to be dominated by hidden and hostile powers – see p. 39. Christ promises the faithful a share of his royal *power over the nations* and their values,

---

x Lydia was an export representative of its dyed goods industry, Acts $16^{14}$.

and the *star* of victory over pagan magic and the powers behind it – which is himself ($2^{28}$, $22^{16}$).

The question of the attitude to the pagan world is raised sharply by the wording of the promise in v. 27, lit. 'he shall *shepherd* them with an iron rod'. The Hebrew verbs 'break' and 'shepherd' are practically identical. At Ps. $2^9$ the former obviously is appropriate. Is John's choice of the latter a grim irony, or an expression of the paradox central in the story of Jesus and in this book (see on $5^{5f.}$), that the divine omnipotence lies in suffering, and that the violent nationalistic hopes of God's people are fulfilled in their apparent frustration? To point out that the victor's *rod of iron* is the same as Christ's (v. 27b) only raises the deeper question, how did John and his hearers understand the death of Christ in its effect on his enemies, constructively or destructively? The answer probably is *both*, but that the constructive is primary; see on $1^7$, $5^{5f.}$.

This letter lies behind the bowls passage ($15^1$–$22^5$), in which the harlot Babylon is replaced by the Bride, new Jerusalem. It is closely linked with the preceding letter, just as Babylon is with the beast (17 and 13), and the bowls with the trumpets. There is a shift of emphasis from idolatry to immorality, but see on v. 26.

༺༝༻

18

*Son of God:* the only occurrence of the term in Revelation, a point of contrast with the other Johannine writings. It connotes obedience and closeness to the Father in activity and function – in this Revelation is at one with the Fourth Gospel in its presentation of Christ (cf. $2^{23}$, $3^{21}$, $5^{6, 13}$, $21^{22}$, $22^3$). The title is perhaps chosen here to express his kingship over the nations – cf. Ps. $2^{6-9}$, alluded to in the promise; Ps. 2 is a *leitmotiv* from $11^{18}$ onwards – perhaps also to echo Dan. $3^{25}$.

*eyes like a flame of fire . . .*: a further step back in the Son of man vision; see on $1^{14f.}$. The *eyes* suggest piercing perception; see $19^{12}$ and note on $2^{16}$. The *burnished bronze* (a special product of the guild of bronze-workers? – Ramsay, pp. 229f.) may evoke the furnace of Dan. 3 in which one like a *son of God* walked with the three who refused to compromise.

**19**

The contrast with the church in Ephesus ($2^{4f.}$) is the more pointed for this church's doctrinal unsoundness (*faith* in Revelation means faithfulness, not belief). Truth is the crux. *Love* is its fruit, as hatred is the fruit of falsehood (see p. 79). The tree is known by its fruits, but if the root is rotten, tree and fruit will wither.

**20**

*the woman Jezebel:* John's nickname. The church's failure lies in *tolerating* a teacher who is corrupting the *heart* (v. 23) beneath the fair exterior. Jezebel is one of the models of the harlot Babylon ($18^{23f.}$; cf. I Kings $18^{13}$, II Kings $9^{22}$).

*who calls herself a prophetess:* i.e. one who exercises inspired leadership in the church.[y] For the difficulty (and danger) in contesting such leadership, with its apparent authority (see on $2^2$), see *Didache* 11–13 (*ECW*, pp. 232–4). 'Any prophet speaking in the Spirit you shall not test or evaluate – "Every sin shall be forgiven, but this sin shall not be forgiven" [i.e. blasphemy against the Holy Spirit, Matt. $12^{31}$] – yet not everyone who speaks in the Spirit is a prophet, only if he has the ways of the Lord' (*Didache* $11^{7f.}$).

*beguiling:* a feature of the Lord's Apocalypse (Matt. $24^{5, 11, 24}$). *Planan* in Revelation is otherwise confined to Satan and his imperial minions – the beast ($13^{14}$), Babylon ($18^{23}$) – another indication that the later chapters are still concerned with the church (cf. Minear, pp. 124–7).

[y] Christian prophetic women were a problem in Asia in the second century. J. M. Ford, 'Proto-Montanism in the Pastoral Epistles', *NTS* 17, 1971, pp. 338–46, suggests that we may see in Rev. and in the letters to Timothy and Titus, which may date from the same time and are concerned with the same area, the beginnings of the 'Phrygian heresy' (Phrygia was in the south-east of the province of Asia), a charismatic and ascetic movement in the second century, led by one Montanus, in which prophetesses were numerous and powerful. This might help explain the sobriety of the Pastorals, their firm regulation of the conduct of women and their support for the regular ministry of elders and deacons (Christian prophets are not even mentioned). See I Tim. $1^{3-7}$, $2^8-3^{13}$, $5^{1-22}$; Stevenson, pp. 107–14; J. L. Houlden, *The Pastoral Epistles*, Penguin Books 1976, p. 43.

Montanism drew inspiration from Rev., especially the letter to Philadelphia, where it may have originated; see W. M. Calder, 'Philadelphia and Montanism', *Bulletin of the John Rylands Library* 7, 1923, pp. 309–54; Hemer, pp. 390–402.

*fornication . . . idols:* see on 2$^{14}$, and note the change in order, congruous with the shift in emphasis between trumpets and bowls.

**21**

*I gave her time . . . .:* how? via John himself (cf. III John$^{10}$)? She was no doubt a sincere, respectable and effective lady; her refusal to *repent*, and their refusal to disown her, raised the issue of discernment in its sharpest form (cf. Minear, p. 55).

**22, 23**

*sickbed:* simply 'bed' (*kline*) in Greek, with obvious *double entendre*. 'Commit adultery with her' presumably means 'flirt with her teaching', while 'her *children*' are the totally converted. They will be struck *dead* (*thanatos* probably means 'pestilence' as at 6$^8$; cf. I Cor. 11$^{30}$?), whereas the former will be thrown into *great tribulation*. *Great* suggests the tribulation of the last days; cf. 7$^{14}$: their infidelity is to receive a fore-taste of its final condemnation, with a view to repentance (cf. I Cor. 11$^{32}$). See on 2$^5$ for the conditional visitation.

*all the churches:* each message is for all, and for the church at large. Perhaps Thyatira was already notorious as a test-case?

*searches mind and heart:* as often, Christ performs what in the OT is a function of God. Of many parallels Jer. 17$^{10}$ is closest; the passage 17$^{5-18}$ is apposite to the whole book, especially the letters and the final chapters where the theme of scrutiny and recompense is taken up (cf. 20$^{12}$, 22$^{12}$).

**24**

*what some call the deep things of Satan:* would any Christian claim such knowledge? The Greek can be punctuated differently: '. . . have not learned the deep things of Satan: as they say "I do not lay upon you any burden".' Then the command to the faithful is *Only hold fast*. Gnostics offered freedom (cf. II Peter 2$^{19}$), and claimed to know the *deep things* – of God, that is (cf. I Cor. 2$^{10}$); *of Satan* would be John's scornful com-ment – perhaps attacking Pauline teaching (e.g. I Cor. 8$^{1, 4}$) as used, or abused, at this time.

On the other hand, in favour of RSV, *I do not lay upon you any burden* is remarkably like 'to lay upon you no greater burden . . . than . . . that you abstain from what has been sacrificed to idols . . . and from fornication' (Acts 15$^{28f.}$). John may be recalling the churches to the old standard of the apostolic decrees, against gnostic compromise. A gnostically influenced Christian might indeed boast experience of the *deep things of Satan* because his 'knowledge' told him such things were unreal and harmless (cf. I Cor. $8^{1-4}$), or because he was so sure of his sinlessness (cf. I John $1^{8f.}$, $3^9$) that he considered himself immune – 'beyond good and evil'.

## 26f.

*power over the nations:* better, 'authority'. When is it to be exercised? Hardly in the new Jerusalem, where the *iron rod* would be out of place, but in the present order (see on $5^{10}$) – not by compromise with the nations and use of their weapons, but in faithful witness and death (see on $11^{3-13}$), reproducing Christ's authority; cf. Matt. $28^{18-20}$, I Cor. $15^{25}$; and see on $12^5$ and $19^{15}$, where Ps. $2^9$ is again cited.

In the letter to Pergamum and the trumpets section witness is primarily verbal: here it is moral (fornication is named before idolatry, and the *conqueror* is he who keeps my *works* to the end), and in the bowls section the Bride, the beacon-city which draws in the *nations*, is clothed with the righteous deeds of the saints ($19^8$). John's concern with Christian behaviour is, as we might say, evangelistic; cf. I Peter $3^{1f.}$, Matt. $5^{14-16}$.

*rule them with a rod of iron:* rule is *poimainein* (as in LXX), 'to shepherd', which in Hebrew is very similar to 'to break'. There is certainly irony, as in Ps. 2 itself, but it may not be simply destructive. The breaking of earthen pots evokes Jer. 19 (destruction) but also Jer. $18^{1-11}$ (reconstruction), and *rod* (or sceptre) figures in several texts which were widely used to expound the birth and death of Jesus: Gen. $49^{9f.}$, significantly cited at $5^5$, Num. $24^{17}$ (see below), Ps. $23^4$, Isa. $11^{1,4,z}$ Micah $5^{2-6}$, $7^{14}$. Does it all represent God's grace, brought to bear in the witness of Christ and his church, which is shepherd's crook to those who respond (cf. $7^{17}$), iron bar to those who do not?

## 28

*the morning star:* the planet Venus had long been a symbol of victory

z 'There shall come forth a shoot (LXX 'rod') from the stump of Jesse, and a branch shall grow out of his roots (cf. Rev. $5^5$, $22^{16}$) . . . he shall smite the earth with the *rod* (LXX 'word') of his mouth, and with the breath of his lips he shall slay the wicked'; cf. 'the sword of my mouth' ($2^{16}$, $19^{15}$) and the 'two witnesses' ($11.^{5f.}$).

and domination. Now Christ is 'the bright, morning star' (22$^{16}$). Previous mention of *Balaam* (see p. 89) and *rod* points to Num. 24$^{17ff.}$: 'a star shall come out of Jacob, and a sceptre (*shebet* = rod, as at Ps. 2$^9$) ... out of Israel', to crush the hostile nations. Christians linked this passage with Isa. 11$^{1ff.}$$^a$ (LXX had *rhabdos* in both places) in reference to the birth of Christ (which at Rev. 12$^5$ is one with his death and exaltation), interpreted as the defeat of *magic*; cf. Ignatius: 'A star shone in heaven brighter than all the stars ... whence all magic was dissolved ... the ancient kingdom (of Satan) was pulled down, when God appeared in human form to bring a new order of everlasting life' (*Eph.* 19; *ECW*, p. 81). John, and other Christians, were not concerned, as might appear, with the literal smashing of their human enemies, so much as with the defeat of magic and idolatry, the power behind pagan wickedness which could infect the church itself from within. This internal reference is subtly suggested by the position of the refrain *he who has an ear*, which in the first three letters preceded the promise, but here follows it, leading into the next message; see on 3$^1$.

3$^{1-6}$        TO THE CHURCH IN SARDIS

3 *'And to the angel of the church in Sardis write: "The words of him who has the seven spirits of God and the seven stars.*

*I know your works; you have the name of being alive, and you are dead.* $^2$*Awake, and strengthen what remains and is on the point of death, for I have not found your works perfect in the sight of my God.* $^3$*Remember then what you received and heard; keep that, and repent. If you will not awake, I will come like a thief and you will not know at what hour I will come upon you.* $^4$*Yet you have still a few names in Sardis, people who have not soiled their garments; and they shall walk with me in white, for they are worthy.* $^5$*He who conquers shall be clad thus in white garments, and I will not blot his name out of th⟨ book of life; I will confess his name before my Father and before his angels;* $^6$*He who has an ear, let him hear what the Spirit says to the churches." '*

*a* Cf. Rev. 22$^{16}$ again and 5$^5$. See Daniélou, *Symbols*, ch. 7.

Sardis was the ancient capital of Croesus' kingdom of Lydia, a symbol of wealth and power – but in the past: the Acropolis was now uninhabited. It should have been an impregnable fortress, but had twice fallen, through over-confidence, to a night attack (v. 3). These facts were well known. In the present it was, like Ephesus, a commercial city on a great trade route, with the shrine of a famous mother-goddess and a powerful Jewish community. As in the letter to Laodi-cea, there is no hint of external oppression or opposition: that suggests compromise and lack of witness (v. 2). City and church have a reputation for liveliness, but in Christ's eyes are dead.

The theme is wakefulness, based on the city's history and Jesus' teaching about nocturnal burglars and returning masters. The 'death' of the Sardians is one of 'sleep' in the face of vast spiritual opportunity and danger. 'Keep awake and pray,' Jesus said to the disciples in Gethsemane (Matt. 26$^{41}$ par.); the thief comes at an hour when he is not expected (Matt. 24$^{43}$, Luke 12$^{39}$); the master has given his slaves *authority* (cf. 2$^{26}$) and to each his *work* (contrast 3$^2$) – he must not return and find them sleeping, far less carousing (Matt. 24$^{49-51}$, Luke 12$^{45f.}$). Christians must be alert and active, in prayer and witness (cf. Eph. 6$^{10-20}$).

The prologue and promises reinforce this message. The speaker is he who dispenses the *Spirit*, the life-giver and activator, over against the deadness and ineffectiveness of the Sardians, and as holder of the *seven stars*, the churches as spiritual entities, he is like the master who calls his slaves to account. The *white garments* promised to the faithful stand for baptismal acceptance ('justification') made final, possession of eternal life confirmed. *Confession* before *Father* and *angels* rewards the few who have confessed Christ on earth (Matt. 10$^{32}$, Luke 12$^8$), in contrast with the majority who have failed to maintain their baptismal confession in discipleship and witness.

∾

3$^1$
*the seven spirits of God:* see on 1$^4$; functionally the same as 'the Holy Spirit', but John is using the model of Zech. 4$^{2, 10}$ (cf. Rev. 4$^5$, 5$^6$), which suits his sevenfold model for the church.

*the seven stars:* see on $1^{20}$; the seven planets, – continuing the challenge to astrology and magic implicit in $2^{28}$ – but the primary reference, as in the Ephesian letter, is to the churches themselves; see on $2^1$. The titles pick up the last words of the preceding letter: *star . . . Spirit . . . churches.*

*the name:* a Greek usage, for an external or superficial estimate; to a Hebrew *name* denotes inner reality. *Name* occurs again in vv. 4 and 5, in different senses – typical Johannine word-play.

**2**

*Awake:* lit. *be wakeful;* an important theme in the synoptic gospels (especially the Gethsemane story) and epistles (e.g. I Thess. $5^{2-6}$).

*strengthen:* cf. Luke $22^{32}$. The whole of Luke $22^{28-34}$, which precedes the account of Gethsemane, is full of parallels with the letters.

*I have not found your works perfect:* lit. 'completed', another link with the first letter ($2^5$). Contrast $2^{19}$, $14^{13}$.

*in the sight of my God:* as opposed to their own eyes or the world's; or perhaps better taken with *I have not found:* Christ judges, in the presence of God (cf. $3^5$, Matt. $10^{33}$). For *my God* cf. $1^6$, John $20^{17}$, and Paul's phrase 'the God and Father of our Lord Jesus Christ' (Rom. $15^6$ etc.). It expresses Christ's special relationship with God in judging the church, as in acknowledging the conqueror (v. 5).

**3**

*Remember:* again present imperative: 'be mindful'; another link with the letter to Ephesus ($2^5$), recalling them to their beginning, the new life they had *received* (cf. John $1^{12, 16}$), the voice they had *heard* (John $10^3$, $^{27f.}$, $18^{37}$; cf. Rev. $3^{20}$).

*keep that:* the Greek has no *that;* rather, *be observant* (present imperative) and *repent* (aorist). *Keep (tērein)* is a key-word (see on $1^3$), signifying earnest attention. Cf. $3^{19}$: this church is too frivolous, as that in Laodicea is too complacent, for repentance to be a live option.

*If you will not awake . . . .:* again this looks like a 'conditional coming' (see on $2^5$), but $16^{15}$ shows that the coming is not in doubt. What is conditional is whether or not he will come upon Sardis unawares, like Cyrus and Antiochus the Great.

*like a thief:* an obvious reference to Jesus' teaching (Matt. 24<sup>42-51</sup>, Luke 12<sup>39-46</sup>) – just as the Ephesian lampstand is threatened with removal from its place, so the careless servant at Sardis may be 'cut in pieces' and 'find his place among the hypocrites' (Matt. 24<sup>50f.</sup>).

**4**

*names:* as at 11<sup>13</sup> simply 'people'. In Pergamum few were at fault, here few are blameless.

*not soiled their garments:* i.e. have not compromised their discipleship to the Christ they 'put on' (Gal. 3<sup>27</sup>) in baptism; cf. I Cor. 6<sup>9-11</sup>, and Rev. 22<sup>14</sup> (and 7<sup>14</sup>): *those who wash* (keep washing) *their robes* are contrasted with those *outside* who have denied Christ not explicitly but by conformity to the world.

*shall walk with me: walk* suggests discipleship, as at John 6<sup>66</sup>.

**5**

*white garments:* in the Bible they denote festivity (Eccles. 9<sup>8</sup>); victory (II Macc. 11<sup>8</sup>; cf. Roman triumphs and processions at imperial festivals); righteousness or 'justification' (7<sup>9ff.</sup>, 19<sup>8, 14</sup>); and the heavenly state or 'glorification' (Dan. 7<sup>9</sup>, Matt. 17<sup>2</sup> par.). All these associations meet here, but justification, which is consummated in glorification (Rom. 8<sup>30</sup>), is dominant in the context.

*the book of life:* cf. 13<sup>8</sup>, 17<sup>8</sup>, 20<sup>12, 15</sup>, 21<sup>27</sup>, Phil. 4<sup>3</sup>. To an Asian it would suggest the list of citizens (a link with the heavenly city theme of chs. 21–22); to a Jew the roll of those in God's favour (Ex. 32<sup>32</sup> etc.), with overtones of predestination.[b] In the OT 'to be blotted out of the book' means simply to die (Ps. 69<sup>28</sup>), but by NT times refers to eternal destiny – cf. the *second death* (2<sup>11</sup>).

*I will confess his name before my Father and before his angels:* the final assize, with the angels as assessors; cf. 3<sup>2</sup>, Matt. 10<sup>32</sup>, Luke 12<sup>8</sup>; and contrast

b In view of the powerful Jewish presence there may be allusion to the 'cursing of the heretics' introduced into the synagogue liturgy, probably in the 80s: 'May the Nazarenes and the *minim* [heretics] perish suddenly and be blotted out from the book of life and with the righteous may they not be inscribed' (*Eighteen Benedictions* 12). The church has not attracted Jewish attacks, as at Smyrna and Philadelphia; presumably it has been afraid to provoke them (Hemer, pp. 339f.).

those who deny Christ and receive the mark of the beast (14$^{10}$). The *conqueror* is one who has *confessed* Christ in baptism and remained true to his confession until death.

7'*And to the angel of the church in Philadelphia write: "The words of the holy one, the true one, who has the key of David, who opens and no one shall shut, who shuts and no one opens.*

8*I know your works. Behold, I have set before you an open door, which no one is able to shut; I know that you have but little power, and yet you have kept my word and have not denied my name.* 9*Behold, I will make those of the synagogue of Satan who say that they are Jews and are not, but lie – behold, I will make them come and bow down before your feet, and learn that I have loved you.* 10*Because you have kept my word of patient endurance, I will keep you from the hour of trial which is coming on the whole world, to try those who dwell upon the earth.* 11*I am coming soon; hold fast what you have, so that no one may seize your crown.* 12*He who conquers, I will make him a pillar in the temple of my God; never shall he go out of it, and I will write on him the name of my God, and the name of the city of my God, the New Jerusalem which comes down from my God out of heaven, and my own new name.* 13*He who has an ear, let him hear what the Spirit says to the churches."* '

Philadelphia and Smyrna have much in common, in particular opposition from those *who say that they are Jews and are not*. Here the issue is primarily theological: 'Who are God's people now?' Christ speaks as he *who has the key of David*, an allusion to Isa. 22$^{15ff.}$, where Eliakim replaces the arrogant Shebna as steward of the royal household: 'I will place on his shoulder the key of the house of David; he shall open and none shall shut; and he shall shut and none shall open', but the reference back to 1$^{18}$, *I have the keys of Death and Hades*, suggests that the key of David should be seen also in the light of the commission to Peter (Matt. 16[18f.]), and to the twelve (John 20[21-23]). It is the issue, as between Jesus and the Pharisees (Matt. 23[13]), of forgiveness and admission to the kingdom, and it turns on the status of Jesus and the interpretation of scripture. He, not the Jewish scribes,[c] is true steward of God's household; by his death he has *ransomed men for God from every nation* (5[9]) and proved himself alone able to *open the scroll* (5[5]). The Jews, who look forward to the Gentile homage promised by Isaiah, will themselves be forced to pay homage to the (largely Gentile) church and acknowledge that the *Holy One* has *loved*, or chosen, them.

It is attractive to see here a prediction that the Jews will be *converted*. Paul uses the expression *open door* of missionary opportunity (I Cor. 16[9], II Cor. 2[12], Col. 4[3]), and Philadelphia had been founded in the second century BC as an apostle of Hellenism in barbaric Lydia and Phrygia; it had a reputation as a missionary city which it would be entirely in character for John to play on (Ramsay, pp. 404f.). If he had written 'I will make them bow down *before God*' (cf. 15[4]), this interpretation might stand, but *before your feet* must mean Christian vindication, not Jewish conversion; and the sense of access for *door*, which is indicated by Christ's title, is confirmed by the promises in v. 12 of secure belonging in the New Jerusalem. The message to Philadelphia complements that to Smyrna thus: Christians must *know* that God has set his love on them, and that arguments which disparage their standing are the work of *Satan*, if they are to bear their witness in face of the *trials* and suffering which lie ahead (cf. Rom. 8[31ff.]).[d]

It may seem odd that Christians should still be vulnerable to such attack, but there was as yet no 'New Testament'; the Old Testament was the church's 'Bible', and the OT *on its own* gives overwhelming support to the Jewish case. Only if Christ is resolutely seen as the key to, and fulfilment of, all the scriptures (5[5]) can the Christian case begin to carry conviction. The letters of Ignatius to the Philadelphians

---

*c open* and *shut* in Isa. 22[22] was sometime taken to refer to the teaching authority of the scribes (S-B I, 741 note *c*).

*d* After the rest of Christian Asia had succumbed to Islam, Philadelphia remained a free and independent bastion of Christianity till AD 1390.

(see on v. 12) and Magnesians show that early in the second century the issue was still very much alive.

❧

**7**

*the holy one, the true one:* cf. $6^{10}$, referring to God. *Holy* means 'set apart', either of God himself (the Holy One of Israel), or of anyone or anything belonging to God – for Holy One as a messianic title, cf. Mark $1^{24}$, John $6^{69}$. *True* to a Greek meant 'real', to a Hebrew 'trustworthy'. Both meanings fit, in view of the false claims of the Jews (v. 9), and the *trial* facing the church (v. 10).

*the key of David:* picking up the Smyrnaean reference to $1^{18}$ (see on $2^8$), together with Isa. $22^{15-25}$ (see above).

**8**

*an open door:* literally 'an opened door', perfect participle (as at $4^1$), suggesting the present consequences of a past action. Jesus, 'the door of the sheep' (John $10^{7-9}$), by his death and resurrection finally 'opened the kingdom of heaven to all believers' ($1^{18}$; cf. I Cor. $15^{17}$). Ignatius calls him 'the door to the Father' in his letter to the Philadelphians ($9^1$, *ECW*, p. 114). See also Isa. $45^{1\text{ff.}}$.

*have not denied my name:* the name of Christ, confessed in baptism; see on $2^{13}$, $3^5$.

**9**

*synagogue of Satan:* see on $2^9$. Exclusion from the earthly Israel's *synagogue* laid Christians open to state persecution.

*bow down before your feet:* Isaiah's prophecies of Gentile subjection to the Jews are reversed ($45^{14}$, $49^{23}$, $60^{14}$). Their true fulfilment is found at $21^{22\text{ff.}}$.

*I have loved you:* Isa. $43^4$ – the *Holy One* of Israel speaking. *Loved* often has the sense of *chosen* in biblical Greek, cf. John $3^{19}$, Rom. $9^{13}$. The Jews will be made to recognize that the Christians are now the real Jews; cf. Rom. $2^{28\text{f.}}$.

10

*my word of patient endurance:* better *the word of my* patient endurance, elaborating the *word* of v. 8 – not merely Jesus' sayings (commands to endure), but his whole self-revelation, characterized as *endurance*; cf. Heb. $5^{7ff.}$, $12^{1ff.}$, II Thess. $3^5$.

*I will keep you from the hour of trial;* cf. John $17^{6, 15}$, Matt. $6^{13}$ (the Lord's Prayer) – safe-keeping rather than exemption. Christians had taken over the Jewish expectation of a final time of world-wide *trial* or testing (*peirasmos*) – see on $2^{9f.}$ – conventionally set out as a series of earthly and heavenly disasters, as in the Lord's Apocalypse (there are echoes of Luke $21^{26, 34-36}$ here) which is one of John's chief models. It would have a double effect,[e] sifting and purifying the elect, who needed special protection (cf. $7^{2ff.}$) and alertness (see on $3^{ff.}$, $16^{15}$) if they were to come through, and showing up God's enemies (cf. $6^{16}$, $9^{20f.}$, $16^{9, 11, 21}$ – the disasters bring out men's opposition to God). *Those who dwell upon the earth* is in Rev. the regular designation of those who follow the beast ($6^{10}$, $8^{13}$, $11^{10}$, $13^{8, 12, 14}$, $17^2$, $^8$). Here as in Luke $21^{35}$ the phrase is neutral, but like 'world' (*kosmos*) in the Fourth Gospel it suggests men set apart from God, in ignorance or opposition; see p. 15.

11

*I am coming soon:* cf. $2^{16}$, $22^{7, 12, 20}$, and see on $2^5$. The *trial* is a sign not of Christ's absence but his nearness.

*seize your crown:* cf. Isa. $22^{17, 21}$ (LXX). The Lord will take away Shebna's glorious *crown* and give it to his faithful successor, i.e. a warning not to go back to Judaism; Ignatius' letter points up the danger. For the Christian significance of *crown*, see on $2^{10}$.

12

*a pillar in the house of my God:* Shebna's successor would be fastened like a peg in a sure place (Isa. $22^{23}$). Philadelphia was troubled by earthquakes, causing frequent evacuation (contrast *never shall he go out* of it) and chronic insecurity, just as the Christians were troubled by Jewish polemics, seeking to 'unchurch' them. Cf. Gal. $2^9$ for the apostles as pillars of the messianic community, conceived as a temple in that it

e See S. Brown, 'Deliverance from the Crucible', *NTS* 14, 1968, particularly pp. 254ff.

enshrines God's presence. Again the Christian is promised the fulness of something he believes to be already the case; cf. 7¹⁵, 22³, ¹⁴.

*I will write on him the name of my God*: for *name* see on 2¹⁷. Philadelphia's name had been changed to Neocaesarea, binding it to the imperial service. There is perhaps an allusion to the Hebrew letter *Tau*, the symbol of the divine name, with which Christians were 'signed' in baptism, cf. 7²ᶠᶠ·, 14¹, 22⁴, and Daniélou, *Symbols*, pp. 143-9.

*the name of the city*: cf. Isa. 62².

*the New Jerusalem which comes down . . .*: see on 21², ¹⁰. The present tense could be future in meaning, *which is to come down*, but perhaps indicates its quality: given by God, not man-made like the Tower of Babel. *New* means belonging to the Age to Come, which is not simply future, but pre-existent in heaven – already present in Christ and available through faith; cf. Phil. 3²⁰.

*my new name*:ᶠ see on 2¹⁷, 19¹².

¹⁴'*And to the angel of the church in Laodicea write*: "*The words of the Amen, the faithful and true witness, the beginning of God's creation.*
¹⁵*I know your works: you are neither cold not hot. Would that you were cold or hot!* ¹⁶*So, because you are lukewarm, and neither cold nor hot, I will spew you out of my mouth.* ¹⁷*For you say, I am rich, I have prospered, and I need nothing; not knowing that you are wretched, pitiable, poor, blind,*

ᶠ Ignatius in his letter to the Philadelphians said of Jewish–Christian controversy: 'If either speak not concerning Jesus Christ, I look on them as tombstones and graves of the dead, whereon are inscribed only the names of men' (6¹). It is hard to see any meaning in these last words, especially 'only', except in allusion to Rev. 3¹², tombstones (*stēlai*) picking up *pillars* (*stuloi*). It is odd that he shows no knowledge of Rev. otherwise, even when writing to Ephesus and Smyrna, but he had visited Philadelphia, and may have heard their letter read in church; cf. his reference to Christ as *door* (9¹); cf. Hemer, p. 387.

*and naked.* [18]*Therefore I counsel you to buy from me gold refined by fire,
that you may be rich, and white garments to clothe you and to keep the
shame of your nakedness from being seen, and salve to anoint your eyes,
that you may see.* [19]*Those whom I love, I reprove and chasten; so be zealous
and repent.* [20]*Behold, I stand at the door and knock; if any one hears my
voice and opens the door, I will come in to him and eat with him, and he
with me.* [21]*He who conquers, I will grant him to sit with me on my throne,
as I myself conquered and sat down with my Father on his throne.* [22]*He
who has an ear, let him hear what the Spirit says to the churches."* '

Laodicea was a prosperous commercial city on a great trade route,
and there are sarcastic allusions to its earthly wealth and pride; in this,
like Jezebel in the fourth letter, it foreshadows the harlot Babylon.
The church is threatened with total rejection: in its complacency it is
insulated from Christ, the Divine Wisdom (v. 14), in whom alone is
real wealth and salvation, and it is useless to Christ, the *faithful witness*
(cf. Antipas in the third letter), in its lack of 'works' (v. 15); as at
Sardis we may guess that prosperity was achieved by accommodation.
But the castigation springs from the divine love, which is stated in
terms which evoke the bridegroom of the Song of Songs, the good
shepherd of John 10, and the Lord's Supper.

The eucharist, as the focus of Christ's presence in judgment and
mercy, and the foretaste and pledge of his final coming (cf. I Cor.
11[23-32]), is the key not only to the letters but the whole book, as
the epilogue indicates (22[17, 20]); see pp. 41f. The promised, or
threatened, coming of Christ is not simply a matter of judgment,
though it must be that to all who are *blind* to his true nature: it is a
matter of divine love, of which judgment is the corollary (cf. John
3[16-21]), and if judgment is anticipated in the present it is to save men
from exclusion when the door is finally shut (Matt. 25[10]).

This letter has special links with the third and fourth, but also
serves as *Amen* to the total message.

ଷଷ

14
*Amen:* signifies divine affirmation and human response, both embodied
in Christ – cf. his characteristic 'Amen, I say to you' in the gospels, and

Paul's words: 'In Christ is the Yes to all the promises of God. That is why we utter the Amen through him to the glory of God' (II Cor. 1$^{20}$). He is the *faithful and true witness;* cf. 1$^5$ and 2$^{13}$ (Antipas) – such witness was lacking in Laodicea – and the *beginning of God's creation,* not 'the first of created things', but 'the origin and principle of creation'.

The title evokes Isa. 65$^{15ff.}$ (already in mind through the promise of a *new name* at 3$^{12}$): 'men will bless themselves by the God of Amen (or truth) . . . because the former troubles are forgotten . . . For behold I create new heavens and a new earth' (cf. 21$^{1-8}$). Like the title at 1$^5$, it also evokes the teaching of Col. 1$^{15-20g}$ and the prologue of the Fourth Gospel that Christ is the Divine Wisdom, the agent of creation. Against Jewish polemic and gnostic speculation,[h] he is unique and all-sufficient.

## 15

*would that you were cold or hot: hot* (boiling) is obviously commendable (Acts 18$^{25}$, Rom. 12$^{11}$), but why *cold*? There is again a clue[i] in the local situation: the water-supply came from hot springs and arrived luke-warm. Water is useful *hot,* or *cold* (cf. Matt. 10$^{42}$), but *lukewarm* it is nauseating. The reference then is not to the spiritual temperature of the Laodiceans, but to the barrenness of their *works,* their lack of witness; cf. 3$^{2b}$.

## 16

*I will spew you out:* better *I am on the point of . . .* (*mellō;* cf. 3$^2$); the threat is with a view to repentance, vv. 18ff.

## 17

*I am rich . . .:* contrast Smyrna (2$^9$), and cf. Babylon (18$^{7,\ 16f.}$) Laodicea, under its self-satisfaction, like Ephesus under its self-righteousness, wears the mark of the beast. *I have prospered* suggests 'by my own efforts'; cf. I Cor. 4$^{7f.}$ After the great earthquake of AD 61 it refused the imperial help offered for rebuilding.

*not knowing:* contrast *I know* (v. 15).

g Colossians was to be read aloud in the church in Laodicea (4$^{16}$).

h See p. 32. The gnostic depreciation of this world involved holding that its creator was not the true God, the Father of Jesus Christ, but an inferior (evil) deity.

i See M. J. S. Rudwick and E. M. B. Green, 'The Laodicean Lukewarmness', *ExpT* 69, 1957–58, pp. 167f.

*you are wretched:* lit. *you* (emphatic) *are the wretched one* – because of your claim to be *rich*; cf. Luke 6²⁴ᶠᶠ·, James 5¹ᶠᶠ·; not that riches in themselves disqualify, but in biblical idiom *rich* connotes trusting in riches, *poor* connotes trusting in God (cf. on 2⁹).

*poor, blind, naked:* Laodicea was a banking centre, and had a medical school, noted for its ophthalmologists, and a famous clothing industry.

18
*buy from me gold:* cf. Isa. 55¹. The true *gold* (=faith? cf. I Peter 1⁷; James 2⁵) cannot be bought with money. There is perhaps deeper irony in that Christians are *bought* by Christ (5⁹, 14³ᶠ·, I Cor. 6²⁰ etc.). *Gold* is the material of the new Jerusalem (21¹⁸, ²¹).

*white garments:* in contrast with the black wool of Laodicea. See on 3⁵ and 16¹⁵. The image covers both baptismal 'justification' and its end in heavenly 'glorification'; *nakedness* was to Jews (unlike Greeks) shameful, and is an obvious symbol for lack of *works* and condemnation at the judgment. Contrast 19⁸.

*salve to anoint your eyes:* contrast the famous Phrygian eye-powder, probably dispensed in Laodicea's medical school. The true giver of sight is Christ; cf. John 9⁶, 'he *anointed* the man's eyes', and 9³⁹⁻⁴¹: 'because you say "We see", your guilt remains.'

19
*Those whom I love . . .:* a condensed quotation of Prov. 3¹¹ᶠ·, used at Heb. 12⁵ᶠ· in a very similar context. Prov. 3 was much used by early Christians, and fits the theme of Christ, the true Wisdom, over against the foolishness of the Laodiceans. *Love* is not the usual Johannine word (*agapō*), which is found at this point in LXX and in Hebrews, but *philō*. It would be rash to press this (see commentaries on John 21¹⁵⁻¹⁷), but it may help the interpretation of the next verse to note that *philō* is the more human and emotional word (cf. John 11³⁶), *agapō* expresses more the direction of the will. For *reprove and chasten* cf. I Cor. 11³².

*so be zealous and repent:* one might expect the reverse order, but for those who lack passion, as for those who are forgetful (see on 3³, 2⁵), repentance is impossible. Ephesus lacked *love*, Laodicea lacks *zeal* or passionate concern (Heb. *qinah*), which is a vital aspect of love in the biblical sense, especially God's love; cf. Song of Songs 8⁶ᶠ·.

20

*I stand at the door and knock:* there are several interlocking allusions:

(i) the crisis of the last judgment (Mark 13²⁹, James 5⁹). This is not a purely present and individual occasion: it is equivalent to the warning of Christ's *coming* or parousia which follows the demands for repentance at 2⁵, ¹⁶, 3³.

(ii) the bridegroom of the synoptic parables: (*a*) Luke 12³⁵ᶠᶠ·; where he makes the servants who *open* at his *knock* sit down at table;ʲ (*b*) Matt. 25¹⁻¹³, with the wise and foolish virgins, the bridegroom's coming·at midnight, the shut door.

(iii) the bridegroom of the Song of Songs: 'The voice of my beloved – he is knocking at the door: "Open to me, my love" . . .' (5² LXX). The context fits, with the bride asleep but her heart awake (5²ᶠ·; cf. Matt. 26⁴¹; like Laodicea she is capable of being roused) and the invitation to eat and drink (5¹). The Song was interpreted allegorically by the Jews at this time, of Yahweh seeking out Israel at the time of the exodus, and was read liturgically at the passover season, when the Messiah was expected to come – the temple doors were opened for him at midnight (cf. Matt. 25⁶).

In other words the image evokes the final crisis of redemption and condemnation, but subordinates it to the love of the Bridegroom seeking out his unsatisfactory Bride, like God recalling fallen Israel to the honeymoon period of the desert wanderings (Hos. 2¹⁴ᶠᶠ·).

*if anyone hears my voice* . . .: cf. John 10²ᶠ·, 18³⁷. The popular picture of Christ asking for admission as a guest to the individual's heart – cf. Holman Hunt's 'The Light of the World' – is hardly intended. The allusion to Jesus' simile at Luke 12³⁶ suggests that the house is his, he comes as master, and invites the servant who is awake to eat with him.ᵏ The focus on the individual is no different from that in the promises to *him who conquers.*

*eat with him and he with me:* in *eat* (*deipnein*) there is inescapable reference back to the Last *Supper* (*deipnon*, John 13²ᶠᶠ·, I Cor. 11²⁰, ²⁵) and forward to 'the marriage *supper* of the Lamb' (19⁹). As before, John is recalling

*j* Note how this simile has influenced the accounts of the Last Supper in John (13²ᶠᶠ·) and Luke (22²⁴ᶠᶠ·).

*k* Cf. R. J. Bauckham, 'Synoptic Parousia Parables and the Apocalypse', *NTS* 23, 1977, p. 173.

Christians to what they already *have* and the imminent fulfilment of all it prefigures. See on 22$^{17, 20}$.

**21**

*sit with me on my throne:* taking up Jesus' promise, made at the Last Supper according to Luke (22$^{30}$), that those who had shared his trials (*peirasmoi*) should 'eat and drink at my table in my kingdom, and sit on thrones judging the twelve tribes of Israel'; cf. 20$^{4-6}$, 22$^{3-5}$. In Matt. (19$^{28}$) the promise follows the story of the rich young man and Peter's question about the reward for 'leaving everything and following' – a context equally significant, cf. v. 17.

*as I myself conquered:* see above on 2$^7$ and 2$^{27}$. This *throne* is reached through witness and death.

# Revelation 4¹–5¹⁴

# The Heavenly Liturgy

The seven letters set the scene on earth; chs. 4 and 5 set it in *heaven*. In Revelation heaven and earth are correlative terms; see p. 16. It is not that heaven is the realm of the real and immutable and earth its transitory shadow, created by an inferior deity, as in the debased form of Platonism then prevalent. In Revelation heaven is the dwelling of God and those who belong to him in contrast to the earth-dwellers who worship the beast (13[6, 8]), but it contains, besides God's throne, the *sea* (4[6]) which is a symbol of chaos and destruction, as well as of purification and redemption, and the *dragon*, the *ancient serpent* the devil (12[7ff.]). The dragon is thrown down from heaven to earth, and when the first heaven along with the first earth has passed away, there is *no more sea* (21[1]). In an age of radical dualism, and in a writer who at first sight thinks entirely in blacks and whites, this thoroughly biblical ambivalence is significant.

In *heaven* is found both the origin and the reflection of earthly events, good and bad. According to Caird's distinction (pp. 60f.) the symbolism may be determinative or descriptive: flags may be pinned on to a military map either to indicate troop-movements which are to take place, or to represent changes which have taken place, on the battle-field. The imagery of ch. 4, expressing the nature and will of the Creator, is determinative of all that happens on earth, right up to the new creation of 21; the imagery of 5 describes the effects of the earthly victory of the cross. The two are dialectically related in that the latter rises out of the former – creation and redemption are not two things, as gnostics believed, but one; the Lamb was slain 'before the foundation of the world', (13[8]) – and heaven's will waits on earth's response: the scroll cannot be opened, and the events of 6[1ff.] be unleashed, until the Lamb has conquered. In worship the two lines intersect; the heavenly will is communicated and becomes fruitful in earthly doing and suffering; the earthly victory is registered (note *the prayers of the saints*, $5^8$) and becomes effective in new heavenly dispositions.

Chapters 4 and 5 are still, then, part of the framework, by which the visions of destruction must be interpreted. But they are also closely linked with chs. 6 and 7, in developing the themes of the letters to Smyrna and Philadelphia: Christian endurance and the assurance on which it is based. The unsealing of the scroll sets out the effects of Christ's conquest in the terms of his own Apocalypse (Matt. 24 par.; see pp. 19–21); the disasters of the time are signs not of God's forgetfulness ($6^{10}$) but of the implementation of his plan; the moment of truth will come ($6^{12-17}$); and those who are now, despite Jewish slander, sealed as the Israel of God will come through the great tribulation ($7^{9-14}$), and find fulfilment in his service ($7^{15-17}$).

**4** *After this I looked, and lo, in heaven an open door! And the first voice, which I had heard speaking to me like a trumpet, said, 'Come up hither, and I will show you what must take place after this.' ²At once I was in the Spirit, and lo, a throne stood in heaven, with one seated on the throne! ³And he who sat there appeared like jasper and carnelian, and round the throne was a rainbow that looked like an emerald. ⁴Round the throne were twenty-four thrones, and seated on the thrones were twenty-four elders, clad in white garments, with golden crowns upon their heads. ⁵From the throne issue flashes of lightning, and voices and peals of thunder, and before the throne burn seven torches of fire, which are the seven spirits of God; ⁶and before the throne there is as it were a sea of glass, like crystal.*

*And round the throne, on each side of the throne, are four living creatures, full of eyes in front and behind: ⁷the first living creature like a lion, the second living creature like an ox, the third living creature with the face of a man, and the fourth living creature like a flying eagle. ⁸And the four living creatures, each of them with six wings, are full of eyes all round and within, and day and night they never cease to sing,*

> *Holy, holy, holy, is the Lord God Almighty,*
> *who was and is and is to come!*

⁹*And whenever the living creatures give glory and honour and thanks to him who is seated on the throne, who lives for ever and ever, ¹⁰the twenty-four elders fall down before him who is seated on the throne and worship him who lives for ever and ever; they cast their crowns before the throne, singing*

> ¹¹*Worthy art thou, our Lord and God,*
> *to receive glory and honour and power,*
> *for thou didst create all things,*
> *and by thy will they existed and were created.*

The vision of an *open door* in heaven, perhaps initiated on the human plane by a striking cloud-formation, leads to renewed inspiration. The chapter is based on Ezekiel's vision of the chariot-throne[1] – it draws also on the temple vision of Isa. 6 and the heavenly judgment scene of Dan. 7⁹ᶠᶠ· – and whatever John actually heard and saw, the account is carefully integrated with the rest of the book. *Door* links back through 3²⁰ to 3⁸, *trumpet* and *spirit* to 1¹⁰, and *what must take place after this* to 1¹. *After this* does not mean that from now on everything is future: John has moved into *heaven* where past, present and future exist as one whole. Thence comes light on what must take place on earth, from realities which in earthly terms are past or present, as much as from those which are strictly future. And as we have seen (on 1¹⁻³, compared with 22⁶ᶠᶠ·), *what must take place* is primarily the coming of Jesus, not events so much as the person from whom the events unroll (6¹ᶠᶠ·).

The setting of the scene cannot be tied down to any one earthly model. One might think of Solomon's temple (cf. II Chron. 3–5) with its cherub throne, its brazen 'sea', its incense and singing, its altar of sacrifice and its great festivals of redemption; or of the synagogue, with its scroll of the law in the central place of honour, its elders, its readings, hymns and prayers; or of a law-court – cf. Dan. 7⁹ᶠᶠ· and

[1] Meditation on Ezek. 1 was a means of inducing mystical experience; public discussion of it was forbidden by some rabbis (S-B I, p. 975, 2.6). See p. 42.

the legal connotations of the scroll and the Lamb's 'victory' in ch. 5; the synagogue served for pronouncing the law as well as for reading it. These and other models[m] would be part of the furniture of John's and his hearers' minds, and one cannot delimit the intended associations and meanings of the imagery.

There is clear reference too to the creation and exodus stories. The *throne*-vision of Ezek. 1 was connected in Judaism with Gen. 1 (Prigent, pp. 51–3); the *rainbow* suggests God's promise after the flood (Gen. 9), and the *sea* suggests the flood's source in the 'waters above the firmament'; the *Sanctus* (*Holy, holy, holy,*) figures in the Jewish *Yotser* (= Creator) liturgy (Prigent, pp. 62–4) and the hymn of the *elders*, which is to be regarded as interpretative comment, worships God precisely as Creator. John is already preparing for the vision of the new heaven and earth in which there is no more *sea* (21$^{\text{I}}$). Is this something quite other than the old order, as the intervening destructions might imply? Or does the emphasis in this strategic position on the God of Genesis, whose identity with the Father of Jesus Christ was denied by gnostics, suggest a fundamental continuity? Already there are hints of the exodus theme of redemption which is stated in ch. 5: the *lightning* and *thunder* suggest God enthroned on Sinai; the *sea* is (among other things) the heavenly counterpart of the Red Sea; the *Sanctus* was probably already part of the Christian celebration of redemption in the eucharist.

But the most important thing about this chapter is the picture it gives, or rather does not give, of God. 'John knows that to ordinary mortals the presence of God becomes real not through direct vision, even in the mind's eye, but through the impact of those to whom God is the supreme reality. So he allows his readers to look on the Eternal Light through the mirror of the worshipping host of heaven' (Caird, p. 63). God is the centre of the scene, and of the book.

༄

m One might think of an oriental throne-room, as at I Kings 22$^{\text{19}}$ (L. Mowry, 'Rev. 4–5 and Early Christian Liturgical Usage', *JBL* 71, 1952, pp. 75–84), or of the Greek theatre (R. R. Brewer, 'The Influence of Greek Drama on the Apocalypse of John', *Anglican Theological Review* 18, 1936, pp. 74–92), or of the gladiatorial games (Stauffer, pp. 169ff., 182ff.).

**I**

*an open door:* a conventional motif in apocalyptic, cf. I Enoch 14¹⁵, Test. Levi 5¹, but if the messages to Smyrna and Philadelphia are being expounded in these chapters, then the link with 3⁸ (and 3²⁰) is more than verbal: access is made possible by Christ's death and resurrection (cf. 1¹⁸) and granted to those who share it (cf. 1⁹, 3²⁰). The 'witness' Stephen sees the heavens opened (Acts 7⁵⁶), and the 'two witnesses' after their death are told *Come up hither* (11¹²). John's experience is in itself a vindication of Christian faith, against Jewish disparagement (3⁹) and Christian anxiety (6¹⁰).

**2**

*the first voice:* see 1¹⁰. There it was heard in ecstasy; here its sound brings on the ecstasy again (v. 2).

*a throne:* contrast the *throne of Satan* (2¹³); God is King of kings. The one *seated on the throne* is John's favourite description of God, and *the throne* as the symbol of his sovereignty is a constant point of origin and reference in what follows, e.g. 5⁶, 7⁹, 8³, 12⁵, 14³, 16¹⁷, 19⁵, 20¹¹, 21³, 22¹, ³. The raw materials for this vision come from Ezek. 1 – for the *throne* see 1²⁶ (itself based on Ex. 24¹⁰, God's appearance at Sinai): 'there was the likeness of a throne, in appearance like sapphire, and seated above the likeness of a throne was a likeness as it were of a human form.' As elsewhere, John simplifies and sharpens Ezekiel, concentrating attention not on the *throne* but on the *one seated*, without suggesting human shape.

**3**

*appeared like jasper and carnelian:* the brilliance of precious stones conveys the presence of God 'who clothes himself in light as with a garment' (Ps. 104²); see p. 70. The precise colour and significance of the gems in Revelation cannot be recovered with any certainty. *Jasper* is perhaps diamond, cf. 21¹¹, 'like a jasper, clear as crystal', and the 'terrible crystal' of Ezek. 1²². *Carnelian* (*sardius* in Greek) was probably red, the colour of fire – a favourite image of God, cf. Ezek. 1²⁷, Ex. 24¹⁷. For the assimilation of white and red, cf. 7¹⁴.

*a rainbow that looked like an emerald:* the *rainbow* is taken from Ezek. 1²⁸, where there is an explicit reference back to Gen. 9¹³. Does John mean to remind the hearer of God's 'everlasting covenant'? 'It warns us not to interpret the visions of disaster that follow as though God had forgotten his promise to Noah' (Caird, p. 63). The addition *like an emerald* might suggest that the rainbow is merely decorative; cf. Sirach 50[7]. But John's use of scripture is never merely decorative, and Caird's view is supported by the Genesis and Exodus echoes of the chapter as a whole; see also notes on 10[1].

**4**

*twenty-four elders*: taken by some to be *angels*, in line with OT pictures of God surrounded by his court (I Kings 22[19], Isa. 6[1]). But (apart from Isa. 24[23] possibly) nowhere are angels called *elders* or said to be *crowned*. More probably they are the OT worthies who already have a place in heaven – the 'men of old' (*presbuteroi*) of Heb. 11[2n] who received divine approval for their faith, as their *white garments* (='justification', cf. 3[5, 18], 6[11], 7[9], 19[8]) and *crowns* (=reward for faithful witness, cf. 2[10], 3[11]) suggest. Their number perhaps stems from the *twenty-four* heads of priestly families (I Chron. 24[4-6]), who must all be present in the temple at the great festivals. Caird emphasizes the kaleidoscopic quality of John's images: the *twenty-four* could also be the twelve patriarchs and twelve apostles of the Lamb (21[12-14]); their *crowns* make them kings as well as priests (cf. 5[10], 20[4]). They have also something of the character of the chorus in Greek drama (cf. 4[11], 5[9], 11[16ff.], 19[4]), and one of them acts as an interpreter at 5[5] and 7[13].

**5**

*lightning, voices, thunder*: cf. Ex. 19[16ff.], Heb. 12[18ff.],: the majesty and terror of God as law-giver and judge; NB the same trio at 8[5], 11[19], 16[18]. According to *Jubilees* 2[2] 'the angels of the voices and of the thunder and of the lightning' were among the things created on the first day; in Jewish tradition exodus and Sinai look back to creation.

*seven torches of fire, which are the seven spirits of God*: these words pick up the trinitarian greeting of 1[4ff.] (see notes there). God's active presence in the world, usually spoken of as (Holy) Spirit, is here expressed on the model of Zech. 4[2, 10]: Zechariah saw seven lamps, and heard that they were 'the eyes of the Lord which range through the whole earth.' God's self-revelation in Jesus (1[5]) is taken up in the next chapter, and there the *seven spirits* are his (5[6]; cf. 3[1], John 14[26], 15[26]).

*n* See also Heb. 12[18-24] for a scene similar to that of Rev. 4–5.

6

*a sea of glass like crystal:* again a variety of possible meanings:

(*a*) decoration: cf. the story in the Quran (xxvii) of the pavement of glass (*clear* glass was an expensive rarity) in front of Solomon's throne and the Queen of Sheba lifting up her skirt to walk through it.

(*b*) temple furniture, like the lights of v. 5; Solomon's temple contained a *sea*, a vast cauldron – originally a cosmological symbol (I Kings $7^{23-26}$) but in II Chron. $4^6$ a bath for ritual washing: 'the fires of the spirit (v. 5) carry with them the waters of regeneration, in virtue of the constant Christian association of water and spirit' (Farrer, pp. 90f.); see on $15^{2f.}$

(*c*) the heavenly analogue of the Red Sea, as in the Targum tradition (McNamara, pp. 201-4), pointing forward to the redemption of $5^{9, \text{ 10}}$; cf. $15^2$.

(*d*) the abyss (Caird,[o] pp. 65-8): 'the reservoir of evil out of which arises the monster ($13^1$)' – the *sea* which in the new order is *no more* ($21^1$). According to the Mesopotamian mythology reflected in the Bible, God at the creation defeated the dragon of the sea and imposed order on chaos, but chaos might always return, e.g. in the form of the heavenly waters of the flood, which were linked with 'the waters under the earth' (Gen. $1^7$, $7^{11}$); see notes on $9^1$ for this 'spiritual' geography, in which heaven comprises both 'above' and 'below'. Christians saw a connection between the waters of the flood which destroyed and of baptism which saved, cf. I Peter $3^{20}$ and (*b*) above. The Red Sea similarly was the occasion of destruction for the wicked and salvation for the righteous; its drying up echoed God's ancient victory over the dragon (Isa. $51^{9f.}$). This interpretation, which is more fully documented by Caird and was, as he says, 'still part of the living language of theology', might seem to founder on the beauty and purity expressed by *glass, like crystal,* cf. $21^{11, \text{ 18}, \text{ 21}}$, $22^1$. But Satan, called *dragon* by John, also had his place in heaven ($12^{7\text{ff.}}$), and like the fallen angel of Isa. $14^{12}$ and Ezek. $28^{12, \text{ 13}}$ was no doubt 'perfect in beauty'. Such ambivalence is to be grasped as characteristic, not rejected as (by Western standards) anomalous. Evil could not seduce if it did not contain real elements of beauty, truth and goodness; cf. II Cor. $11^{14}$.

None of these possibilities excludes any of the others.

*round the throne, on each side of the throne:* RSV is struggling with difficult

[o] See also Caird, 'On Deciphering the Book of Revelation', *Exp T* 74, 1962, pp. 103-5.

Greek. *On each side of* is literally *in the middle of*, and may be a Hebraism for 'between', – the *living creatures* are perhaps arranged in a semi-circle round the throne, between it and the *sea*. An accurate picture is not, of course, important. The *creatures* are a composite, already familiar in Jewish tradition, of the cherubim supporting the enthroned Glory in Ezekiel, and the seraphim singing *Holy, holy, holy*, in Isaiah.

*full of eyes:* cf. the wheels of the chariot-throne (Ezek. $10^{12}$); II Enoch $21^{1}$ (A): 'the creatures with six wings and many eyes overshadowed all his throne singing . . . Holy, holy, holy'. *Eyes* are connected with *spirit* at $5^{6}$; they symbolize probably wakefulness: 'those who sleep not bless thee . . . saying 'Holy, holy, holy . . .' (I Enoch $39^{12}$); cf. Argus, the many-eyed watchman of the Greek gods.

**7**
*lion, ox, man, eagle:* cf. Ezek. $1^{10}$. 'Man is exalted among creatures, the eagle among birds, the ox among domestic animals, the lion among wild beasts; all of them have received dominion . . . Yet they are stationed below the chariot of the Holy One' (*Midrash Shemoth* R. 23). The *creatures* represent the universe's praise of its Creator, and are associated with the outworking of the divine wrath ($6^{1-7}$, $15^{7}$).

**8**
*never cease to sing:* lit. *have no rest singing;* contrast the worshippers of the beast, $14^{11}$. *Rest* is one of the great rewards set before men in their earthly ordeals, cf. $6^{11}$, $14^{13}$, Matt. $11^{29}$, but it turns out to be not inactivity but unresting worship, cf. $7^{15}$, $22^{4}$.

*Holy, holy, holy:* cf. the angelic worship (I Enoch $39^{12}$, II Enoch $21^{1}$), which was regarded as the prototype of the earthly. The hymn was already part of the Jewish liturgy, and almost certainly of the Christian, cf. I Clement $34^{6}$. Isaiah has 'Holy, holy, holy is the Lord of hosts' ($6^{3}$); John, who always adapts his allusions, substitutes his favourite formula *Lord God Almighty* – see on $1^{8}$.

*who was and is and is to come:* see on $1^{4}$. Here there is the same peculiar grammar, but the conventional order, (past, present, future), as befits the worship of God as Creator.

**9–11**
This is the language of court ceremonial, cf. Dan. $4^{34-37}$, and the doxologies of I Enoch.

10

Tacitus tells how the Parthian Tiridates placed his diadem before an image of Nero (*Annals XV*.29).

11

*our Lord and God:* in the east a common form of address to the emperor, affected especially by Domitian.

*to receive:* these things belong to him already as Creator, but it is the proper part of subjects to ascribe them to their king, cf. I Chron. 29$^{11}$.

*thou didst create:* better 'it was thou who . . . and it was by thy will that they came to be' (lit. 'were' – God said, and it was so, Gen. 1), which is filled out by *and were created*.

It has been remarked that there is nothing specifically Christian in this chapter, but we move on at once from creation to redemption, the Lamb's victory through death, in which Christians share. The great OT redemptions from Egypt and Babylon were seen as repetitions of God's victory at the creation: Christians are to understand that 'their coming ordeal will be part of the process by which the chaotic world is to be brought within the compass of the divine sovereignty' (Caird, p. 69), a process which has already been decisively inaugurated by the birth and death of Christ.

$5^{-14}$ THE ENTHRONEMENT OF THE LAMB

5 *And I saw in the right hand of him who was seated on the throne a scroll written within and on the back, sealed with seven seals;* $^2$*and I saw a strong angel proclaiming with a loud voice, 'Who is worthy to open the scroll and break its seals?'* $^3$*And no one in heaven or on earth or under the earth was able to open the scroll or to look into it,* $^4$*and I wept much that no one was found worthy to open the scroll or to look into it.* $^5$*Then one of the elders said to me, 'Weep not; lo, the Lion of the tribe of Judah, the Root of David, has conquered, so that he can open the scroll and its seven seals.'*

*'And between the throne and the four living creatures and among the elders, I saw a Lamb standing, as though it had been slain, with seven horns and with seven eyes, which are the seven spirits of God sent out into all the earth;* ⁷*and he went and took the scroll from the right hand of him who was seated on the throne.* ⁸*And when he had taken the scroll, the four living creatures and the twenty-four elders fell down before the Lamb, each holding a harp, and with golden bowls full of incense, which are the prayers of the saints;* ⁹ *and they sang a new song, saying,*

> *'Worthy art thou to take the scroll and to open its seals,*
> *for thou wast slain and by thy blood didst ransom men for God*
> *from every tribe and tongue and people and nation,*
> ¹⁰*and hast made them a kingdom and priests to our God,*
> *and they shall reign on earth.'*

¹¹ *Then I looked, and I heard around the throne and the living creatures and the elders the voice of many angels, numbering myriads of myriads and thousands of thousands,* ¹²*saying with a loud voice, 'Worthy is the Lamb who was slain, to receive power and wealth and wisdom and might and honour and glory and blessing!'* ¹³*And I heard every creature in heaven and on earth and under the earth and in the sea, and all therein, saying, 'To him who sits upon the throne and to the Lamb be blessing and honour and glory and might for ever and ever!'* ¹⁴*And the four living creatures said, 'Amen!' and the elders fell down and worshipped.*

In the Jewish morning liturgy the praise of God as Creator led on to celebration of the Torah (Law) and thanksgiving for redemption at the Red Sea, a pattern reflected in the heavenly worship of Rev. 4–5 which perhaps itself reflects the worship of the Asian churches (Prigent, pp. 61–76). This may guide us in the interpretation of the *scroll* and the *Lamb*, for which there are again several overlapping models.

## (i) The scroll (biblion)

What sort of document is it? *Written within and on the back* suggests an 'opisthograph', a scroll with writing on both sides as at Ezek. 2¹⁰ (John is working through Ezekiel more or less in order). But there is a variant reading *written inside and outside*, which would indicate a folded and sealed document (Latin *diploma*) of a kind familiar throughout the ancient world; cf. the sale deed of Jer. 32$^{9-14}$. Unsealing would let the contents be given effect, as in the case of a will, which in Roman law had to be sealed by at least seven witnesses. The contents here might be a legal bond, of man's debt or guilt before God.[p]

Most probably, however, this variant is secondary and *biblion* means scroll or book, as at 1$^{11}$, 6$^{13}$, 10$^2$. Some think of the Book of Destiny or 'heavenly tablets' – an idea going back to Babylonian religion and common in the apocalypses: a prophet ascends into heaven and is shown the book, in order to communicate God's plans to men; e.g. I Enoch 81, 93. This fits 4$^1$ well, but Ezekiel's scroll was 'in my mouth as sweet as honey' (Ezek. 3$^3$) which suggests the law (Ps. 19$^{10}$); cf. the two tables of the decalogue, 'written on both sides' (Ex. 32$^{15}$). Perhaps in the heavenly as in the earthly synagogue the Torah scroll is the central object, and one might think of the law's indictment of man's disobedience, unsealed and executed in 6$^{1ff.}$.

But why, then, the grief before the Lamb took the scroll and the rejoicing after? It must contain not just the law but the prophets' interpretation as well. Isaiah had said that their visions had become 'like the words of a book that is sealed', and looked forward to a time when 'the deaf shall hear the words of a book' (Isa. 29$^{11, 18}$). It must be the total revelation of God's will and plan in scripture, which Christ can 'open' because he is the subject of the book, himself the Word of God, and his sacrifice is the foundation of the whole plan (cf. 13$^8$, Heb. 1$^{1-4}$). Scripture is indeed a 'sealed book' until 'the veil over men's minds' has been removed (II Cor. 3$^{14ff.}$); the letter to Philadelphia has prepared us to think of Christ as opening both the scriptures and the kingdom of heaven. To reveal is not only to make plain but also thereby to make effective. The relation between 4–5 and 6$^{1ff.}$ can then be seen in Pauline terms: the revelation (and execution) of God's righteousness (his saving action to right the wrong) in the gospel is bound up with the revelation of his wrath (the recoil of his righteousness on all who ignore it.)[q] Salvation and wrath are two sides of one coin.

---

[p] Cf. O. Roller, 'Das Buch mit den sieben Siegeln', *ZNW* 26, 1937, pp. 98–113.

[q] Rom. 1$^{16-18}$; cf. G. Bornkamm, *Early Christian Experience*, pp. 47–9, 62–5.

If it be asked why God could not have opened the scroll himself, the answer may be found in the biblical conviction that he had given dominion over the world to man, and however deeply man had abused his trust would not bypass man in bringing his purposes to completion (cf. Rom. 5$^{11ff.}$, Heb. 2$^{5-10}$); and in the further conviction that 'man' was truly embodied only in Israel and in the Man who was to come, the Messiah. Thus the Lamb is introduced in allusion to famous messianic prophecies as *the Lion of the tribe of Judah*, the *Root of David*, and *the prayers of the saints* (v. 8) hint at the part played in his victory by the expectant faithfulness of God's people.

### (ii) *The Lamb (arnion)*

But what is implied by seeing the Messiah as a 'slain lamb'? Does it continue the sense of military might in *Lion* and *David*, as the *seven horns* (symbols of power) imply, and as his wrath (6$^{16}$) and his victorious warfare (17$^{14}$, 19$^{11ff.}$) seem to confirm? Or does it turn the old ideas of power upside down?

In I Enoch David appears as a lamb (*arēn*) which grows into a ram, and the Messiah is a great horned sheep, battling victoriously against hostile beasts (89$^{45f.}$, 90$^{9-16}$; cf. Test. Joseph 19$^{8}$; one Jewish expectation was of a Messiah, son of Joseph, who would die in battle). No doubt John and his hearers were familiar with this concept, but, on our view, he has reinterpreted it in the light of Jesus' death. *Arnion* is the diminutive of *arēn*, used by LXX for the defenceless lamb of Jer. 11$^{19}$, and *slain* is *esphagmenon*, a word used for the slaughter of a sacrificial victim. The two ideas are combined in Isa. 53$^{7, 10-12}$ – the servant of the Lord is like 'a lamb led to the slaughter . . . an offering for sin . . . he bore the sin of many' – and Isa. 53$^{9}$ is applied to the 144,000 who follow the Lamb at 14$^{5}$. There are also obvious echoes in vv. 9f. of the Passover lamb, whose blood redeemed Israel in Egypt; cf. 1$^{5f.}$ Jesus was 'the Lamb of God that takes away the sin of the world' and died at the time when the Passover lambs were being sacrificed (John 1$^{29}$, 19$^{31}$; cf. I Cor. 5$^{7}$, I Peter 1$^{18f.}$, 2$^{21-25}$).$^{r}$

*r* The Passover lamb was not technically a 'sin-offering', but by the first century AD it had attained enormous significance: expiation of sin, atonement with God, the crossing of the Red Sea and the covenant at Sinai all sprang from its virtue.

*(iii) Hearing and seeing*

For the interpretation of the Lamb, it is important to grasp the relation of hearing and seeing. What is heard, the 'voice', represents the inner reality, the spirit; what is seen, the 'appearance', represents the outward, the flesh. Mary Magdalene saw Jesus in the garden, but did not recognize him until she heard his voice (John 20$^{14ff.}$; see Lohmeyer on Rev. 13$^{11}$). But as with 'heaven' and 'earth' (p. 113), it is not a simple 'Platonic' distinction to the effect that the outward and bodily is the shadow of the inward and spiritual, which is alone real. Equally, the fact that Hebrew imagery is auditory rather than visual (pp. 14 and 70) does not mean that what is seen is unimportant or inferior. To the Jew the outward world is the locus of God's 'speaking', his self-revelation and action, so that there is a dialectical relationship between inward and outward, spirit and flesh, hearing and seeing. Thus the slain Lamb (which John *sees*) is interpreted by the Lion of Judah (of which he *hears*): its death is not weakness and defeat, as it seems to be, but power and victory (cf. I Cor. 1$^{23ff.}$). But the Lion of Judah, the traditional messianic expectation, is reinterpreted by the slain Lamb: God's power and victory lie in self-sacrifice (in contrast with Satan's; his beast 'looks like a lamb but speaks like a dragon', 13$^{11}$). Similarly in ch. 7 John *hears* (v. 4) the number of the 144,000 who are 'sealed' (i.e. the spiritual truth of Israel's 'election'), which interprets what he *sees* (v. 9), a multitude drawn from all nations: i.e. 'salvation is of the Jews'. But the outward reality of the church, in which there cannot be distinctions between Jew, Greek and barbarian (Col. 3$^{11}$), reinterprets the traditional theological truth of Israel's priority.

We may agree, then, with Caird that what John *hears*, the traditional OT expectation of military deliverance, is reinterpreted by what he *sees*,[s] the historical fact of a sacrificial death, and that the resulting paradox is the key to all his use of the OT, 'as if John were saying to us . . . "Wherever the Old Testament says *Lion*, read *Lamb*". Wherever the Old Testament speaks of the victory of the Messiah or the overthrow of the enemies of God, we are to remember that the Gospel recognizes no other way of achieving these ends than the way

[s] Caird, p. 73; cf. also his comment on 7$^{4, 9}$ (p. 96).

of the Cross' (p. 75). If the visions of destruction (6–20) are to be interpreted by the framework of creation and redemption (4f. and 21f.) and not vice versa, then the apparent violence of the Lamb in 6–20 must be interpreted by the *slain* Lamb of 5$^6$ and not vice versa.

Can we go further with Caird and say that the Lamb is 'the symbol of self-sacrificing and redemptive love' (p. 74)? To the Jews the death of a martyr expiated the sins of the people and guaranteed his own resurrection. It also guaranteed for the persecutors eternal punishment far worse than the temporal pains they had inflicted (cf. II Macc. 7$^{1-19}$, 3$^{0-38}$). If we had only chs. 6–20 it would be hard to see more than this in Revelation – an attitude poles apart from the love for enemies which Jesus taught. But again the framework changes the perspective. The Lamb's death ransomed men for God *from every nation*, to be *a kingdom and priests* (5$^{9f.}$) – i.e. to bring God to men and men to God – and finally the nations and their kings, the victims of the destructions of 6–20, will walk by the light of the city's lamp, which is the Lamb, and the leaves of the tree which grows in the city's street are for their healing (21$^{24}$–22$^3$). The word 'love' seems a mockery applied to the terrible Lamb of the intervening chapters, but his eternal purpose is the redemption of all men, and his severity to those who choose the beast is a function of that purpose. In both Old Testament and New, in gospels and epistles, God's love cannot be separated from his severity, which is often expressed in terms the opposite of loving.[t]

Finally we may note that the hymns which John *hears* at vv. 11–13 are again specifically connected with what he *sees* and convey its deepest meaning: the unification of the whole cosmos in the worship of God and Christ. They point us not to the victory of the cross or the opening of the scroll, but to the enthronement of the Lamb. Verse 11 evokes Daniel's vision (7$^{9-14}$) of thrones and the 'ancient of days' surrounded by thousands of thousands, myriads of myriads, and one like a son of man receiving dominion, glory and a kingdom. Verse 13 speaks the same language as the hymn of Phil. 2$^{5-11}$: 'Therefore God has highly exalted him . . . that at the name of Jesus every knee should

---

[t] Cf. John 3$^{16-19}$, $^{36}$, Rom. 11$^{22-32}$, Song of Songs. 8$^6$: 'love is strong as death, jealousy (passionate concern) is severe as Sheol . . . fiercer than any flame.' See pp. 51, 108.

bow, in heaven and on earth and under the earth, and every tongue confess that Jesus is Lord, to the glory of God the Father'. This chapter is the most powerful statement of the divinity of Christ in the NT, and it receives its power from the praise of God the Creator which precedes it: this is the divinity which Christ has achieved, through suffering, and this divinity, so achieved, is the power behind all that follows.

ಣಌ

**1**

*I saw:* this may be part of John's genuinely visionary experience – visionary emotion (v. 4) is one of the criteria (Lindblom, *Gesichte und Offenbarungen*, p. 219).

*within and on the back:* the best attested of several readings, all of which could easily have arisen from it but not vice versa. Roller argued for *inside and outside* on the grounds that the sense demands a legal document, which would naturally be *sealed*, not a book (*scroll*) which would not. But John's imagery is impressionistic and exploits a variety of models. Ezek. 2$^{10ff.}$ is primary, but he may also have in mind Dan. 12$^4$, 'But you, Daniel, shut up the words, and seal the book, until the time of the end.' *Sealing* in apocalyptic signifies that God's plan for the world is put into cold storage because of men's unworthiness, until the appointed time.

For the relation of this scroll to the 'little scroll' of 10$^{2ff.}$, see notes there.

**2**

*open the scroll and break its seals:* as often in the Bible, the end is put before the means.

**2f.**

The scene is set in heaven but the whole cosmos is involved; John's cosmology is not to be spatially understood. For angelic incapacity cf. I Peter 1$^{12}$.

**5**

*one of the elders:* see on 4$^{14}$.

*the Lion of the tribe of Judah:* an allusion to Gen. 49$^{9f.}$, a favourite Jewish messianic text, bloodthirstily embroidered in the Targums with motifs from Isa. 63$^{1-6}$ (see on 7$^{14}$, 14$^{20}$, 19$^{15}$).

*Root of David* cites another stock Messianic passage, Isa. 11$^{1-10}$, about the 'branch from Jesse's root', who will be equipped with the spirit of wisdom and insight (cited again at 22$^{16}$).

*Conquered* (*nikan*) can have a forensic as well as military or athletic sense (cf. 12$^{10f.}$, Rom. 3$^4$), but the purpose of the titles is not only to assert Jesus' authority to open the scriptures (in the face of Jewish 'slander', 3$^{7-9}$), but also to set up the contrast with the master-title *Lamb*: conquest is through sacrificial suffering and apparent defeat (see on 2$^7$). *Lion* and *Root* over against *Lamb* is a symbolic equivalent of 'we preach Christ crucified . . . the power of God and the wisdom of God' (I Cor. 1$^{23f.}$).

**6**
*between the throne . . . and among the elders:* in the light of Hebrew idiom the correct translation is probably 'between the throne and the creatures (which form a unit) and the elders' (cf. NEB margin), but NEB's 'in the very middle of the throne' is true to John's theology (3$^{21}$, 22$^1$, $^3$), and the wording of 7$^{17}$ is similar.

*a Lamb: arnion,* a dimunitive; the usual word is *amnos.* The diminutive sense was no longer prominent and could not alone disqualify the militant interpretation, but in the NT the only other occurrence of *arnion* is significantly at John 21$^{15}$, 'Feed my lambs.'

*standing, as though it had been slain:* i.e. alive, though 'with the marks of slaughter upon him' (NEB; cf. John 20$^{25ff.}$); it does not mean that the death was only apparent. *Slain* (*esphagmenon*), like Paul's 'crucified', is the perfect participle, expressing a present state based on a past action: it suggests the present and eternal reality of the historical death on the cross; cf. 13$^8$, I Peter 1$^{18-20}$. The death of Christians is linked with it by the use of the same word (6$^9$, 18$^{24}$). Some scholars hold that the phrase is not sacrificial but simply signifies Christ's triumph over apparent defeat, which promises like triumph for Christians. *Sphazō* can certainly be used for slaying enemies, but the sacrificial sense was prominent in secular Greek and predominant in LXX.

*seven horns:* a symbol of power, answering to *Lion* (contrast 13$^1$, 17$^3$). The *seven eyes* symbolize wisdom, answering to *Root.* John is interpreting

Isa. 11 by Zech. $3^{8-10}$, where Zerubbabel is called 'branch', and Zech. $4^{2-10}$, where 'the seven lamps' are equated with 'the seven eyes of the Lord which range through the whole earth'.[u] 'Range through' here becomes *sent out into: sent* (*apestalmenos*) is a keyword in John's Gospel, cf. $20^{21f}$, 'As the Father has sent me out, so I send you . . . Receive the Holy Spirit.' The hearers would understand the symbolism in terms of their own mission and witness; see on v. 10 and $11^{3ff}$. Already the *seven spirits* have been linked with the seven torches or lamps ($4^5$), which symbolize the churches ($1^{20}$, $2^1$, $3^1$).

**7**

*he went:* not yet enthroned; cf. Dan. $7^{13}$: 'there *came* one like a son of man'.

**8**

*which are the prayers of the saints:* for the association of incense with prayers cf. Ps. $141^2$. Some regard the phrase as inappropriate here, perhaps a gloss from $8^{3-5}$, but it is characteristic of John to indicate the earthly realities which lie behind heavenly scenes; cf. $1^{20}$. The *saints* are God's faithful people, whether of the Old Covenant, like Simeon and Anna in Luke 2, or of the New – it is the normal NT expression for 'Christians'. John may have in mind Dan. 7 where the 'one like a son of man' is a personification of 'the saints of the Most High', who are oppressed by the beast (cf. Rev. $13^7$). The Lamb does not *take the scroll* and open it apart from their prayers; see on $6^{10}$, $8^{3-5}$, cf. Luke $1^{10}$, $18^{1-8}$.

**9**

*a new song:* like the *harps* (v. 8) the *song* is associated with redemption at $14^{2f}$, $15^{2f}$, and often in the Psalms (e.g. $33^3$, $40^3$, $98^1$). In ancient religion hymns, especially *new* and secret ones, were thought to have power to rescue man from his earthly prison (cf. Jonah 2, Acts $16^{25f}$) and open the gates of heaven.[v] The praise of God in itself weakens Satan's power (see on $1^{5f}$, p. 62). For *new* as not just fresh but connoting the New Age, see on $2^{17}$; cf. Isa. $42^{9f}$, which in Judaism was linked with Ps. $98^1$ as a reference to the messianic era (Prigent, p. 76).

u The gist of the vision is 'Not by might, nor by power, but by my Spirit, says the Lord of hosts' (Zech. $4^6$); cf. also II Chron. $16^9$.

v T. Arvedson, *Das Mysterium Christi*, Uppsala 1937, pp. 18f, 50f. The song which accompanied a sacrifice was thought to have the same power (p. 233).

*worthy art thou:* see on $4^{11}$. As at vv. 12f., Christ is addressed in the same terms as God. Pliny in his examination of Christians in Bithynia (*c.* AD 112) learned that 'they recited a hymn antiphonally to Christ as a god' (*Letters* X. 96.7).

*thou didst ransom:* a Pauline word (*ēgorasas*) with echoes of the slave market. For a Jew the supreme emancipation was from slavery in Egypt. Here the point of the metaphor is both the fact of liberation, which is for God's service (a *kingdom and priests*), as in the exodus usage (see on $1^5$), and the means of liberation, Christ's *blood* replacing that of the passover lamb – perhaps also the cost of liberation, as at I Cor. $6^{20}$.

*from every tribe:* note the universal scope of Christ's redemption; see on $1^7$, $7^9$.

10

*a kingdom and priests:* a slight alteration of Ex. $19^6$, 'a kingdom of priests'. *Kingdom* in biblical Greek means 'active rule' rather than 'realm': they are set free to be both kings and priests ($1^6$, $20^6$). But when? *They shall reign on the earth* – presumably in the millennium, the interim period after the parousia ($20^{4-6}$), or on the renewed earth ($21^1$, $22^5$): 'as often in the book, the hymn of praise anticipates the finished result' (Beckwith). But there is MS support for *they reign*, which as the 'harder reading' is to be preferred: a scribe with ch. 20 and millennial ideas in mind would naturally change the present tense, which at first sight is puzzling, to the future (by adding one letter), but there is no apparent motive for change from future to present. The present in fact fits the context well: Christ is praised for what he *has* achieved; the ransomed are already *a kingdom* ($1^5$), sharing Christ's pattern of kingship ($1^9$) in faithful 'witness to the truth' (cf. John $18^{37}$); see notes on $2^{26f.}$, $6^2$. The hymn expresses the heavenly reality behind their outward weakness – 'Blessed are the poor in spirit for theirs *is* the kingdom of heaven' (Matt. $5^3$). Nicolaitans might forget the qualification of suffering and endurance ($1^9$), like the Corinthians (I Cor. $4^{8-13}$), but the present tense would be no puzzle to the hearers. As *priests* they are to bring the obedient worship of the nations to God, again through their witness;[w] cf. Rom. $15^{16}$, 'a minister of Christ Jesus to the Gentiles in the priestly service of the gospel of God'.

[w] See on $11^{1-4}$ below: the 'two witnesses' are the two olive-branches of Zech. $4^{3, 11ff.}$, which represent Zerubbabel and Joshua, *king* and *priest*; cf. on v. 6 above.

Their kingship and priesthood have indeed still to be *fulfilled*, but it is vital for our understanding of John to recognize that he can regard it as a present fact.

**11**

*I looked, and I heard:* see on $9^{16}$ and pp. 125ff. – the hymns interpret the whole vision.

*myriads of myriads:* the number, or rather innumerability, of the *angels* evokes Dan. $7^{10}$ and Ps. $68^{17f.}$ – a passage applied by the early Christians to Christ's exaltation and pouring out of the gifts of the Spirit (Acts $2^{33}$, Eph. $4^{8-11}$.)

**12**

*to receive power and wealth . . .:* the same attributes can be ascribed (*received* does not imply previous lack) to Jesus as to God ($4^{11}$), and to Jesus as *the Lamb that was slain*, again the perfect tense. This is tantamount to the developed Christian belief that 'it is in the Cross that God discloses the essence of what it is to be God' (A. M. Ramsey). The power and homage which Rome takes for granted belong in reality to the Lamb, by right of self-sacrifice, not self-assertion.

**13**

*I heard every creature:* the whole of creation outside the circle of elders and angels unites in the worship for which it was created (ch. 4) and redeemed (ch. 5). In *hearing* as opposed to *seeing*, the End is already present.

We may draw some conclusions from our study of ch. 4 and 5. Prigent (pp. 61–76) has demonstrated their remarkable similarity with the Jewish morning liturgy: it prasies God as Creator (*Yotser*), it celebrates the Torah (not just as a series of commandments but as the history of salvation), and it gives thanks for redemption (*Geullah*) with a reference to the *new song* on the bank of the Red Sea (Ex. 15). Whether or not these chapters are based, as Prigent suggests, on the paschal liturgy of John's own church, the concepts of new creation and new exodus, which the church celebrates in baptism and eucharist, are clearly meant to control all that follows:

(i) John is setting out God's creative act of redemption in Christ as the ground and guarantee of final redemption from archetypal Egypt and Babylon (just as Isaiah grounded rescue from earthly Babylon in

God's exodus revelation, $43^{16-17}$, $5^{19ff.}$), even though all the plagues of Egypt must be recapitulated before the latter-day Pharaoh will 'let my people go'.

(ii) As in Isaiah, there is no narrow concern with a 'chosen people'; on their glorification hangs the destiny of the whole of God's creation (cf. Rom. $8^{19-21}$).

(iii) The author of the plagues that follow is the God of Genesis, who 'saw everything that he had made, and behold, it was very good', the God who says 'Behold, I make all things new' ($21^5$).

(iv) The scene is timeless. Even the historical event of the Lamb's slaughter is later implied to have been 'before the foundation of the world' ($13^8$). The events and scenes of the following chapters cannot be plotted on a time-scale, though historical reference is not lacking. It is the essence of Jewish and Christian worship that the lines of eternity and historical event cross, and man is admitted to heaven where past, present and future are alike in God *who was, and is, and is to come*.

# Revelation 6¹–7¹⁷

# The Seven Seals Opened

The unsealing of the scroll is at first sight a bizarre sequel to the build-up of expectation in ch. 5. The first unsealing, on its own, suggests the triumphant progress of God's cause in the gospel, but then war, famine, plague and every kind of death parade before us, performing however only a partial destruction, and the souls of the martyrs ask how long before they will be avenged. Only then, in the sixth unsealing, are we given a picture of what they want to see. The seventh should surely now present the finale of the New Age, but there is delay while God's servants are sealed against supernatural attack, and the unsealing dissolves into a further sevenfold series of disasters.

But the first hearers would have been prepared by their knowledge of Ezekiel for the scroll to contain 'lamentation, mourning and woe'; Moses had foretold sevenfold punishment, to be repeated if not followed by repentance (Lev. 26$^{18-28}$); and Jesus in his 'opening' of the future on the Mount of Olives[x] had warned of just such a series of disasters – 'the beginning of birth-pangs' (of the New Age) – but 'he who endures to the end will be saved'. In line with the messages to Smyrna and Philadelphia these chapters encourage the patient endurance of the saints, in face of the apparent triumph of God's enemies. They are shown Christ's victory taking effect in the world in ch. 6, and in ch. 7 they are given assurance of protection and final bliss. The sealing of 7$^{4-8}$ takes up another theme of those letters, assuring Christians under physical and theological attack that they are indeed God's people.

x Matt. 24, Mark 13, Luke 21; see pp. 19–21 and the tables in Charles, I, p. 158. John is drawing either on all three gospels or on the common underlying tradition. We will normally refer to Matthew.

6 *Now I saw when the Lamb opened one of the seven seals, and I heard one of the four living creatures say, as with a voice of thunder, 'Come!'* [2]*And I saw, and behold, a white horse, and its rider had a bow; and a crown was given to him, and he went out conquering and to conquer.*

[3]*When he opened the second seal, I heard the second living creature say, 'Come!'*

[4]*And out came another horse, bright red; its rider was permitted to take peace from the earth, so that men should slay one another; and he was given a great sword.*

[5]*When he opened the third seal, I heard the third living creature say 'Come!' And I saw, and behold, a black horse, and its rider had a balance in his hand;*

[6]*and I heard what seemed to be a voice in the midst of the four living creatures saying, 'A quart of wheat for a denarius, and three quarts of barley for a denarius; but do not harm oil and wine!'*

[7]*When he opened the fourth seal, I heard the voice of the fourth living creature say, 'Come!'* [8]*And I saw, and behold, a pale horse, and its rider's name was Death, and Hades followed him; and they were given power over a fourth of the earth, to kill with sword and with famine and with pestilence and by the wild beasts of the earth.*

There is no sign here of ecstatic experience, rather John's own meditation on the Lord's Apocalypse in the light of OT prophecies and recent events. The Roman defeat by the Parthians in AD 62 and the year of civil war following the suicide of Nero in 68 perhaps lie behind the first two riders. The eruption of Vesuvius in AD 79 terrified the Roman world and was taken as a warning of imminent divine judgment (Stauffer, pp. 147ff.). The year after, the city of Rome suffered a devastating fire and then the worst plague in its history. In 92 there was severe grain famine in Asia.

This is the world, insecure beneath its affluence and power, which the four horsemen evoke. But the nature of the series is determined by the cry of the *creatures*, 'Come', which may be interpreted by the same cry at $22^{17, 20}$: there it is the believers' liturgical response to the Lord's promise, 'I am coming soon'; here, as often in Revelation, earthly liturgy has its parallel in heaven (see p. 113). In accordance with Jesus' own revelation, his coming must be heralded by signs and catastrophes, just as in the letters it was clear that it must bring judgment as well as blessing. The disasters are the overture for the parousia, set in motion by the slain *Lamb* and invoked by the creatures which form God's throne. Creator and Redeemer are united behind the world phenomena which might seem to deny their power and concern.

This understanding is confirmed by the model in Zechariah. He saw men on horses of four different colours, identified as 'those whom the Lord had sent to range through the earth', who were involved in God's punishment of the nations which oppressed his people ($1^{8-15}$, $6^{1-8}$). Here, then, they signify that the natural and political disasters of the contemporary world are God's own agents for the vindication of his people.

But what is the significance of the first rider? *White* horse, *crown* and *conquering* suggest a divine agency; the early commentators took him to be either Christ himself or the proclamation of the Word of God in the gospel, in the light of $19^{11ff.}$, which says in identical words *and behold, a white horse, and he who sat on it* and names him as the Word of God. The Lord had mentioned, along with wars and famines, testimony before governors and kings: 'the gospel must first be preached to all nations' (Matt. $24^{14}$, Luke $21^{12}$).

This interpretation is rejected by most modern scholars: the rider cannot be Christ since he opens the seal, and the context gives no hint of gospel. The horsemen form a quartet like the first four trumpets and bowls, and the first must represent not the beneficent activity of evangelism but a maleficent power like the rest – either the Parthian[y] menace, or the lust for conquest out of which international strife (v. 4) and its consequences in famine etc. arise (vv. 6, 8). Or perhaps in line with Matt. $24^5$, 'Many will come in my name, saying "I am the Christ", and will lead many astray', he represents Antichrist.[z] The

[y] See Introduction, p. 24 note *l*.

[z] Brilliantly argued by M. Rissi in 'The Rider on the White Horse: a study of Revelation $6^{1-8}$, *Interpretation* 18, 1964, pp. 413–18; cf. *Time and History*, pp. 72–4.

white horse, crown and conquering are then all part of the Satanic parody which comes into the open in ch. 13 (see p. 214), and the *bow* is the weapon of the demonic Gog, the account of whose destruction is applied to the defeat of Antichrist and his armies in $19^{17-21}$ (Ezek. $39^{3-6, 17-20}$).

But the 'Satanic parody' has not yet been set up. The imagery, if interpreted by what has gone before rather than by what is yet to come, points unequivocally to something heavenly. This rider's function is simply *conquering*, which must be interpreted by the Lamb's conquest ($5^5$). He must be both divine agency and maleficent power, and a clue has been found in God's '*arrows* of judgment' in Ezek. $5^{16f.}$: famine, wild beasts, pestilence, and sword. Jesus' victory on the cross is the 'judgment of this world' (John $12^{31-33}$).[a]

But in this light we may return to the ancient view. The gospel in the NT is not simply beneficent. It declared God's victory in Christ and warned of coming judgment by the God who searches men's hearts – to the alarm of the governor Felix (Acts $24^{25}$; cf. Rom. $2^{16}$, Rev. $14^{6-11}$). In their witness before governors and kings Christians were promised the Holy Spirit, which 'convicts' the world (John $16^{8ff.}$); the two witnesses were a 'torment' to the earth-dwellers with the 'fire from their mouth' (Rev. $11^{5-10}$). In the OT bow and arrows, like sword and rod, can be a metaphor for God's word. Finally, $6^2$ is on any showing closely related to $19^{11-16}$. The rider cannot be Christ, but Christ is followed by the armies *of heaven* in *white linen* on *white horses* – the 'faithful witnesses'. It may be they whom this rider represents; we can read of their *conquering* in the Acts of the Apostles.

There is no direct reference to Christian witness as in $11^{3-13}$: the seals are an overture, a sketch, filled out in trumpets and bowls, and the Antichrist interpretation cannot be ruled out. But our interpretation must not be ruled out simply because to list witness with war, famine and pestilence is 'unthinkable'. For John the work of the Lamb and his followers is destructive – for a world in the grip of 'false consciousness' (*pseudos*) it must be torment (the 'steel which questions the distempered part'; see p. 51); equally, all destructive

---

a So A. Feuillet, 'Le premier cavalier de l'Apocalypse', *ZNW* 57, 1966, pp. 243–50.

powers, even *Death and Hades* which are finally thrown into the lake of fire, are in God's service.

ᚱᚲᚱ

**I**

*I saw ... I heard:* what is heard interprets what is seen (p. 125). The call for Christ's final *coming* ($22^{17, 20}$) points to the meaning of what looks like mere carnage. The *voice of thunder* suits the *lion*, first in the list of *creatures* ($4^7$), and in ch. 10 a voice like a *lion's* and seven *thunders* introduce the *little scroll* (= the gospel – some support for the view that this *rider* represents Christian witness), but the other three *creatures* do not obviously fit their horsemen.

**2**

*a white horse:* the colours, unlike Zechariah's ($1^8$, $6^{2f.}$) are significant; see notes on $2^{17}$, $3^5$ for *white*, and $2^{10}$, $3^{11}$ for *crown*.

*bow:* in the OT the weapon of kings, and of cavalry and chariot troops, especially the Assyrian and Babylonian invaders. In Roman times the Parthians were the only known mounted archers. But the significance of *bow*, which occurs only here in the NT, must match that of *white*, *crown* and *conquer* which is already clear. It could well suggest God's word[b]. *Sword* would make the point more clearly (see on $2^{12}$), but is needed for the next rider.

*was given:* frequent in Rev. for divine gift (v. 11) or divine permission (vv. 4, 8 – see on $13^{5f.}$).

*and to conquer:* the witness of the church is the means of Christ's reign on earth ($2^{26f.}$, $5^{10}$, I Cor. $15^{25}$). Or does this phrase represent 'the imperfect victory of the adversary which will never reach its goal' (Rissi, *Future*, p. 95, n. 51)?

*b* Perhaps John had Hab. $3^{5-9}$ in mind. There God appears preceded by plague and pestilence, and the shaking of nations and mountains. The Hebrew consonants for 'plague' (*dbr*) are the same as those for 'word', which was read here by LXX and the rabbis (Hebrew words were written without vowels), and the passage continues: 'thou didst ride upon thy *horses*, thy chariot of victory; thou didst strip the sheath from thy *bow* and put the arrows to the string.' See also Ps. $45^{4f.}$, which lies behind $19^{11-16}$.

**4**

*red:* the colour of bloodshed, and of the dragon ($12^3$).

*peace from the earth:* 'do not think I have come to bring peace on earth: I have not come to bring peace but a sword' (Matt. $10^{34}$) – part of Jesus' instructions to the twelve before sending them out to preach. This passage lies behind $11^{1-13}$ (the two witnesses) – another hint that the first rider may represent Christian witness?

**5–6**

*balance:* a symbol of famine; cf. Lev. $26^{26}$, Ezek. $4^{16}$, 'they shall eat bread by weight'. The voice *in the midst of the creatures* reinforces their cry 'Come!': all proceeds from God's throne. A *quart* of grain is a day's ration, a *denarius* a day's wage; *barley* is cheaper than *wheat* and is the food of the poor: the famine then is severe but not extreme. *Oil and wine*[c] are not luxuries, as is often maintained (as if the divine irony were anticipating Marie Antoinette's 'Let them eat cake'); they are staples along with corn (Deut. $7^{13}$ etc.) but having deeper roots could survive when corn failed. The picture is of limited famine, cf. a *fourth* (v. 8).

**8**

*pale: chlōros* means green or livid, chosen in place of Zechariah's 'dappled' to fit *Death, thanatos,* which also means *pestilence* (cf. the Black Death) as at the end of the verse and at $2^{22}$. John has emphasized the *double entendre* by adding *Hades,* the companion of Death at $1^{18}$, $20^{13f.}$. Their instruments are traditional: the trio of Jeremiah ($14^{12}$ etc.), to which John adds *wild beasts* to make Ezekiel's quartet ($14^{21}$; cf. $5^{16f.}$) – perhaps also as a bridge to the next vision, evoking the arena in which Christians were put to death. The quartet recapitulates the second and third riders, but not the first – as is to be expected, if he represents Christian witness, not a traditional plague.

*the fourth:* the trumpets affect a *third* ($8^{7ff.}$), the bowls the whole (16). The seals are 'the beginning of birth pangs' (Matt. $24^8$).

c Many see allusions to Domitian's edict, in connection with the famine of AD 92, reducing the number of vines to stimulate grain production. Hemer points out that this would have been particularly disastrous for Philadelphia: the volcanic soil is ideally suited to vines, which were the staple crop; 'do not harm *wine*' is then a limitation of the disaster for Philadelphia by divine grace. Such local references are characteristic, and the seals section is related to the letters to Smyrna and Philadelphia (see p. 45) – but why 'do not harm *oil*'?

THE FIFTH SEAL:
             THE CRY OF THE MARTYRS

⁹*When he opened the fifth seal, I saw under the altar the souls of those
who had been slain for the word of God and for the witness they had
borne;* ¹⁰*they cried out with a loud voice, 'O Sovereign Lord, holy and true,
how long before thou wilt judge and avenge our blood on those who dwell
upon the earth?'*

¹¹ *Then they were each given a white robe and told to rest a little longer,
until the number of their fellow servants and their brethren should be
complete, who were to be killed as they themselves had been.*

This passage is built on two stock themes of apocalyptic – the cry of
innocent blood for vengeance and the fixed amount of evil and
suffering which must be endured before the End – which are already
combined in the words of Jesus preceding his Apocalypse: 'I send you
prophets . . . whom you will kill . . . that upon you may come all the
innocent blood shed on earth, from the blood of innocent Abel
[Gen. 4¹⁰] . . . all this will come upon this generation' (Matt. 23³⁴⁻³⁶).

The spirit of the cry seems regrettably pre-Christian. This, however,
is not a matter of attitudes to people in daily life, but of God's cause
which seems to go by default; it is 'the language not of private revenge
but of public justice'ᵈ (Caird, p. 85). *Avenge* (*ekdikein*) has the sense of
'vindicate', as at Luke 18¹⁻⁸, where Jesus demands of the living just
such prayer as this; 'Will not God *vindicate* his elect who cry to him
day and night?' And the answer to the prayer comes not in the
punishment of individual enemies but in the 'judgment of the great
harlot' who deceives the nations (17¹–19²), and the coming of a new
order, symbolized by the Bride. To this final deliverance their
sacrifice contributes invisibly, not piecemeal but as part of God's total
plan: they must wait for their visible vindication till their *number* is
*complete*.

※

ᵈ In the Bible abstract ideas are expressed in concrete and personal terms.

**9**

*under the altar:* the blood of a sacrifice, which is its life or *soul* in biblical thought, drains down under the *altar*. The death of a martyr was conceived as a sacrifice on the altar of the heavenly temple, which combined the attributes of the earthly temple's incense altar, inside the sanctuary (*naos*), and its altar of sacrifice outside. So in Revelation the altar at 8³, ⁵, 9¹³, 14¹⁸ is for incense, here and at 16⁷ for blood. In each case it is linked with vindication for the righteous in answer to their prayers which rise, like incense (5⁸), before God.

Does John fall short of Heb. 12²⁴, 'the blood that speaks more graciously than the blood of Abel'? See his picture of the heavenly Jerusalem (21²⁴–22³).

*for the word of God . . .:* the phrase could include the OT martyrs, but probably refers to Nero's victims. The *witness* is not that which they *bore* but which they 'held' (*echein*) – the witness of Jesus which they maintained; cf. 1², ⁹, 12¹⁷, 20⁴. *Slain* is *esphagmenōn*, echoing 5⁶.

**10**

*holy and true:* cf. Christ's title in the Philadelphian letter (3⁷).

*how long?:* an OT formula, e.g. Ps. 13¹ᶠ·, Isa. 6¹¹, Zech. 1¹², following the horsemen vision.

*judge and avenge:* cf. 16⁵, 18²⁰, 19², ¹¹. *For those who dwell upon the earth* see on 3¹⁰ and p. 15. It is a stock expression for the 'worldly'.

**11**

*white robe:* see on 3⁵; cf. 7⁹, ¹³. For *rest* cf. 14¹³.

*until the number . . . complete:* cf. II Esd. 4³³⁻³⁷. There the point is the fixity of the divine programme – delay is not slackness or weakness. Here it is the divine programme as embodied in Christ's sacrifice in which his people must share; cf. Col. 1²⁴. Protection from the 'hour of trial' (3¹⁰) does not give bodily immunity, as the Lord had warned (Matt. 10²⁸, 24⁹,). See 11⁷ᶠᶠ·.

THE SIXTH SEAL:
THE WRATH OF THE LAMB

$^{12}$*When he opened the sixth seal, I looked and, behold, there was a great
earthquake; and the sun became black as sackcloth, the full moon became like
blood, $^{13}$and the stars of the sky fell to the earth as the fig tree sheds its
winter fruit when shaken by a gale; $^{14}$the sky vanished like a scroll that is
rolled up, and every mountain and island was removed from its place.*

$^{15}$*Then the kings of the earth and the great men and the generals and the
rich and the strong, and every one, slave and free, hid in the caves and among
the rocks of the mountains, $^{16}$calling to the mountains and rocks, 'Fall on us
and hide us from the face of him who is seated on the throne, and from the
wrath of the Lamb; $^{17}$for the great day of their wrath has come, and who can
stand before it?'*

The traditional cry of the martyrs' blood is answered in a traditional
picture of the Day of the Lord, with a new twist at the end in *the
wrath of the Lamb*. In the Lord's Apocalypse failure of the heavenly
lights and powers precedes the coming of the Son of man; this scene
is an anticipatory glimpse of that moment of truth, and it is important
to grasp the sense of the traditional imagery. In the OT passages
which John draws on, the prophets were declaring the punishment of
human pride and folly, usually with reference to contemporary
disasters, in terms of God undoing his work of creation: bringing back
chaos, opening the windows of heaven to pour down the flood waters,
quenching the lights of heaven and rolling up the sky. This, however,
was not mere destruction but clearing the decks for a new order.
'Creation' in biblical thought is the imposition of order on chaos,
understood morally rather than physically. Human pride and refusal
to acknowledge the Creator bring chaos back: therefore men must be
made to recognize God before a new order is possible, and his
appearance or 'coming' is the climax of the picture.

It is equally important to grasp the NT understanding of the divine
*wrath*. In the OT there are two main strands: God's passionate
indignation at man's sin, but also the more impersonal sense of the

disastrous effects in history of man's sin.[e] In both cases it is pre-eminently a feature of the End, when sin, at present apparently over-looked, reaps its reward. In the NT the second strand is dominant. God is never said to 'be angry' (though often to be gracious etc.), and 'the wrath' often occurs on its own as a technical term for the recoil of sin upon the sinner, rather than as an emotion in God; NEB often translates it by 'retribution' or 'vengeance'. But the impersonal aspect must not be over-stressed: it is still God's wrath, not just Nemesis. When man is blinded and corrupted by his refusal to acknowledge God, it is God who hands him over to the effects of his refusal (cf. Rom. $1^{24-28}$) – in order that he may repent (Rev. $9^{20}$, $16^{9-11}$). For ultimately man must face the God he has refused to acknowledge.

It is this final confrontation which John here depicts. But what of *the wrath of the Lamb*? To many commentators this phrase proves that *wrath*, at least in Revelation, stands squarely for the divine anger, and confirms the violent interpretation of 'Lamb' at $5^{5-6}$; it is a grim irony, like 'shepherding with an iron rod' ($2^{27}$). Others see in it the same paradox as in the conjunction of 'Lion' and 'Lamb' (Caird, pp. 90–92); the irony lies in men's rejection of the gracious initiative of God which the slain Lamb symbolizes (cf. John $3^{16-19, 36}$). This is the consummation of the moment of truth on Calvary;[f] John evokes the crucifixion by his echo of Jesus' words to the women of Jerusalem, 'The days are coming when . . . they will say to the mountains "Fall on us", and to the hills "Cover us" ' (Luke $23^{28-31}$);

*e* The biblical writers do not distinguish between what God directly wills, and what he allows – e.g. the consequences of human freedom to sin (see Caird, *Powers*, pp. 38–40). Against any sort of 'dualism' – belief in two ultimate powers behind good and evil – they stoutly maintain God's responsibility for everything (cf. Job 1, 2, Isa. $45^7$, Amos $3^6$). Caird quotes John of Damascus (*Fid. Orth.* II. 29): 'God's original wish was that all should be saved and come to his kingdom. . . . But inasmuch as he is a just God, his will is that sinners should suffer punishment. The first then is called God's antecedent will and pleasure, and springs from himself, while the second is called God's consequent will and permission, and has its origin in us.' Though John makes no such sormal distinction, the logic of his book's structure places 'God's wrath' in the fecond category. See also D. E. H. Whiteley, *The Theology of St Paul*, Blackwell and Fortress Press 1964, pp. 64–72.

*f* Cf. A. T. Hanson, *The Wrath of the Lamb*, SPCK and Macmillan, New York, 1957, ch. 7.

see pp. 63f. on 1⁷. God must be experienced either as love or as wrath. In the present he may let men keep him at arm's length, but in the last resort there can be no middle ground.

Is *wrath* the last word for these deluded earth-dwellers? John has no doubt of their culpability and its terrible consequences (cf. 14⁹⁻¹¹). But in his final vision *the kings of the earth*, who here cower in terror, bring their glory into the new Jerusalem, and the leaves of its tree are for the healing of the nations. There is no formal resolution of the paradox – see on 21²²ff. (pp. 308f.).

ॐ

**12**
*earthquake*ᵍ: a recurring symbol of the dissolution of the godless world at God's self-manifestation (Isa. 2¹⁹ etc.; Rev. 8⁵, 11¹³, 16¹⁸, at the climax of each septet) – an *earthquake* accompanied the death and resurrection of Jesus (Matt. 27⁵⁴, 28²). Asia Minor was subject to terrible earthquakes, then as now.

**12–14**
*Sun, moon and stars* suggest 'the host of Heaven', the powers behind the godless world; cf. Isa. 34²⁻⁴, 24¹⁹⁻²³. John has woven together various OT motifs – *sackcloth* perhaps from Isa. 50³, suggesting mourning; *blood* from Joel 2³¹; the *fig tree* and *rolling up* of the *sky* from Isa. 34⁴; the moving of the *mountains* from Jer. 4²⁴ (etc.). As the continuing presence of *mountains* in vv. 15, 16 shows, these motifs are symbolic. Is there a memory of the withered *fig tree* and the moving of *mountains* at Matt. 21¹⁸⁻²¹ par., which intepret the cleansing of the temple as God's judgment on Israel? See on 8⁸. Does the rolling up of the sky signify the removal of the veil between God and man? cf. 20¹¹ff.

**15f.**
The model is Isa. 2¹²ff., where 'the Lord has a day against all that is proud' – here not only against the *rich and strong* but *everyone*, the 'earth-dwellers' (v. 10). Isa. 2¹⁹, 'then men shall enter the caves of the rocks . . . from before the terror of the Lord', links naturally with Hos. 10⁸, where the corrupt rulers of Israel 'shall say to the mountains, Cover us, and the hills, Fall on us' – words applied by Jesus to those responsible for his

g See R. J. Bauckham, 'The Eschatological Earthquake in the Apocalypse of John', *NovT* 19, 1977, pp. 224–33.

crucifixion (Luke 23$^{28-31}$; see on 1$^7$). Men will try to *hide*, like Adam, from the God they have disobeyed, whom their own conscience invests with terror (Gen. 3$^{8f.}$). The *wrath* of the Lamb could refer to the cosmic disasters he has unsealed, but the parallel with the *face* of the Enthroned shows that the Lamb himself is meant: he must appear as disaster to those whose horizons are bounded by this earth; see on 1$^7$, 14$^{9-11}$.

**17**

*the great day:* cf. Joel 2$^{11}$, Nahum 1$^6$, Mal. 3$^2$. The letters have already shown the conditions for *standing*; cf. 7$^9$ and Luke 21$^{34-36}$.

7$^{1-8}$     THE SEALING OF GOD'S SERVANTS

7 *After this I saw four angels standing at the four corners of the earth, holding back the four winds of the earth, that no wind might blow on earth or sea or against any tree.* $^2$*Then I saw another angel ascend from the rising of the sun, with the seal of the living God, and he called with a loud voice to the four angels who had been given power to harm earth and sea,* $^3$*saying, 'Do not harm the earth or the sea or the trees, till we have sealed the servants of our God upon their foreheads.'*

$^4$*And I heard the number of the sealed, a hundred and forty-four thousand sealed, out of every tribe of the sons of Israel,* $^5$*twelve thousand sealed out of the tribe of Judah, twelve thousand of the tribe of Reuben, twelve thousand of the tribe of Gad,* $^6$*twelve thousand of the tribe of Asher, twelve thousand of the tribe of Naphtali, twelve thousand of the tribe of Manasseh,* $^7$*twelve thousand of the tribe of Simeon, twelve thousand of the tribe of Levi, twelve thousand of the tribe of Issachar,* $^8$*twelve thousand of the tribe of Zebulun, twelve thousand of the tribe of Joseph, twelve thousand sealed out of the tribe of Benjamin.*

Instead of a seventh and final unsealing there is now a delay while the servants of God are *sealed* – a characteristic play on words. A *seal* is a sign of ownership, and of protection, – cf. today the registering of a letter – and the word is widely used in early Christian writings, often in connection with Christian initiation, as probably here. As in the letters, John is bringing out for Christians the significance of their baptism both as present reality and as promise for the future: this sealing is not to provide something extra, specially for martyrs – as the enumeration of those sealed (vv. 4–8) shows. All Christians, not some, constitute the true Israel already; John's purpose is to make them realize this, in spite of Jewish 'slanders' (2$^9$, 3$^9$). Hence the symbolic numbers and (to us) laboured repetition; for the relation of the 144,000 to the *great multitude*, see on v. 9.

Against what are they sealed? Attacks on *earth, sea and trees* apparently, cf. the first two trumpet blasts (8$^{7-9}$), but the protection promised must be from spiritual attack (cf. 9$^4$); Christians were never promised immunity from physical danger, to which they have already presumably been subject (6$^{1-11}$). *The four winds of the earth* do in fact suggest demonic powers: in Daniel's vision 'the four winds of heaven were stiring up the great sea. And four great beasts came up out of the sea . . .' (7$^{2ff}$); cf. the *four angels* of Rev. 9$^{14}$. The unsealings were a prelude. Now we are coming to the real thing, the *great tribulation* (v. 14) culminating in the emergence from the *sea* of the beast, Antichrist (13$^{1ff}$), which is the climax of the trumpets section. For what are they sealed? For the role of the true Israel – witness – as will be brought out in the balancing 'delay' between the sixth and seventh trumpets (10$^1$–11$^{13}$).

✿

**7$^1$**
*After this:* the scene is not part of the sixth unsealing; it relates to the present time, while vv. 9–17 belongs to the Age to Come.

*four winds of the earth:* not 'of heaven' as in Dan. 7$^2$, perhaps because of the belief that it is the winds which blow from 'the corners of the earth' (conceived as a square) which are destructive; cf. I Enoch 76, and see on 20$^8$.

*on earth or sea or against any tree:* this seems to suggest natural disaster, but the source is supernatural; see on 8$^{6ff}$. *Trees* are mentioned presumably as the most obvious victims of *wind*, cf. 6$^{13}$.

2

*another angel:* cf. the angel of 10¹ – representing the direct will of God. The four wind-angels personify cosmic forces.

*from the rising of the sun:* the quarter both of danger (16¹²) and of deliverance. The Messiah was expected to appear from the east (cf. Matt. 2¹ᶠᶠ·), and Jesus was himself called 'dayspring' (*anatolē = rising*, Luke 1⁷⁸), and 'morning star' (Rev. 22¹⁶).

2–3
*the seal of the living God:* the OT model is again to be found in Ezekiel – John is working through his book roughly in order (see pp. 39f.). God orders a mark to be put on the *foreheads* of the penitent in Jerusalem, before the executioners pass through (9⁴ᶠᶠ·); cf. the blood of the passover lamb on the Israelite doorposts to avert the destroyer of the Egyptians (Ex. 12); and for similar stay of execution in apocalypses, cf. II Baruch 6⁴ and I Enoch 6⁶, where the angels of the waters are told to hold them back while Noah's ark is built. Ezekiel's mark (*tau*, the last letter of the Hebrew alphabet – written in the old script + or X) was currently taken by Jews as the Divine Name; so also probably by Christians in connection with baptism,ʰ in which a man took on himself the Name, and acknowledged Christ's ownership – see notes on 3¹², 'I will write on him the name of my God'. At 14¹ the 144,000 have the name of the Lamb and of his Father '*written on their foreheads*' (cf. 22⁴), in contrast with those who have 'on the right hand or the *forehead*' the mark, that is the name, of the beast (13¹⁶ᶠ·). 'Mark', with its suggestion of the branding or tattooing of pagan religion, goes well with the beast, and *seal* (*sphragis*) had a rich range of meaning in Christian usage: ownership (II Cor. 1²²), authentication (John 6²⁷), protection leading to final salvation (Eph. 1¹⁴, 4³⁰). It may already have been the custom in baptism, as it was later, to make the *tau* sign on the candidate's forehead; Paul refers to circumcision, which is replaced in the New Covenant by baptism, as a *seal* (Rom. 4¹¹), and 'the *sphrāgis*' is one of the names given to baptism in the Jewish Christian community.ⁱ Like the *name* references

h The *tau* was soon connected with the cross, and baptism signified dying with Christ (Rom. 6³ᶠᶠ·). The *seal* then would imply not simply protection but commitment to reproducing Christ's witness (cf. 12¹⁷, 14⁴).

i J. Daniélou, *Theology of Jewish Christianity*, E. T. Darton, Longman & Todd 1964, p. 329. See also his *Symbols*, ch. 9, and G. W. H. Lampe, *The Seal of the Spirit*, Longmans 1951, pp. 15–18, 284ff. The *seal* usually designated the Holy Spirit, which was held to be poured out in baptism.

in the letters, the *sealing* would bring out for a Christian the permanent meaning of his baptism, which under worldly pressure he might forget. $7^{14}$ probably alludes to another aspect of the same many-sided fact.

**4**

*I heard the number*: cf. $9^{16}$. What John *hears* often gives theological comment on what he *sees* (v. 9), and numbers had anyway a qualitative sense for Hebrews (see pp. 14f.). *Twelve* is the number of the tribes of Israel, a *thousand* intensifies it (and is itself a military formation), a squared number expresses perfection: *twelve times twelve thousands*, therefore, means that the *sealed* are the totality of God's Israel, brigaded for his service.j *Out of every tribe* might seem to indicate some, not all, but again the sense is not quantitative: they are the 'first fruits' ($14^4$), the first and best of the harvest, not in disjunction from the whole but representing and including it (see notes on $1^5$ and $14^{1-5}$).

**5–8**

The list of the twelve tribes, which for centuries had been a purely theological concept, corresponds to no known arrangement; probably it is John's own variation on a traditional theme.k *Judah* is put first, not *Reuben*: the true Israel is led by *the lion of the tribe of Judah* ($5^5$, referring to Gen. $49^{10}$). Dan is omitted: from him would spring Antichrist, according to one interpretation of Gen. $49^{17}$, cf. Test. Dan $5^6$. *Manasseh* is anomalous along with his father *Joseph*, whom he and his brother Ephraim replace in some lists: he is probably brought in here as substitute for Dan.

$7^{9-17}$ BEYOND THE GREAT TRIBULATION

$9$*After this I looked, and behold, a great multitude which no man could number, from every nation, from all tribes and peoples and tongues, standing before the throne and before the Lamb, clothed in white robes, with palm*

*j* Some commentators take them to be the faithful remnant of the old Israel, over against the Christian church (v. 9), but this means distinguishing them from the 144,000 at $14^1$. For John 'Israel' is now the followers of the Lamb; see pp. 45–7.

*k* For a brilliant exposition see Farrer, pp. 106–8.

*branches in their hands,* ¹⁰*and crying out with a loud voice, 'Salvation belongs to our God who sits upon the throne, and to the Lamb!'*

¹¹*And all the angels stood round the throne and round the elders and the four living creatures, and they fell on their faces before the throne and worshipped God,* ¹²*saying, 'Amen! Blessing and glory and wisdom and thanksgiving and honour and power and might be to our God for ever and ever! Amen.'*

¹³*Then one of the elders addressed me, saying, 'Who are these, clothed in white robes, and whence have they come?'*

¹⁴*I said to him, 'Sir, you know.' And he said to me, 'These are they who have come out of the great tribulation; they have washed their robes and made them white in the blood of the Lamb.*

¹⁵*Therefore are they before the throne of God, and serve him day and night within his temple; and he who sits upon the throne will shelter them with his presence.*

¹⁶*They shall hunger no more, neither thirst any more; the sun shall not strike them, nor any scorching heat.* ¹⁷*For the Lamb in the midst of the throne will be their shepherd, and he will guide them to springs of living water; and God will wipe away every tear from their eyes.'*

In the previous vision we were, in imagined time, before *the great tribulation*: now we are given an anticipatory glimpse beyond it. There has been much discussion of the relation between the *great multitude which no man could count* and the *hundred and forty-four thousand* enumerated in the previous verses. Some take the *multitude* to represent Gentile Christians alongside Jewish, but the *hundred and forty-four thousand* are unlikely to be simply Jewish Christians; for John, as for the other NT writers, all Christians, whatever their origin, now constitute 'the Israel of God' (Gal. 6¹⁶; cf. Eph. 2¹⁹), 'the twelve tribes in the dispersion' (James 1¹; cf. I Peter 1¹, 2⁹). The clue is to be found in the relation between *seeing* and *hearing*. John *heard* the counting of the sealed (the theological truth); he *saw* a countless multitude (the outward reality). Salvation is *from* the Jews, *for* all nations (John 4²², Rom. 15⁸⁻¹²), in accordance with the promise to Abraham that in his 'seed' all the nations of the earth should be blessed, and that his progeny should be past counting. John seems to share Paul's view that this 'seed' is not the Jewish nation, or the faithful remnant of it, but Christ and those who belong to him (Gal. $3^{16, 29}$, Rev. $14^{1-5}$). So there are not two different groups, but the one group seen under two aspects: its ultimate empirical extension (cf. $21^{24}-22^5$), and the divine purpose which marked it out.[1]

The scene in these verses is the same as in chs. 4 and 5: the heavenly congregation, arranged in concentric circles round the *throne*, in which the men *from every nation*, whose ransoming was then celebrated, now themselves have their place. *One of the elders* reveals their identity: they are those who *have come out of the great tribulation* (the crisis for which John is preparing the churches); they have gained the *white robes* of final justification and victory through sharing the Lamb's sacrificial death. Does this mean martyrdom? Not necessarily: *they have washed their robes* refers to the sharing of Christ's death which is begun in baptism. The approaching crisis will indeed demand faithfulness *up to death* ($2^{10}$, $12^{11}$), but it is the pattern, not the physical dying, which matters: 'Blessed are those who wash their robes [present participle of ongoing action]. They will have the right to the tree of life' ($22^{14}$; cf. $2^7$ and comment there).

The picture of heavenly blessedness in vv. 15–17 draws on passages from Isaiah and the Psalms, and is taken up in the final visions ($21^{3-6}$, $22^{1-5, 17}$). Its essence is worship, *serving God day and night in his temple* (cf. $4^8$), in vivid contrast with the fate of those who worship the beast and bear his mark instead of God's seal on their foreheads ($14^{9-11}$), and it is dominated by the imagery of the feast of Tabernacles. For Jews this was *the* feast, the crown of the year, when all harvesting was complete; it celebrated the joy of God's presence and protection in Israel's desert wanderings, and looked forward to its consummation in the messianic age. For Christians it provided many motifs for their own hopes and the liturgies in which they expressed them.[m] This chapter also is illuminated by Prigent's suggestion that John is using the language of apocalyptic to draw out the significance of the church's worship and the sacraments on which it centred (see p. 42).

[1] Or to put it in terms of $14^{1-5}$, being ransomed by the Lamb's blood out of the nations of the world ($5^9$) depends on *the hundred and forty-four thousand* who follow the Lamb and share his sacrifice; they are 'first fruits' ($14^4$).

m See Daniélou, *Symbols*, ch. 1.

ന്ദ

**9**

*after this:* another change of stance, as at v. 1.

*multitude which no man could number* (in modern English *count*): the actuality which the 144,000 in God's providence symbolizes. For the relation of *seeing* and *hearing*, see p. 125.

*from every nation . . . :* a Danielic phrase; cf. 5$^9$. It is the same totality as that to which the witnesses testify (11$^9$) and over which the beast is given authority (13$^7$).

*standing before the throne and before the Lamb:* contrast 6$^{16f.}$

*white robes:* cf. 6$^{11}$. See on 3$^5$, and on v. 14.

*palm branches:* these were gathered at the feast of Tabernacles (= tents), to symbolize the time Israel had spent in tents under God's protection in the desert, and the hope for the future of which this 'tenting' was an image. They appeared on Jewish, and Christian, funerary monuments, probably as a symbol of the resurrection.[n]

There are Tabernacles motifs in vv. 15–17, but there is perhaps a closer model in the *palm branches* carried at the feast of Dedication, at which the Tabernacles liturgy was used to celebrate the Maccabean cleansing of the temple from the 'desolating sacrilege' of Antiochus Epiphanes (II Macc. 10$^{6f.}$, I Macc. 4$^{54-59}$; cf. 13$^{51}$). Palms were carried at Jesus' triumphal entry into Jerusalem (John 12$^{23}$; it preceded his cleansing of the temple according to the synoptic gospels), perhaps to evoke the spirit of the feast of Dedication. This scene in heaven celebrates the defeat of the kingdom of the beast and its 'desolating sacrilege' (Dan. 11$^{31}$, Matt. 24$^{15}$, etc.), of which Antiochus and Nero have been historical agents. The hymn that follows brings out this meaning.

**10**

*salvation:* cf. Ps. 3$^8$. The Hebrew word can also mean *victory* – so NEB here and at 12$^{10}$ and 19$^1$ – but *salvation* fits well the Greek *sōtēria*, total well-being, in this world and beyond, of which the official source was

n See Daniélou, *Symbols*, p. 20.

Caesar. The shout answers, in the age of fulfilment, to the *Hosanna!* ('Save us', Ps. 118²⁵) of the *palm*-bearing *multitude* which acclaimed Jesus (Matt. 21⁸ᶠ·, John 12¹²ᶠ·). Ps. 118 was one of the Hallel Psalms, used at the great festivals, including Tabernacles and Dedication; see on 19¹ᶠᶠ·.

**11f.**

Cf. 4⁶⁻¹⁰, and 5¹¹ᶠ· where there is a similar sevenfold doxology, addressed to the Lamb. From here on worship is addressed only to God; see on 22³⁻⁵.

**13**

*one of the elders:* as at 5⁵. For the *elders*, see note on 4⁴.

**14**

*the great tribulation:* see notes on 2¹⁰, 3¹⁰. The word (*thlipsis*) is used at Matt. 24²¹, ²⁹ for the troubles connected with the 'desolating sacrilege'; cf. Dan. 12¹.

*washed their robes:* salvation is not effected without their co-operation, cf. 22¹⁴ – maintaining the baptismal pattern of dying with Christ.

*made them white in the blood of the lamb:* cf. 12¹¹ and Dan. 12¹⁰. The picture is theological, not visual: sacrificial blood cleanses, Heb. 9²², I John 1⁷ (and Rev. 1⁵, on the inferior reading). For *blood* making *white*, see p. 70 above on the dynamic understanding of colour. Red and white can be opposites – 'though your sins are like scarlet, they shall be as white as snow' (Isa. 1¹⁸) – or complementary – 'Judah washes his garments in wine, and his vesture in the blood of grapes; his eyes shall be red with wine, and his teeth white with milk' (Gen. 49¹¹ᶠ·; cf. Lam. 4⁷, and see on 14²⁰).

**15**

*serve him: latreuein,* which means carry out cultic duties and is translated *worship* at 22³. Like the *four creatures* (4⁸), they take no rest *day and night,* in contrast with the worshippers of the beast, who have no rest. day and night, from their torment (14¹¹).

*will shelter them:* the present tense of the *elder* in heaven gives way to the future of the prophet on earth. *Shelter them with his presence* translates *skēnōsei,* = 'spread his tent over them', or as at 21³, 'dwell with them' in the new order: God's presence and protection are the same thing.

The word evokes the *Shekinah*,$^o$ the glorious presence of God in the cloud which accompanied the Israelites in the desert and settled in the temple (Ex. 13$^{21}$, 40$^{34}$, I Kings 8$^{10}$; cf. Isa. 4$^{5f.}$); it evokes also the incarnation, when the Word 'dwelt among us' (*eskēnōsen*, John 1$^{14}$), and the feast of Tabernacles (*skēnai*), which celebrated the future enjoyment of God's presence finally restored (see on 2$^{10}$).

### 16f.

In Isaiah the returning exiles 'shall not hunger or thirst, neither scorching wind nor sun shall smite them, for he who has pity on them will lead them, and by springs of water will guide them' (49$^{10}$; cf. Pss. 23, 121$^6$). John foresees the return of the victims of latter-day Babylon;$^p$ contrast the worshippers of the beast, 16$^{4-9}$. The end of *hunger and thirst* would remind Christians of Jesus' promise in John 6$^{35}$ and of their own eucharistic experience; and the *springs of living water* (lit. *water of life*) would evoke Jesus' conversation with the Samaritan woman (John 4$^{10ff.}$) and his words at the feast of Tabernacles (John 7$^{37-39}$), at which *water* and light$^q$ were the leading themes; cf. Rev. 21$^6$ and 22$^1$, in passages where the Tabernacles influence is again evident, and 22$^{17}$, which is plainly eucharistic.

*the Lamb will be their shepherd:* a striking reversal of roles, but already prepared for in the apocalyptic literature; see p. 124. Compare Ezek. 34$^{23}$, Ps. 23 and John 10$^{10f.}$ For the 'shepherding' of the nations with a rod of iron, see on 2$^{27}$, 19$^{15}$.

*wipe away every tear:* cf. 21$^{3f.}$ John picks up the promise of Isa. 25$^8$; the context, 'a feast for all peoples' (25$^6$), supports his implicit eucharistic theme.

---

*o* The Hebrew verb is *shakan*, to dwell, which has practically the same consonants as the Greek verb *skēnoun*.

*p* The victims of her seductions as well as of her violence? See on 21$^{24}$–22$^3$, and note the allusion in the last line of 7$^{17}$ to Isa. 25$^{6-8}$, which foretells the destruction of 'the veil that is spread over all nations'.

*q* Cf. Zech. 14$^{7f.,}$ $^{16}$, John 8$^{12}$.

Revelation $8^1$–$14^{20}$

# The Seven Trumpets

The seals section (cf. pp. 45, 135) corresponds to the 'beginning of birth-pangs' (Matt. 24[8]), and takes up the themes of assurance and endurance from the second and sixth letters. The trumpets section culminates in the expulsion of Satan from heaven and his setting up on earth the kingdom of the beast (ch. 13) – the 'third woe' (12[12]) which follows the seventh blast (11[14f.]). This surely corresponds to the 'desolating sacrilege', the consequent 'tribulation' and the 'false Christs and false prophets' (Matt. 24[15-24]) of the Lord's Apocalypse; and the themes of the third letter, to Pergamum, are evident: the throne of Satan (13[1-8]), Balak and Balaam, false king and false prophet (13[1ff.], 11[ff.]), and the danger of compromise with idolatry (13[14-18]).

There is a long lead up to this climax in the first six trumpet blasts. They signal the self-destruction of idolatry; they are modelled on the plagues of Egypt and have a similar effect in hardening men's hearts (9[20f.]). As in the previous series, the last three, characterized as the *three woes* (8[13], 9[12], 11[14]), differ in form and weight from the first four, and the sixth is followed by an interlude (10[1]-11[13]). This takes up the theme of the *scroll*, now *open*, from ch. 5, and issues in the work of the *two witnesses* – witness is the positive theme of the third letter (2[13]), taken up in the seventh (3[14]). The penitence in which it ends (11[13]) contrasts with the hardening effect of the demonic plagues.

In the OT the hardening of Pharaoh after the death of the first-born led to a deliverance like a new birth at the Red Sea, but Israel's wilderness journey was threatened by the worship of the golden calf and the seductions of Balaam and Balak: just so the death of which the sixth trumpet warns is followed in ch. 12 by a new exodus, which is threatened in ch. 13 by the worship of the beast and the seductions of the false prophet.

Finally, just as in ch. 7 we are given anticipatory glimpses beyond the *great tribulation*, so after the final *woe*, which corresponds to it, ch. 14 adumbrates the triumph of the Lamb and his followers, the fate of the beast's city and worshippers, and the final coming of the Son of man (cf. Matt. 24$^{27}$).

The concluding section, the bowls, goes over much of the same ground, but it is not simply a more explicit recapitulation. It has a new focus: the final doom of Satan's work, now seen as embodied in the *harlot*, Babylon, and the final triumph of God's work, embodied in the *Bride*, New Jerusalem – themes already stated in the fourth and seventh letters. The Lord's Apocalypse is still in view: the coming of the Son of man, the conquering Bridegroom, is the centre of the picture (19$^{11ff.}$).

**8** *When the Lamb opened the seventh seal, there was silence in heaven for about half an hour.* $^2$*Then I saw the seven angels who stand before God, and seven trumpets were given to them.* $^3$*And another angel came and stood at the altar with a golden censer; and he was given much incense to mingle with the prayers of all the saints upon the golden altar before the throne;* $^4$*and the smoke of the incense rose with the prayers of the saints from the hand of the angel before God.* $^5$*Then the angel took the censer and filled it with fire from the altar and threw it on the earth; and there were peals of thunder, loud noises, flashes of lightning, and an earthquake.*

After the judgment scene introduced by the sixth unsealing, the seventh might be expected to usher in the consummation, or at least spell out the contents of the *scroll*, but in fact there is *silence*, followed by a further septet of disasters.

This *half-hour silence* has caused much speculation. Stauffer explains it from the ritual of the Games,[r] but we are on firmer ground with

r Which he seems to have invented. His reconstruction (pp. 184ff.) is attractive but lacks evidence.

the ritual of the daily sacrifice in the Jewish temple, as set out in the Mishnah (*Tamid*). It began with the trimming of the sevenfold lamp (Rev. 1–3), then came the slaughter of the lamb (5⁶) and the blood-offering poured at the base of the altar (6⁹), then the incense-offering (8³⁻⁵) – a time of prayer (cf. Luke 1¹⁰), to which the *silence* might correspond. The liturgy continued with the burnt-offering of the lamb and a drink-offering (cf. 16¹) accompanied by the blowing of *trumpets* (8⁶), and the singing of psalms (cf. 19¹⁻⁸). Charles explains the *silence* by reference to a Talmudic tradition (*Hagigah* 12 b) that in the fifth heaven angels sing praises by night, but are silent by day so that Israel's praises may be heard. Here, 'the prayers of the highest orders of angels in heaven are hushed that the prayers of *all* the suffering saints on earth may be heard before the throne' (I, p. 224).

Rissi (*Time and History*, pp. 3–6) suggests, more convincingly, the primeval *silence* out of which issues the Word of God, to create the world (II Esd. 6³⁹, 7³⁰, II Baruch 3⁷, Gen. 1³ in Jewish exegesis); or to punish the Egyptians (Wisd. 18¹⁴⁻¹⁶); or to dwell among men (John 1¹⁴, Ignatius, *Magn.* 8²). So now *silence* precedes the final Egyptian punishment and the re-creation of the world (cf. II Esd.7³¹).

The *trumpets* which follow the half-hour of prayer do not give the contents of the scroll – for that see ch. 10. They are warning blasts, summoning the world to repentance (cf. 9²⁰f.). Here is another word of multiple associations: *trumpets* were used in liturgy and in war, for warning, for assembly, for victory (cf. e.g. Ex. 19¹⁶, Josh. 6⁴ff., Isa. 27¹³, Ezek. 33³, Amos 3⁶, Joel 2¹, ¹⁵). They were blown on New Year's Day, to initiate a penitential season leading up to the Day of Atonement ten days later. They were part of the imagery of the Day of the Lord, with its themes of gathering, battle, judgment and a new order (cf. Matt. 24³¹, I Cor. 15⁵², I Thess. 4¹⁶).

ﬡﬡ

1

*silence:* Jewish expectation was that the world would return to primeval chaos (cf. 6¹²⁻¹⁴); out of it a new world would arise (cf. II Esd. 7²⁹ff.).

2

*The seven angels:* the seven archangels of Judaism, who 'present the prayers of the saints' (Tobit 12$^{15}$). They are named Uriel, Raphael, Raguel, Michael, Sariel, Gabriel, Remeiel (I Enoch 20).

**3**

*the altar:* combining the earthly temple's altar for sacrifice and altar for incense. See on 6$^9$.

*incense to mingle with the prayers of all the saints:* lit. 'to put on the prayers', as if they are the burning charcoal on which grains of incense are poured to make smoke. Through the sacrifice of the Lamb the prayers of the saints (cf. 5$^8$) have access to God's presence (cf. John 14$^{13}$, 16$^{23}$), and are poured out as coals of wrath on the earth (v. 5). Not that the saints pray for the plagues that follow. They ask for *justice* (6$^{10}$), and it was a commonplace that 'the instruments of a man's sin are the instruments of his punishment' (Wisd. 11$^{16}$; cf. Rev. 16$^{4-7}$). But that is God's business, as Paul told the Romans (12$^{19-21}$). The saints do not specify what should happen to their persecutors as the psalmists do. They pray in accordance with Jesus' teaching (Luke 18$^{1-8}$), and 11$^{15}$ suggests that 'Thy kingdom come!' was their prayer.

**4**

*Smoke* hides the glory of God (15$^8$, Isa. 6$^4$). Contrast the *smoke* of the torment of those who worship the beast (14$^{11}$).

**5**

*fire . . . threw it on the earth:* John again draws on Ezekiel. After the marking of the penitent (9$^4$; cf. Rev. 7$^3$) and the smiting of the rest, the man clothed in linen is told to take 'burning coals from between the cherubim [= God's throne], and scatter them over the city' (10$^2$). *Fire* figures prominently in the following plagues (Rev. 8$^{7f.,}$ $^{10}$, 9$^2$, $^{17}$); cf. also Luke 12$^{49-51}$.

*peals of thunder* etc.: cf. 11$^{19}$ and 16$^{18}$; each of the three septets concludes with the *son et lumière* proper to the divine throne (4$^5$), being manifestations of its hidden power in the rebellious world. The model is Mount Sinai and the giving of the law (Ex. 19$^{16ff.}$). See on 6$^{12}$ and p. 145 note *g*.

THE FIRST FOUR TRUMPETS

$^6$ Now the seven angels who had the seven trumpets made ready to blow them. $^7$ The first angel blew his trumpet, and there followed hail and fire, mixed with blood, which fell on the earth; and a third of the earth was burnt up, and a third of the trees were burnt up, and all green grass was burnt up.

$^8$ The second angel blew his trumpet, and something like a great mountain, burning with fire, was thrown into the sea; $^9$ and a third of the sea became blood, a third of the living creatures in the sea died, and a third of the ships were destroyed.

$^{10}$ The third angel blew his trumpet, and a great star fell from heaven, blazing like a torch, and it fell on a third of the rivers and on the fountains of water. $^{11}$ The name of the star is Wormwood. A third of the waters became wormwood, and many men died of the water, because it was made bitter.

$^{12}$ The fourth angel blew his trumpet, and a third of the sun was struck, and a third of the moon, and a third of the stars, so that a third of their light was darkened; a third of the day was kept from shining, and likewise a third of the night.

$^{13}$ Then I looked, and I heard an eagle crying with a loud voice, as it flew in midheaven, 'Woe, woe, woe to those who dwell on the earth, at the blasts of the other trumpets which the three angels are about to blow!'

The *trumpets* are primarily for warning, summoning the earth to repentance (cf. Amos 3$^6$). They signal plagues modelled on those of Egypt (Ex. 8–12), a model already used by Amos (one of John's chief sources for chs. 8–10), and imaginatively expanded in the Wisdom of Solomon 11–19 (early first century AD?), which contrasts the providential disciplining of God's people with the recoil of nature upon the idolatrous. The latter theme is taken up by Paul in Rom. 1$^{18ff.}$, where God's 'wrath' is the consequences of men's idolatry, to which he hands them over. Rom. 1$^{16-18}$, with its connection of the manifestation of God's righteousness with the manifestation of his wrath, is a vital clue to the proper understanding of Revelation, and Wisdom[s] lies behind them both.

The first blasts, like the first four unsealings, form a distinct group, each of about the same length and structure: each time the destruction is of a *third*, detailed *three* times over – an intensification of the *quarter* devastated by the horsemen ($6^8$). The group is concluded by the scream of the *eagle* (or vulture), introducing the last *three* blasts as three *woes* ($8^{13}$; cf. $9^{12}$, $11^{14}$, $12^{12}$): the weight of the series lies in the last *three*. The first four plagues are supernatural, in contrast with those of the horsemen, and the last *three* are explicitly demonic (see on $7^{1-8}$; the true believers are *sealed* against them). The first four fall not directly on men but on the sources of men's life (poisoned, as we shall see, by their idolatry); the last *three* plague men themselves. Their purpose is to bring them to repentance ($9^{20f.}$), just as the Egyptian plagues were aimed at Pharaoh's hardened heart. The point of the Egyptian model is not the plaguing of the impenitent but the exodus which follows; human stubbornness is the locus of God's greatest victory, as at the cross.

ॐ

## 6

The incense-liturgy (the heavenly dynamic) completed, the trumpeters may *blow* (the earthly effects). In the daily liturgy the *trumpets* accompanied the drink-offering, but John follows none of his models slavishly, and the *trumpet* plagues prefigure those of the *bowls* (16).

## 7

*hail and fire, mingled with blood: fire* picks up v. 5; it is also the punishment of sin in Amos ($1^4$ etc.; cf. $7^4$ 'it devoured the great deep, and was eating up the land'). The mingling of *hail and fire* (= lightning, Ex. $9^{23f.}$) stuck the Jewish imagination as a miracle within a miracle: Wisdom took it as the supreme example of nature serving God in the punishment of the godless and protection of the righteous ($16^{15-24}$) – see Sirach $39^{24-31}$ for the basic theme which Wisdom and Revelation

---

*s* A detailed comparison with Rev. was worked out by G. Kuhn, 'Beiträge zur Erklärung des Buches der Weisheit', *ZNW* 28, 1929, pp. 334–8. See also G. Bornkamm, *Early Christian Experience*, pp. 47–9, 62–5, and above on $6^{12-17}$. For the links of apocalyptic with the Jewish wisdom tradition, see G. von Rad (references in the Introduction, p. 40 note *i*).

embroider. Is that why John has taken what was the seventh Egyptian plague for his first trumpet blast? He adds *mixed with blood* in reminiscence of the first plague, when the Nile was turned to *blood* (Ex. 7¹⁷ᶠᶠ·), which is the model for the second and third trumpets and bowls.

7

*all green grass:* Ex. 9²⁵. Why *all*? Is it to break up the monotony of *a third* – cf. *many men* (v. 11)?

8f.

*the sea became blood: blood* links with v. 7 and the first Egyptian plague, in which the fish died (Ex. 7¹⁸).

*a great mountain, burning with fire:*ᵗ cf. Amos 7⁴ again. John weaves in the fall of Babylon, a latter-day Egypt, from Jer. 51, another of his main sources: 'Behold I am against you, O destroying mountain, says the Lord, . . . which destroys the whole earth [cf. Rev. 11¹⁸]; I will . . . make you a burnt mountain' (51²⁵). Later he describes the fall and *burning* of present-day Babylon (18², ⁸ᶠ·), and the destruction of the *ships* here prepares for the lament of the merchants and shipmasters there (18⁹⁻¹⁹). Jesus, after cleansing the temple, said that faith can throw a mountain into the sea (Matt. 21²¹); his parable about praying for vindication ended, 'When the Son of man comes, will he find faith on earth?' (Luke 18⁸). Rome no doubt seemed as divine and invincible to most Christians as did the Jewish religious establishment to the disciples. But both were under divine sentence. Does the throwing down of the mountain hint at the spiritual 'fall' behind Rome's present glory? Verse 10 confirms it. Enoch saw 'seven angels, like great mountains, burning with fire' bound together in a place chaotic and horrible, because they had transgressed the Lord's command (I Enoch 18¹³ᶠᶠ·, 21³ᶠᶠ·); Rome also had its 'command' (cf. Rom. 13¹ᶠ·) – see on ch. 13.

10

*a great star fell from heaven:* here the 'fall' is clear, drawn this time from the dirge on the king of Babylon in Isa. 14: 'How are you fallen from heaven, O Day Star, son of Dawn! . . . you who laid the nations low' (14¹²). We have already heard of the *fall* of the church in Ephesus,

---

ᵗ A volcano? The eruption of Vesuvius in AD 79 terrified the world, and was followed by a series of catastrophes in which men saw the wrath of the gods (Stauffer, pp. 147ff.).

whose *angel* is a *star* in Christ's hand ($1^{20}$-$2^5$), and of the promise of the *morning star* (which is Christ himself – $22^{16}$) to the *conqueror*, along with *power over the nations* ($2^{26, 28}$). Jesus said, 'I saw Satan fall like lightning from heaven' (Luke $10^{18}$), but this star, like the star-angel of $9^{1, 11}$, is an aspect of Satan rather than Satan himself: his fall is reserved for the *third woe* ($12^{1-12}$).

**11**

*Wormwood*: *apsinthos* (= *absinthe*; wormwood = *vermouth*). The naming connotes more than *bitterness*. It evokes Amos again: 'Seek the Lord and live ... you who turn justice to *wormwood*, and cast down righteousness to the earth' ($5^{6f.}$). 'You have turned justice into poison and the fruit of righteousness into *wormwood*' ($6^{12}$). Satan is the false accuser ($12^{10}$); his perversion of justice (through Jewish and Roman agents – see on $2^9$) poisons the earth. One versed in the scriptures would also remember Jeremiah: 'Because they have gone after the Baals ... I will feed this people with *wormwood* and give them poisonous water to drink' ($9^{15}$; cf. $23^{15}$ – the same threat made against the prophets, because from them 'ungodliness has gone forth into all the land'). Idolatrous adulation of its rulers, who usurp God's place (cf. Isa. $14^{14}$), is the source of the world's torments, and has its prophets even within the church (see on $13^{11}$; and cf. Balaam, $2^{14}$, and Jezebel, $2^{20}$). 'Wormwood is the star of the new Babylon which has *poisoned* by its idolatry the *springs* of its own life' (Caird, p. 115).

**12**

*a third of the sun was struck*: cf. Amos $8^9$: 'I will make the sun go down at noon, and darken the earth in broad daylight' (cf. $5^{18ff.}$). The repeated *third* builds up an auditory rather than visual impression (cf. p. 14). The diminishment of the heavenly bodies and of the 'ordinances of day and night' which depend upon them (Gen. $1^{14-18}$, Jer. $31^{35f.}$) signals the return of chaos; see on $6^{12-17}$ above.

*Darkness* was the penultimate Egyptian plague (Ex. $10^{21-29}$), not in itself destructive but the realm of the chaos-powers (Gen. $1^2$) and the breeding-ground of fears and conscience pangs (Wisd. $17^{11-15}$). It is thus a bridge to the *woe* of the fifth trumpet ($9^{2ff.}$).

**13**

The remaining *three* blasts bring even more terrible disaster *to those who dwell on the earth.* The *eagle* (or vulture; cf. Hos. 8¹) evokes Jesus' words about the Day of the Son of Man (Matt. 24²⁸, Luke 17³⁷): 'Where the body is, there will the eagles be gathered together.'ᵘ The world of the earth-dwellers (see on 3¹⁰) is already, under its apparent vitality, a corpse. Farrer (p. 116) suggests a parallel with the fifth un-sealing (6⁹⁻¹¹), and the blood of all earth's Abels (Matt. 23³⁴⁻³⁶) under the altar: where murder has been done judgment will fall.

*in midheaven:* cf. 19¹⁷, and contrast 14⁶ – the *angel with an eternal gospel to proclaim to those who dwell on earth.* The plagues are not God's primary will but the fruit of its rejection; cf. p. 144 note *e.*

## THE FIFTH TRUMPET AND FIRST WOE – LOCUSTS

**9** *And the fifth angel blew his trumpet, and I saw a star fallen from heaven to earth, and he was given the key of the shaft of the bottomless pit;* ²*he opened the shaft of the bottomless pit, and from the shaft rose smoke like the smoke of a great furnace, and the sun and the air were darkened with the smoke from the shaft.* ³*Then from the smoke came locusts on the earth, and they were given power like the power of scorpions of the earth;* ⁴*they were told not to harm the grass of the earth or any green growth or any tree, but only those of mankind who have not the seal of God upon their foreheads;* ⁵*they were allowed to torture them for five months, but not to kill them, and their torture was like the torture of a scorpion, when it stings a man.* ⁶*And in those days men will seek death and will not find it; they will long to die, and death flies from them.*

⁷*In appearance the locusts were like horses arrayed for battle; on their heads were what looked like crowns of gold; their faces were like human faces,* ⁸*their hair like women's hair, and their teeth like lions' teeth;* ⁹*they had scales like iron breastplates, and the noise of their wings was like the noise of many chariots with horses rushing into battle;* ¹⁰*they have tails like scorpions, and stings, and their power of hurting men for five months lies in*

ᵘ An allusion to Job 39³⁰. The book is in John's mind in chs. 9 and 13.

*their tails.* [11] *They have as king over them the angel of the bottomless pit;
his name in Hebrew is Abaddon, and in Greek he is called Apollyon.* *
[12] *The first woe has passed; behold, two woes are still to come.*

* Or *Destroyer.*

The first four plagues attacked the sources of men's life, and the
imagery suggested demonic corruption and the return of chaos. Now
the attack is explicitly demonic, and directed against *men* who lack
God's *seal* (v. 4; cf. $7^{1ff.}$ and contrast $13^{16ff.}$, the *mark* of the beast).
The *star fallen from heaven* (v. 1) keeps up the motif of coals of wrath
falling to earth ($8^{5, 8, 10}$), and prepares for the climax of the woes –
the fall of Satan ($12^{9, 12}$) and the appearance of the beast ($13^{1ff.}$).
The *tortures* of *darkness* (vv. 2ff.) are followed by *death*, the *second woe*
(vv. 14ff.) – cf. the ninth and tenth Egyptian plagues (Ex. $10^{21ff.}$)
– but the *third woe* is worse than death itself, for all that it is a source
of *wonder* and *worship* ($13^{3ff.}$), since it brings men to eternal torture
($14^{9-11}$), the *second death* ($20^{14}$, $21^8$).

The torture is inflicted by locusts, the eighth Egyptian plague (cf.
Amos $7^{1ff.}$), but the direct model is Joel 2: an army of locusts, presented as the demonic 'foe from the north', *in appearance like horses*
($2^4$, Rev. $9^7$; cf. $9^{17-19}$). Joel's locusts instigated a liturgy of penitence
(note the *trumpet*, $2^1$, $^{15}$), but the survivors of these plagues did not
repent (Rev. $9^{20f.}$).

Both models are horrifically enhanced, but John is probably drawing on traditional materials rather than his own visions, as the notes
will show. He is depicting the fruits of godlessness – cf. Jesus' parable
of the seven worse devils which take over the empty house (Matt.
$12^{43-45}$) – painting in traditional terms the horrors to which faithless
men subject themselves (cf. Wisd. $11^{15, 16}$, $12^{23ff.}$, $14^{12, 22}$, $17^{3ff.}$;
Rom. $1^{24ff.}$). Verse 1 perhaps gives the first hint of the Satanic parody
of divine reality which dominates chs. 13 and 17: the *key* of the *pit*
is *given* to the *fallen* one; the *keys of Death and Hades* are *held* by the
*risen* one ($1^{18}$). For John as for Paul these obscene parodies have no
independent power, but are allowed by God as part of his total plan
which they believe will triumph in the end (I Cor. $15^{24-28}$, Rom.
$11^{32-36}$). The ugliness of the one is a foil to the beauty of the other.

John's vision requires him to paint both – many of his hearers are dazzled by the *deep things of Satan* ($2^{24}$) – but the ugliness is encapsulated within the overarching beauty (chs. 4 and 5; $21^1$–$22^5$; see p. 13).

ෆ

1

*a star fallen:* see on $8^{10}$. Clearly it is an angel, perhaps the same angel who at $20^1$ *comes down* with *the key of the bottomless pit* to bind the dragon, Satan. *Fallen* need not have a sinister sense: Charles shows from parallels in Enoch that it need mean no more than 'having come down', and suggests that it is Uriel, who was set over 'the world and Tartarus' (= the nether world; I Enoch $20^2$). If so, he unlocks *the angel of the bottomless pit* (v. 11), just as the heavenly trumpeter *releases* the *four angels* of destruction (v. 14).

Nevertheless, the parallel with $8^{10}$ strongly suggests the sinister sense, and the perfect participle hints that fallenness is part of his character. It is natural to identify him with the *angel of the bottomless pit* in v. 11, and to contrast him with the angel who *comes down* at $10^1$. In that case he too is not Satan himself, but is an aspect of Satan, in deliberate contrast to Christ ($1^{18}$), and prepares us for the definitive *fall* of Satan in ch. 12.

*he was given:* cf. vv. 3 and 5, and $13^{5,\ 7,\ 14}$. Whether good or evil, he is still under the divine permission.

*bottomless pit:* lit. the 'abyss', the 'waters under the earth' of the old Mesopotamian world-view, the source of the chaos powers and the destined place of evil spirits (Luke $8^{31}$). This is spiritual geography (see pp. 15f.), signifying the reservoir of evil, out of which the *beast ascends* ($11^7$, $17^8$): it is thus one with the *sea*, out of which John saw the beast ascending ($13^1$), which has its analogue in heaven (see on $4^6$, $15^2$), and which in the new order is *no more* ($21^1$). Such geography is confusing to the Western mind, to which 'above' is good, 'below' bad, but according to Gen. $1^{6f.}$ God made a 'vault' to separate the waters of the abyss below from those above, and in one Jewish picture the rebel angels are imprisoned in the abyss (cf. II Peter $2^4$), in another in one of the heavens (as probably in I Peter $3^{19-22}$). 'Heaven', as the spiritual reality behind earthly phenomena and choices, comprises both 'above' and 'below', and Satan, like the *sea*, is found in both.

It was commonly believed that the world was full of demons, luring men into idolatry and sexual sin (e.g. I Enoch 19), but according to Caird John has no thought of a pre-cosmic fall of angels corrupting the earth. The *angels of the churches* represent their corporate life (see on $1^{20}$); thus 'a fallen angel represents some aspect of the corporate life of men which is in open revolt against the purpose of God' (Caird, p. 118). The *abyss* likewise does not threaten men from outside: it represents 'the cumulative power and virulence of evil to which all men contribute, and by which all men, whether they choose or not, are affected' (p. 119).

**2**

*the sun and the air were darkened:* picking up $8^{12}$. Darkness was the ninth Egyptian plague, magnified in Wisd. 17 as the source of phantoms and the terrors of conscience. The *smoke of a great furnace* picks up the sixth plague: 'Take handfuls of soot from a kiln [LXX *furnace*]. Moses shall toss it into the air . . . and it will turn into a fine dust over the whole of Egypt . . . It will become festering boils on man and beast' (Ex. $9^{8f.}$). The reference to boils is confirmed by the allusion to Job in v. 6 (see Job $2^7$), and by the fifth bowl plague ($16^{11}$). Sodom also went up like the *smoke of a furnace* (Gen. $19^{28}$): it was linked with Egypt by John ($11^8$) as by Wisd. $19^{14ff.}$.

**3**

*locusts:* the eighth plague (Ex. $10^{12-20}$), cf. Amos $7^{1ff.}$; but the chief model is now Joel 2, itself a series of ghastly improvisations on the exodus theme. These are demonic locusts, *given* the *power* of earthly *scorpions* (cf. v. 10, and Sirach $39^{30}$; for a plausible zodiacal explanation, see Farrer, p. 118).

**4**

*not to harm the grass:* contrast the earthly locusts of Exodus ($10^{12ff.}$). The discrepancy with $8^7$ is of no importance: the point is that men, not nature, are now the target.

*the seal of God:* see on $7^3$ and $13^{16}$ – the *mark* of the beast on his worshippers' *foreheads*. God's people are protected as they were in Egypt (Ex. $8^{22ff.}$, $9^{4ff.}$, $10^{23}$, Wisd. $18^1$); cf. the two witnesses: 'if anyone should *harm* them fire pours from their mouth' ($11^{5ff.}$). Jesus said, 'I saw Satan fall like lightning from heaven. Behold I have given you *power*

to tread upon serpents and *scorpions* . . . and nothing shall *harm* you'
(Luke 10$^{18f.}$): this was to the returning missionaries whose number
(seventy) foreshadowed the Gentile mission. We suggested (p. 147)
that the sealing was for the task of witness, and this is confirmed by
11$^{1-13}$; witness is the positive theme of the letter to Pergamum. See
also on v. 19.

**5**

*torture them for five months:* the normal extent of locusts' activity, and a
conventional 'round number'.$^v$ It signifies limitation, like the *ten days* of
2$^{10}$. The point is *torture*, not death as in the next plague, to bring them
to repentance (vv. 20f.); a method offensive to us, but a commonplace
of John's world. *Torture* is a keyword in Wisd. 11–19 for the effects of
men's own sin (e.g. 12$^{23}$) – sin in the religious sense of withholding
attention and worship from God, which entails bestowing it elsewhere
and being vulnerable to the deceptions and destructions of evil (see on
14$^{9-11}$). The punishment of evil by evil is a fact, and one of John's
themes (cf. 17$^{16f.}$), but it is subordinate to the theme of the 'witness of
Jesus'. This also is *torture* (11$^{10}$), but has a different end (11$^{13}$).

**6**

*men will seek death:* cf. Job 3$^{21}$. Job, whom the Lord had allowed Satan
to smite with boils (Job 2$^7$ – see on v. 2 above), spoke of those 'who
long for death, but it comes not, and dig for it more than for hid
treasures', because it would be a release from their pains. Is the *torture*
the effect of flight from God? cf. 6$^{16}$.

**7–10**

*the locusts were like horses:* see Joel 2$^{4ff.}$ for this and other motifs. John
intensifies the horror: *golden crowns* signify victory, a parody of the
Son of man (14$^{14}$). He represents true humanity: they have as it were
*human faces* and *women's hair* – classic horror images, but drawn from
tradition rather than John's unconscious mind; an eighteenth-century
German traveller was given a very similar comparison of locusts with
other creatures by a desert Arab (cited by Beasley-Murray, p. 162).

**10**

*stings:* lit. 'goads', as at Acts 26$^{14}$; a metaphor for spiritual pains, cf.
Hos. 13$^{14}$, I Cor. 15$^{56}$.

   $v$ Farrer observes that 'there are five months, or zodiacal signs, from the
Scorpion to the end of the zodiacal year' (p. 118).

**11**

*king:* according to Proverbs the locusts 'have no king' ($30^{27}$); according to Amos $7^1$ in the LXX version their king is Gog (cf. Ezek. 38-39, which John will use in chs. 19 and 20). These locusts have *the angel of the abyss* - not the archangel Uriel (see on $9^1$), but a minion or aspect of Satan.

*Abaddon:* a word almost confined to Job and Proverbs (which are in John's mind here), linked with Sheol, the pit. The LXX renders it *apōleia*, 'destruction', but John personifies it: *Apollyon*, the destroyer (cf. I Cor. $10^{10}$, a different word). There may be a punning dig at claims of Nero and Domitian to be incarnations of Apollo (cf. pp. 70f. on the *seven stars*); Paul makes a similar dig at the Apollos party (I Cor. $1^{18f.}$).

**12**

See $8^{13}$, $11^{14}$: John is building up to the third *woe* ($12^{12ff.}$).

## $9^{13-21}$ THE SIXTH TRUMPET AND SECOND WOE – CAVALRY

[13] *Then the sixth angel blew his trumpet, and I heard a voice from the four horns of the golden altar before God,* [14] *saying to the sixth angel who had the trumpet, 'Release the four angels who are bound at the great river Euphrates.'* [15] *So the four angels were released, who had been held ready for the hour, the day, the month, and the year, to kill a third of mankind.* [16] *The number of the troops of cavalry was twice ten thousand times ten thousand; I heard their number.* [17] *And this was how I saw the horses in my vision: the riders wore breastplates the colour of fire and of sapphire\* and of sulphur, and the heads of the horses were like lions' heads, and fire and smoke and sulphur issued from their mouths.* [18] *By these three plagues a third of mankind was killed, by the fire and smoke and sulphur issuing from their mouths.* [19] *For the power of the horses is in their mouths and in their tails; their tails are like serpents, with heads, and by means of them they wound.*

[20] *The rest of mankind, who were not killed by these plagues, did not*

*repent of the works of their hands nor give up worshipping demons and idols of gold and silver and bronze and stone and wood, which cannot either see or hear or walk;* ²¹*nor did they repent of their murders or their sorceries or their immorality or their thefts.*

★ Greek *hyacinth.*

Darkness and death were the last two Egyptian plagues. Out of John's 'darkness' came *locusts, like horses arrayed for battle; the horses* of an innumerable demonic *cavalry* (always an image of terror to the Jews, like the army of Gog, Ezek. 38⁴ᶠ·) are the agents of his 'death' – *three* plagues which again smite a *third* of mankind (v. 18). See the introductory notes to the fifth trumpet (9¹⁻¹²). Joel's army of locusts like horses instigated *repentance*: these plagues do not (vv. 20f.). Idolatry, with the crimes it breeds, continues and comes to a climax of deception in the *third woe* (12¹² and 13), which issues in torment worse than death itself (14⁹⁻¹¹).

We may find these plagues revolting, like pictures of the effects of nuclear war or ecological arrogance, but their aim is to shock people into avoiding the action, or inaction, which would bring them about. John is not threatening pagans but revealing to Christians the spiritual nature and destiny of the world to which they are tempted to conform. It is a deeper diagnosis than that of many of our contemporary prophets of doom, and it is encapsulated within a more positive vision – see again pp. 13ff.

ॐ

**13**
*I heard a voice:* what John *hears* (vv. 13–16) interprets what he is going to *see* (v. 17); see p. 125.

*the four horns of the golden altar:* i.e. the incense altar, suggesting again the prayers of the saints as the dynamic behind this visitation (8³⁻⁵). *Four* is omitted by many authorities; if original, it is to balance the *four angels* of v. 14.

**14**
*saying to the sixth angel:* for the first time the trumpet archangel is

involved. Like the *voice from the altar* and the *number* which John *hears* at v. 16, it emphasizes divine control.

*Release the four angels:* an echo of the four angels at the four corners of the earth, holding back the four winds (7$^1$). The supernatural powers of chaos which they represented are now found concentrated at the *river Euphrates* – in Old Testament times the frontier across which came invaders from the East; now Rome's frontier with the Parthians, who since the defeat of Crassus in 53 BC had been a source of worry and fear. Cf. the sixth bowl (16$^{12-16}$). *Bound* suggests the wicked angels of the apocalypses, which are the 'cause' of evil on earth.

## 15

*held ready for the hour, the day, the month and the year:* another stock motif of apocalyptic. Everything is minutely and immutably laid down in advance – 'by measures and number and weight thou didst order all things' (Wisd. 11$^{20}$). Apparent failure and delay are within God's plan.

*to kill: to* depends on *released*, not *held ready*.

*a third of mankind:* John does not say those who lack *God's seal* as at 9$^4$, but v. 20 shows that it is intended.

## 16

*troops of cavalry:* the *four angels* have become 200,000,000 *cavalry* without explicit mention. The locust-horses of Joel become the demonic cavalry of Gog, the locusts' *king* according to Amos 7$^1$ LXX – see on v. 11, and Ezek. 38$^{4ff}$. The Parthians were celebrated horser · · · see on 6$^2$.

*I heard their number: heard* seems to be significant, as at 7$^4$, in juxtaposition with *saw* in v. 17. The angels round the throne were 'myriads of myriads and thousands of thousands' (5$^{11}$; cf. Dan. 7$^{10}$), but even closer are the chariots of God, '*twice* ten thousand and thousands upon thousands', at Ps. 68$^{17}$: does the *number* imply that in spite of their appearance they are in divine service? or perhaps simply that 'God knows the numbers he has marked for salvation, and the numbers he has armed with destruction' (Farrer, p. 121)? Caird finds the clue in the Gog myth of Ezek. 38–39: an inexhaustible reservoir of evil beyond the confines of the civilized world (pp. 122f.). John takes up this passage explicitly in chs. 19 and 20.

**17**

*the colour of fire and of sapphire* (Greek *hyacinth*) *and of sulphur:* the colours of the *riders' breastplates* balance the colours of the last three *horses* of $6^{5-8}$, *red, black* and *pale* (another indication that the *first* horseman is different in kind from the three disaster-bearers? see pp. 137ff.). *Fire* dominates the whole series from $8^5$ on, like the recurrent *threes*. *Sulphur* (*theion*) is translated *brimstone* at $14^{10}$; cf. $19^{20}$, $20^{10}$, $21^8$, *the lake of fire and brimstone.*

*the heads of the horses were like lions:* cf. v. 8, *teeth like lions' teeth.* But their bite is the torment of hell, *fire, smoke and sulphur* (cf. v. 2), which fell on Sodom and Gomorrah (Gen. $19^{24, 28}$). Since Job is in mind, it is possible that his Leviathan has contributed to the picture ($41^{19-21}$, LXX $41^{10-12}$). Leviathan and Behemoth ($40^{15}$) lie behind the beasts of ch. 13.

**19**

*The power of the horses* . . .: cf. vv. 3 and 10. Now the *tails* are like *serpents.* But *serpents and scorpions* go together as in Sirach $39^{30}$ and Luke $10^{19}$; cf. also Ps. $91^{13}$, which links *lions* and *serpents* as no terror to the faithful. Is the sting in the tail a reference to the 'Parthian shot' of the mounted archer? Scorpions and serpents wounding idolatrous and lawless men also suggest Gen. $3^{15}$ – see on $12^{17}$. According to the Targum (see p. 40) there would be a remedy (the *seal*, v. 4?) for the woman's offspring, but none for the serpent, in the days of the Messiah.

**20**

*did not repent:* repentance is God's object, as in Joel and Amos; cf. Wisd. $12^{10, 19ff.}$, Rom. $2^{4-5}$, II Peter $3^{15}$.

*works of their hands:* a common phrase for idolatry; cf. Acts $7^{41}$, referring to the golden calf.

*demons and idols:* see I Cor. $10^{14-22}$, based on Deut. $32^{16-21}$. 'Strong' Christians said 'an idol has no real existence' (I Cor. $8^4$); Paul agreed but warned them of the *demons* behind. That which is not God, if worshipped, becomes a demonic power (see on $13^3$).

*gold and silver . . .:* cf. Dan. $5^{23}$, Belshazzar's feast.

**21**

*murders . . .:* for idolatry as the root of immorality and crime see Wisd. $14^{12, \ 24-27}$, Rom. $1^{18-32}$. For *sorceries* cf. $18^{23}$. They are linked with idolatry (Gal. $5^{20}$) and were common in Ephesus (Acts $19^{18f \cdot}$). There are similar lists at $21^8$ and $22^{15}$: their destiny is 'the lake that burns with fire and brimstone, which is the second death'.

*The Little Scroll and the Two*
*Witnesses*

The sixth trumpet brings us, like the Egyptian plagues, to the end of
a cul-de-sac: Pharaoh's heart is still hardened (Ex. 14$^{5, 8}$); a break-
through is needed (see the general introduction to 8–14). But before
this exodus (ch. 12) comes the enigmatic interlude which is explicitly
bound in with the *second woe* by 11$^{14}$; the repentance of 11$^{13}$, therefore, must balance the impenitence of 9$^{20f.}$, and the theme seems to
be the gospel (ch. 10) and the church's witness (ch. 11) over against
the visitations of divine wrath on idolatry. Gospel and wrath were
already two sides of one coin in Christian tradition, cf. Rom. 1$^{16-18}$
and notes on Rev. 6$^{2}$; and the parallel delay between the sixth and
seventh unsealings, when the servants of God were sealed (7$^{3ff.}$),
suggests that the bearing of witness is what they were sealed *for*;
chs. 8 and 9 have told us what they were sealed against. Witness and
idolatry are the themes of the letter to Pergamum (see p. 45).

We must now see how ch. 10 introduces this theme.

10 *Then I saw another mighty angel coming down from heaven, wrapped
in a cloud, with a rainbow over his head, and his face was like the sun, and
his legs like pillars of fire.* $^{2}$*He had a little scroll open in his hand. And he
set his right foot on the sea, and his left foot on the land,* $^{3}$*and called out
with a loud voice, like a lion roaring; when he called out, the seven thunders
sounded.* $^{4}$*And when the seven thunders had sounded, I was about to write,
but I heard a voice from heaven saying, 'Seal up what the seven thunders*

*have said, and do not write it down.'* ⁵*And the angel whom I saw standing on sea and land lifted up his right hand to heaven* ⁶*and swore by him who lives for ever and ever, who created heaven and what is in it, the earth and what is in it, and the sea and what is in it, that there should be no more delay,* ⁷*but that in the days of the trumpet call to be sounded by the seventh angel, the mystery of God, as he announced to his servants the prophets, should be fulfilled.*

⁸*Then the voice which I had heard from heaven spoke to me again, saying,* '*Go, take the scroll which is open in the hand of the angel who is standing on the sea and on the land.'* ⁹*So I went to the angel and told him to give me the little scroll; and he said to me,* '*Take it and eat; it will be bitter to your stomach, but sweet as honey in your mouth.'* ¹⁰*And I took the little scroll from the hand of the angel and ate it; it was sweet as honey in my mouth, but when I had eaten it my stomach was made bitter.* ¹¹*And I was told,* '*You must again prophesy about many peoples and nations and tongues and kings.'*

The *little scroll* (v. 2) is explicitly linked with the *sealed scroll* of ch. 5 by the *mighty angel* who delivers it (5²), and by the allusion to Ezekiel's commission (Ezek. 2⁸–3³) in the terms in which John is told to *eat* it (v. 9). These features suggest that the great scroll of God's purpose, opened now in heaven by the Lamb's death, is committed (suitably scaled down) to his servants on earth. 'It is not when earth ascends, but when heaven comes down, that revelation is complete' (Farrer, p. 125). If that scroll represented the scriptures, God's will and purpose under the guise of law, then the *little scroll* is the law fulfilled in the gospel, the scriptures opened by Christ – John is commissioned like the disciples at Luke 24⁴⁵⁻⁴⁹. This is confirmed, perhaps, by the *angel's* trappings: the *rainbow*, symbol of God's covenant with the earth, and the *cloud* and *pillars of fire*, symbols of the exodus and the covenant with Israel, to which all nations are to be admitted on the Christian understanding of Ex. 19⁵ᶠ· (I Peter 2⁹, Rev. 5⁹ᶠ·).

The *seven thunders* set rolling by the angel's voice may reinforce the point. The proclamation of God's commands and penalties in the trumpets and thunder of Sinai (Ex. 19¹⁶ᶠᶠ·, Heb. 12¹⁸ᶠᶠ·) might echo on and on for ever, but again in clear reference back to ch. 5 John is told to *seal up*, not record and pass on, what the *thunders have said*

(v. 4). Instead, the angel (in allusion now to Dan. 12^{7ff.}) gives divine assurance that there shall be *no more delay* (v. 6), but that when the seventh trumpet has sounded, God's secret plan, the subject of *good news* to the prophets, will be fulfilled (v. 7).

John, like Jeremiah and Ezekiel, is told to *eat* and digest the message, and *prophesy about many nations* (v. 11, cf. 11^3, 9); its reception is *sweet* (good news), its assimilation *bitter* (its effects, on hearers and proclaimers). Another theme of ch. 5, that man's redemption can be achieved only by man (see p. 124), is also carried forward: Christ's victory depends for its earthly completion on Christians *eating* the message (which in Johannine terms is himself, cf. John 6^{53-63}, 15^{7f.}, 17^{14-19}); they must share his bitter cup (John 18^{11}, Mark 10^{18}) and baptism (Luke 12^{49-53}): their saving *seal* is the sign of the cross. All this is worked out in ch. 11, and summed up at 12^{11}: 'They have conquered him by the blood of the Lamb and by the word of their testimony, for they loved not their lives even unto death.'

ॐ

<sup>1</sup>

*another mighty angel:* cf. 5^2. His oath (vv. 5f.) links him with the angel Gabriel, which means 'strong man of God', in Daniel (12^{7ff.}; cf. 8^{16}, 9^{21}, 10^5).

*coming down from heaven:* contrast 9^1. If that fallen angel represented God's indirect will, in letting men's sin recoil upon them (cf. p. 144 note *e*), this one represents his direct will, revealed in the gospel, and thus is decked out with the divine splendour – cf. the description of the 'one like a son of man' (1^{15f.}). The earthly origin of the picture is perhaps a storm, with the sun shining through the rain-clouds (Farrer, p. 124), but the theological overtones are what matter: *cloud* veiled God's glory at Sinai (Ex. 19^{16}) and with *pillars of fire* evokes the exodus (13^{21} etc.); *rainbow* evokes God's promise to Noah after the flood (see on 4^3). In spite of the terrible impasse in which the previous chapter ended, the God of creation and redemption is still in control.

<sup>2</sup>

*a little scroll open:* the diminutive *biblaridion* both distinguishes it from and links it with the *biblion* of 5^{1ff.}, which is now fully unsealed and communicated to the prophet. (He is now back on earth; consistency of time and place is not to be expected in apocalyptic.)

**2**

*right foot on the sea, and his left foot on the land:* emphasizing the universal scope of his mission (cf. 14$^6$).

**3**

*like a lion roaring:* a frequent OT image for God bestirring himself to judgment (Amos 1$^2$, 3$^{4-8}$, Hos. 11$^{10}$, Jer. 25$^{30}$, Joel 3$^{16}$).

*the seven thunders: the* may indicate an apocalyptic cliché, unknown to us, but probably like the other 'sevens' it is John's own coinage from traditional materials, such as the sevenfold voice of the Lord in Ps. 29. *Thunder* in Revelation is a sign of the divine presence and judgment (4$^5$, 6$^1$, 8$^5$, 11$^{19}$ etc.). It is linked with *trumpet* in the account of the lawgiving at Sinai (Ex. 19$^{16}$; cf. Heb. 12$^{19}$).

**4**

*seal up what the seven thunders have said:* this puzzling prohibition may simply originate in John's visionary experience, cf. Paul's at II Cor. 12$^3$, but as it stands it serves to focus attention away from God's judgments on to his positive message in the *little scroll*, as if he should 'in wrath remember mercy' (Hab. 3$^2$). In view of the promise of *no more delay* (v. 6), it may be a symbolic representation of the Lord's promise that the days of the 'great tribulation' would be shortened for the elect's sake (Matt. 24$^{22}$); so Farrer and Caird. Farrer (p. 125) points out that the unsealings affect a *quarter*, the trumpets a *third*, the bowls (ch. 16) the *whole*: it is as if the expected *half* has been providentially omitted. The number *two* dominates ch. 11 as *three* dominated 8 and 9.

**5**

*lifted up his right hand:* the standard gesture in oath-taking (Gen. 14$^{22}$ etc.). The closest parallel is Dan. 12$^7$, but note also God's oath to avenge his people in the Song of Moses: 'For I lift up my hand to heaven, and swear, As I live for ever . . .' (Deut. 32$^{40}$).

**6**

*who created heaven . . .:* for the description of God, by whom the angel swears, cf. 4$^9$, $^{11}$. No more here than there is it empty verbiage: it is God the *Creator*, who made the world according to his will, whose final will is to be done.

*no more delay:* lit. 'no more time (*chronos*)', but this is clearly not a metaphysical statement. Rather it is an answer to the saints' cry, 'How long?' ($6^{10}$), reminiscent of Hab. $2^3$ (quoted at Heb. $10^{37}$) 'Still the vision awaits its time; it hastens to the end – it will not lie. If it seem slow, wait for it; it will surely come, it will not delay (*chronisei*)'. This replaces the angel's words in Daniel 'that it would be for a time, two times, and half a time; and that when the shattering of the power of the holy people comes to an end all these things would be accomplished' ($12^7$). Daniel's mysterious 'three and a half' period of desolation will dominate chs. $11$-$13$ (see p. 182 below); the angel's words here promise that this will not be just a prolongation of heart-break but the fulfilment of the *mystery of God*.

### 7

*in the days . . .:* the seventh *trumpet* call does not introduce an atomic moment; the consummation is itself a process. The chronology is not that of actual history, but of the drama; we can expect the period of the seventh blast to be longer than the sixth, as the sixth was longer than the fifth, and the end is in fact sketched in ch. $14$ (Farrer, p. $126$).

*the mystery of God:* 'Surely the Lord God does nothing, without revealing his secret to his servants the prophets' (Amos $3^7$). In the NT *musterion* stands for the hidden purpose of God, or some part of it, now being made known in the *gospel*, cf. Rom. $16^{25}$, Eph. $3^{2-10}$, Col. $4^3$. John has changed Amos's 'reveal' to *announced* (*euēngelisen*), lit. 'proclaimed the good news'. The longed-for fulfilment is not simply vengeance, it is *gospel*. For what John means by that, see $14^{6f.}$. *Fulfilled* is the same Greek verb as *finished* at $11^7$; cf. Matt. $24^{14}$.

### 8

*Go, take the scroll:* Amos continued, 'The Lord God has spoken; who can but prophesy?' ($3^8$). Now a prophet is commissioned – John himself (v. $11$), and symbolically the whole church ($11^3$) under the guise of the two witnesses.

### 9

*Take it, and eat:* The echoes of $5^7$ suggest the inseparability of Christ's heavenly work and its earthly assimilation; men, not angels, are needed to carry it through to external completion. God's *servants the prophets* (John and his fellow-Christians, $1^{1f.}$, $22^9$) are not merely to listen to his revelations but to digest and proclaim them.

9f.

*bitter to your stomach:* Ezekiel's scroll, with the writing on front and back (cf. Rev. 5$^1$), words of lamentation and mourning and woe, was *sweet as honey in* his *mouth* – the phrase evokes the law (Ps. 19$^{10}$ etc.) – but he was sent with it to a stubborn and rebellious people (Ezek. 2$^8$–3$^{11}$). Behind Ezekiel lies the experience of Jeremiah (15$^{16-18}$), who is also John's model. *My stomach was made bitter* is John's addition, intelligible enough: in a rebellious world the gospel too is destructive to both hearers and proclaimers – see 11$^{6-10}$. But this is a different bitterness from that of 8$^{11}$, both in origin and results (see 11$^{13}$; cf. II Cor. 7$^{8-10}$).

11

*You must again prophesy: again* – after the moratorium of v. 4?

*peoples and nations and tongues:* a Danielic formula (3$^4$, 6$^{25}$, 7$^{14}$; cf. Rev. 5$^9$, 14$^6$). The addition of *kings* may evoke Jeremiah's commission (1$^{10}$), or the Lord's commissioning of the twelve: 'you will be dragged before governors and *kings* for my sake, to bear testimony before them and the Gentiles (= *nations*; Matt. 10$^{18}$). Both Matt. 10 and Luke 10 seem to be in John's mind in the next chapter.

II$^{1-14}$      THE TWO WITNESSES

I I Then I was given a measuring rod like a staff, and I was told: 'Rise and measure the temple of God and the altar and those who worship there, *2but do not measure the court outside the temple; leave that out, for it is given over to the nations, and they will trample over the holy city for forty-two months. 3And I will grant my two witnesses power to prophesy for one thousand two hundred and sixty days, clothed in sack-cloth.'*
*4These are the two olive trees and the two lampstands which stand before the Lord of the earth. 5And if any one would harm them, fire pours from their mouth and consumes their foes; if any one would harm them, thus he is doomed to be killed. 6They have power to shut the sky, that no rain may fall during the days of their prophesying, and they have power over the waters to turn them into blood, and to smite the earth with every plague,*

*as often as they desire.* <sup>7</sup>*And when they have finished their testimony, the beast that ascends from the bottomless pit will make war upon them and conquer them and kill them,* <sup>8</sup>*and their dead bodies will lie in the street of the great city which is allegorically\* called Sodom and Egypt, where their Lord was crucified.* <sup>9</sup>*For three days and a half men from the peoples and tribes and tongues and nations gaze at their dead bodies and refuse to let them be placed in a tomb,* <sup>10</sup>*and those who dwell on the earth will rejoice over them and make merry and exchange presents, because these two prophets had been a torment to those who dwell on the earth.* <sup>11</sup>*But after the three and a half days a breath of life from God entered them, and they stood up on their feet, and great fear fell on those who saw them.* <sup>12</sup> *Then they heard a loud voice from heaven saying to them, 'Come up hither!' And in the sight of their foes they went up to heaven in a cloud.* <sup>13</sup>*And at that hour there was a great earthquake, and a tenth of the city fell; seven thousand people were killed in the earthquake, and the rest were terrified and gave glory to the God of heaven.*

<sup>14</sup>*The second woe has passed; behold, the third woe is soon to come.*

\* Greek *spiritually.*

As we have already observed (p. 175), v. 14 (*the second woe has passed*) binds in 10 and 11<sup>1-13</sup> with the sixth trumpet blast and second woe: the repentance of 11<sup>13</sup> balances the impenitence of 9<sup>20f.</sup>, and the gospel (10) proclaimed by Christ's witnesses (11<sup>3ff.</sup>) is set over against the visitations of divine wrath on idolatry. Witness and idolatry are the themes of the letter to Pergamum.

S. Giet[w] found many allusions in these chapters to the course of events in the war of AD 66–70; and Charles had already detected, from peculiarities of language and style, two independent fragments in 11<sup>1f.</sup> and 11<sup>3-13</sup> – perhaps Jewish oracles from Zealot circles before AD 70: one concerned with the fate of the temple, one with a ministry of Moses and Elijah in fulfilment of Malachi's prophecy (4<sup>4-6</sup>). But Charles rightly observed that John has completely re-interpreted this material. Even if he was writing close to AD 70, when readers might be

---

[w] S. Giet, *L'Apocalypse et l'Histoire*, Paris 1957. See pp. 22–4 above for an outline of events.

able to pick up the historical references, he has so universalized the historical starting point (11$^8$) that any literal reference to the fate of Jerusalem and its temple, or to a prophetic ministry to the Jews, must be ruled out. 11$^8$ warns us that the interpretation of the entire passage must be symbolic, and relate to the church and the world. See pp. 45–7 above for Feuillet's view[x] and reasons for rejecting it.

We begin, then, with an echo of Ezekiel 40$^3$: the measuring of Jerusalem there, as in Zech. 2 and Rev. 21$^{15}$, signifies restoration; here it means preservation. But the *court outside the temple* is excluded: the clue here may be Luke's version of the Lord's Apocalypse in which Jerusalem, after its 'desolation', 'will be trodden down by the Gentiles, until the times of the Gentiles are fulfilled' (21$^{24}$), combined with Dan. 12$^{11}$: 'from the time that . . . the abomination that makes desolate is set up, there shall be a thousand two hundred and ninety days' – i.e. roughly the *forty-two months* for which the nations will *trample over the holy city* (v. 2). Jesus was concerned with the fate of Jerusalem and its temple, but John (whatever the pre-history of his material) is thinking of the spiritual temple which in God's eyes has replaced it (cf. John 2$^{19f.}$, 4$^{21-24}$), and of *those who worship there* (v. 1). Inwardly this community is preserved from Satanic attack (cf. the sealing of 7$^{1-8}$, and the preservation of the woman at 12$^{6, 14}$); outwardly it is given over to the violence of the Gentiles (cf. 12$^{17}$: the dragon makes war on the woman's offspring), though armed with the powers of Moses and Elijah (11$^{5f.}$) it more than holds its own, for a time.

The time references, enigmatic enough at first sight, clarify John's perspective. The time of this trampling, *forty-two months* = three and a half years, is the time of the beast's authority and war against the saints (13$^{5-7}$); it is equivalent to the *one thousand two hundred and sixty days* that the witnesses prophesy (11$^3$) and the woman is nourished in the wilderness (12$^6$). As *three and a half years* it represents the mysterious *three and a half times* of Dan. 7$^{25}$; 12$^7$ (Rev. 12$^{14}$; see on 10$^6$) – the divinely limited period of oppression before final victory, which also lies behind the *three and a half days* of the earth-dwellers' triumph over the dead witnesses (11$^9$)

x A. Feuillet, 'Essai d'interprétation du ch. 11 de l'Apocalypse', *NTS* 3, 1957, pp. 183–200.

and the half-week of Jesus' own eclipse (cf. Farrer, pp. 7ff., and on the significance of numbers pp. 14f. above).

In other words, John is urging the church to see its whole life and work under the sign of *three and a half*. He is expressing symbolically what was set out historically in Jesus' own career, in his instructions to the twelve (Matt. 9³⁷–10⁴²) and the seventy (Luke 10¹⁻²⁰), and in the stories of Stephen, Peter, Paul and no doubt others: a pattern of witness, opposition, invulnerability and success for a time, defeat and death, but final vindication and triumph of the cause. His three and a half covers the time both of invulnerability (11³⁻⁶) and of eclipse (11⁷⁻⁹; 13⁵⁻⁷): the implication is that *both* are of the church's essence. There can be *no* period at which the church is simply at peace in the world, much less simply triumphant, or simply crushed. But he does foresee a final three and a half days when what so far has been the fate of individuals – Moses, Elijah, John the Baptist, Jesus, Stephen, Peter, Paul, Antipas (2¹³) – must be faced by all Christians (12¹²–13¹⁸). The stories of these individuals are prophetic anticipations of the final crisis, for which John is trying to alert Christians too ready to be at peace in the world, or perhaps looking for divine intervention of the kind promised in the Jewish oracles which he has re-used (cf. 13¹⁰ᵇ·). The true and only pattern of divine intervention (apart from the self-destruction of godlessness which God *allows*) has been laid down in Jesus, and witnessed to by prophets and saints. Their *seal* is the sign of the cross. If Christians are not living this pattern *now*, they will not be ready when the time comes (see on 12¹⁷, 13¹⁰, ¹⁸, 14¹², 16¹⁵, 18⁴). It is this pattern, not the plagues God allows, which breaks through human obstinacy (11¹³).

❦

**1f.**

*Measure the temple:* a metaphor for 'put under divine protection and control'. The man whom Ezekiel saw (40³ᶠᶠ·), like John's angel at 21¹⁵ᶠᶠ·, measured the whole city. John measures the central shrine (*naos*) and altar, and *those who worship there*, but is told to *leave out the court outside*. This too must signify people, not buildings (it was widely held that the true temple was the holy community; cf. I Cor. 3¹⁶, Eph. 2²¹), because *leave out* is *ekbale* – 'throw or send out'. Many take the *naos* to be the church, the true Israel (cf. John 2^{19f.}, Rev. 3^9), and the *court outside* to be the old Israel, the sons of the kingdom now *thrown out* (Matt. 8^{12} etc.) – a reference to the destruction of Jerusalem in AD 70. But the historical fate of the Jews is not John's concern; for him the Danielic *trampling* (Dan. 8^{13}; cf. 7^{21, 25}) is over the *saints* (13^7), and the *holy city* is no longer the earthly Jerusalem, which has identified itself with the *great city* (v. 8), but the heavenly (21^{2ff.}).

The distinction must be between the church in its inward being, *measured* as the 144,000 were *sealed* (7^{1-8}), and the church in its outward life, already the *holy city* (cf. 3^{12}), but not yet *measured* as it will be (21^{15}): it is *given over to the nations* – engaged in the mission to the Gentiles (Matt. 10^{17f.}, 24^{9-14}). *Ekbale* then has other possible associations: Jesus told the twelve to 'pray the Lord of the harvest to *send out (ekbalei)* labourers into his harvest' (Matt. 9^{38}, Luke 10^2, see also on 14^{13-16}). *Ekbale exōthen* (= *throw outside*) also hints at the results of bearing witness: as for Jesus at Nazareth (Luke 4^{29}), the man born blind (John 9^{34}), the son of the vineyard-owner (Mark 12^8, Matt. 21^{39}, Luke 20^{15}), and Stephen (Acts 7^{58}). 'Outside the city' was perhaps a watchword for the Christian vocation, cf. Heb. 13^{11-14} (which may point to the true interpretation of Rev. 14^{20}).

3

The Greek is lit. 'I will give to my two witnesses, and they shall prophesy 1260 days', which echoes v. 2: lit. 'it was given to the nations, and they shall trample the holy city forty-two months'. The parallelism is intentional: the being trampled which is allowed by God, and the witnessing comissioned by God are two sides of one coin. For the significance of the two periods, see above. *Two* is the minimum for valid witness (Deut. 19^{15}; cf. John 8^{17}); the seventy, like rabbinic delegates, were sent out in twos (Luke 10^1; cf. Acts 13^2, 15^{39f.}); see also on v. 4. *Prophesy* means 'speak and act for God', and picks up 10^{11}. *Sackcloth* befits prophets who are heralds of repentance, like Elijah (II Kings 1^8), whom Christians saw as a type of John the Baptist (Mark 1^6); it is a sign of penitence (Jonah 3^{6, 8}, Matt. 11^{22}). The church is powerful only when itself penitent. 'A comfortable easy-minded church has no power to stir the world either to salvation or to opposition' (Morris, p. 148).

4

*the two olive trees and the two lampstands:* Zechariah had seen a *lampstand* of gold, with *seven lamps* on it (4²), a model which John used for the church in chs. 1–3. On either side of it Zechariah saw *two olive trees* (4³) which his angel explained as 'the two anointed who stand by the Lord of the whole earth' (4¹⁴) – Zerubbabel, the scion of David, and Joshua (= Jesus in Greek), the high priest, prototypes both of Jesus and of his church which he has made a *kingdom and priests* (1⁶, 5¹⁰). 'The seven branched lamp was carried in triumph by Titus; the twofold lamp of witness$^y$ continues to shine' (Farrer, p. 131). The two witnesses represent not particular individuals, though Elijah and Moses (vv. 5f.), and perhaps James and John (v. 5) and Peter and Paul, who died in Rome (vv. 7f.), contribute to the picture$^z$; they represent the role of the church, as laid down at Acts 1⁶⁻⁸, where the expected 'kingdom' is redefined in terms of witness in the power of the Spirit (cf. Zech. 4⁶, 'Not by might, nor by power, but by my Spirit').

**5**

*if anyone would harm them:* 'I have given you authority to tread upon serpents and scorpions . . . and nothing shall *harm* you', Jesus told the seventy (Luke 10¹⁹).

*fire pours from their mouth:* Elijah called down fire from heaven on the soldiers sent to arrest him (II Kings 1¹⁰ff.), but Jesus, just before the sending of the seventy, rebuked James and John's request to bid fire come down on the people who would not receive him (Luke 9⁵³⁻⁵⁵). It is a 'reborn' image: *from their mouth* recalls Sirach 48¹, 'Elijah, a prophet like fire, whose word flamed like a torch' (cf. Rev. 4⁵), and suggests *the sword of the mouth* (2¹⁶, 19¹⁵), the Spirit-empowered words with which Christ and his witnesses are armed (Matt. 10²⁰, Acts 6¹⁰ etc.). Contrast the beast's parody of the Pentecostal fire (13¹³).

**6**

*power to shut the sky:* like Elijah (I Kings 17¹). John echoes the words of Jesus' sermon at Nazareth (Luke 4²⁵), which records the famine as lasting three and a half years (on three and a half, see p. 182 above).

$y$ Cf. Matt. 5¹⁴⁻¹⁶, Luke 11³³⁻³⁶; the danger in John's churches is that their light may become darkness.

$z$ The role of Moses and Elijah, preparing Israel for the coming of the Messiah, is transferred to the church preparing the world for Jesus' final coming. James and John asked for places on either side of Jesus, and were told they would share his cup and baptism (Mark 10³⁷⁻³⁹). For Peter and Paul, see J. Munck, *Petrus und Paulus in der Offenbarung Johannis*, Copenhagen 1950.

*power over the waters:* like Moses (Ex. 7$^{14-25}$, the first of the ten plagues). To *turn them into blood* recalls Rev. 8$^{8f.}$ (see notes) and the fall of the *destroying mountain,* Babylon (is Zech. 4$^7$ also in mind?).

*smite the earth with every plague:* echoing the words of the Philistines, when they heard that the ark of the covenant (cf. v. 19) had come into the Israelite camp (I Sam. 4$^8$). The Spirit-filled scion of David was to '*smite the earth* with the rod of his mouth' (Isa. 11$^4$): the church's only weapon is its message inspired by the Holy Spirit, who 'convicts the world' (John 16$^{8ff.}$) – a *torment* (Rev. 11$^{10}$) to its conscience (cf. Acts 24$^{25}$, I Cor. 14$^{24f.}$). This is not merely destructive: *smiting* may imply *healing* as at Hos. 6$^{1-5}$, referring to apostate Israel (cf. Rev. 22$^2$ – the leaves of the tree for the healing of the nations); see on v. 13.

As Farrer says (p. 134), it is odd that John should seem to confirm the pagan charge that Christians are the cause of fire, famine and plague (see p. 31); but whereas the pagans say it is by their vicious atheism, John follows the Wisdom of Solomon's line: Christian witness provokes heathen attacks, which in their turn bring down the forces of nature on the attackers (Wisd. 16$^{17, 24}$, 18$^{4f.}$, 19$^{1-6}$).

**7f.**

*when they have finished their testimony:* see on 10$^7$; *finished* is the same verb as *fulfilled.* See also Matt. 10$^{23}$, 23$^{34-39}$ and 24$^{14}$; Christian witness is to come to a bloody climax in Jerusalem, crowned by the 'end', the coming of the Son of man. For John Jerusalem has become *the great city;* see on v. 12 for the link with the Son of man.

**7**

*the beast that ascends:* who he is will be made clear in ch. 13: he belongs to the *third woe.* The present tense *ascends* could be a vivid future ('is to ascend'), but may indicate the *beast's* nature; cf. the New Jerusalem which 'comes down' (3$^{12}$).

*from the bottomless pit:* lit. the abyss. See on 9$^1$, 13$^1$.

*make war ... conquer ... kill:* cf. 12$^{17}$, 13$^{7, 15}$. Contrast the Lamb, who *makes war* with the sword of his mouth (2$^{16}$, 19$^{11, 15}$), and *conquers* by dying, not *killing* (see on 2$^7$). *Make war* shows that the two witnesses are in fact an army, like the 144,000 (7$^4$, 14$^1$); cf. v. 11.

**8**

*their dead bodies will lie in the street:* cf. Ps. 79$^{2f}$. Contrast the *street* of the New Jerusalem, where the water of life flows, and the leaves of the tree are for the healing of the nations (22$^{1f}$.).

*the great city which is allegorically called Sodom and Egypt:* not to be found in any one place on the map. To assume from *where their Lord was crucified* that it must be Jerusalem is to misunderstand all John's 'geography'. Jerusalem is indeed called *Sodom* by the prophets (e.g. Isa. 1$^{10}$, 3$^9$), and *Sodom* is linked with *Egypt* (Wisd. 19$^{14}$), but he is speaking *allegorically,* lit. *spiritually,* in the symbolic language in which divine secrets must be handled (I Cor. 2$^{6-16}$). In this language Christ was crucified by 'the rulers of this age' (I Cor. 2$^{6-8}$), who at that moment were embodied in Caiaphas, Herod and Pilate, and it was in the *great city,* which was located at that moment in Jerusalem. The *city* is the social and political embodiment of human self-sufficiency and rebellion against God. Its most powerful image is Babylon (16$^{19}$), which inspired the ironic account of the Tower of Babel in Gen. 11; its present location is Rome (chs. 17, 18), but it has been preceded by *Sodom* and *Egypt* (and has many successors!), in their arrogant vice and oppression of God's servants (the two angels, Gen. 19$^1$, and God's two witnesses, Moses and Aaron). See again the sending of the seventy (Luke 10$^{10-12}$).

*where their Lord was crucified:* 'A servant is not greater than his *Lord.* If they persecuted me, they will persecute you' (John 15$^{20}$).

**9**

*three days and a half:* ' "Destroy this temple, and in three days I will raise it up" . . . he spoke of the temple of his body' (John 2$^{19-21}$). The *half* makes a link with the Danielic three and a half (see p. 182 above).

**9**

*peoples and tribes . . . :* cf. 10$^{11}$, 13$^7$, 14$^6$. The witnesses' work is universal (cf. Matt. 24$^{14}$).

*their dead bodies:* here and in v. 8 it is the collective singular *ptōma,* which recalls Jesus' words, 'Where the *body* is, there the eagles will be gathered together' (Matt. 24$^{28}$); see on 8$^{13}$.

**10**

*rejoice over them:* as the Jews rejoiced over the death of Haman (Esth.

9<sup>19, 22</sup>) and as Jesus said the world would rejoice over his death (John 16<sup>20</sup>); contrast the heavenly rejoicing at the defeat of Satan (12<sup>12</sup>) and the vindication of God's witnesses (18<sup>20</sup>).

*a torment:* like Elijah (I Kings 18<sup>17</sup>, 21<sup>20</sup>), cf. John 16<sup>8ff.</sup>, and to good effect in the end (v. 13). Contrast the destructive *torments* of 9<sup>5ff.</sup>, 14<sup>10f.</sup>.

## 11

*a breath of life:* in the valley of dry bones, which signified Israel's captivity in Babylon, 'the breath came into them, and they lived, and stood upon their feet, an exceedingly great army' (Ezek. 37<sup>10</sup>). Faithful Christians, confronted by the power of the Roman world, may well have felt 'our bones are dried up, and our hope is lost' (37<sup>11</sup>).

*great fear fell on those who saw them:* as at Jesus' resurrection (Matt. 28<sup>4</sup>).

## 12

*Come up hither:* see on 4<sup>1</sup>.

*They went up to heaven in a cloud:* lit. *the cloud*, the traditional vehicle of assumption, as for Jesus (Acts 1<sup>9</sup>, cf. I Thess. 4<sup>17</sup>). Elijah was *taken up* (II Kings 2<sup>11</sup>), and tradition embroidered Moses' mysterious death (Deut. 34<sup>5f.</sup>) on similar lines. Clouds are also the vehicle of the coming of the Son of man.

*in the sight of their foes:* lit. 'and their foes *saw* them'. This *seeing* has been emphasized in vv. 9 and 11: John is perhaps applying to them the prophecy of Zech. 12<sup>10</sup>, 'when they look on him whom they have pierced, they shall mourn for him', which he has already applied to the coming of Jesus *with the clouds* (1<sup>7</sup>; cf. Acts 1<sup>11</sup>), and which the Fourth Gospel applied to the crucifixion (19<sup>37</sup>). The description of this coming has its proper place in John's plan in ch. 19; it is adumbrated in the picture of 'one like a son of man' at 14<sup>14-16</sup>, again in connection with the reward of those who have died in his service (14<sup>13</sup>). See again Matt. 24<sup>14</sup>: the end does not come apart from faithful witness.

## 13

*a great earthquake:* as at Jesus' death, and resurrection (Matt. 27<sup>51-54</sup>, 28<sup>2</sup>). *Earthquake* in the OT commonly expresses the shaking of the godless world's foundations, and forms part of the climax of each of

John's series of plagues (6¹², 8⁵, 11¹⁹, 16¹⁸); cf. the article by R. J. Bauckham (see note g on 6¹²⁻¹⁷).

*a tenth of the city fell; seven thousand people were killed:* factually the numbers make sense – the population of Jerusalem may well have been about 70,000. They may have had symbolical significance for John (see Caird, p. 140), but the main point is that it is again a limited destruction as with the plagues of chs. 6, 8 and 9. But whereas the plagues hardened men, *witness* thus consummated breaks down their resistance; the total destruction by plagues (16¹⁹) is balanced by the total destruction by the word (19²¹). But is it barren remorse, as at Wisd. 5¹⁻¹⁴, or constructive repentance? We raised the same question at 1⁷ over the 'mourning' of Zechariah, which has just been hinted at. *Terrified* might indicate only the barren reaction of Felix (Acts 24²⁵), but the same word is used of the effect of Jesus' resurrection on the women and disciples (Luke 24⁵, ³⁷); and *gave glory to God* regularly expresses repentance in the OT; e.g. the Philistines, already alluded to at v. 6, are told by their priests to 'give glory to the God of Israel . . . Why should you harden your hearts as the Egyptians . . .?', and to return the captured ark (I Sam. 6⁵⁻⁸).ª John uses similar words, meaning 'turn from idols and acknowledge God', at 14⁷, and at 15⁴ (with reference to *all nations*) – contrast 16⁹, ¹¹, where men cursed the *God of heaven* for their pain.

A verdict must depend on one's reading of the book as a whole. It is often assumed that 'John was another Jonah, who would have resented the idea that the inhabitants of the great city might repent and be forgiven' (Caird, p. 139). Certainly John recognizes the possibility that men may so identify themselves with falsehood, with the beast, that they share his eternal torment (14⁹⁻¹¹, 20¹⁰⁻¹⁵, 21⁸, 22¹⁵). But his book is addressed not to the nations but to Christians who are in danger of identifying themselves with the beast, in order that they may maintain Christ's witness to the nations, for their salvation (see below on chs. 13 and 14). In his final vision the nations and their kings do (like Nebuchadnezzar, Dan. 4³⁴⁻³⁷) give glory to God in the New Jerusalem (21²⁴).

**14**

*The second woe is passed:* all that precedes has set the stage for the *third woe* – outwardly Satan's final triumph, but in reality his death-throes (12¹²).

ª For the evidence of Enoch see on 21²⁶.

The seventh trumpet blast does not in itself effect the End, but introduces the *days* (10⁷) in which it is consummated. According to one view, 11¹⁵⁻¹⁹ is the content of the seventh blast and third woe, but this heavenly liturgy is hardly comparable to the preceding woes. According to another, the third woe consists of the bowl-plagues, *the seven plagues, which are the last, for with them the wrath of God is ended* (15¹), just as the seventh unsealing expands into the trumpet-plagues; in that case the unnumbered visions of chs. 12–14 are a series of 'close-ups', which expound the inwardness of this climax.

But at 12¹², *woe to you, O earth and sea, for the devil has come down to you in great wrath,* John refers back (as we shall argue) to the *third woe* of 11¹⁴ (cf. 8¹³). If he is following the Lord's Apocalypse (see pp. 19–21), then the climax of the trumpets section should be the 'desolating sacrilege', the setting up of the kingdom of Antichrist (ch. 13); it would be odd if this were in the no-man's-land between two septets. The *bowls* in fact represent a further 'moment' in the drama (see p. 158): the collapse of the beast's city and its replacement by the City of God. It seems best, therefore, to take 12¹³–13¹⁸ as the *third woe*. As we have seen (p. 175), the *second woe* is a cul-de-sac like the plagues of Egypt: the break-through is not the bowls of wrath (which are also modelled on the Egyptian plagues), but the gospel – the witness of Jesus and his church, which lies behind the heavenly defeat of the dragon (12⁷⁻¹²) and his setting up the beast on earth (13¹ff.).

This theme is introduced by heavenly liturgy (11¹⁵⁻¹⁹; cf. 4–5, 8³⁻⁵) and followed by visions and voices (14¹ff.), which declare the eternal significance of what is unfolded; and ch. 14, like ch. 7, gives anticipatory sketches of the consummation.

^{15} *Then the seventh angel blew his trumpet, and there were loud voices in heaven saying, 'The kingdom of the world has become the kingdom of our Lord and of his Christ, and he shall reign for ever and ever.'* ^{16}*And the twenty-four elders who sit on their thrones before God fell on their faces and worshipped God,* ^{17}*saying,*

*'We give thanks to thee, Lord God almighty, who art and who wast,*
*    that thou hast taken thy great power and begun to reign,*
^{18}*The nations raged, but thy wrath came*
*    and the time for the dead to be judged,*
*for rewarding thy servants, the prophets and saints,*
*    and those who fear thy name, both small and great,*
*and for destroying the destroyers, of the earth.'*
^{19} *Then God's temple in heaven was opened, and the ark of his covenant was seen within his temple; and there were flashes of lightning, loud noises, peals of thunder, an earthquake, and heavy hail.*

The fulfilling of *the mystery of God* (10^7) is celebrated as the inauguration of his kingdom, one of the themes of the Jewish New Year and its trumpet-blowing: the *elders* significantly drop the future element in God's triple title (v. 17). They take up Ps. 2, the messianic enthronement psalm,[b] and sing as if all that it implies has happened, though it is not until ch. 20 that the dead are judged, the servants of God rewarded and the destroyers of the earth destroyed. The themes of Ps. 2 keep reappearing in the meantime (12^5, 14^1, 16^14, 17^18, 19^15, 19),

---

*b* Psalm 2 was probably used originally in Solomon's temple at the annual celebration of the king's accession, understood as his enthronement as God's 'son' or vice-gerent. This may have been accompanied by a ritual combat between God, represented by the king, and the powers of evil (often symbolized by a dragon), a triumphal procession and a 'sacred marriage', in line with the Near Eastern 'myth and ritual' pattern investigated by S. H. Hooke. Many of its elements recur in the apocalyptic writings, especially Rev.; see his essay in *The Labyrinth* (Introduction, p. 41 note *k*). After the demise of the monarchy Ps. 2 was referred to the future enthronement of the King Messiah, and is frequently cited in the NT.

and the divine irony (Ps. 2$^4$) is seen in the Satanic parodies which God allows.

*Destroying the destroyers* (v. 18; cf. 19$^2$) is the key to the destructiveness of Revelation. John's concern is essentially constructive. God is Creator and Redeemer (chs. 4, 5, 10). and the destructions signify, as with the OT prophets, God allowing his work in creation to be undone in order that the earth may be purged and remade (chs. 21-22; see on 6$^{12-17}$). And it is not as if God were himself descending to the level of the destroyers: he allows their work to have its effects (human free-will), but his own direct action is different. The *ark of the covenant* (v. 19) evokes the redemption from Egypt, and the Day of Atonement for which the New Year trumpets prepared, when God wipes out the sins of the repentant.

༄༅

15

*The kingdom of the world . . .:* NEB 'the sovereignty of the world has passed to our Lord . . .', bringing out the dynamic sense of *basileia*; cf. Ps. 47$^{5-8}$. The sovereignty of Satan has been terminated at source, even if externally it has achieved its summit (12$^{7-12}$).

*our Lord and his Christ:* see notes on 1$^{4f.}$ and 12$^{10}$.

16

*the twenty-four elders:* see on 4$^4$.

17

*Lord God almighty, who art and who wast:* John's favourite formula (see on 1$^8$), but omitting *who is to come* (cf. 10$^7$).

*hast taken thy great power:* God had allowed satanic authority in the world (Luke 4$^6$). His resumption of 'direct rule', so to speak, dates from the birth of Jesus (Rev. 12$^{1ff.}$; cf. Matt. 2$^{2ff.}$, Luke 1$^{32ff.}$, 2$^{11ff.}$); there is a period of overlap, but the issue for which Jesus taught his disciples to pray (Matt. 6$^{9f.}$) is, since the victory of the Lamb, secured and can be celebrated already in the heavenly (as in the earthly) eucharist or *giving of thanks* (v. 17).

18

*the nations raged:* Greek *ōrgisthēsan*, an allusion to the LXX version of

Ps. 2$^1$ (cf. Acts 4$^{25}$) phrased so as to introduce an allusion to Ps. 2$^5$: *Thy wrath (orgē) came*. This seems to be an anticipatory glimpse forward, like 7$^{9-17}$. God is Alpha and Omega (1$^8$), and the *elders* who share his perspective can praise him for the events of chs. 19 and 20 as if they had already happened.

*the time for the dead to be judged*: described 20$^{11}$ff..

*rewarding thy servants*: see 20$^{4-6}$, 22$^{3-5}$, $^{12}$.

*those who fear thy name*: cf. 19$^5$, quoting Pss. 113$^1$, 115$^{13}$.

*destroying the destroyers of the earth*: described at 19$^{15-21}$, 20$^{9f.}$, where it is clear that the arch-destroyers are the beast and false prophet who deceived the nations; they lie behind the *destroying mountain*, Babylon, which *destroys the whole earth* (Jer. 51$^{25}$); see on 8$^8$, 11$^6$.

### 19
*God's temple in heaven was opened*: correlative to the rending of the veil over the Holy of Holies in the earthly temple at Jesus' death, which was followed by an *earthquake* (Matt. 27$^{51f.}$); it is a symbol of God's presence available to men – fulfilled at 21$^3$.

*the ark of his covenant*: the symbol of his presence, and the place of atonement (Lev. 16$^{2}$ff., Heb. 9$^3$ff., 10$^{20}$); also the source of the Philistines' plagues (see on 11$^6$, $^{13}$) and Jericho's fall (Joshua 6$^{1-20}$): the priests marched round seven days, blowing *trumpets* and followed by the *ark*, and at their shout the walls fell down; so here the appearance of the *ark* follows the blowing of the *seven trumpets* (Farrer, p. 137).

*flashes of lightning . . .*: see on 8$^5$, and 16$^{17-21}$ (for *hail*). Each septet ends with these manifestations of the sovereignty of the divine throne (4$^5$).

12$^{1-6}$  THE WOMAN AND THE DRAGON

12 *And a great portent appeared in heaven, a woman clothed with the sun, with the moon under her feet, and on her head a crown of twelve stars;*

²*she was with child and she cried out in her pangs of birth, in anguish for delivery.* ³*And another portent appeared in heaven; behold a great red dragon, with seven heads and ten horns, and seven diadems upon his heads.* ⁴*His tail swept down a third of the stars of heaven, and cast them to the earth. And the dragon stood before the woman who was about to bear a child, that he might devour her child when she brought it forth;* ⁵*she brought forth a male child, one who is to rule all the nations with a rod of iron, but her child was caught up to God and to his throne,* ⁶*and the woman fled into the wilderness, where she has a place prepared by God, in which to be nourished for one thousand two hundred and sixty days.*

The enthronement psalm cited at 11¹⁸ goes on: 'The Lord said to me, You are my son; today I have begotten you . . . I will give you the nations as your inheritance . . . you shall shepherd them with a rod of iron' (Ps. 27⁻⁹ LXX). We are told here of the Redeemer's birth and enthronement, but the main theme is the Woman, the community which gives him birth – John's whole message is for that same community which, somewhat waveringly, maintains his testimony (v. 17).

The imagery contains a multiplicity of allusion which is remarkable even for John. Striking parallels have been found in Babylonian, Persian, Egyptian and Greek mythology, and in astrological lore; Beasley-Murray gives an excellent survey (pp. 191–7). John was well aware of the mythologies influential in the Graeco-Roman world (e.g. the story of Leto and Apollo – see on 9¹¹), and of the links between the goddess Roma and the Great Mother (Cybele)ᶜ of the local cults, links exploited in the imperial coinage. Cosmic myths of light attacked by darkness, summer by winter and life by death, and of the young god's victory over the dragon, are in the background. But the dominant imagery is biblical, and the dominant themes (as in chs. 4 and 5) are from Genesis – the serpent's defeat of the woman reversed (Gen. 3¹⁵⁻²⁰) – and from Exodus: God's historical defeat of the dragon Egypt and rescue of his people.

The true centre is the Woman, whose seed bruises the dragon's head (cf. 13³) and on whose seed the dragon makes war (v. 17, Gen. 3¹⁵⁻²⁰). She is the bride of Yahweh (S. of Sol. 6⁴′ ¹⁰); Zion out of whom will

---

ᶜ See P. Touilleux, *L'Apocalypse et les cultes de Domitien et de Cybele*, Paris 1935, pp. 109–31.

come the Messiah (cf. II Esd. 9$^{38}$–10$^{55}$). She is Mary, but only in so far as Mary embodies faithful Israel, and mothers the Messiah and his community (John 19$^{26f.}$). She is the church, but only in so far as the church is continuous with God's people from the beginning and with Eve, 'the mother of all living' (Gen. 3$^{20}$).

The attempt to destroy the child by the Power of whom he is the destined destroyer is again a familiar theme – as in the story of Herod (Matt. 2$^{1ff.}$). But the *catching up to God* (v. 5) has nothing to do with the flight to Egypt. The whole life of Jesus[d] from conception to ascension is condensed in these few words. This child was not physically preserved to return and destroy the usurper: humanly speaking he was swallowed by the dragon; his road to safety was the cross. Nor is his return to defeat the usurper simply awaited: it has already been accomplished – that is the burden of the next section (vv. 7–12). In the meantime the woman is safe in *the wilderness*, like Israel after the exodus, for the significant period of 1260 days.

ॐ

1

*A great portent appeared in heaven:* the tableau suggests a Greek myth in which the characters are elevated to the stars – though here they return to earth to carry on their story. No doubt a genuine vision lies behind, but the details evoke scriptural passages, like Joseph's dream, in which the sun and the moon and the eleven stars bowed down to him (Gen. 37$^9$), and the bride in the Song of Solomon (6$^{10}$) 'like the dawn, fair as the moon, bright as the sun, terrible as an army with banners'.

*A woman clothed with the sun . . .:* the ideal glorified Israel. Her celestial array finds point later in the contrast between the *woman arrayed in purple and scarlet* who is Rome (17$^4$, 18$^{16}$), and *the Bride, the holy city Jerusalem,* coming down with *the glory of God* (21$^{10}$). 'The coinage . . . declared that Roma was the new queen of the gods and mother of the world's saviour. John is going to portray her as the new Jezebel, the seducer of the world, clad in all the finery of earth. She who claims to be queen of earth (18$^7$) must be seen to be a travesty of the resplendent Queen of Heaven' (Caird, p. 148).

*d* See Introduction, p. 9 note *d*. For the connection with vv. 7–12, see Farrer, pp. 56f. For Jung on woman and child, see pp. 43f.

**2**

*she was with child and she cried out in her pangs* . . .: the closest parallels are with scripture: Eve, who is to bring forth children in pain (Gen. 3¹⁶); the Immanuel prophecy (Isa. 7¹⁴); Israel in travail, in respect of 'the beloved', i.e. the Messiah (Isa. 26¹⁷ LXX – followed by the smiting of the *serpent* or *dragon* Leviathan, 27¹); Zion bringing forth a male child (Isa. 66⁷), indeed many sons (66⁸), in virtue of God's new creation (65¹⁷ᶠᶠ·, 66²²).

In other words John is evoking the idea of Zion as mother of many sons, like Eve, in the new age (cf. Ps. 87), but this by virtue of bearing the Son, through bitter danger and travail (the 'birth-pangs of the Messiah')ᵉ, the Man who is to smite the dragon (Gen. 3¹⁵, Isa. 27¹) and *shepherd the nations* (v. 5 = Ps. 29 LXX).

**3**

*a great red dragon: drakōn* means serpent, and is used by LXX for the sea-monster Leviathan (as at Isa. 27¹). His appearance links him with the *scarlet* beast of 17³, and the ten-horned beast of Dan. 7⁷· ²⁰ – the model for the *seven-headed* beast which the dragon summons from the sea (Rev. 13¹). Daniel's beasts also rise from the sea (7²ᶠᶠ·): they represent God's primeval enemy, the dragon of watery chaos, Tiamat, Leviathanᶠ (many-headed according to Ps. 74¹⁴), or Rahab (= Pride), which the Jews saw embodied in the idolatrous empires which oppressed them – Egypt, called Rahab by the prophets (Isa. 30⁷, 51⁹, Ezek. 29³, 32²), Babylon (Jer. 51³⁴· ³⁶) and more lately Rome, in the person of Pompey (Psalms of Solomon 2²⁹).

**4**

*His tail swept down a third of the stars:* cf. Dan. 8¹⁰. A *third* recalls the earlier trumpet blasts (8⁷⁻¹²), and the destruction of cosmic order by the new Babylon's idolatry and violence: here is the power behind it.

*that he might devour her child:* cf. Moses threatened by Pharaoh, and

---

*e* 'Birth-pangs of the Messiah': a Jewish metaphor for the terrible sufferings which must precede his advent; cf. Matt. 24⁸ par.

*f* Leviathan had seven heads according to an Ugaritic text (F. F. Bruce, *This is That*, Paternoster Press 1968, p. 44). The ancient Mesopotamian and Canaanite mythology lived on, and is often alluded to in the OT; it was probably still alive in John's time; see S. H. Hooke in *The Labyrinth* (see Introduction, p. 41 note *k* above), pp. 229–33.

Jesus by Herod, against the background of the enmity between the serpent and the woman's seed (Gen. $3^{15}$).

5

*a male child*: cf. Isa. $66^7$ LXX. Pharaoh ordered the drowning of the male Israelite babies (Ex. $1^{15}-2^{10}$).

*to rule all the nations with a rod of iron*: these words from Ps. $2^9$, the messianic enthronement psalm quoted at $11^{18}$, are repeated at the Son's return ($19^{15}$). See too the promise to the faithful at Thyatira, who do not hold the teaching of Jezebel, the deep things of Satan ($2^{24-27}$): the *rest* of the true woman's *offspring* (v. 17) share both his sufferings and his sovereignty.

*Rule* is *poimainein*, lit. 'shepherd', as in the LXX of Ps. $2^9$, and Micah $5^{2-4}$, quoted at Matt. $2^6$. For the irony of shepherding with *a rod of iron*, see on $2^{27}$ (p. 93).

*but her child was caught up to God and to his throne*: this covers allusively Jesus' death and exaltation. In John's Gospel he is 'lifted up' or 'glorified' on the cross, and this is linked with the expulsion of 'the ruler of this world' (John $12^{31-33}$; cf. Rev. $12^{7-11}$); according to Luke he is 'taken up', like Moses and Elijah (Luke $9^{31, 51}$, Acts $1^9$), and exalted at God's right hand (Acts $2^{33-36}$). It may seem strange that his death and resurrection,[g] normally the centre of the story, are not actually mentioned, but John is writing for the church, which knows it, and here the church is the centre of the story – attacked by Satan ($2^{13}$) and called to share in Jesus' sacrifice by its witness. Its struggle is therefore shown to be primeval, its victory, which is his, already achieved. The words *and to his throne* recall the promise to the *conqueror* at Laodicea ($3^{21}$). Contrast Satan's *throne*, threatening the church at Pergamum ($2^{13}$).

6

*and the woman fled into the wilderness*: cf. v. 14. In the myths the *woman* drops out of the story once her child is safely born, but John is concerned with God's miraculous provision for his witness people through the ages. The *wilderness* is where Israel was guided by *cloud* and *fire* (cf. $10^1$)

g But Ps. 2, in which 'begetting' is a metaphor for the enthronement of the king, is quoted in reference (seemingly) to the resurrection at Acts $13^{33}$; cf. Rom. $1^4$.

and *nourished* for forty-two years with *manna* (cf. the promise to the *conqueror* at Pergamum, 2¹⁷), after escaping from the dragon Egypt. It is the place of Israel's *first love* for Yahweh (Jer. 2²; see on Rev. 2⁴, p. 79), over against the *great city*, the place of Jezebel's seductions. See also on 17³.

*a place prepared:* cf. John 14²ᶠ·, and God's provision for Elijah (I Kings 17²⁻⁴, ⁸ᶠ·) in the three-and-a-half year drought – see on 11⁶.

*one thousand two hundred and sixty days:* cf. 11²ᶠ·, 12¹⁴, 13⁵; see p. 182 above. Christians suffer, but the church is preserved.

## 12<sup>7-12</sup>   THE EXPULSION OF THE DRAGON

⁷*Now war arose in heaven, Michael and his angels fighting against the dragon; and the dragon and his angels fought,* ⁸*but they were defeated and there was no longer any place for them in heaven.* ⁹*And the great dragon was thrown down, that ancient serpent, who is called the Devil and Satan, the deceiver of the whole world – he was thrown down to the earth, and his angels were thrown down with him.* ¹⁰*And I heard a loud voice in heaven, saying, 'Now the salvation and the power and the kingdom of our God and the authority of his Christ have come, for the accuser of our brethren has been thrown down, who accuses them day and night before our God.* ¹¹*And they have conquered him by the blood of the Lamb and by the word of their testimony, for they loved not their lives even unto death.* ¹²*Rejoice then, O heaven and you that dwell therein! But woe to you, O earth and sea, for the devil has come down to you in great wrath, because he knows that his time is short!'*

We now learn more about the woman's adversary and his activities. But (i) what is the meaning of *war in heaven*? (ii) How is the victory Michael's, not Christ's? And (iii) why does it bring *woe* to the earth? Again what John *hears* (vv. 10–12) gives the inner meaning of what he *sees* (vv. 7–9); see on 5⁵ᶠ·, 7⁴, ⁹.

(i) The *war* is not military but moral and legal: Satan is the *accuser of our brethren* (v. 10). *Satan* means in Hebrew 'adversary', in a legal sense, and he has his 'place in heaven' as a kind of Public Prosecutor (Zech. $3^{1\text{ff.}}$); in rabbinic thought he is the 'attribute of justice' in God over against the 'attribute of mercy'. But he is also *agent provocateur* (I Chron. $21^1$; Job 1; 2), and undergoes a 'rake's progress', as Caird puts it,[h] so that he ends up the personification of enmity to God and his people, the leader of all the powers of evil; both *deceiver* and *accuser* of men, both instigator and punisher of sin (see on $9^{1\text{ff.}}$).

But because he represents justice he cannot simply be removed by military force; there is conflict in heaven itself. As long as there are sinners to be accused, he has his 'place' (Caird, p. 155).

(ii) His defeat therefore is not military but forensic: *nikan* 'to conquer' has both connotations (cf. Ps. $51^4$ as quoted at Rom. $3^4$). *They have conquered him by the blood of the Lamb* (John was told that the military Lion of Judah had *conquered*, and saw a *slaughtered Lamb*, $5^{5\text{f.}}$). The victory then is not Michael's but Christ's. Michael is the defending barrister, who pleads Christ's sacrifice 'for the sin of the whole world' (I John $2^2$) against the *deceiver of the whole world*. Or in Caird's metaphor he 'is not the field officer who does the actual fighting, but the staff officer who is able to remove Satan's flag from the heavenly map because the real victory has been won on Calvary' (p. 154) – see p. 113 above.

But how can sinners be rendered innocent by another's death? Only if it is also somehow theirs: 'there is therefore now no condemnation for those who are in Christ Jesus' (Rom. $8^1$). He is the new Adam, and his brethren (Rom. $8^{29}$), fellow-*offspring* of the *woman* (v. 17), have *conquered* their accuser by his *blood*, and *by the word of their testimony, for they loved not their lives even unto death* (v. 11). It is Paul's doctrine of 'justification by faith' in pictorial form.

(iii) Why cannot all live happily ever after? Because sin is not only unbelief and alienation from God, which his gracious initiative can heal: it has set up a counter-reality, a vicious circle of consequence for a prose version of which we can again look to Romans ($1^{18-32}$). Paul calls it 'the wrath of God', in that God 'hands men over' to the

h *Principalities and Powers*, pp. 31ff.

consequences of ignoring him. For John it is also Satan's wrath (v. 12), in that he is the executor; see on 6[16] (p. 144) and 14[8-11] (p. 227). This *wrath* must run its course, and the brunt is borne by Christ's brethren, who maintain his *testimony* (v. 17; cf. I Tim. 6[12-14], Col. 1[24]), but its *time is short* (three and a half!). Its violence is Satan's death throes.

A final point about the burst of thanksgiving: according to Paul refusal to acknowledge God and give him glory and thanks lies behind idolatry, the root sin (Rom. 1[21-23], contrast 4[20-22]), and Ignatius told the Ephesians (13[1], *ECW*, p. 79) to 'meet more often to give thanks and glory to God, for when you meet frequently, Satan's powers are thrown down and his destructiveness is nullified in the harmony of your faith'. Liturgy plays the part it does in Revelation because of the conviction that what men do in their worship lies behind what they do in the world: if God is truly acknowledged, the *war* at the heart of things is resolved.

נצח

### 7
*war arose in heaven:* some think of the fallen *stars* (v. 4) as the dragon's *angels*, storming heaven like the Titans attacking Mount Olympus; cf. Isa. 14[13f.]. But this *war* is shown by v. 10 to be a conflict *in* heaven over the fate of man; cf. Satan's conflict with Michael over the body of Moses (Jude 9).

*Michael and his angels: Michael* (= 'who is like God?') was perhaps the most important figure in contemporary Judaism after God – chief of the archangels, promulgator of the law, captain of God's army, Israel's champion and advocate in court (cf. Dan. 10[13, 21], 12[1]). For Christians Jesus replaced Michael and took over his functions – he is our advocate in heaven, I John 2[1ff.]. Here, while Jesus is on the cross, Michael must still function in heaven[i] – but it is, so to speak, a mopping-up operation.

### 8
*they were defeated:* lit. 'had no strength', cf. Gen. 32[25].

*no longer any place for them:* cf. 20[11] – an allusion to Dan. 2[35].

[i] For Michael cf. the Qumran *War Rule*, where a correspondence between heavenly and earthly events is also found: 'He will raise up the kingdom of Michael in the midst of the gods, and the realm of Israel in the midst of all flesh' (1QM xvii 7f.; Vermes, p. 146).

9

*the great dragon was thrown down:* see on v. 3, and see John 12$^{31-33}$ and Luke 10$^{18}$. It is the language of falling stars (= angels): the physical damage they can do is a symbol of the evil effected by a spiritual fall – see on 2$^4$, 8$^8$–9$^1$.

*that ancient serpent:* cf. 20$^2$ – identifying him with the *serpent* of Gen. 3; cf. Isa. 27$^1$. *Devil* (*diabolos*) means 'informer', 'slanderer'.

*deceiver of the whole world:* cf. 16$^{14}$, 20$^3$, $^8$, II Thess. 2$^{9ff.}$. In Jewish thought the nations were each allotted to one of the 'sons of God' or angels, whereas Israel was God's own portion (Deut. 32$^{8f.}$) – in Dan. 10$^{13ff.}$ Michael acts for him. These 'princes' had their authority from God (Rom. 13$^{1ff.}$), but in so far as the nations were idolatrous and hostile to God and his people, their angels were thought of as rebellious and deceiving spirits, under Satan their chief, who had gone beyond their commission (see on 8$^9$; cf. Luke 4$^{5-8}$). The symbolism reflects the ambivalence inherent in human institutions: both God-given and God-resistant, vehicles of both illumination and deception.

10

*Now: now* and *henceforth* (14$^{13}$) are key NT words (see Rissi, *Time*, pp. 29f.). They refer not to the time of writing but to the cross as the turning point in world history (cf. Matt. 26$^{64}$, John 12$^{31}$, Rom. 5$^{11}$, 8$^1$) – the longed-for time when God's 'direct rule' replaces Satan's abuse of his powers, and *authority* passes to God's *Christ* (through his refusing to follow Satan, Luke 4$^{5-8}$). Christ is now enthroned at God's right hand, but on earth the usurping *authorities* must still be fought (I Cor. 15$^{24-26}$, Eph. 6$^{12-17}$, I Peter 5$^{8f.}$); see on v. 17.

*his Christ:* cf. 11$^{15}$ comment on 1$^{4f.}$. *Christos* = anointed, Hebrew *Messiah*, quickly became merely a proper name in the Greek-speaking churches, but John is well aware of its meaning. Jesus is the fulfilment of the messianic hope, but only through suffering, which he shares with his church, the messianic community; cf. 20$^4$, $^6$.

*the accuser of our brethren:* the roles of deception, accusation and destruction are combined in Jewish texts (I Enoch 40$^{7ff.}$ 69$^{4ff.}$, Jubilees 1$^{20}$, 10$^{2-5}$, 48$^{25ff.}$).

*day and night before our God:* cf. 14$^{10f.}$, and contrast 4$^8$, 7$^{15}$: Satan is defeated in God's being praised *day and night*.

### 11

*they have conquered:* see on 2$^7$; contrast Satan's conquering (11$^7$, 13$^7$).

*by the blood of the Lamb:* see on 5$^9$, 7$^{14}$ and 22$^{14}$. It is a picture of 'justification' (Rom. 3$^{24}$) – 'faith' appears in the *word* of *their testimony*; see on v. 17.

*loved not their lives:* cf. John 12$^{25}$, Mark 8$^{35}$ and parallels. *Even unto death* picks up the words to Smyrna (2$^{10}$).

### 12

*Rejoice then, O heaven:* or 'keep festival'; cf. 18$^{20}$ and contrast 11$^{10}$.

*But woe to you, O earth and sea:* the *third woe*, following the seventh trumpet (11$^{14f.}$). Contrast Isa. 49$^{13}$, 'Sing for joy, O heavens, and exult, O earth . . . for the Lord has comforted his people.' The justification of sinners and the devil's expulsion do not lead to earthly bliss, but to the setting up of the kingdom of the beast (13$^{1ff.}$). It has been objected that this cannot be the *third woe*, because it affects the church (v. 17) not the 'earth-dwellers' (8$^{13}$); the third woe, like the first and second, should be 'a terrible supernatural agency working in the visible world and inflicting agony and horror on the enemies of God' (Beckwith, p. 669). But the whole point is that though the 'earth-dwellers' *take* it for bliss (11$^{10}$, 13$^{3ff.}$), it is in fact their deadliest plague (14$^{9-11}$; cf. II Thess. 2$^{8-12}$).

## 12$^{13-17}$     THE WOMAN AND THE DRAGON – CONTINUED

$^{13}$*And when the dragon saw that he had been thrown down to the earth, he pursued the woman who had borne the male child.* $^{14}$*But the woman was given the two wings of the great eagle that she might fly from the serpent into the wilderness, to the place where she is to be nourished for a time, and times, and half a time.* $^{15}$*The serpent poured water like a river out of his mouth after the woman, to sweep her away with the flood.* ¹⁶*But the earth came to the help of the woman, and the earth opened its mouth and swallowed the river which the dragon had poured from his mouth.*¹⁷*Then the dragon was angry with the woman, and went off to make war on the rest of her offspring, on those who keep the commandments of God and bear testimony to Jesus. And he stood\* on the sand of the sea.*

\* Other ancient authorities read *And I stood*, connecting the sentence with 13.1

The woman's offspring has bruised the serpent's head (cf. 13³). The serpent, having *pursued* the woman to no effect, turns against the *rest of her offspring*, to bruise its heel, and this operation against the church turns out to be the earth-dwellers' crowning disaster. Israel, the mother of the Messiah, now appears as God's Israel, the church, mother of the 'many brethren' of whom he is 'the first-born' (Rom. 8²⁹, Gal. 6¹⁶). The symbolic link is no doubt Mary. The *anguish* of her travail was repeated at the cross; cf. Luke 2³⁵. Jesus, seeing his mother and the disciple he loved standing near, said 'Woman, behold your son' and to the disciple, 'Behold your mother' (John 19²⁶f.). But Gen. 3¹⁵⁻²⁰ dominates this chapter. The *woman* is described in terms of Eve, and represents primarily the people of God. And this, we may add, in no exclusive sense; not over against humanity but as the nucleus of true humanity. Eve is the 'mother of all living', though only a remnant now acknowledge their affiliation (see on 14¹⁻⁵).

The model for her flight is again the exodus story. God brought his people on *eagles' wings* into the *wilderness* (Ex. 19⁴, Deut. 32¹¹), where they were nourished for *forty-two* years. The *river-flood* evokes Pharaoh's attempt to destroy male Israelites in the river (Ex. 1²²) and his pursuit of Israel between the waters of the Red Sea (Ex. 14²¹ff.). Finally the dragon's next move, the sending of the two *beasts* (13¹, ¹¹), corresponds with the test which met Israel at the entry to the promised land, at the hands of Balak and Balaam, as the letter to Pergamum has already warned (see p. 89).

The *flight* motif may, like the motifs of 11¹f., have its origin in the events of the Jewish war with Rome – the Jerusalem church's flight to Pella recorded by Eusebius (*Hist. Eccl.* III, 5; Stevenson, pp. 6f.)

– but is now, like $11^{1f.}$, entirely symbolic; indeed it symbolizes the same thing. The *woman*, like the *temple*, is the inward church and invulnerable; but the outward church, the *rest of her offspring*, is given over to the dragon's minions, like the *court outside* ($11^1$). The *wilderness*, like the *great city*, has no precise place on the map (see on v. 6): John is not counselling physical withdrawal from the world (any more than at $18^4$) – witness must be given in *the street of the great city* ($11^8$). And the time of the sojourn cannot be plotted on a date-chart: *a time, times and half a time* refers us to Daniel ($7^{25}$, $12^7$), it denotes the reign of evil as permitted, limited and overcome by God (see pp. 182f. on three and a half).

In this chapter are the clearest pointers to astrological symbolism (see Farrer, p. 148).[j] John's contemporaries were certainly versed in zodiacal lore and assumed that earthly destinies were determined by, and reflected in, the stars. But this merely reinforces the general point about *heaven* (see p. 16), so we may be excused from trying to explain the obscure by the (to us) more obscure.

☙

**13**

*he pursued:* like Pharaoh (Ex. $14^8$); the word also means 'persecute'. For *the woman*, see on $12^{1-6}$.

*the two wings of the great eagle:* see Ex. $19^4$, Deut. $32^{11}$.

*the wilderness:* see on v. 6, and on $17^3$.

**15**

*water like a river:* the dragon is a water-monster, and 'waters' often signify evil – 'the floods of Belial assailed me' (Ps. $18^4$).

*out of his mouth:* the phrase, repeated in v. 16, suggests that the *flood* is Satan's 'river of lies' (Caird); cf. $16^{13}$, and contrast the sword issuing from the *mouth* of the Son of man ($1^{16}$ etc.), and the fire from the *mouth* of the two witnesses ($11^6$), which represents the word and Spirit of truth.

[j] E.g. Virgo escaping from the claws of Scorpio is rescued by *the* Eagle (NB the article in v. 14), who has replaced the ill-omened Scorpion among the *four creatures* (see on $4^{6ff.}$), which represent the four faces of the sky. The Milky Way, which goes up from the Scorpion and sweeps over the Eagle, is the model for the *river* (v. 15).

16

*the earth came to the help of the woman:* the *earth* to which Satan has come down (v. 12) does not receive him as her inhabitants do (13$^{4, 8}$): she *opens her mouth to swallow* his lies. The immediate reference may be to Ex. 15$^{12k}$ and Num. 16$^{30}$, but the best commentary is Wisd. 1$^{13-16}$, 2$^{23f}$. The *earth* is created by God, and good; Satan is derivative and destructive, a parody given reality by those who 'take his part'.

17

*the dragon was angry:* lit. 'raged' (ōrgisthē, cf. 11$^{18}$). The *great wrath* of v. 12 bursts out in *war* (cf. 11$^7$, 13$^7$, Dan. 11$^{30ff}$.) against the woman's *offspring,* lit. 'seed' (*sperma*); cf. Gen. 3$^{15}$, 'I will put enmity between you and the woman, and between your seed and her seed; he (or it) shall bruise your head, and you shall bruise his heel.' John follows the Targum, taking the *seed* collectively: it reads 'When the sons of the woman *keep the commandments* of the law . . . they will smite you on the head (13$^3$!); when they abandon the commandments you will wound them in the heel' (cf. 9$^{3-5, 10, 19-21}$).

*the rest of her offspring:* the Greek suggests the concept of the faithful remnant, the nucleus of restoration after disaster (cf. Isa. 6$^{13}$ RSV; Rom. 9$^{27-29}$). But the remnant stands only by faith and obedience. The *wilderness* is also the place of temptation and disobedience, and the 'wilderness generation' was used as a warning to Christians over-confident of their exodus victory (I Cor. 10$^{1-13}$, Heb. 3$^7$-4$^{13}$).

*testimony to Jesus:* lit. *of* Jesus. The parallel *commandments of God* shows this is the primary meaning (the Greek can mean both) – maintaining the *testimony* Jesus bore (cf. I Tim. 6$^{13}$; see on 1$^2$).

*And he stood on the sand of the sea:* many ancient authorities read *I stood . . .,* as the first words of 13$^1$, but nowhere else does the seer change position without instructions, and the evidence for *he stood* is weightier. Satan summons from the sea (= abyss, 11$^7$) his instruments. His stand is on *sand:* contrast the *Lamb* and his followers on the rock of Mount Zion (14$^1$; cf. Matt. 7$^{24-27}$, 16$^{18}$?).

k When God brought back the Red Sea over the pursuing Egyptians, 'the waters swallowed them'. The Targum paraphrase has Rev.'s actual wording, 'the earth opened its mouth and swallowed them' (McNamara, *Palestinian Targum,* p. 226).

**13** *And I saw a beast rising out of the sea, with ten horns and seven heads, with ten diadems upon its horns and a blasphemous name upon its heads.* <sup>2</sup>*And the beast that I saw was like a leopard, its feet were like a bear's, and its mouth was like a lion's mouth. And to it the dragon gave his power and his throne and great authority.* <sup>3</sup>*One of its heads seemed to have a mortal wound, but its mortal wound was healed, and the whole earth followed the beast with wonder.* <sup>4</sup>*Men worshipped the dragon, for he had given his authority to the beast, and they worshipped the beast, saying, 'Who is like the beast, and who can fight against it?'*

<sup>5</sup>*And the beast was given a mouth uttering haughty and blasphemous words, and it was allowed to exercise authority for forty-two months;* <sup>6</sup>*it opened its mouth to utter blasphemies against God, blaspheming his name and his dwelling, that is, those who dwell in heaven.* <sup>7</sup>*Also it was allowed to make war on the saints and to conquer them.** And authority was given it over every tribe and people and tongue and nation,* <sup>8</sup>*and all who dwell on earth will worship it, every one whose name has not been written before the foundation of the world in the book of life of the Lamb that was slain.* <sup>9</sup>*If any one has an ear, let him hear:*
<sup>10</sup>*If any one is to be taken captive,*

  *to captivity he goes;*
*if any one slays with the sword,*

  *with the sword must he be slain.*
*Here is a call for the endurance and faith of the saints.*

\* Other ancient authorities omit this sentence.

We are now shown the nature both of Satan's attack on the woman's *offspring* ($12^{17}$) and of the *third woe* ($12^{12}$), the climactic disaster for the earth and its inhabitants. This is not genuine vision but a predictive allegory woven from a variety of threads; the *beast* itself is a composite of the four beasts and 'little horn' of Dan. 7, as artificial as the scorpion-locusts of the *first woe* ($9^{1-11}$) and the lion-cavalry of the second ($9^{16-19}$).

The allegory is usually decoded as the Roman empire, personified in its *heads*, blasphemously demanding worship and persecuting those who stand by the true God; the *beast* from *the earth* then represents the emperor cult's local propagandists. The linked allegory in $17^{9-17}$ seems to confirm it. But these verses may be a later interpolation, giving a political interpretation of what was originally spiritual (Rissi, *Time and History*, pp. 75–83), and both chapters in any case admit of an entirely spiritual understanding (Lohmeyer; Minear, pp. 113–27, 235–60):

(i) Though the 'little horn' of Dan. 7 referred originally to Antiochus IV, the historical references of Daniel have here been ironed out. Likewise the 'desolating sacrilege' (Dan. $8^{12f.}$, $11^{30-36}$), which is at the centre of the Lord's Apocalypse and provides the climax of the trumpets section in John's, is related to the Roman destruction of Jerusalem and its temple by the synoptic gospels but is spiritualized in the Johannine writings: the true temple, the church, is desecrated by false teaching and schism within (I John $2^{18ff.}$, $4^3$, II John$^7$); and the trampling of Jerusalem has been transferred by our John to the church ($11^{1f.}$). And in II Thess. $2^{3-7}$ the Antichrist is a demonic figure of lawlessness (remarkably like the *beast*) whose appearance from beyond history is restrained for the time by (as most commentators take it) the Roman empire itself.

(ii) In the Lord's Apocalypse the 'sacrilege' and 'tribulation' are linked with the appearance of 'false Christs and false prophets' (Matt. $24^{24}$). 'False prophet' is the designation of the second *beast* (v. 11) in later chapters; the first *beast*, then, is a parody of the true Christ, and all the supposed references to Rome and the emperor cult can be taken as part of this parody, which dominates the chapter and the rest of the book.

The *beast's* most striking feature, the *head healed* from its *mortal wound* (vv. 3, 12, 14), is a test case. On the 'Roman' view this refers to the myth of *Nero redivivus* ('come back to life'). He stabbed himself in the throat in AD 68, but at once there were rumours that he was not really dead, and later it was believed that he would return from the dead with a demonic army of vengeance. But is not this too trivial? *Beast* and *head* are at one with the *dragon* (v. 2): how could Nero's suicide be a death-blow to him? Only Christ's life and death could qualify, as ch. 12 has already told us, and the wounded head must, in the light of 12$^{17}$, refer primarily to God's words to the serpent 'her seed shall bruise your head' (Gen. 3$^{15}$). The *beast*, like the *great city* (11$^8$), personifies all opposition to God and his people from the beginning, and apes the true Man's death and resurrection.

But as the commentary will show, references to Rome and the emperor cult are plausible and pervasive. In ancient thought political institutions and the spiritual powers behind them were inseparable.[1] Pergamum was an example, as the letter to it confirms (see on 2$^{12-17}$). Pergamum is *Satan's throne* (2$^{13}$, 13$^2$), both as provincial capital and as centre of pagan religion. There the faithful witness, Antipas, was killed, presumably by Caesar's sword (cf. 13$^{7, 15}$), and there Balak, the heathen king, and Balaam, the false prophet, trip Christians into idolatry and immorality (and thus into the camp of the earth-dwellers), just as they tripped Israel in the wilderness (see p. 89 above).

So the *beast* is (at this moment) the Roman empire, but its real threat to the church is not its sword, but its divine pretensions supported from within the church, which may lead Christians to take the wrong side when the final attack on the saints comes (v. 7), and thus expose them to a more deadly sword (2$^{12, 16}$). See on 13$^{11ff.}$ for the Nicolaitan position – cf. Dan. 11$^{30-36}$. Likewise the supreme disaster for the earth-dwellers is the Roman empire which, as the inscriptions show, they take to be their supreme blessing. For it involves them in a love of darkness and hatred of the light which must bring a recoil worse than the scorpion's sting (9$^{5f.}$, 14$^{9-11}$).

It is usually assumed that the 'earth-dwellers' are the non-Christians, who lack God's *seal* (9$^4$). But they must also include those who compromise it (cf. 2$^{16}$ and 19$^{21}$): thus the call to discernment (v. 9) and fidelity (v. 10). The challenge, *If any one has an ear . . .*, as on the lips of Jesus and in the letters to the churches, indicates not inability to understand but unwillingness to listen and act. Christians must accept what lies ahead, as Jesus accepted his 'cup', without recourse to the earthly sword (cf. John 18$^{11}$, Matt. 26$^{52}$; but see note *r* on 13$^{10}$ on the reading of v. 10b). This gives a final clue to John's stance. He is 'demythologizing' the Antichrist myth and referring it back to the

*1* See C. D. Morrison, *The Powers that Be*, SCM Press and Allenson 1960.

Roman state – not now as desecrating the outward temple at Jerusalem but as threatening and corrupting the true temple, the church, in unholy alliance with false Christians. But in attacking those who compromise with the state and mocking its pretensions he is careful not to align himself with the advocates of violent resistance. There is a formal parallel in the stance of the 'Confessing Church' over against the 'German Christians' who supported Hitler in the 1930s, and of von Moltke over against those who plotted to assassinate Hitler in the 1940s.[m]

‰

**1f.**

*A beast rising out of the sea:* Daniel saw four beasts rising out of the *sea* ($7^{2ff.}$ = the primeval waters = the *abyss*, Rev. $11^7$). They represented empires, and the fourth and worst (Alexander's) had *ten horns*, among which sprouted a 'little horn' – the Seleucid king Antiochus IV who in 167 BC savagely attacked the Jews, their temple and their law – with help from within Judaism (Dan. $11^{30-36}$). John's beast acts like the 'little horn' (vv. 5ff.) but has attributes of Daniel's first three – *lion, bear* and four-headed *leopard*. As a composite of all four it has a total of *seven heads*, and it is signalled by the number of its *heads* and *horns* as being the 'incarnation' of the dragon ($12^3$). The heads wear *a blasphemous name* because they represent emperors ($17^{9ff.}$) who assumed titles of divinity – Son of God, Lord and God, Saviour etc. (see Introduction, p. 25 above).

*to it the dragon gave his power and his throne:* it is at one with the *dragon*, as Jesus is at one with his Father and shares his *throne* ($3^{21}$; note also *Satan's throne* at Pergamum, $2^{13}$).

**3**

*One of its heads seemed to have a mortal wound:* the parody of Jesus continues; literally *one* (or *the first*) *of its heads was as though it had been slaughtered (esphagmenēn) to death* – cf. $5^6$. A false Nero appeared in AD 69 soon after his death (Tacitus, *Hist.* II.8), and another about ten years later was welcomed by the Parthians. For the myth of Nero's return from the dead to punish Rome's crimes against the East, see *Sibylline Oracles* IV and V, which can be dated to the end of the first

*m* See M. L. G. Balfour and J. Frisby, *Helmuth von Moltke: a Leader against Hitler*, Macmillan 1972.

century.[n] John is certainly referring to Nero, who had claimed divine honours, and had savaged the church in Rome (AD 65; Tacitus, *Annals*, XV.44, quoted in Introduction, pp. 22f.), setting a deadly precedent for the future. But in the light of ch. 12 the primary reference for the Christian reader must be to Gen. $3^{15}$, as it was for Irenaeus *c.* 180.

*its mortal wound was healed: its* in the Greek refers not to the *head* but the beast (cf. vv. 12, 14). This *first head* expresses the beast's whole character. The *healing* is on a superficial level Nero's return, but again $12^{17}$ and Gen. $3^{15}$ (in the Targum version – see p. 40) must be primary: the *obedience* and *testimony* of Jesus and his saints wound the beast's *head* (*wound* is *plēgē* = *plague* as at $11^6$); immorality and idolatry (as at Pergamum), and lack of witness (as at Laodicea) restore its power to wound their heel, and *the whole earth follows it with wonder* (contrast John $12^{19}$). Worship of that which is 'not God' releases demonic powers – see on $9^{20}$. Failure to maintain the *testimony of Jesus* is deadly not only to the church but to the world it is meant to save, by its testimony, from the dragon's deceit.

**4**
'*Who is like the beast?*': a parody of Ex. $15^{11}$, 'Who is like thee, O Lord, among the gods?'; cf. Ps. $89^6$ and many other passages, and Leviathan (Job $41^{33}$). The provincials' worship of Rome and emperor arose out of genuine gratitude for the 'salvation' they brought.

'*who can fight against it?*': the feeling no doubt of many Christians – see $14^{1ff.}$, $17^{14}$, $19^{11ff.}$ for the answer.

**5f.**
*the beast was given a mouth*: like the 'little horn' (Dan. $7^{8, 11, 20, 25}$).

*it was allowed to exercise authority for forty-two months*: but not by the dragon. He *gave* (vv. 2, 4), but *allowed* is the same word as *was given* (*edothē*) – the 'passive of divine action' (vv. 7, 14f.; cf. $9^{1, 3, 5}$). *Forty-two months* reinforces the sense of divine control (see pp. 182f.). The witnesses' *authority* was for the equivalent 1260 days, ended by the beast's appearance ($11^{3-7}$), and its *forty-two months* (= three and a half years) links

n Bo Reicke, 'Die jüdische Apokalyptik und die johanneische Tiervision', *Recherches de science religieuse* 60, 1972, pp. 181–8, gives full references. Charles, *AP* II, gives the text of the *Sibylline Oracles*.

with the time of the witnesses' defeat (11⁹, 13⁷). But it also corresponds
with the *trampling* of the outward church (11²), which is co-terminous
with the witnesses' work. That is, John sees the time from the cross
onwards as one both of being trampled and of giving witness, but
foresees a final recapitulation of this pattern which will be total and
sharp, before Christ comes (14¹⁴ᶠᶠ·; cf. II Thess. 2⁸⁻¹²).

*to exercise authority:* lit. 'it was given authority to act (*poiesai*)'; *poiein*
(= 'make', 'do') occurs ten times in this chapter. Frantic activity is
characteristic of the *beasts,* as of the 'little horn' (Dan. 8¹²; cf. 11³⁰, ³⁶)
and the men of Babel (Gen. 11³⁻⁵).

**6**

*blaspheming his name:* the assumption of divine names in documents and
inscriptions and on coins?

*and his dwelling, that is, those who dwell in heaven:* 12¹² suggests that the
heaven-dwellers are the angels (cf. Dan. 8⁹⁻¹², Jude 8ᶠᶠ·), but as in
Daniel the 'host of heaven' is the analogue of the army of *saints* on
whom the beast is *allowed to make war* (v. 7). God's dwelling, like his
temple (11¹ᶠ·), is people, not a place; cf. 18²⁰. Though the beast can hurt
their bodies on earth, its blasphemies have no effect in *heaven,* because
of the Lord's victory (12⁷⁻¹²).

**7**

*and to conquer:* by killing (v. 15). The Lamb and his followers *conquer*
by dying (5⁵ᶠ·, 12¹¹).ᵒ

**7-8**

The extent of the beast's *authority* and of its *worship* is world-wide, as
was the witnesses' prophesying and the relief of their victims (11⁶⁻¹⁰).
But *earth-dweller* and *written in the Lamb's book of life* (i.e. 'of the living')
are not hard and fast categories. Names can be expunged from the
latter – those who deny Christ (cf. 3⁵) – and the *nations* and *kings of the
earth* find a place in the City reserved for those *written in the Lamb's
book* (21²⁴⁻²⁷).

ᵒ The omission of this sentence by some ancient authorities is probably due
to a copyist's eye having jumped from *was allowed (kai edothē)* to *was given*
*(kai edothē).*

*everyone*[p] *whose name has not been written before the foundation of the world:* RSV has changed the order of the Greek (which runs 'whose name has not been written in the book of life of the Lamb that was slain before the foundation of the world'), because of $17^8$ where the same words are found, with 'the Lamb that was slain' omitted. *Before the foundation of the world* certainly can be taken with *written*, but it goes so closely with *slain* that it is wrong to expunge the clear implication here that the Lamb's atoning death has its place in God's plan from the beginning (cf. I Peter $1^{20}$), in contrast with the death of 'the beast that was slain' in v. 3. If we may take a hint from the other Johannine writings (John $1^{29}$, $3^{16}$, I John $2^2$ – for their relationship to Rev. see p. 40), the Lamb's death is *for* those who are not *written* in his *book*, excluded by their worship of the beast like Israel by its worship of the golden calf (Ex. $32^8$, $32^{f.}$).

In any case, 'not written' does not mean that they have no chance. The language of 'predestination' occurs in Jewish and Christian writings alongside clear statements of human free-will and responsibility. It serves to express both God's control over a seemingly chaotic world – nothing that happens is in fact unforeseen or accidental – and the un-varying quality of his intention: his discountenancing of sin and his provision for salvation (cf. Matt. $25^{34}$, $^{41}$, Rom. $8^{28-30}$). 'Not written from the foundation of the world' expresses the constitutional and eternal incapacity for *life* of those whose treasure is on earth. For the *book of life* see on $3^5$, $20^{12}$.

**9**

*If anyone has an ear:* the reference to the present Israel is brought sharply home by the closing formula of the letters (cf. Ps. $95^{7ff.}$); see on $2^7$.

**10**

*If anyone is to be taken captive:* text and interpretation are uncertain. RSV is probably right, but can be taken in two ways. (i) John is alluding to Gethsemane, and to Jer. $15^2$, $43^{11}$ (but with a significant shift of meaning). Peter said he was willing to go to *prison* and *death* with Jesus (Luke $22^{33}$), but when the time came, *denied* him; and in the garden the

p *Everyone* is supplied by RSV. The Greek could mean 'all the earth-dwellers whose names have not been written . . .', paraphrased by NEB 'all on earth except those whose names the Lamb keeps in his roll of the living'. But the 'earth-dwellers' in Revelation are one inclusive category of those whose horizons are bounded by this earth, in contrast to the 'heaven-dwellers' (v. 6), those whose treasure is in heaven (see above, pp. 15f. and on $3^{10}$).

disciples took to the *sword*, but then fled – in both ways avoiding what the scriptures required (Matt. 26^51–56). Jeremiah speaks of the irrevocability of the doom God has laid down for the sinful – which is to be borne now, as at Calvary, not by the sinful but by the faithful.q See also Matt. 26^39, John 18^11, and below on *cup* (14^10). Christians are not to save their earthly skins (cf. 2^10) by compromise, like the Nicolaitans, or by the earthly *sword* like Jewish Zealots or Roman conspirators. *Here is a call for the endurance and faith of the saints.* (ii) But this last sentence literally translated runs, 'Here *is* the endurance ...' (so too at 14^12), and v. 10 could be taken (as by some early copyists) as promise of retribution on the 'earth-dwellers': 'this is the vindication for which the saints have trustfully waited' (cf. 6^9–11; 14^12 could be taken the same way). Then *if anyone has an ear* would introduce a threat in contrast with the promises to the faithful in the letters, and the allusion to Jeremiah would be in line with the original meaning.r

If the chapter is primarily a *warning* to the church, then (i) is preferable. But John's Greek is oracular enough for him to mean both!

THE BEAST FROM THE EARTH

11*Then I saw another beast which rose out of the earth; it had two horns like a lamb and it spoke like a dragon.* 12*It exercises all the authority of the first beast in its presence, and makes the earth and its inhabitants worship the first beast, whose mortal wound was healed.* 13*It works great signs, even making fire come down from heaven to earth in the sight of men;* 14*and by*

q For the idea of vicarious suffering, see above, p. 126.

r Some MSS read 'if anyone *takes* captive, to captivity he goes', but this looks like an attempt to make sense of a difficult saying by introducing the idea of retaliation from v. 10b.

It is possible that retaliation was introduced by copyists in v. 10b also from passages like Matt. 26^52. One good MS (Codex Alexandrinus) reads, 'If anyone [is] to be slain with the sword, [he is] to be slain with the sword': this is not Greek, but is the literal translation of a distinctive Hebrew idiom (Charles II, p. 355). The sense would then be that of Jer. 15^2, as in v. 10a: acceptance of the divine sentence. This difficult reading could have given rise to the other variants, but equally it could have arisen from a copyist aligning v. 10b with v. 10a in the light of Jer. 15^2.

*the signs which it is allowed to work in the presence of the beast, it deceives those who dwell on earth, bidding them make an image for the beast which was wounded by the sword and yet lived;* <sup>15</sup>*and it was allowed to give breath to the image of the beast so that the image of the beast should even speak, and to cause those who will not worship the image of the beast to be slain.* <sup>16</sup>*Also it causes all, both small and great, both rich and poor, both free and slave, to be marked on the right hand or the forehead,* <sup>17</sup>*so that no one can buy or sell unless he has the mark, that is, the name of the beast or the number of its name.* <sup>18</sup>*This calls for wisdom: let him who has understanding reckon the number of the beast, for it is a human number, its number is six hundred and sixty-six.*\*

\* Other ancient authorities read *six hundred and sixteen*.

The satanic parody continues. The second *beast*, whose title hereafter is 'false prophet' (16<sup>13</sup>, 19<sup>20</sup>, 20<sup>10</sup>), could be simply a mock-up to ape the Holy Spirit, a personification of false prophets as the first beast is of false Christs. It comes not from the *sea* but the *earth*, which helped the woman (12<sup>16</sup>), and its gentle appearance is betrayed only by its voice (the inner reality; see Lohmeyer, p. 115) – 'beware of false prophets who come to you in sheep's clothing but inwardly are ravenous wolves' (Matt. 7<sup>15</sup>). Its *great signs* and *fire from heaven* (v. 13) parody the activity of the Pentecostal Spirit and the true prophets (11<sup>3-13</sup>; cf. II Thess. 2<sup>9ff.</sup>). As Preston and Hanson point out (p. 96), this chapter gives a parody of the whole Christian dispensation: a trinity (dragon, beast and false prophet), a death and resurrection, and a universal church with its sacrament of membership (v. 16).

But there may be a wider reference. Pagan religion also had its signs and wonders, and the emperor cult its propagandists, drawn from the pagan priesthoods, and in vv. 14–17 the Roman reference is hard to avoid: the *image* suggests imperial statues and coins (as well as Nebuchadnezzar's image in Dan. 3), and the sanctions of vv. 15–17 allude to political possibilities, even if there is no evidence that things had yet reached this pitch.

But if this *beast* represents propaganda for the emperor cult, how could it be lamb-like enough to deceive Christians? The answer probably lies in the tenets of the Nicolaitans, which we can only infer (see pp. 32ff., 88ff.): they may have upheld the divine authority of the state, for which they could appeal to Jesus ('Render to Caesar'), Peter (I Peter 2$^{13-17}$) and Paul (Rom. 13$^{1-7}$), and emphasized Christian 'knowledge' – 'an idol has no real existence' (I Cor. 8$^{1-4}$). There would also be genuine patriotism and admiration for Rome and for Greek city culture, which John would see in terms of Dan. 11$^{32-36}$ as succumbing to seduction.

John's attack, then, is on Rome primarily as the means whereby Satan is active within the church. The final *call* (v. 18) is not for crossword-puzzle ingenuity: if 666 = Nero, John's readers *knew it already* (see below). He rams home the Roman reference for those who see Rome as God's gift to the world, to keep chaos at bay (cf. II Thess. 2$^{6f.}$, I Thess. 5$^3$; cf. also Hitler seen in the 1930s as a bulwark against Bolshevism), but calls for deeper *wisdom* (cf. I Cor. 2$^{6ff.}$) in understanding the number itself. Briefly, *six* is one short of *seven*, which signifies completeness, perfection (see Introduction, pp. 14f. above); 666 is thus penultimacy intensified, and 'the penultimate claiming ultimacy' is a fair definition of Antichrist; cf. 'Lucifer', Isa. 14$^{12-14}$, and the 'little horn', Dan. 11$^{36}$. This is an age-old thing: Rome and Nero are merely contemporary expressions. So the reference of ch. 13 is spiritual rather than simply Roman, but the spirit cannot be separated from the flesh in which it operates.

৯৩

## 11

*another beast which arose out of the earth:* the two beasts are no doubt distant relatives of Job's Leviathan (41$^{1ff.}$), and Behemoth (40$^{15ff.}$), which in later texts are linked with Beginning and End (as in the Targum version of Gen. 1$^{21}$). The first arose out of the sea across which lay Rome; this one represents Rome's local enthusiasts. If an individual is in mind, it is only as a representative of the system. Its *two* horns are a parody of true witness (11$^{13}$). It *looks* like a *lamb*, but *speaks* like a *dragon* (= 'serpent' in Greek; cf. the seductive speech of Gen. 3$^{1-5}$, and see p. 125 on the relation between hearing and seeing).

## 12

*It exercises all the authority of the first beast in its presence:* the *authority* of the first *beast* is the dragon's (v. 4). Christians have the authority of

Christ which is God's. The true prophet stands in God's presence (11$^4$; cf. Elijah, I Kings 17$^1$); the emperor cult is performed in the *presence* of Caesar's representative. The *earth and its inhabitants* echoes the universal scope of Pentecost (Acts 2$^{5ff.}$), and *whose mortal wound was healed* takes up the parody of Christ (see on v. 3) and of Christian witness to his resurrection (Acts 17$^{30, 31}$).

13f.

*it works great signs: signs and wonders* were to mark both the Day of the Lord (Acts 2$^{19}$, quoting Joel) and the 'great deception' (II Thess. 2$^9$, Matt. 24$^{24}$ – the elect had already been warned of their ambivalence by Moses, Deut. 13$^{1ff.}$). The *fire from heaven* is a parody of the Holy Spirit (Acts 2$^{3f.}$), who inspires Christian prophets (Rev. 11$^5$); cf. Elijah's competition with the prophets of Baal (I Kings 18$^{38}$).

14

*an image of the beast:* cf. Aaron's golden calf (Ex. 32$^8$), and the *image* set up by Nebuchadnezzar which Shadrach, Meshach and Abed-nego refused to worship, braving the furnace (Dan. 3). Antiochus' 'sacrilege' was a statue of Zeus, perhaps made in his own likeness (Dan. 11$^{31}$); a colossal statue of Domitian was erected in a new temple in Ephesus. *Image* also suggests the coinage, bearing the emperor's portrait (cf. Matt. 22$^{20}$ par.).

*which was wounded by the sword:* the Greek is *who*, indicating the beast's embodiment in a person; cf. Mark 13$^{14}$ NEB. *By the sword* alludes on one level to Isa. 27$^1$, God's sword (which is his Word), on the other to the manner of Nero's death. In John's vision he has *come to life* (better than *lived*; contrast 2$^8$, where the same word *ezēsen* is used) in a final emperor, who as the *eighth* (17$^{10f.}$) is a parody of the risen Christ.

15

*allowed to give breath to the image:* contrast the true Spirit which gave breath to Israel's dead bones and to the two witnesses (Ezek. 37, Rev. 11$^{11}$). Statues were made to speak in pagan temples by ventriloquism, and magic no doubt had its place in the emperor cult (as at the proconsul's court, Acts 13$^{6ff.}$).

*to cause those who will not worship:* in the Greek the *image* is the subject, itself ordering execution (so NEB), but the allusion to Dan. 3$^{4-6}$ suggests

that John meant what RSV says. There was no such direct demand until
the third century, but men accused before a Roman magistrate might be
required to deny Christ and burn incense or pour wine before a bust of
the emperor (as by Pliny in Bithynia, see Introduction, p. 29) and
be executed if they refused. As a prophet John sees the way things are
going.

### 16

*to be marked on right hand or forehead:* a parody of the *seal* ($7^3$, $14^1$). Pagan
cults, like that of Cybele, used tattooing as a mark of the God's ownership, like the branding of a slave; cf. Gal. $6^{17}$, Isa. $44^3$. *Mark (charagma)*
is the technical term for the imperial stamp on documents, etc.

### 17

*no one can buy or sell:* there was no such ban in John's time, but he may
have seen the seeds of it in provincial zeal and Christian unpopularity.
His model may be the Jewish ban on all dealings with those excom-
municated from the synagogue (Farrer, p. 157). The equation of the
*mark* with the beast's *name* or *number* shows the whole picture is metaphorical.

### 17f.

*the number of its name:* Greek and Hebrew letters had numerical equivalents (there were no Arabic numerals) – a = 1, b = 2, etc. – so that a
name could be *reckoned* as the sum of its letters (*isopsēphia*), e.g. *Iēsous*
= 888;[s] this might be related to the numerical value of other names
or words (*gēmatria*) – a kind of arithmetical punning – e.g. 'Nero' =
'he murdered his mother' (Suetonius, *Nero*, 39.2). Clearly there were
too many possibilities in a large number for one to calculate the name
from the number – unless one knew it already. A graffito at Pompeii
which reads: 'I love her whose number is 545', meant nothing except
to the lady and her friends. So the call for *wisdom* is not to decipher the
number, but to recognize its significance, and act – cf. Matt. $24^{15f.}$.

### 18

*it is a human number:* i.e. not an apocalyptic riddle beyond human wit?
cf. $21^{17}$? But *human* is literally *of a man*, and it may mean just that –
most probably Nero (already by *gēmatria* reckoned as 'matricide'). By
Irenaeus' time the identification was forgotten, but this was perhaps

s I = 10, $\bar{e}$ = 8, s = 200, o = 70, u = 400, s = 200.

because the sum works only if the Greek *Neron Kaisar* is transliterated into Hebrew.[t] It was probably an identification made by Jews or Jewish-Christians[u] – in the eyes of both groups Nero had earned the title of Antichrist – and valued for the qualities of the number itself, on which we follow Farrer's exposition (pp. 158f.):

(i) Six being one less than seven is the number of incompleteness and evil; 666 is its intensification. Jews put together the seven 'days' of Gen. 1 with Ps. 90⁴ to get seven thousand-year periods (millennia) of world history. The sixth, the penultimate, is the time of Antichrist, leading into the final millennium of the Messiah.

(ii) The numerical value of Jesus in Greek is 888, which would be well-known to any Christian (cf. the Christian *Sibylline Oracles*, I. 324ff.). This fits the 'first day/eighth day' pattern (see on 1¹⁰), in which the eighth is the first day of the age to come, the new creation, and recapitulates the first day of the old creation. Jesus rose on the 'first day of the week', which could also be seen as the eighth. Antichrist had his apparent triumph on the *sixth*.

(iii) The ancients talked of 'triangular' as well as square numbers. The triangular of a given number is the sum of the whole numbers up to

---

*t* There is a variant reading, 616 – the sum of the Latin form (*Nero Caesar*) transliterated into Hebrew. Irenaeus took it as *Gaios Kaisar* (Caligula) – obviously an attempt to find a suitably blasphemous emperor while working from the Greek. There have been countless other identifications, from Domitian (Stauffer) to Pio Nono and the World Council of Churches.

*u* B. Reicke, op. cit., pp. 189ff., thinks it was a familiar political slogan for the tyranny introduced by Nero. There are striking parallels to this treatment of Nero in Christian writings which can be dated to mid-second century or earlier. In the Ascension of Isaiah 4¹ff. (Hennecke II, pp. 648–50) Isaiah 'foretells' the future to his sons: 'Beliar . . . shall descend . . . in the form of a man, a lawless king, a slayer of his mother, who . . . will persecute the plant which the Twelve Apostles of the Beloved have planted . . . He will act and speak in the name of the Beloved and say "I am God and before me there has been none else." And all the people in the world will believe in him, and will sacrifice to him . . . And the majority of those who have united to receive the Beloved will turn aside to him, and the power of his miracles will be manifest . . . and he will set up his image before him in every city, and he shall rule three years, seven months and twenty-seven days [i.e. 1332 = 2×666 days; roughly 3½ years] . . . a few will remain as [Christ's] servants, fleeing from desert to desert and awaiting his coming.' If the passage is dependent on Revelation, it shows how Revelation was understood at the time. See also the Christian *Sibylline Oracles*, e.g. VIII. 65ff. (Hennecke II, pp. 727ff.; see also pp. 707f.).

and including it; e.g. 10 is the triangular of 4, and the formula is $n^{tr} = \dfrac{n(n+1)}{2}$. John $21^{11}$ ($153$ fish $= 17^{tr}$) and Acts $27^{37}$ ($276$ persons $= 23^{tr}$) are NT examples, which may or may not be significant, but 666 is a triangular of a triangular: $8^{tr} = 36$ and $36^{tr} = 666$. So 666 is a power of 8, and Antichrist parodies Christ in being himself an *eighth* ($17^{11}$) – the penultimate claiming ultimacy.

(iv) A doubly triangular number expresses three-sidedness (*three* has dominated the trumpet plagues, $8^{7ff.}$), which contrasts with the square number of Christ's flock ($14^1$).

# The Triumph of the Gospel

Chapter 14 looks back over the trumpets section, and forward to the bowls. As in Dan. 7, beasts give way to the true man.

1–5 After the unholy alliance of church and world in ch. 13, John sees the true Lamb and his followers. Their purity anticipates the themes of harlot and bride, and the shift from the Pergamene to the Thyatiran letter (see p. 45).

6–13 After the *third woe*, the great deception, comes the true perspective of the gospel – just as it followed the first two woes (10<sup>1</sup>–11<sup>13</sup>). This perspective introduces the final plagues (15<sup>3f.</sup>).

13–20 After the 'sacrilege' and 'tribulation' comes, as in the Lord's Apocalypse, the picture of the Son of man on a cloud, picking up the vindication of the two witnesses (11<sup>11-13</sup>), and sketching what is to be the centre-piece of the final section (19<sup>11-21</sup>).

14<sup>1-5</sup>    THE FOLLOWERS OF THE LAMB

*Then I looked, and lo, on Mount Zion stood the Lamb, and with him a hundred and forty-four thousand who had his name and his Father's name written on their foreheads. ²And I heard a voice from heaven like the sound of many waters and like the sound of loud thunder; the voice I heard was like the sound of harpers playing on their harps, ³and they sing a new song before the throne and before the four living creatures and before the elders. No one could learn that song except the hundred and forty-four thousand who had been redeemed from the earth. ⁴It is these who have not defiled themselves with women, for they are chaste;* ★ *it is these who follow the Lamb wherever he goes; these have been redeemed from mankind as first fruits for God and the Lamb,* ⁵*and in their mouth no lie was found, for they are spotless.*

\*Greek *virgins*.

The nations raged (11$^{18}$), but the Lord has them in derision: 'I have set my king on Zion, my holy hill' (Ps. 2$^{1-6}$). Satan *stood* on the *sand*: up came a beast with a *slaughtered* head, and another that looked *like a lamb*. But the Lamb is *standing* (as at 5$^6$) on the rock and, over against the multitude who take the *name* and *number* of the beast (13$^{16f.}$), the army of the twelve tribes of Israel stands foursquare with the *name* on their foreheads. But the church is not simply in opposition to the world: some Christians have joined the beast (see the letters to Pergamum and Thyatira), and the 144,000 have been *redeemed from mankind* as *first fruits* of a great harvest from every nation. This chapter might seem merely to contrast the reward of the faithful with the punishment of those who worship the beast, but the *new song* here suggests, and at 15$^{3f.}$ declares, the ingathering of *all nations* to the true worship of God (cf. 5$^{9f.}$, 7$^{9ff.}$, 21$^{24ff.}$).

But this ingathering depends on the purity of the *first fruits*, on *following the Lamb wherever he goes*, on reproducing not only the witness but the ways of Jesus (cf. 12$^{17}$). In this context the reference to *chastity* is not a monkish interpolation (Charles, II p. 9): it represents religious fidelity over against the idolatry and fornication of 'Jezebel' and the Nicolaitans (2$^{14, 20}$). *In their mouth no lie was found* (=Isa. 53$^9$) identifies them with their leader as the sacrificial Lamb, who 'bears the sin of many' (Isa. 53$^{12}$). The sacrifice to be valid must be *spotless*, unblemished by compromise with the *lie*.

࿓

1  *on Mount Zion stood the Lamb*: *stood* is a participle, *standing*; contrast the frantic activity of ch. 13. *Mount Zion* is the heavenly counterpart of the earthly Jerusalem, where the nations gather for attack, and God, or his Messiah, appears to confound them, as in II Esd. 13$^{5-11, 34-38}$ (a passage about contemporary with Rev.; cf. II Esd. 2$^{42ff.}$, a later Christian composition) and Joel 3$^{12ff.}$ – see on vv. 14–20, and cf. Heb. 12$^{22-24}$.

*his name and his Father's name:* the *seal* which the 144,000 received (see on 7<sup>3ff.</sup>) is identified thus in contrast with the beast's *mark* (13<sup>17</sup>); cf. 15<sup>2</sup>, and the promise to *the conqueror* (3<sup>12</sup>).

### 2–3

*I heard a voice from heaven:* as at 5<sup>11</sup>, what John *hears* interprets what he *sees* (see p. 125). The *many waters* remind us of the Son of man (1<sup>15</sup>), but with the *loud thunder* they link the *voice* with the throne of God (4<sup>5</sup>, Ezek. 1<sup>24–26</sup>). *Harps* accompany the elders' *new song* of redemption at 5<sup>8–10</sup> (see the commentary there), and the conquerors' song of Moses and of the Lamb at 15<sup>2–4</sup>. Here the harping comes, by allusion, from the throne itself, and confirms the redemptive sense of John's vision.

### 3

*No one could learn that song:* in ancient thought the power of a hymn, as of a name (cf. 2<sup>17</sup>, 19<sup>12</sup>), lay in its being secret (see on 5<sup>9</sup>), but the Christian point is different: the redemption which the *song* celebrates is a mystery beyond men of 'this age' (cf. I Cor. 2<sup>6–9</sup>).

### 4

*have not defiled themselves with women:* perhaps the most misunderstood words in the book. Unchastity is a regular biblical metaphor for religious infidelity (see on 2<sup>15</sup> and on Jezebel, 2<sup>20</sup>), and John is preparing for the harlot-bride contrast (17–22). But there is a positive point. For orthodox Jews (and Christians) marriage and sexual intercourse were good, but the latter was temporarily defiling (Lev. 15<sup>18</sup>) and thus a disqualification for priestly or military duty (war was 'holy' in the OT; cf. Deut. 23<sup>9–14</sup>, I Sam. 21<sup>5</sup>). The men who gathered at Qumran in military and priestly guise to prepare for the final War of Yahweh were (mostly) celibate; and Christians, who also saw the Day of the Lord as imminent and themselves as metaphorically on military and priestly service ('a kingdom and priests', 1<sup>6</sup>, 5<sup>10</sup>) may have lived as celibates where possible (cf. Matt. 19<sup>10–12</sup>) – in order to be at the Lord's disposal without distraction (I Cor. 7<sup>32–35</sup>). The next words here suggest that the point is undivided devotion, in a religious task for which purity is essential (cf. 3<sup>4</sup>).

Their maleness is simply part of the military metaphor; they represent the whole church.

*for they are chaste:* Gk *parthenos*, which can be used of men as well as women. Usually it means 'virgin', but it can be used of the married also, meaning 'married only once' and thereafter celibate. It is used metaphorically by Philo (*On the Cherubim* 49f.) for detachment from earthly concerns.

*follow the Lamb wherever he goes:* go (*hupagein*) is often used in John's Gospel with double meaning, of Jesus' death; cf. the conversation with Peter ($13^{36-38}$). His failure was hinted at above (Rev. $13^{10}$).

*first fruits for God and the Lamb:* the priests become the offering. *First fruits* (*aparchē*) can mean simply the *best* of the crop, offered as a gift to God, or on the Hebrew understanding of the *first* of a series, it can mean the *first* sheaf as being in germ the *whole* harvest (cf. I Cor. $15^{20ff.}$, $45^{ff.}$, $16^5$). 'It designates the Church as a promise for all men' (Rissi, *Time and History*, p. 104 note 171) – cf. the relationship between 144,000 and the great multitude at $7^{4, 9}$.

5

*in their mouth no lie was found:* an allusion primarily to Isa. $53^9$, but see also Zeph. $3^{13}$ in its context.

*spotless:* a technical term for a sacrificial victim. For Christians the ritual requirement has become moral.

## THE GOSPEL

[6]*Then I saw another angel flying in midheaven, with an eternal gospel to proclaim to those who dwell on earth, to every nation and tribe and tongue and people;* [7]*and he said with a loud voice, 'Fear God and give him glory, for the hour of his judgment has come; and worship him who made heaven and earth, the sea and the fountains of water.'*

*v* See J. M. Ford, 'The Meaning of "Virgin"', *NTS* 12, 1966, p. 294, and Anchor Commentary on Rev., p. 242. A contrast may be intended with the *Galli*, the emasculated priests of Cybele, the Great Mother, who was widely worshipped in Asia Minor. The *Lamb* may likewise be contrasted with the young god Attis. See Touilleux, op. cit. (see p. 194, note *c*), pp. 131ff.; 106ff.

<sup>8</sup>*Another angel, a second, followed, saying, 'Fallen, fallen is Babylon the great, she who made all nations drink the wine of her impure passion.'*
<sup>9</sup>*And another angel, a third, followed, saying with a loud voice, 'If any one worships the beast and its image, and receives a mark on his forehead or on his hand,* <sup>10</sup>*he also shall drink the wine of God's wrath, poured unmixed into the cup of his anger, and he shall be tormented with fire and brimstone in the presence of the holy angels and in the presence of the Lamb.* <sup>11</sup>*And the smoke of their torment goes up for ever and ever; and they have no rest, day or night, these worshippers of the beast and its image, and whoever receives the mark of its name.'*
<sup>12</sup>*Here is a call for the endurance of the saints, those who keep the commandments of God and the faith of Jesus.*

Three angels proclaim a counter to the three *woes*.

(i) The angel *flying in midheaven* recalls the *eagle* of 8<sup>13</sup>; it proclaims the good news of God's victory and summons the earth-dwellers to worship their Creator.

(ii) The second spells out the good news as the *fall of Babylon*, the cause of the earth-dwellers' fatal intoxication. It is implicitly a warning to 'come out of her' (18<sup>4</sup>; Isa. 52<sup>7–12</sup> and Jer. 51<sup>6–10</sup> lie behind).

(iii) The third underlines the warning by spelling out the terrible results of this intoxication: her *wine* is the *wine of God's wrath*.

John introduces a new motif, the cup or *bowl* which gives shape to the final section of the book (see on 15<sup>7</sup>). Several passages of scripture must be read to give the background: Ps. 75<sup>8</sup>, Isa. 51<sup>17–23</sup>, Jer. 25<sup>1ff.</sup>, 51<sup>6–10</sup>, Deut. 32<sup>32f.</sup> (Jer. 51 and Deut. 32, the Song of Moses, are two of John's primary sources). 'Babylon is a golden cup in the Lord's hand, making all the earth drunken' (Jer. 51<sup>7</sup>). Here is an answer to the question *why* men ignore the *eternal gospel* (v. 6) and take the mark of the beast to their *eternal torment* (v. 11). II Thess. 2<sup>10–12</sup> gives a negative answer: 'they did not open their minds to love of the truth' (NEB), and so had no resistance to the power of the lie. John gives a positive answer: Roman city civilization, which corrupts men as the Phoenician cities corrupted Israel in the time of Elijah (Jezebel came from Tyre; see on 2<sup>20</sup>).

So God punishes Babylon and the beast on which she rides (17<sup>3</sup>) – and anyone who refuses to give up his identification with them. Her wine is in fact the wine of his *wrath*. Again, what the earth-dwellers take to be blessing is final disaster (cf. 12¹²). But where is the 'good news' for them in that? Many would say there is none: *gospel* for John means simply proclamation of *judgment* and summons to submit (v. 7). But there is another possibility. *Judgment* may mean not only sorting men out, but also the expulsion of Satan, the deceiver and accuser, by Jesus' death on the cross (John 12³¹⁻³³; see on Rev. 12⁷⁻¹², p. 199) – now to take final effect.

ॐ

### 6

*flying in midheaven:* cf. 8¹³, 19¹⁷. God's throne would appear in *midheaven* for the judgment (S-B III, p. 815). What in ordinary experience is individual and local is now represented as universal and brought home to all.

### 6

*an eternal gospel: eternal (aiōnios)* means 'of the age (*aiōn*) to come', 'with eternal consequences'; cf. II Cor. 4¹⁷ᶠ. and contrast the transient gospel of the emperor cult, leading to eternal *torment* (v. 11) – e.g. the inscription of 9 BC at Priene near Ephesus: 'The birthday of the god [= Augustus] was the beginning for the world of the good news (*euangelia*) which was because of him.' It made the beginning of a new provincial era for Asia, which was to be for ever.

*to every nation:* cf. 10¹¹, 11⁹ᶠ. – the same constituency as rejoiced over the dead witnesses.

### 7

The good news (*euangelion*) for the Gentiles, as we gather from Acts and Paul, was God's victory over the evil powers by Christ's death and resurrection, and its imminent consummation in a day of judgment, with Christ as agent (cf. Rom. 2¹⁶). It ended with a call to repent and turn from idols to God (Acts 17²⁹⁻³¹; cf. I Thess. 1⁹ᶠ.). The *song* of redemption at 15³ᶠ. suggests the call had effect, but the rest of ch. 14 shows the gravity of the issue and the cost of the redemption.

*give him glory:* see on 11¹³; cf. 15⁴, and contrast 16⁹.

*the hour of his judgment has come:* cf. 10⁷. The language is reminiscent of the Fourth Gospel, in which *krisis* (lit. 'sifting') has two senses: sorting into already determined categories (3¹⁹⁻²¹), and changing the categories – upsetting the old balance of power (12³¹⁻³³). Normally the NT makes no distinction between the final coming of Christ and the day of judgment, when the new alignments brought about by his first coming are finally ratified. But our John does separate the two, and we should be open to the possibility that he sees Christ's final coming not simply as classificatory, like the judgment of 20¹¹ᶠᶠ·, but as creative, bringing to final effect what his first coming initiated, as 'first fruits' – see on vv. 4, 14–20 and 19¹¹ᶠᶠ·.

*heaven and earth, the sea and the fountains of water:* the elements smitten at 8⁷⁻¹², 16²⁻⁸. Contrast 9²⁰.

**8**
*Fallen, fallen is Babylon the great:* see Isa. 21⁹ and the 'good news' of 52⁷ᶠᶠ· which leads into the 'suffering servant' passage (52¹³–53¹²) already evoked at v. 5. See also Jer. 51⁸ and Dan. 4²⁸⁻³². The *great city* of 11⁸ is now given, still by allusion, its current identification; cf. I Peter 5¹³.

*drink the wine of her impure passion:* lit. 'the wine of the wrath (*thumos*) of her fornication' (cf. 17²; 17⁶ suggests that her wine is *the blood of the saints* – see on v. 20). It could be interpreted 'the wine of God's wrath upon her fornication' (NEB margin), but *thumos* can mean strong feeling or desire as well as anger, and this is clearly a condensed allusion to Jer. 51⁷: 'Babylon has been a golden cup in the Lord's hand, to make all the earth drunk; . . . her wine . . . has made them mad.' See notes on 8⁸⁻¹². The *cup* motif is taken up at v. 10. John adds *fornication* to make clear the allusion to Jezebel (II Kings 9²²) and the idolatry, with its consequent immorality, which was integral to city civilization in the near East. Her *fall*, then, is good news – 'there is no hope for the rehabilitation of the alcoholic until the source of his supply is cut off' (Caird, p. 184) – but also a warning to the seduced (cf. 2²⁰⁻²³).

**9**
*If any one . . .:* the true nature of the beast's kingdom as *woe* (12¹²) is spelt out. Verses 9–11 are a 'prediction' in the logical sense 'if p then q'.

10

*drink the wine of God's wrath:* the motif from Jer. 51⁷ is taken a step further. Babylon's seductive wine is in fact retribution, here for her victims, at 18⁶ for herself; cf. the Greek tragic sequence of satiety, arrogance, infatuation, retribution (*koros, hubris, atē, nemesis*).

*the cup of his anger:* cf. pp. 143f. for *anger* (*orgē*, which is used interchangeably with *thumos*, translated *wrath* above. In the NT it is not a feeling or passion in God, but his reaction against sin, and the effects of that reaction. According to the scriptures God is man's *cup*, or destiny – blessing to those who accept him (Pss. 16⁵, 23⁵), ruin to those who do not (Ps. 75⁸); not that he *gives* them ruin, simply, but that to turn away from truth and embrace falsehood *is* ruin, which he *allows* to take effect. His instruments are Babylon, who is allowed to prostitute God's *cup*, and Satan, who is allowed to exercise *great wrath* (12¹²); they personify the recoil of sin upon itself. But that is not all: John links *God's wrath* with the cross (A. T. Hanson, *Wrath of the Lamb*, pp. 159ff.). God's *cup* has already been drunk – by Jesus (John 18¹¹, etc.; see on Rev. 13¹⁰); the winepress is trodden *outside the city* (v. 20); and Babylon's wine is the blood of the *witnesses of Jesus* (17⁶). The nature of the link is harder to state – see pp. 50f., 232.

*fire and brimstone:* the fate of Sodom and Gomorrah (Gen. 19²⁴); see on 9¹⁷, and on 19²⁰, 20¹⁰, 21⁸.

*in the presence of the holy angels and the Lamb:* the *presence of the beast* (13¹⁴) is a delusion which must give way to the truth – the *presence of the Lamb*. Those who accept him he will 'confess in the presence of his Father and his angels' (3⁵); to those who do not he, like his witnesses (11¹⁰), is *torment*. See on 6¹⁶, and cf. II Esd. 7⁷⁹⁻⁸⁷, where at death the supreme torment of the 'scorners' is to see the glory of the Most High against whom they sinned.

11

*the smoke of their torment:* cf. Gen. 19²⁸. The fate of the individual is depicted in terms of the fate of the city which has corrupted him; cf. 19²ᶠ·, 20¹⁰.

*for ever and ever:* a liturgical phrase (cf. 4⁹, 15⁷) – a terrible contrast with the ceaseless worship of heaven.

*they have no rest, day or night:* contrast the *rest* of those who *die in the Lord* (v. 13), and the *living creatures* who *have no rest, day or night, singing Holy, holy, holy* ($4^8$). When the veil of time is removed God must be either man's supreme joy or his supreme torment – see on $6^{16}$. John's severity is diagnostic: *these worshippers of the beast* are a hypothetical category (v. 9), which may include Christians, and it is for Christians this 'apocalypse' is written, removing the veil and revealing the nature and destiny of beast-worship, so that they may see and act now, before it is too late.

This picture of eternal torment is the most terrible in the book. Eternal *torture* is elsewhere reserved for abstractions – Babylon, the devil and the beasts ($19^{3, 20}$, $20^{10}$) – and it can be held that the fate of the people who follow them is eternal *destruction* (see on $20^{15}$, $21^8$). But it makes little difference. To ask 'what does Rev. teach – eternal torment or eternal destruction?' is to use (or misuse) the book as a source of 'doctrine', or of information about the future. John uses pictures, as Jesus used parables (cf. Matt. $18^{32-34}$, $25^{41-46}$), to ram home the unimaginable disaster of rejecting God, and the unimaginable blessedness of union with God, while there is still time to do something about it.

12

*Here is a call:* as at $13^{10}$ this could be a statement 'Here (*hōde*) is the vindication the saints prayed for' ($6^{9-11}$); then v. 13 would follow on. But *those who keep the commandments of God and the faith of Jesus* echoes $12^{17}$ and suggests a warning against seduction, in line with our interpretation of vv. 9–11 and of $13^{9f.}$.

$14^{13-20}$    THE SON OF MAN:
HARVEST AND VINTAGE

$^{13}$*And I heard a voice from heaven saying, 'Write this: Blessed are the dead who die in the Lord henceforth.' 'Blessed indeed,' says the Spirit, 'that they may rest from their labours, for their deeds follow them!'* $^{14}$*Then I looked, and lo, a white cloud, and seated on the cloud one like a son of man, with a golden crown on his head, and a sharp sickle in his hand.* $^{15}$*And another angel came out of the temple, calling with a loud voice to him who sat upon the cloud, 'Put in your sickle, and reap, for the hour to reap has come, for the harvest of the earth is fully ripe.' ¹⁶So he who sat upon the cloud swung his sickle on the earth, and the earth was reaped.*

*¹⁷And another angel came out of the temple in heaven, and he too had a sharp sickle. ¹⁸Then another angel came out from the altar, the angel who has power over fire, and he called with a loud voice to him who had the sharp sickle, 'Put in your sickle, and gather the clusters of the vine of the earth, for its grapes are ripe.' ¹⁹So the angel swung his sickle on the earth and gathered the vintage of the earth, and threw it into the great wine press of the wrath of God; ²⁰and the wine press was trodden outside the city, and blood flowed from the wine press, as high as a horse's bridle, for one thousand six hundred stadia.\**

\* About two hundred miles.

This vision is linked by the *cloud* with the vindication of the two witnesses ($11^{12}$) – it is perhaps to the completion of their *labours* that the *Spirit* refers – and it is linked by the *wine press* (vv. 19f.) with the appearance of Christ and his witnesses in $19^{11ff.}$, but the pictures are so vague and evocative that various meanings are possible (and perhaps intended). Charles simplifies by excising vv. 15–17 as an interpolation, on grounds of linguistic peculiarities. But John's Greek is a shaky basis for such judgments, and it is harder to explain the mind of the interpolator than the text as it stands.

The chief model is Joel $3^{13}$: the nations have gathered outside Jerusalem, and God pronounces judgment:

> Put in the sickle, for the harvest is ripe.
> Go in, tread, for the wine press is full.
> The vats overflow, for their wickedness is great

– a single harvest (of grapes), and a single picture of judgment. But John, no doubt following Jesus' parable of the seed growing secretly (Mark $4^{28f.}$), has taken the first line to refer to the grain harvest. The harvester, *one like a son of man*, suggests as at $1^{13}$ both the human figure of Dan. $7^{13}$, who supersedes the beasts, and 'the Son of man', whose coming on the clouds is to be followed by the gathering of his elect

(Matt. 24³⁰f·). Many take that gathering to be John's meaning here; then the vintage conducted by mere angels, signifying the indirect action of God, would be the judgment of wrath on the nations, as in Joel. But John may mean the gathering in of both the 144,000 elect and the nations, the *harvest of the earth* (v. 15), of which the elect are the *first fruits* (v. 4). Verse 13 fits the former view well enough, but if we were right to see the two witnesses as 'labourers sent out into the harvest' (11²), and their death as crowned by success (11¹³), then the *labours* from which they rest may be harvest labours as at John 4³⁵⁻³⁸, and the *deeds* or 'works' which follow them may allude to the results of their labours, as seen at 21²⁴ff·.

Is the vintage then simply destructive judgment? The *vine of the earth* (v. 18), in parallel with the harvest of the earth (v. 15), is hardly evil in itself, but John may have 'the vine of Sodom' (Deut. 32³²) in mind. Certainly it is harvested by angels, not directly by Christ, and the angel who has *power over fire* (v. 18) evokes 8³⁻⁵, the prayers of the saints for vindication and the trumpet plagues. Certainly the grapes are thrown into the *winepress of the wrath of God*, and its being *trodden outside the city* evokes the terrible picture of Yahweh's vengeance in Isa. 63¹⁻⁶.

But *outside the city* also evokes the crucifixion, and the death of the first witness, Stephen (see Heb. 13¹²⁻¹⁴ and the passages cited in our comment on 11²), and Isa. 63¹⁻⁶ is perhaps being reinterpreted in the light of the slaughtered Lamb (5⁵f·); see below on v. 19. It all turns on John's use of the OT. If there is a 'rebirth of inages' at 5⁵f·, there is the same rebirth here, and at 19¹⁵. The manlike figure on the cloud represents the traditional expectation; the bloodbath is the earthly reality, by means of which (as in ch. 12) the heavenly picture comes true. This is not to deny the destructive judgment – John is quite clear about the cost of redemption to both redeemers and redeemed – only to deny that it is merely destructive; that would make nonsense of 1⁷, 11¹³, 15⁴ and 21²⁴ff·.

ॐ

13
A link verse:ʷ the *voice* declares the blessedness of those who have heeded

*w* The reward of the faithful at death is contrasted with that of the 'scorners' in II Esd. 7⁷⁵ff·.

the call for *endurance* (v. 12), and *the Spirit* states its effect, expressed symbolically in the following visions (*hearing* again interprets *seeing*). The command to *write* and the *Spirit's* comment recall the letters to the churches (2<sup>1, 7</sup>, etc.).

## 13

*henceforth: ap' arti.* It might be read *aparti* ('assuredly') and taken with what follows, as by NEB; cf. 6<sup>11</sup>. But RSV is probably right – see on 12<sup>10</sup>. Not that those who died in the Lord's service were not *blessed* before. The time reference, as with the three and a half period (see pp. 182f., 210f. above) is to the new era begun by Christ's life and death. What was then initiated is now, through the *labours* of his witnesses, to achieve its final effect. Their *rest* contrasts with the *no rest* of the beast-worshippers (v. 11), who *trample* them in this life (11<sup>2</sup>).

For *labours* (*kopoi*) and *deeds* (*erga*) see 2<sup>2, 19</sup>, 3<sup>3</sup>. *Kopos* is used for missionary labours by Paul; so at John 4<sup>35-38</sup>, with the *harvest* metaphor. The primary suggestion is of reward for work done in God's field, cf. I Cor. 3<sup>8f.</sup>; but Paul then talks of *work* (*ergon*) in building on the foundation of Christ with gold, silver, precious stones (3<sup>10-16</sup>), and John may also be implying that their *works* will come through the test – see on 21<sup>15ff.</sup>.

## 14

*I looked, and lo, a white cloud:* cf. 11<sup>12</sup>, 1<sup>7</sup>. The traditional *pictures* of the Day of the Lord which follow have already been interpreted by the preceding *words*: both harvest and vintage are to be seen as the consummation of *witness* (see on 11<sup>7</sup>; cf. Matt. 24<sup>14</sup>). *White* is the colour of Christ and his followers; cf. the *white* horse, and its rider's *crown* (6<sup>2</sup>; cf. 19<sup>11, 14</sup>). *One like a son of man* alludes primarily to Dan. 7<sup>13</sup>, where the human figure represents the saints trampled by the beasts. Jesus 'judges' as true *man*; cf. John 5<sup>27</sup>, 19<sup>5</sup>.

## 15

*another angel:* the figure on the cloud is not identified as *the* Son of man, and some take *another angel* to mean he is one too, but the reference is back to v. 9; three angels appear on either side, as it were, of the man. How can an *angel* give orders to Christ? He had said that not even the Son knows of that day and hour (Matt. 24<sup>36</sup>), and Farrer points to the liturgy which governed Jewish harvesting: the *first fruits* sheaf (v. 4) to be offered in the *temple* (whence the *angel* comes, v. 15) could only be cut when the time and tools were declared to be right (p. 165).

**16**

*the earth was reaped:* this can hardly refer simply to the gathering of the elect, who are united with the Son of man in his work. It must mean also the ingathering of the world for judgment, as at Joel 3¹³.

**17-20**

Grain suggests the blessedness of the barn (Matt. 3¹², 13³⁰); *wine* has already been given a sinister significance, as in Joel (though to a Christian neither *wine* nor *cup* could be wholly sinister, after what Christ had made of his *cup*). The sequence parallels the grain harvest, but all is done by *angels* until the 'passive of divine action' in v. 20 hints at Christ's involvement.

**19**

*the great wine press of the wrath of God:* 'I have trodden the wine press alone . . . I trod down the peoples in my anger, I made them drunk in my wrath, and I poured out their lifeblood on the earth' (Isa. 63³, ⁶). 'How noble is the king, Messiah, who is going to rise from the house of Judah . . . killing kings . . . reddening the mountains with the blood of their slain. With his garments dipped in blood, he is like one who treads grapes in a press' (Gen. 49¹¹, Targum). If, as is likely, John and many of his hearers knew the scriptures through the Targum paraphrase (see p. 40), then reinterpretation of the Lion of Judah in Gen. 49 would carry with it reinterpretation of Isa. 63. In the light of 5⁵ᶠ· can John be simply echoing the OT? Can Christ finally conquer in the manner of the beast? See on 19¹³⁻¹⁵, and cf. Heb. 12²⁴. Gen. 49¹¹, 'washing his vesture in the blood of grapes', also evokes 'they have washed their robes in the blood of the Lamb' (7¹⁴) – as if the vat in which the *multitude's* clothes have been made *white* is the wine press filled with the blood of Christ and his witnesses, who have been *trampled outside the city* (see on 11²). The wine of God's wrath, with which Babylon and her people are intoxicated to their ruin, is the *blood of the saints* and *Jesus' witnesses* (17⁶). This ruin (17–18) is succeeded by the vision of Bride, Holy City and Nations (21⁹–22⁵), via the *winepress* of 19¹⁵. Is it succession, or transformation (21⁵)? (cf. Caird, pp. 192–5).

*blood . . . high as a horse's bridle:* the bloodbath in the valley *outside the city* is a stock image which goes back to the goddess Anath in the Canaanite texts from Ugarit – cf. I Enoch 100¹⁻³ (the self-destruction of sinners). Contrast *the river of the water of life* flowing from the new City (22¹). For *horses* cf. 19¹¹, ¹⁴.

*1600^x stadia:* roughly the length of Palestine, which has become a symbol of the *world* ($4 \times 4$ – the four corners), just as Jerusalem has become a symbol of the *city* ($11^8$).

x The square number, in contrast with the triangular number of the beast (see on $13^{18}$), may confirm a positive interpretation of the vintage (cf. Caird, p. 195).

# Revelation 15$^1$–22$^5$

# The Seven Bowls:
# The Harlot and the Bride

The 'seven last plagues' provide a thread which carries through to ch. 22; for their relation to the trumpet plagues of 8–14 see pp. 157f. above. Their immediate target is the beast's city (16¹⁹–19⁵), but a bowl-angel shows John both the judgment of the harlot (17¹ff.) and the descent of the Bride (21⁹ff.), linking them together as two aspects of one reality. In between is the coming of the Bridegroom or Son of man (19¹¹ff.), the climax of the traditional scheme which John is following (see pp. 19–21 above). But his central concern is the church. He elaborates the 'gathering of the elect', which traditionally follows the coming, as the adorning of the Bride (19⁸, 21⁹ff.), and prefaces the coming with the opposite theme of the dismantling of the harlot (17–18); ch. 14 has hinted that the elect may, by the mysteries of *first fruits* (v. 4) and *wine press* (v. 20), come to include the nations whom the harlot has seduced.

The relevance of this for the church has been stated in the letter to Thyatira (2¹⁸⁻²⁹). Its theme is discernment ('eyes like a flame of fire', v. 18), seeing beyond the church's good works (v. 19), to the works in accordance with which God who searches the heart will judge (v. 23). The harlot is not simply an external enemy but is enthroned as a false queen (Jezebel, v. 20; cf. 18²³ᶠ.) with many followers in the church itself. The issue is obedience to the apostolic teaching (vv. 24f.) – cf. 12¹⁷: if the 'trumpets' section is concerned with idolatry and witness, the 'bowls' section centres on fornication (which is put first at 2²⁰, in contrast to 2¹⁴) and purity (19⁸). Purity also is a testimony (cf. I Peter 3¹⁻⁴) and the theme of influence over the nations (2²⁶⁻²⁸) is woven in. We may see here a reference to the sorceries of Jezebel (18²³, II Kings 9²²): instead of the deep things of Satan (2²⁴), by which some seek power, Christ promises to the conqueror, who keeps his works to the end, power over the nations (2$^{26}$), and the bright morning star before which magic fades (2$^{28}$) – which is himself (22$^{16}$).


15$^{1-8}$  THE SONG OF MOSES AND OF THE LAMB

15 *Then I saw another portent in heaven, great and wonderful, seven angels with seven plagues, which are the last, for with them the wrath of God is ended.*

*²And I saw what appeared to be a sea of glass mingled with fire, and those who had conquered the beast and its image and the number of its name, standing beside the sea of glass with harps of God in their hands. ³And they sing the song of Moses, the servant of God, and the song of the Lamb, saying,*

 '*Great and wonderful are thy deeds,*
  *O Lord God the Almighty!*
 *Just and true are thy ways,*
  *O King of the ages!*★
 ⁴*Who shall not fear and glorify thy name, O Lord?*
  *For thou alone art holy.*
 *All nations shall come and worship thee,*
  *for thy judgments have been revealed.*'

*⁵After this I looked, and the temple of the tent of witness in heaven was opened, and out of the temple came the seven angels with the seven plagues, robed in pure bright linen, and their breasts girded with golden girdles. ⁷And one of the four living creatures gave the seven angels seven golden bowls full of the wrath of God who lives for ever and ever; ⁸and the temple was filled with smoke from the glory of God and from his power, and no one could enter the temple until the seven plagues of the seven angels were ended.*

★Other ancient authorities read *the nations.*

Since the *seven last plagues* end in total impenitence and disaster (16$^{9,11,21}$), like the trumpet plagues (9$^{20f.}$), and the plagues of Egypt on which both series are modelled, it is significant that they are introduced by a *song* which celebrates a new and greater exodus. God's direct action in Christ and his saints carries the *first fruits* promise (see on 14$^{1-7}$) that *all nations will come to worship*, beyond the carnage which he allows men to bring down on themselves. But to John, as to Paul, this indirect action is still *God's* and is initiated from the temple with all the terrors of the divine Presence (vv. 5–8; see pp. 143f. on 'wrath').

శ్రీ

1

*another portent:* cf. 12$^{1, 3}$ – 'as though everything in 12–14 had been the working out of that mighty conflict, and the next act were now to begin' (Farrer, p. 169).

*seven plagues, which are the last:* the mystery of God was to be *ended* in the days of the seventh trumpet, or third woe (10$^7$), which was the kingdom of the beast: these plagues bring that kingdom's collapse (at least the last three, 16$^{10-21}$, which parallel the 'three woes'). The number *seven* is traditional; cf. Lev. 16$^{21}$.

*what appeared to be a sea of glass:* see on 4$^6$. The *sea* is a kaleidoscopic image which now represents the Red Sea, and perhaps the brazen 'sea' of Solomon's temple, with its waters for washing (II Chron. 4$^6$, I Kings 7$^{23ff.}$ – see Farrer, pp. 170–2). Christians saw their baptismal washing as passage through the Red Sea (I Cor. 10$^{1ff.}$), and as sharing Christ's death (Rom. 6$^{3ff.}$, Col. 2$^{12}$). The 'great tribulation' of the *third woe* was indeed a baptism of blood and *fire* – passed through by the saints, now to be poured out on the earth-dwellers; *mingled with fire* suggests a fiery mixture for the *bowls of wrath* (see Luke 12$^{49f.}$ for the connection of fire and baptism). If this is right, then *sea* has the same ambivalence as *cup* and *wine press* in ch. 14. 'Can you drink the cup that I drink or be baptized with the baptism I am baptized with?' Jesus asked (Mark 10$^{38}$).

*those who had conquered:* lit. *those conquering*. The present is timeless as at 14$^4$, and expresses the character of conqueror, not the fact of conquest (Swete); see on 2$^7$. For the beast's *image* and *name* see 13$^{14-18}$.

*with harps of God:* cf. 5$^8$, 14$^2$; they evoke the *new song* of redemption.

239

**3**

*the Song of Moses . . . and . . . of the Lamb:* Moses and Israel praised God by the Red Sea (Ex. 15$^{1-18}$), and Deut. 32$^{1-43}$, one of John's and the early church's favourite texts, was known as 'the Song of Moses'; at 32$^{44}$ he is associated with Joshua (= Jesus in Greek) in singing it. It is a bloodthirsty celebration of divine vindication and vengeance, and the characterization of Jesus as the *Lamb* suggests the same 'rebirth of images' we argued for at 5$^{5f.}$ and 14$^{20}$; the words of the song confirm it.

**3-4**

The *song* contains phrases from Deut. 32$^4$, the Psalms (111$^2$, 86$^{8f.}$) and Jeremiah (10$^{6f.}$, 16$^{19}$), and though those from Jeremiah have a punitive sense (see Jer. 10$^{10}$, 16$^{21}$), the total effect is of God's greatness breaking through heathen blindness and *all nations* coming to his worship – because his *judgments have been revealed.* 16$^7$ suggests these *judgments* are punitive, but the word here is *dikaiōma*, which means 'righteous act (19$^8$) or decree' (Luke 1$^6$), and Rom. 5$^{18}$ – one man's 'act of righteousness' leading to acquittal and life for all – suggests also the sense of 'deliverance' which 'righteousness' often has in Hebrew. The context requires reference to the exodus deliverance (5$^{5f.}$, 12$^{1-11}$), rather than the plagues which harden men (9$^{20f.}$, 16$^{9, 11, 21}$). This final exodus *is* punitive (11$^{13}$, 12$^5$, 14$^{20}$, 19$^{11ff.}$), but not *simply* punitive.

**3**

*O King of the ages: aiōnōn;* i.e. 'eternal King'; cf. v. 7; 14$^{6, 11}$, I Tim. 1$^{17}$. The variant reading *king of the nations (ethnōn)* is well supported, but an editor is more likely to have corrected the text by Jer. 10$^7$ ('who would not fear thee, O King of the nations?') than to have assimilated it to I Tim. 1$^{17}$, especially as *nations* is picked up in v. 4. In either case the sense is that the true king is God, not Caesar.

**4**

*For thou alone art holy:* in the sense of unapproachably great (cf. Ps. 111$^9$). The reason for *fearing* and *glorifying* God is that this greatness has come near (cf. 11$^{13, 17}$, and 16$^5$ where *holy* replaces *is to come* in the threefold title).

**5**

*the temple of the tent of witness in heaven was opened:* cf. 11$^{19}$, which initiates the *third woe*. Here the point is not access to God's presence won by Christ's death (as set out in 12$^{1-11}$), but the manifestation of that presence to all the world. Moses' *tent* contained the ark with the tables of 'the testimony' (= witness) – the ten commandments which set out God's nature and will (Ex. 25$^9$, $^{16}$, 34$^{29}$) – but Christians would think of the *testimony of Jesus* alongside the *commandments* (12$^{17}$).

## 6

*out of the temple came the seven angels with the seven plagues:* God-with-us (cf. John 1$^{14}$) is disaster to those who worship false gods before it can be blessing; cf. the effect of *witness* at 11$^{10}$, and see on 6$^{16}$. The *temple*, with its incense-altar, was the source of the trumpet-plagues (8$^{3-5}$).

*robed in pure bright linen . . .:* cf. the Son of man (1$^{13}$), the Bride (19$^8$) and the armies of heaven (19$^{14}$). The word for *linen* is not the usual *bussinon* but *linon* = flax, for which there is a well-supported variant *lithon* = (precious) *stone*. This makes possible sense; cf. Ezek. 28$^{13}$, a passage which was in John's mind (17$^4$, 18$^{16}$, 21$^{19-21}$). But *linen* fits so much better – cf. also Ezek. 9$^1$–10$^2$, the passage which lies behind Rev. 8$^{3-5}$ – that RSV is right to read it, even though it is the 'easier reading'. The 'harder reading' is normally to be preferred (because copyists tend to smooth out difficulties rather than create them), unless, as here, it may be due to a mechanical error of transcription; cf. 5$^{10}$.

## 7

*seven golden bowls full of the wrath of God:* the *third woe* was dragon's wrath (12$^{12}$, Deut. 32$^{33}$ LXX); this is God's – ministered like the horsemen-plagues (6$^{1-8}$) by one of the *living creatures* which form his throne, but linked with the dragon's by the *bowls* (*phialai*, vials) or cups; see on 14$^8$, $^{10}$. The Targum in fact introduces the Aramaic loan-word *piyilē* = *phialai* at Isa. 51$^{17}$, $^{22}$. There God takes the 'cup of staggering' and 'bowl of his wrath' from Israel and gives it to her tormentors.

*who lives for ever and ever:* cf. 4$^{9f.}$, 10$^6$; contrast 14$^{11}$.

## 8

*the temple was filled with smoke:* cf. Isa. 6$^4$. *No one could enter*, as when God's glory filled the *tent* (Ex. 40$^{35}$) and the *temple* (I Kings 8$^{11}$).

**16** *Then I heard a loud voice from the temple telling the seven angels, 'Go and pour out on the earth the seven bowls of the wrath of God.'*

*2 So the first angel went and poured his bowl on the earth, and foul and evil sores came upon the men who bore the mark of the beast and worshipped its image.*

*3 The second angel poured his bowl into the sea, and it became like the blood of a dead man, and every living thing died that was in the sea.*

*4 The third angel poured his bowl into the rivers and the fountains of water, and they became blood. 5 And I heard the angel of water say,*

*'Just art thou in these thy judgments,*
*  thou who art and wast, O Holy One.*
*6 For men have shed the blood of saints and prophets,*
*  and thou hast given them blood to drink.*
*It is their due!'*
*7 And I heard the altar cry,*
*'Yea, Lord God the Almighty, true and just are thy judgments!'*
*8 The fourth angel poured his bowl on the sun, and it was allowed to scorch men with fire; 9 men were scorched by the fierce heat, and they cursed the name of God who had power over these plagues, and they did not repent and give him glory.*

The first four of *the seven bowls of the wrath of God* are closely modelled on the first four trumpet plagues (8^{7-12}). They fall on *earth, sea, rivers* and *sun*; they echo the plagues of Egypt, after the manner of the Wisdom of Solomon (see on 8^{6-13}); they are set in motion from the *temple* (cf. 8^{3-5}); and they are the punishment of idolatry: what was there stated symbolically (see on 8^{8-11}) is here stated directly (v. 2).

But they are more than a mere recapitulation:

(i) The trumpets gave warning by smiting a *third*: here the effect is total.

(ii) The wickedness which recoils upon the idolatrous is focused on the murder of God's spokesmen which their idolatry involves (vv. 5-7; cf. Jezebel again, I Kings 16^{31}, 18^4).

(iii) The trumpets section covered the great 'sacrilege' and 'tribulation' in the Lord's apocalypse: the beast showed its colours in killing the saints who refused to worship its image and take its mark ($13^{15-17}$). The bowls section covers the vindication of the Son of man and his elect, which involves the punishment of the beast's followers (the first four bowls), and the demolition of its kingdom and city (the last three).

The theme is God's retributive justice, executed by the elements: his creation taking vengeance on his enemies, according to the principle 'whereby a man sins, thereby is he punished' (Wisd. $5^{17}$, $11^6$). Here is the vindication of the souls under the altar, who were slain for their witness ($6^{9-11}$), as the *altar* itself *cries* (v. 7).

These punishments which their crimes bring down make men *curse* God (vv. 9, 11, 21), lit. *blaspheme*, thus laying bare their identification with the beast (cf. $13^{1,5f.}$, $17^3$). But this is not the whole picture. It is clear that such identification may be final (see on $14^{9-11}$), but the passages envisaging ultimate repentance must not be ignored ($1^7$, $11^{13}$, $14^7$, $15^{3f.}$, $21^{24ff.}$); the section $10^1-11^{13}$ represents another 'story', which overlaps that of the septets of plagues – see on $16^{19}$. The *blood* which men are made to drink (v. 6) is here simply punitive, but at $14^{20}$ and $19^{13-15}$ there is at least the hint that it may be ultimately redemptive. But retribution must have its place. Redemption is not achieved at its expense in John's thought any more than Paul's (cf. Rom. $1^{18ff.}$). See also pp. 49–51 on divine vengeance.

ഇരു

1

*a loud voice from the temple:* presumably God's (cf. $15^8$), as at v. 17. 'A voice from the temple! The voice of the Lord, rendering recompense to his enemies!' (Isa. $66^6$).

*pour out on the earth* ...: 'Pour out thy wrath upon the nations that know thee not ... for they have devoured Jacob' (Jer. $10^{25}$; cf. Ps. $69^{24}$, Zeph. $3^8$). But see the allusions to Jeremiah at $15^{3f.}$, which suggest that there is hope in the end for the nations.

*the seven bowls of the wrath of God:* see on $15^{1,7}$. They evoke both the *cup* of God's wrath, and the libation which completed the Jewish daily liturgy (see p. 159).

**2**

*the first angel . . . poured his bowl on the earth:* cf. the first trumpet ($8^7$). But the effect, *foul and evil sores* or boils, links with the fifth trumpet (see on $9^2$, and on the fifth bowl, $16^{10f.}$). The *sores* come first because they match the beast's *mark* (cf. Wisd. $11^{16}$). What was a deficiency, lack of God's seal ($9^4$), which laid men open to deception (cf. II Thess. $2^{10ff.}$), has now broken out in a deadly infection.

**3**

*the second angel poured his bowl into the sea:* the second trumpet caused a *third* of the *sea* to become *blood*. Now the effect is total. 'Blood of a corpse' both enhances the horror and prepares for v. 6.

**4-7**

*the third angel poured his bowl into the rivers . . . :* the fresh waters now become *blood* too (this was the first Egyptian plague, Ex. $7^{17ff.}$). The third trumpet caused the *waters* to be made bitter by the fall of the star Wormwood, symbolizing 'the new Babylon which has poisoned by its idolatry the springs of its own life' ($8^{10f.}$; Caird, p. 115). Now the poison is specified: their murder of God's witnesses, the *saints and prophets*; cf. $11^{7ff.}$, $13^7$, $^{15}$, $17^6$, $18^{24}$, $19^2$. Nero's terrible pogrom of AD 65 (see pp. 22f. above), not current persecution, explains the violence of the language.

**5**

*the angel of water:* cf. the 'angels over the powers of the waters' at I Enoch $66^2$, and the angels over winds and fire (Rev. $7^1$, $14^{18}$). In contemporary thought spiritual powers represented and controlled earthly realities (see p. 16 above).

*Just art thou in these thy judgments:* this is the *hour of judgment* of him who made heaven and earth, the sea and the *fountains of waters*, proclaimed by the angel with the eternal gospel ($14^{6f.}$). But its immediate effect, in line with the warnings that followed ($14^{8-11}$), is that men refuse to *give God glory* ($14^7$, $16^9$) – though according to the Song of Moses and the Lamb that will be the ultimate result ($15^{3f.}$; cf. $11^{13}$).

*thou who art and wast, O Holy One:* as at $11^{17}$ the future element, 'art to come', is dropped from the threefold title. God's *holiness* (see on $15^4$) is now present, unmitigated by space and time.

**6**

*It is their due:* lit. 'they are worthy' (*axios* – a keyword in Wisd. 11–19, e.g. 16⁹). Contrast 3⁴ and 5⁹: the Lamb was *worthy* because he ransomed men by his *blood*. They have *shed blood*, lit. *poured out*, echoing the *pouring out* of the bowls.

**7**

*I heard the altar cry:* cf. 6⁹, 8³⁻⁵, 9¹³, 14¹⁸. The source and the validation of God's judgments is the *altar*: the place of incense (= the prayers of the saints) and of sacrifice (= God's own provision for atonement).

**8**

*the fourth angel poured his bowl on the sun:* at the fourth trumpet a *third* of the sun was struck, so that its light was impaired. Here its heat is intensified (*it was allowed* signifies divine control, cf. 9², 13⁵, etc.) and *men* are *scorched* – 'who worship the beast's image' is understood, like 'who lack God's seal' at 9¹⁵. Contrast 7¹⁶, and Dan. 3²², ²⁷: the three who refused to worship Nebuchadnezzar's image were not even singed by the scorching furnace.

**9**

*they cursed the name of God:* lit. *blasphemed*, as at vv. 11, 21 – a mark of the beast (13¹, ⁵ᶠ·, 17³; Caird, p. 202). At least they recognize the ultimate source of *these plagues*, though not the immediate cause in their own sin: to men blinded by false allegiance God's law, and the punishments its transgression entails, are intolerable.

*they did not repent and give him glory:* contrast 11¹³. As with Nebuchadnezzar (Dan. 3²⁸), it is the resurrection of God's witnesses which makes the beholders give glory to God.

16<sup>10-21</sup>    THE LAST THREE BOWLS

¹⁰*The fifth angel poured his bowl on the throne of the beast, and its kingdom was in darkness; men gnawed their tongues in anguish* ¹¹*and cursed the God of heaven for their pain and sores, and did not repent of their deeds.*

¹²*The sixth angel poured his bowl on the great river Euphrates, and its water was dried up, to prepare the way for the kings from the east.* ¹³*And I saw, issuing from the mouth of the dragon and from the mouth of the beast and from the mouth of the false prophet, three foul spirits like frogs;* ¹⁴*for they are demonic spirits, performing signs, who go abroad to the kings of the whole world, to assemble them for battle on the great day of God the Almighty.* ¹⁵(*'Lo, I am coming like a thief! Blessed is he who is awake, keeping his garments that he may not go naked and be seen exposed!'*) ¹⁶*And they assembled them at the place which is called in Hebrew Armageddon.*

¹⁷*The seventh angel poured his bowl into the air, and a great voice came out of the temple, from the throne, saying, 'It is done!'* ¹⁸*And there were flashes of lightning, loud noises, peals of thunder, and a great earthquake such as had never been since men were on the earth, so great was that earthquake.* ¹⁹*The great city was split into three parts, and the cities of the nations fell, and God remembered great Babylon, to make her drain the cup of the fury of his wrath.* ²⁰*And every island fled away, and no mountains were to be found;* ²¹*and great hailstones, heavy as a hundredweight, dropped on men from heaven, till men cursed God for the plague of the hail, so fearful was that plague.*

The first four bowls struck the elements of nature, and through them all who followed the beast. The last three are more directly political, directed not against individuals but the forces of deception and persecution. The *fifth* strikes the beast's *throne*, the directing centre of the brilliant *kingdom* in which men had put their trust. This confidence shattered, the *pain* of the fourth bowl and the *sores* of the first cause unmitigated *anguish*. *Darkness*, echoing the fifth trumpet and the ninth Egyptian plague as elaborated at Wisd. 17, is the realm of fears and conscience pangs (see on 9²).

The *sixth bowl* echoes the sixth trumpet, with the *Euphrates* as the starting point of a destructive army (9¹⁴), but its plague is different from the rest: not the *drying up* of the river, but the *frog-spirits* which gather *the kings of the whole world* to their doom; as with the 'third woe' the damage lies in the deception. Here v. 15 is crucially significant. It breaks in so roughly that some think it has been displaced, from the letter to Sardis (3³). But how? and why? It is in fact a sharp reminder of the concerns of the letters, which we have argued lie all the time behind the apocalyptic part. Such interruptions are typical of John's use of apocalyptic for his pastoral purposes, jolting his hearers out of any comfortable fantasies they may have been enjoying (see on $13^{9f.}$, $^{18}$, $14^{12f.}$, $18^4$, $19^9$). The danger of deception and the threat of Christ's coming is primarily for *them* – lest he come and find them asleep in spite of warning, like the disciples in Gethsemane (Mark $13^{36}$, $14^{37ff.}$). John describes God's judgments not only in order to comfort Christians but to 'counter the insidious arguments being used by leaders within the church to reduce the rigour of Christ's demands . . . [cf. p. 92]. They stand between the call to battle and the assembling of the soldiers: will they answer the frog's call or the Messiah's?' (Minear, pp. 148f.). Christ's coming and God's judgment are, contrary to conventional expectation, inseparable from contemporary world events.

The *seventh bowl* moves the drama on, just as the series as a whole marks an advance on the trumpets (pp. 158 and 242f. above). The seventh trumpet introduced, as the third woe, what the earth dwellers took to be their supreme blessing, the kingdom of the beast. This is now shattered in its social base, the *great city*; the next chapters spell out its ruin, at the hand of the beast itself and its confederates ($17^{16f.}$). Here, *lightning*, *thunder*, *earthquake* and *hail* pick up the adumbrations of the final manifestation of God's will which have already been given at $4^5$, $8^5$ and $11^{19}$, while v. 20 picks up $6^{14}$ and looks forward to $20^{11}$: cosmic demolition prepares for judgment and a new order. As at v. 9, and $9^{20f.}$, these plagues do not make men *repent*, which is God's overriding purpose, but make them show their identification with the beast in *blaspheming God* (vv. 11, 21); contrast $11^{13}$.

ॐ

**10**

*The fifth angel poured his bowl on the throne of the beast:* Satan's *throne*, which he shared with the beast ($13^2$), was at Pergamum ($2^{13}$), the Roman provincial capital. It suggests destruction of the central administration of the empire – something like the chaos of the civil wars of AD 68–69 (see p. 23).

*its kingdom was in darkness:* lit. 'was put into darkness' (perfect participle). Men's *anguish* reminds us of the torture of the locusts' sting ($9^{5ff.}$), symbolizing the torment of spiritual darkness – cf. Wisd. $17^{11-21}$, Eph. $4^{18}$, Matt. $8^{12}$, etc.

## 11

*cursed the God of heaven:* lit. *blasphemed* – see on v. 9. Is there an echo of Isa. $8^{22ff.}$, where those who had forsaken the law 'cursed their king and their God', which leads into the passage, 'the people who walked in darkness have seen a great light'? *God of heaven* may suggest the futility of human *kingdoms* over against God's (Dan. $2^{19ff.}$, $^{44}$); contrast $11^{13}$.

*did not repent of their deeds:* cf. $9^{20f.}$. *Deeds*, or *works*, suggest both idolatry (*works of their hands*) and its criminal consequences.

## 12

*the great river Euphrates:* see on $9^{14}$ – the starting point for invasion of Palestine in OT times and of the Roman empire by the Parthians; see pp. 23f., 209f., on the *Nero redivivus* myth. Cyrus had taken Babylon by *drying up* the Euphrates (Herodotus I. 191; cf. Jer. $50^{38}$, $51^{36}$), but the primary echoes are biblical: the *drying up* of Red Sea and Jordan for the sake of Israel (Ex. $14^{21}$, Josh. $4^{23}$), which Isaiah had reapplied to Israel's rescue from Babylon by Cyrus (Isa. $44^{27}$, $50^2$, $51^{10}$). This is now applied to the new Babylon, in line with another of the book of Wisdom's principles, that the godless are punished by what helps the godly (Wisd. $11^5$, $16^{24}$).

*to prepare the way:* cf. Isa. $40^3$, Mark $1^3$, another counter-echo. It is not for King Messiah but for the *kings* from the barbarian *east* (contrast also the wise men of Matt. $2^{1ff.}$).

## 13f.

*from the mouth of the dragon . . . .:* the satanic trinity of ch. 13. The identity of the *false prophet* and second beast is confirmed by $19^{20}$ compared with $13^{14}$.

*three foul spirits like frogs: foul* is *akatharta*, the usual word for 'unclean spirits' in the synoptic gospels. *Frogs* from the river penetrated the whole of Egypt (Ex. $8^{2ff.}$), and their 'magicians did the same by their secret arts' (8⁷). The magic which captivates the heathen in the end destroys them, for it comes from *demonic spirits, performing signs*; cf. 13¹³ᶠᶠ·, Acts 8⁹ᶠᶠ·, II Thess. 2⁹ᶠᶠ·. The repeated *out of their mouth* reminds us of Satan's 'river of lies' (12¹⁵ᶠ·), in contrast with the Son of man's sword (1¹⁶, etc.) and the fire of the witnesses (11⁵).

*to assemble them for battle:* as the 'lying spirit' enticed Ahab to Ramoth-Gilead (I Kings 22²⁰⁻²²). See also Zech 14²ᶠᶠ·. Kings and rulers are *gathered together* against the Lord and his anointed (Ps. 2², LXX; see p. 191).

*the great day of God the Almighty:* cf. Joel 2¹¹, ³¹, 3⁹ᶠᶠ·, Zeph. 1¹⁴ᶠᶠ·, and see on 6¹⁶. *Almighty* (*pantocratōr*) represents Hebrew *sebaōth*, 'of hosts'; see on 1⁸.

### 15

*Lo, I am coming like a thief:* arguments – e.g. by Charles and Lohmeyer – for displacement from 3³ miss the point; the Christ of the letters breaks in here in case the churches should miss it. 'False Christs and false prophets will arise and show great signs and wonders so as to lead astray, if possible, even the elect' (Matt. 24²⁴ par); the Son of man will come unexpectedly like a thief in the night (Matt. 24⁴³ᶠᶠ·, I Thess. 5¹ᶠᶠ·). The churches must *keep awake*, spiritually and morally *clothed*. At Sardis, where Cyrus had also come like a thief, most have *soiled their garments* (3⁴). Here the tense of *go naked* and *be seen* is present subjunctive = 'go about naked habitually'. The danger is of being caught not momentarily but habitually off guard – not, to put it crudely, with trousers down, but without trousers at all. *Be seen exposed*, lit. 'lest men see your indecency', reminds us of the Laodiceans who do not realize their lack of clothing (3¹⁸); as with the Sardians, their *works* (witness and morality) are deficient. Clothing signifies the righteousness and holiness which God will accept (cf. 19⁸); nakedness signifies its lack.

*Blessed is he:* 'Beatitudes' were used by Jewish and Christian prophets both to embody proverbial wisdom and to support an emergency appeal (Minear, pp. 149ff.). Unlike a direct command ('Wake up!') it calls the hearer to examine himself ('Am I awake?').

### 16

*at the place which is called in Hebrew Armageddon:* like 666 (see pp. 217f.), this may have been a commonplace for Jewish Christians, but soon

became a puzzle. It should be spelt Har-mageddon, = mountain of
Megiddo. Megiddo (LXX Mageddon) was a famous battle-field, but
it was in the plain (Zech. 12¹¹), which may explain why some ancient
authorities omit (h)ar, and it has been suggested that John meant the
mythological 'mount of assembly' (har mo'ed; the Hebrew letter ayin is
often represented in Greek by gamma), where Lucifer, King of Babylon,
tried to set his throne above God's (Isa. 14¹³). But this is philologically
dubious, and the OT allusions to Megiddo are highly congenial to
John's concerns (see Farrer, p. 178). Its nearest mountain was Carmel,
where Elijah confronted the prophets of Baal in the time of Ahab and
Jezebel (I Kings 18¹⁹ᶠᶠ·). At Megiddo King Josiah met his end (II Kings
23²⁹), which the Chronicler describes in terms of Ahab's (II Chron.
35²⁰⁻²⁵, I Kings 22 – see on v. 14 above). There was great mourning,
which in Zechariah was associated with the 'mourning for him whom
they have pierced' (cf. Rev. 1⁷), and was followed by the removal of
false prophets and the unclean spirit (Zech. 12¹⁰–13⁴). At Megiddo 'the
stars in their courses fought for Israel' (Judg. 5¹⁹ᶠ·; cf. Wisd. 5¹⁷ again),
and the floods swept the invincible enemy away.

**17**

*the seventh angel poured his bowl into the air:* Satan was 'the prince of the
power of the *air*' (Eph. 2²); the sub-lunar belt was thought to be his
'sphere of influence'. Christ's victory over him on the cross is brought
to completion; see on 12⁷⁻¹². *'It is done!'* echoes 'It is finished!' (John
19³⁰). For *the voice from the temple,* see 15⁸. *'It is done!'* is repeated at 21⁶:
these *last plagues* (15¹), which are worked out in detail in 17–20, are the
dark side of God's new creation.

**18**

For this evocation of Sinai (Ex. 19¹⁶ᶠᶠ·) cf. Heb. 12¹⁸⁻²⁹ – 'the removal of
what is shaken ... in order that what cannot be shaken may remain'.
*Earthquake* in the Bible often signifies the shattering and removal of a
corrupt political order (see on 6¹² and note *g*).

*such as had never been:* cf. Dan. 12¹, Joel 2², Matt. 24²¹, and see Ex.
9¹⁸, ²⁴ for similar language about the *hail* (v. 21).

**19**

*The great city was split into three parts:* probably John's interpretation of
the splitting of Jerusalem at Zech. 14⁴ᶠ·. But what is the relation to the
earthquake which destroyed *a tenth* of the *great city* at 11¹³? Some

distinguish the *great city* = Jerusalem from *great Babylon*, but it includes both, and Sodom and Egypt as well (11^8). At 11^13 men *gave glory to the God of heaven*, here the opposite (vv. 9, 11, 21); the cross-reference is deliberate. It might be supposed that 11^13 was a partial shattering, causing temporary repentance, and that now, the *witnesses* having been removed, the earth is totally given over to beast-worship, leading to total destruction – but to what end, then, promises like 15^3f. and warnings like 16^15 and 18^4? It is more likely that 10^1–11^13, and the series of plagues, describe different but overlapping realities. *This* earth can never finally be without the lies of Satan and the universal destruction they entail (even the binding of ch. 20 is only temporary). Nor can it be without 'the testimony of Jesus' (unless the churches succumb to Balaam and Jezebel), with its spiritual 'earthquake' (cf. Matt. 27^51-54, 28^2) in which lies hope of *a new heaven and a new earth* (21^1).

*the cities of the nations fell:* in dependence on the *great city*, as if involved in the same tremor. 17^16 shows that no literal earthquake is in mind.

*God remembered great Babylon:* see on 14^8. The Greek – 'Babylon was remembered before God' – avoids anthropomorphism; the time had come (11^18) to take account, and let her sins recoil upon her.

*drain the cup:* lit. 'to give her the cup of the wine of the fury of his wrath'. See on 6^16 and 14^8, ^10.

## 20

*every island fled away ...:* as at the opening of the sixth seal (6^14ff.) all refuge is removed; *mountains* may also signify false religion (e.g. Ezek. 20^28). The structures men have erected in their flight from God themselves *flee*. The process is complete when *earth and sky flee away* (20^11) and individual judgment takes place.

## 21

*great hailstones:* cf. Ex. 9^18ff. Very heavy hail, such as had never been (cf. v. 18 above), smote the Egyptians who did not go in to safety. Their *cities having fallen* (v. 19), there is no protective veil between men and God's presence; see on 6^16, 15^5. Like Pharaoh and the Egyptians, they are only hardened. Contrast the earthquake and rending of the veil in the other 'story', represented by 10^1–11^13.

*men cursed God:* see on v. 9.

17 *Then one of the seven angels who had the seven bowls came and said to me, 'Come, I will show you the judgment of the great harlot who is seated upon many waters, <sup>2</sup>with whom the kings of the earth have committed fornication, and with the wine of whose fornication the dwellers on earth have become drunk.' <sup>3</sup>And he carried me away in the Spirit into a wilderness, and I saw a woman sitting on a scarlet beast which was full of blasphemous names, and it had seven heads and ten horns. <sup>4</sup>The woman was arrayed in purple and scarlet, and bedecked with gold and jewels and pearls, holding in her hand a golden cup full of abominations and the impurities of her fornication; <sup>5</sup>and on her forehead was written a name of mystery: 'Babylon the great, mother of harlots and of earth's abominations.' <sup>6</sup>And I saw the woman, drunk with the blood of the saints and the blood of the martyrs of Jesus.*

*When I saw her I marvelled greatly.*

Through the bowl-angel who introduces the vision John will later link the *harlot* with the *Bride* (21<sup>9</sup>), the true city of which the *harlot* is the parody; by her *array* (v. 4) she is already revealed as a parody of the glorious *woman* of 12<sup>1ff.</sup>; cf. the Laodicean church in its imagined finery (3<sup>17f.</sup>). His central concern is the relation of the church to the world: he expounds the 'gathering of the elect' of the traditional scheme as the adorning of the Bride, which must be preceded by the dismantling of the *harlot*, in order that those she has seduced may (duly chastened; cf. 3<sup>17f.</sup>) be gathered in.

The *many waters* on which she is *seated*, and the *golden cup* in her hand (v. 4) link her with *Babylon*, even without the *name* on her *forehead* (v. 5) – see Jer. 51<sup>13</sup> (cf. 'the waters of Babylon', Ps. 137<sup>1</sup>), and 51<sup>7</sup>. Her *fornication* is elaborated in ch. 18 in terms of Ezekiel's lament over the commerce of Tyre (Ezek. 27). The OT saw a connection between civilization and commerce and a fall from religious and moral simplicity – Ahab was led astray by his Phoenician queen, Jezebel (I Kings 18, 21). Thyatira, the city of 'Jezebel' (2<sup>20</sup>), and Laodicea were commercial cities, as were all the seven. The churches were not immune to the glamour of the civilization in which they had to bear their witness; their sites today reveal something of its real splendour and beauty.

In order that he may see her (and show her to the churches) in her true colours, John is carried away *in the Spirit into a wilderness*, like Jesus for his encounter with Satan (Matt. 4¹ par.). Unlike Jesus, and in spite of her *beast* (v. 3), *cup* (v. 4), *name* (v. 5) and *drunkenness* (v. 6), John (like many Christians?) is almost overcome: *I marvelled greatly* (cf. v. 8 and 13³). As we have said, his concern is with the church, and with discernment – see the letter to Thyatira, and pp. 92 and 237f. Chapters 17 and 18 are a tirade not primarily against contemporary civilization, but against those who, having been entrusted with light for the world, act as if contemporary civilization is itself that light. It is in John's view a prostitution of it, but his chief concern is that prostitution within the church.

☙❧

**1**

*the judgment of the great harlot:* this is in fact described by the angel (vv. 16f.); John is *shown* simply the *harlot* herself. She has many antecedents besides Babylon and Jezebel: Nineveh (Nahum 3⁴), Tyre (Ezek. 26, 27), the Cities of the Plain (Gen. 19), perhaps Cleopatra (Stauffer, pp. 58, 188), certainly Jerusalem (Ezek. 16 and 23), which is the model of the church: 'How has the faithful city become a harlot!' (Isa. 1²¹).

*seated upon many waters:* they are allegorized as her tributary nations (v. 15). Her seat on the beast is a different allegory (vv. 3, 9). The allegories may well stem from an actual vision (see p. 42 and note *m*).

**2**

*with whom the kings of the earth have committed fornication:* see on 2¹⁴, 14⁸ for *fornication* as a metaphor of religious infidelity, and 18³ for the commercial angle. Contrast the *Bride* adorned for her *husband* (21²). For *the kings of the earth* see v. 18 and 18⁹ᶠᶠ·; they are to be distinguished from the *kings* of 16¹⁴ and 17¹²ᶠᶠ·. Ultimately they will bring their glory into the holy city (21²⁴).

**3**

*he carried me away in the Spirit:* this is not merely a renewal of inspiration (cf. 1¹⁰, 4² and 21¹⁰ – another verbal link with the vision of the *Bride*), but an echo of Jesus' temptations. The *wilderness* has many associations (see on 12⁶, and see Isa. 21¹ff.): it is the place of demons and temptation, and of spiritual perception and preservation. There is a counter-echo of the glorious woman (12⁶, ¹⁴).

*sitting on a scarlet beast . . .:* see notes on 12³ and 13¹. She is in fact riding a tiger (v. 16).

4
*purple and scarlet:* cf. Jerusalem (Jer. 4³⁰, Ezek. 16¹¹⁻¹³) and the 'great city' (18¹⁶). Contrast the *linen* of the *Bride* (19⁸), which represents the *righteous deeds of the saints* over against the *abominations* and *impurities* of heathen worship (cf. 3⁴f.) and the false confidence of some Christians (3¹⁷f.).

*gold and jewels and pearls:* cf. Tyre (Ezek. 28¹³) and the 'great city' again, and contrast the Bride (21¹¹ff.). The architecture and adornment of the true city also represents the lives of her citizens; cf. 3¹² and notes on 14¹³.

*golden cup:* 'Babylon was a golden cup in the Lord's hand, making all the earth drunken' (Jer. 51⁷); see on 14⁸, ¹⁰.

5
*on her forehead . . . a name:* perhaps an oblique reference to Roman prostitutes (cf. Juvenal VI. 122ff.), but it may simply be a counter-echo of 14¹: the 144,000 have the Lamb's *name* and his Father's *written on their foreheads*; cf. 13¹⁶f., the mark and *name* of the beast.

*a name of mystery:* lit. 'a name written, mystery'. *Mustērion* could be taken as part of the title, as by RV, but, as at 1²⁰, it indicates that the name is a symbol; cf. the Jerusalem Bible: 'a cryptic name'. *Mystery* in the Bible means something hidden from men of 'this world' but revealed by God to his prophets (cf. Dan. 2²⁹f., I Cor. 2⁶⁻¹⁰) – here it is the *mystery* not of God (10⁷) but of lawlessness (II Thess. 2⁷).

*earth's abominations:* lit.. 'detestable things', used of the practices of idolatry, as at v. 4; cf. Daniel's 'abomination of desolation' (Matt. 24¹⁵). She personifies all prostitution of God's creation, and is embodied at the moment in Rome.

**6**

*drunk with the blood of the saints:* see on 16⁴⁻⁷ and cf. Jezebel (I Kings 16³¹, 18⁴). The reference is to Nero's massacre.

*the martyrs of Jesus: martures,* lit. 'witnessess'; see on 11³⁻¹³.

*When I saw her I marvelled:* cf. 13³. *Seeing* on its own often suggests the deceptiveness of appearances; cf. 13¹⁰ and p. 125. He *hears* the *mystery* from the angel (vv. 7ff.).

## 17^{7-11}     THE HARLOT AND THE BEAST

⁷*But the angel said to me, 'Why marvel? I will tell you the mystery of the woman, and of the beast with seven heads and ten horns that carries her.* ⁸*The beast that you saw was, and is not, and is to ascend from the bottomless pit and go to perdition; and the dwellers on earth whose names have not been written in the book of life from the foundation of the world, will marvel to behold the beast, because it was and is not and is to come.* ⁹*This calls for a mind with wisdom: the seven heads are seven hills on which the woman is seated;* ¹⁰*they are also seven kings, five of whom have fallen, one is, the other has not yet come, and when he comes he must remain only a little while.* ¹¹*As for the beast that was and is not, it is an eighth but it belongs to the seven, and it goes to perdition.'*

John's *marvelling* at the sight of the woman is rebuked by the angel who explains her *mystery*, but in terms of the *beast* – as if to say 'look not at her, or you will be dazzled, but at the blasphemous power that *carries her,* the parody of him "who is and who was and who is to come" (1⁸)'. He gives a decoding of the allegory of ch. 13, which on the face of it should answer our questions about time and circumstances of writing, but only complicates them. His hearers, of course, knew the answers to our questions. Their difficulty was moral: to see Rome and the empire in bestial terms. *This calls for a mind with wisdom* (v. 9; cf. 13⁹ᶠ·, 1⁸).

On our view the *mystery* cannot help with the dating of Rev. (see pp. 21ff.); the numbers are primarily symbolical.

(i) At first the decoding looks simple. The beast who is an *eighth* but *belongs to the seven* (v. 11) is the *Nero redivivus* of ch. 13. He is to succeed a series of *seven kings*, = emperors, of which Nero was *one*, or perhaps the *first* (see on 13³); the sixth is now reigning and the seventh will last *only a little while* (v. 10). Nero (54–68) was succeeded in quick succession (*five have fallen*) by Galba, Otho, Vitellius and Vespasian (69–79), then Titus (79–81), Domitian (81–96), Nerva (96–98) and Trajan (98–117). If Nero was *first*, John wrote in the time of Titus and was proved wrong: Domitian lasted not 'a little while' but fifteen years.

Intrinsically it is quite possible that Revelation was written in AD 79–81: Titus was dazzlingly popular, and during his reign, which was cut short to general grief, the churches could well have been (in John's view) asleep. But this clashes with Irenaeus' date 'towards the end of Domitian's reign' (p. 21) and it is not agreed that Nero is to be taken as the *first*; various attempts have been made to work with the series of emperors from the beginning, taking Nero as simply *one* of the heads. But then there is no agreement where to begin – Julius Caesar? Augustus? Caligula, the first 'Antichrist' Emperor? – and no agreement how many (if any) of the short-lived emperors of 68–69 to include. Working forward gets us nowhere, unless we know where we are already.

(ii) Other scholars work back from Domitian, in the light of Irenaeus' information and Domitian's later reputation as a second Nero (see pp. 24f.). The correspondence of the short-lived Titus with the seventh, who is to last *a little while*, points to Vespasian as the one who now *is*. This can be reconciled with Irenaeus's statement that John saw his vision 'towards the end of Domitian's reign' on one or other of two theories:

(*a*) A first draft was written in Vespasian's reign (cf. the work of S. Giet; see p. 81 and note *w*), when things were quiet; it was reissued with additions, when things sharpened, to identify Domitian as the returning beast. So Rissi, *Time and History*, pp. 75–82; he thinks 13¹⁸ᵇ and 17⁹ᵇ⁻¹⁷ were added by the editor. Some of his arguments will be mentioned in the commentary.

(b) Revelation was indeed put together under Domitian, but was given a fictitious date in the past, just as Daniel was composed under Antiochus IV (in the second century BC) but purported to come from Babylon during the captivity (in the sixth). This was a conventional device of apocalyptic. It made possible a 'forecast' of future events most of which was right because it had already happened; this lent (temporary) authority to the actual predictions. But quite apart from this passage being a tardy and obscure way of establishing such a stance, there is no sign that 'John' is a pseudonym, and in the letters there is an immediacy which is quite inconsistent with a fictitious stance in the past (see pp. 37f., 77f.).

(iii) But are not these calculations misconceived? John's history, like his geography and arithmetic, is *spiritual* ($11^8$); his hearers needed to be told not *who* was reigning but his spiritual affiliations. The number *seven* is symbolic – there were many more *churches* than *seven* – though it can refer to actual entities. John 'means to represent the Roman power as a historic whole' (Beckwith, p. 708; his discussion, pp. 704–08, is excellent). His readers knew all about Nero, but were as unlikely to have known the succession of emperors as readers now are unlikely to know that of the Presidents of the United States. Students 'have worried over the five kings whereas John was concerned only with the eighth' (Beasley-Murray, p. 256).[γ]

All we can safely say is that the perspective is that of the *sixth* in a series of *seven*, the penultimate moment. The seventh is only a *little while*, a point without magnitude (but of central significance – see on three and a half, pp. 182f.). It gives way to an *eighth*, which is the *first* raised to a new order of magnitude. But the beast, which is identified with the *first* of its heads, which *seemed* to *have a mortal wound* ($13^3$, $^{12}$, $^{14}$), is a parody of the true Eighth, who is *the first-born of the dead*, the *first* and the *last* ($1^5$, $17$f.). It is 666 over against 888, the penultimate claiming ultimacy (see p. 215). *It goes to perdition*

γ Robinson (*Redating the NT*, pp. 245–7) argues from parallels in contemporary writings like II Esd. 11, 12, the *Letter of Barnabas* $4^4$ (*ECW*, p. 196) and *Sibylline Oracles* V.1–50, that reference to actual men and events must have been intended. This may well have been so, but our point is that it is impossible now to be sure how the details of the series would have been understood then and that in any case the spiritual reference is primary.

(v. 11): that is its abiding characteristic, just as Christ is characterized as the Coming One.

At the time of writing the beast is not openly present in its true guise; the only contemporary martyr is Antipas (2¹³); the churches are asleep. John probably did write under Domitian, as Irenaeus says, but it is wrong to appeal to Domitian's Neronic traits as evidence. They were evident only to disgruntled aristocrats in Rome: in Asia the Flavians were popular (see pp. 24ff. and notes *m* and *n*). He could have written under Trajan (cf. Farrer, pp. 34–7), who carried on the Flavian policies, including the acceptance of divine honours, or at any time after Nero's death long enough for the idea of his return to have become current, and for the memory of the terrible years 64–70 to have softened – otherwise Christians would hardly have needed to have had their eyes opened to the nature of the empire and the nearness of the End.

༄

**7**

*why marvel?:* the natural response to the divine, which may be evoked by false divinity, as in v. 8, and 13³ff..

*I will tell you the mystery:* see on v. 5; cf. I Cor. 15⁵¹, 2⁷.

*seven heads and ten horns:* see on 12³, 13¹ff..

**8**

*was, and is not, and is to ascend:* a parody of the divine title of 1⁴. God is 'he who is': the beast *is not*. The *wounded head* has not yet come back to life (13¹⁴). It is a time when Christians can think the victory of Gen. 3¹⁵ has been safely won (see on 12¹⁷, 13³), and that they are repossessed of Eden (thus the warning of 2⁵, ⁷).

*from the bottomless pit:* lit. 'the abyss', the home of demons – see on 9¹. The beast is both demonic and personal (see on 13¹⁴).

*go to perdition: apōleia,* destruction – see on 9¹¹. It is described as the *lake of fire* at 19²⁰, 20¹⁰, ¹⁴.

*whose names have not been written:* a summary of 13⁸ – see there on predestination and the *book of life* (or of the living).

*will marvel . . . because it was and is not and is to come:* cf. 13³, ¹⁴. They will marvel at the power of recovery which the beast will have shown by its return. *Is to come* is *parestai*, the verb corresponding to the noun *parousia*, which was used for Jesus' final coming.

## 9
*This calls for a mind with wisdom:* see on 13¹⁸. This is hardly, as some suggest, veiled language to escape the censor: any outsider could see in *seven hills* a reference to Rome.

## 10
*they are also seven kings:* easily grasped from Dan. 7¹⁴ff.. Such a double interpretation of a vision is unparalleled – for Rissi an indication of secondary material – but it simply makes the point that the *kings*, who are the nub, are Roman (Beckwith, p. 698).

*five of whom have fallen: fallen* would be especially appropriate if the Year of the Four Emperors was in mind; it can also suggest the throwing down of spiritual powers (see on 8⁸, ¹⁰, 9¹).

*one is:* this is not meant to tell the hearers who is reigning – they know. John is presenting the emperors as a symbolic *seven*, and placing himself and his readers at the *sixth* for symbolic reasons: at the *sixth* trumpet and *sixth* bowl forces are gathered for the final showdown, while the *seventh* each depict a short but crucial moment of crisis leading into it – see 12¹² and 17¹², and indeed 8¹, the seventh seal ('half an hour'!). John's churches are not yet at the moment of crisis, but in the approach to it on which the outcome depends; cf. Gethsemane (Matt. 26⁴⁰ par.). If they do not *keep awake* (16¹⁵) now, when the crisis comes they will be among the earth-dwellers captivated by the beast – the Antichrist they do not discern.

## 11
*it is an eighth but it belongs to the seven:* it appears claiming the transcendence that *eighth* expresses (cf. Matt. 24²⁴, II Thess. 2³ff.), but in fact it is one of the old firm; its being is as derivative as theirs. All who commit themselves to it must follow it to *perdition* (cf. 20¹⁵).

$^{12}$'And the ten horns that you saw are ten kings who have not yet received royal power, but they are to receive authority as kings for one hour, together with the beast. $^{13}$These are of one mind and give over their power and authority to the beast; $^{14}$they will make war on the Lamb, and the Lamb will conquer them, for he is Lord of lords and King of kings, and those with him are called and chosen and faithful.'

$^{15}$And he said to me, 'The waters that you saw, where the harlot is seated, are peoples and multitudes and nations and tongues. $^{16}$And the ten horns that you saw, they and the beast will hate the harlot; they will make her desolate and naked, and devour her flesh and burn her up with fire, $^{17}$for God has put it into their hearts to carry out his purpose by being of one mind and giving over their royal power to the beast, until the words of God shall be fulfilled. $^{18}$And the woman that you saw is the great city which has dominion over the kings of the earth.'

The instruments of the *judgment* of the harlot (v. 1) are now explained: the *ten horns*, identified as *kings* as at Dan. 7$^{24}$, but not now the central line of emperors. They are barbaric/demonic forces from outside the civilized Roman world (16$^{12ff.}$), but spiritually they are related to its rulers: both draw their power from the beast and its master (13$^{2, 4}$). These apparently disparate forces are to be united *for one hour* in an attack on the *Lamb* and his followers (v. 14), which, because it is the derivative attacking the real, must be their own destruction. But before that, they will have served God's *purpose* (v. 17) by destroying the *harlot* who has been, through history, the means of Satan's influence over men (v. 18).

In other words John sees the apparently invincible and eternal empire destroyed by a coalition of barbaric forces from outside it, unified by the satanic power on which the empire is itself based. It is a house built on *sand* (cf. 13$^1$), on which the floods are soon to descend. His purpose is to warn Christians infatuated or overawed by Rome of the fragility of the *dominion* she exercises over *the kings of the earth* (v. 18).

༺༻

**12**

*the ten horns:* in Dan. 7 they were the *kings* who succeeded Alexander the Great, the fourth beast. John's beast is a composite of Daniel's four, embodying all human arrogance and rebellion against God: it includes the elements which were left outside the Graeco-Roman concept of 'the world', except in its nightmares. These chaotic powers will be articulated for *one hour* (an Aramaism better translated 'for a moment', cf. Dan. 4¹⁹ NEB) in accordance with the Jewish belief that all evil within God's creation must be brought to a head before it is finally destroyed. As at 16¹⁴, they echo the *kings* of Ps. 2².

**13**

*These are of one mind:* a cliché of local politics;ᶻ see on v. 17 – a rational and deliberate alliance to attempt the height of unreason. *These*, repeated in v. 14 (RSV *they*) echoes the repeated *these* in 14⁴, referring to the followers of the Lamb.

**14**

*they will make war on the Lamb:* i.e. the war of 16¹⁴, which is described from the opposite point of view at 19¹¹ᶠᶠ·. The beast was allowed to *make war* on the saints and *conquer* them (11⁷ᶠᶠ·, 13⁷); this is their revenge; cf. the vindication of the two witnesses (11¹¹⁻¹³). Rissi claims that for the Lamb to conquer in battle is contrary to John's usage and theology: he *has* conquered already, by dying. But his status as *Lord of lords* and *King of kings* in virtue of which, here, he *will conquer* was won by his *faithful witness* (1⁵), in which those *with him* share; cf. 12¹¹. The last battle is the final working out of that victory won on the cross (see on 1⁷, pp. 62–4).

*called and chosen and faithful:* not all who are *called* confirm their calling by *faithful* following: 'many are called but few are chosen' (Matt. 20¹⁶, 22¹⁴).

ᶻ W. C. van Unnik, '*Miā gnomē*, Apocalypse of John xvii, 13, 17', in *Studies in John* (*NovT* Suppl. 24), 1970, pp. 209–20.

**15**

*The waters that you saw:* actually they were only alluded to (v. 1); what
he *saw* was the woman sitting on a beast in a *wilderness* – for Rissi
another mark of secondary composition. But this is to demand a consistency inconsistent with the genre; cf. Isa. $21^{1ff.}$, 'the oracle concerning
the *wilderness* of the *sea*', which culminates him 'Fallen, fallen is
Babylon' and is an amalgam of hearing and seeing.

*peoples and multitudes . . . :* this recurrent formula underlines the ecumenical scope of beast and woman (cf. $13^7$), in rivalry with the true woman's
offspring ($12^{17}$) in their witness (cf. $10^{11}$, $11^9$, $14^6$). It also hints at the
insecurity of her seat: the *waters* will become a destroying flood (cf.
Isa. $8^7$, Jer. $47^2$).

*they will hate the harlot:* the *ten kings* are not the same as *the kings of the
earth* (v. 18): they mourn over her ($18^9$).

*make her desolate and naked:* the language is taken from Ezek. $16^{37-41}$,
$23^{25-29}$ on the punishment of adulterous Jerusalem; cf. Jesus' words on
the failed Jerusalem at Laodicea ($3^{17}$). The point here is the self-destruction of evil. *Desolate* is *erēmōmenēn* (perfect participle) = 'rendered
desert' – of a city, laid waste or depopulated. The noun is used of the
destruction of Jerusalem at Luke $21^{20}$: the 'desolating sacrilege' or
*abomination* (vv. 4f.) now recoils upon the desolator.

*devour her flesh:* cf. $19^{17-21}$, based on Ezek. $39^{4, 17-21}$.

*burn her up with fire:* cf. $18^{8f.}$, and Ezek. $16^{41}$, $23^{25}$; it is the punishment
of a harlot (Lev. $21^9$).

**17**

*for God has put it into their hearts: put* is lit. *given,* a common Hebraism,
underlining here the sense of divine control (see on $13^5$): their *giving*
over their power is itself *given*; cf. $13^{2, 4}$. The *heart* in Hebrew and
Greek is the seat of mind and will – thus NEB: 'put it into their heads'.

*to carry out his purpose by being of one mind . . . :* lit. 'to effect his mind
and effect one mind (as v. 13) and give . . .'. Their rational and con-
certed plan operates until God's plan (his *words* express his purpose),
which works through theirs, is *fulfilled,* or completed (cf. $10^7$, $15^{1, 8}$).

18

*And the woman that you saw:* the angel at last returns to the ostensible subject (vv. 1, 7). But the concentration on *beast, heads* and *horns* is not a mark of secondary authorship (against Rissi). The angel was to *show* the *judgment* of the harlot, and though that can be depicted in terms of natural disasters (18^{8ff.}), which can be seen as the hand of God (16^{9, 11, 21}), it is immediately, and must be shown to be, the work of the *beast*. God allows (*gives*) evil to destroy itself, but his own 'proper work' (the Lamb) is other. See on 6^{16}.

*dominion over the kings of the earth:* not the *ten kings*, but the tributaries and paramours of the false queen, who mourn over her burning (18^9). Contrast 21^{24}.

*The Lament over Babylon*

The harlot now becomes Babylon, as the Bride later becomes Jerusalem. The chapter is based on the taunt-songs or dirges of the OT prophets, but is an elaborate and powerful composition in its own right. It is like a triptych within a triptych: the lament (vv. 9–19) is flanked by two proclamations of judgment (vv. 1–8, 20–24), and within it the lament of the *merchants* (vv. 11–17) is flanked by that of the *kings* (vv. 9f.) and *shipmasters* (vv. 17–19). Thus the reader's mind is focused on the world's grief for so much power and wealth so suddenly laid waste, and more precisely on the *merchandise*: all this varied and precious material going to waste.

Caird detects a note of genuine admiration and regret for 'the grandeur that was Rome' – John was 'no Manichaean or eremite, contemptuous of the beauties and amenities of the civilized world' (p. 227); there was nothing sinful about them until they were used by the harlot to seduce men into materialism. To other ears it may sound more like a 'taunt' than a lament, but the proclamations of judgment by which it is framed make it clear that it is not wealth but the arrogant use of it which is condemned, and the lament makes a foil to the glorious fulfilment of the world's potential in the true city (21<sup>24ff.</sup>).

18<sup>1-8</sup>   THE JUDGMENT OF BABYLON (1)

18 *After this I saw another angel coming down from heaven, having great authority; and the earth was made bright with his splendour.* <sup>2</sup>*And he called out with a mighty voice,*

*'Fallen, fallen is Babylon the great!*
*It has become a dwelling place of demons,*
*a haunt of every foul spirit,*
*a haunt of every foul and hateful bird;*
<sup>3</sup>*for all nations have drunk\* the wine of her impure passion,*
*and the kings of the earth have committed fornication with her,*
*and the merchants of the earth have grown rich with the wealth of her*
*wantonness.'*
<sup>4</sup>*Then I heard another voice from heaven saying,*
*'Come out of her, my people, lest you take part in her sins,*
*lest you share in her plagues;*
<sup>5</sup>*for her sins are heaped high as heaven,*
*and God has remembered her iniquities.*
<sup>6</sup>*Render to her as she herself has rendered,*
*and repay her double for her deeds;*
*mix a double draught for her in the cup she mixed.*
<sup>7</sup>*As she glorified herself and played the wanton,*
*so give her a like measure of torment and mourning.*
*Since in her heart she says, "A queen I sit,*
*I am no widow, mourning I shall never see,"*
<sup>8</sup>*so shall her plagues come in a single day,*
*pestilence and mourning and famine,*
*and she shall be burned with fire;*
*for mighty is the Lord God who judges her.'*

\*Other ancient authorities read *fallen by.*


The explanations of ch. 17 give way to proclamation and singing, much as the action in a Greek Tragedy was balanced by the comments and songs of the Chorus. Caird points out that Babylon's destruction is not actually described: just as in ch. 4 John showed us God 'only through the hymns of the worshipping host of heaven, so now he allows us to see the fall of Babylon only through the laments of the heavenly and earthly spectators' (p. 227).

His theme, as in the letter to Thyatira, is the church and the world, and consideration of the OT allusions in these verses may help us to see what he has in mind, though it is always hard to know how far the context can be pressed.

(i) The *angel* with *great authority* evokes Ezek. 43$^{2ff.}$, where the glory of the Lord came to the restored Jerusalem and 'the earth shone with his glory'. Ezekiel connects this vision with those which concerned the destruction of the city (which John has already used[a] – see on 7$^3$, 8$^{3–5}$), and is told that this is the place of God's throne where he will dwell with Israel for ever (cf. 21$^3$), and that Israel will no more defile his name with her kings, her harlotries and her abominations – cf. the language of 17$^{2–5}$, and the application to Babylon at 17$^{16}$ of Ezekiel's words about the punishment of adulterous Jerusalem. Ezek 40–48 is clearly behind the visions of 21$^{10ff.}$, and this allusion to 43$^{2ff.}$ may suggest that the desolation of Babylon (Rev. 18$^{2ff.}$, $^{21ff.}$) is to be seen in the light of God's scouring Jerusalem to prepare it for his everlasting presence. The *great city*, which is Jerusalem (11$^8$) as well as Babylon, is not wholly discontinuous with the true city, any more than the redeemed are discontinuous with the earth-dwellers. The discontinuity is moral, as v. 4 makes clear.

(ii) Another voice summons God's people to *come out of her*, as Lot was summoned from Sodom and the exiled Jews from Babylon. Some scholars object that God's people have all been killed – Babylon is drunk with their blood (17$^6$, 18$^{24}$) – and even if we note that the time-stance is that of the 'sixth head' (17$^{10}$), before the final emergence of the beast and its conquest of the saints, a problem remains: God's people are not required to escape from the world but to maintain the witness of Jesus in the *street of the great city* (11$^8$).

The answer is to recognize overlapping perspectives. From one point of view the holy city is given over to Gentile trampling and the witnesses follow the Faithful Witness to death (11$^{2ff.}$, 12$^{17}$–13$^{18}$). From another the temple is measured (11$^1$) and the woman is preserved in the desert (12$^{6, 14}$). From another God's people are urged to wake up (16$^{15}$), and now to detach themselves from the city in which they sojourn, before they are corrupted and share its punishment: this is the perspective of the letters – moral wakefulness and moral, not literal, separation (cf. 2$^{20ff.}$). For sin is about to recoil in retribution (v. 5).

a For John's use of Ezekiel, see Introduction, p. 40 note *g*.

(iii) But why *repay her double for her deeds* (v. 6)? Consideration of the OT background may confirm both the points just made. In accordance with Jeremiah's prophecy 'First I will recompense their ... sin *double* because they have polluted my land with ... their idols ... and abominations' (Jer. 16¹⁸), Jerusalem in exile 'received of the Lord's hand *double* for all her sins' (Isa. 40²), but was to be restored: 'instead of your shame you shall have a *double* portion' (Isa. 61⁷). There were plenty of OT threats against Sodom, Egypt, Nineveh, Tyre and the historical Babylon: does John's use of passages declaring the punishment and restoration of *Jerusalem* imply the possibility, first of restoration for the *great city*, which is also Jerusalem (11⁸), and, secondly, of punishment for the church, the *holy city's* earthly nucleus, if she identifies herself with Babylon? At any rate the self-assurance of v. 7, *in her heart she says* ..., recalls the church at Laodicea (3¹⁷) – both passages hark back to the Babylon of Isa. 47⁷ᶠ· – and the plagues of v. 8 recall the threats to Jezebel's paramours at Thyatira (22²²ᶠ·).

ℵℵ

**1**

*another angel coming down from heaven:* cf. 10¹. His *great authority*, in contrast with that which the *dragon* gave to the beast (13²), echoes that of God himself, who made the earth shine with his glory (Ezek. 43²).

**2**

*with a mighty voice: mighty* links him again with the *mighty angel* of 10¹, who brought the *little scroll*. It contained the *gospel*, of which *Fallen, fallen is Babylon* is a part; see on 14⁸. *Fallen* is the 'prophetic perfect' of certainty about what is still future.

*a dwelling-place of demons* ...: there are echoes of several OT passages about Babylon: Isa. 13²¹ (the satyrs become *demons* in the LXX); Jer. 50³⁹, 51³⁷; cf. Zeph. 2¹⁴ᶠ· (about Nineveh) and Isa. 34¹¹⁻¹⁴ (about Edom, which is to become a second Sodom: Edom was a rabbinic term for Rome). This is formally inconsistent with both *burning* (v. 8) and *drowning* (v. 21): they are all metaphors of desolation.

*a haunt of every foul spirit: foul* is *akatharton*, 'unclean' – cf. 16¹³. John 'thinks doubtless of the demon-powers represented by the idols of paganism (cf. 9²⁰, 16¹⁴) which will haunt the wrecked temples of Rome' (Swete, p. 224).

**3**

*all nations have drunk:* the majority reading is 'have fallen by' (*peptōkan*). This represents an easy correction of *pepōkan*, 'have drunk', a rare form which is surely right; cf. 14⁸.

*the wine of her impure passion:* lit. 'the wine of the wrath (*thumos*) of her fornication'; see on 14⁸. It is a pregnant phrase: *thumos* can mean anger – her rage against the saints (17², ⁶) as the instrument of the devil's *thumos* (12¹²) – or desire, passion. It is the passionate luxury and materialism of the Roman world which John here develops.

*the wealth of her wantonness:* lit. 'the power of her arrogance' – Gk. *strēnos*, a rare word, but closer to *hubris* than lewdness; cf. II Kings 19²⁸, about the Assyrian King: 'because you have raged against me, and your arrogance (LXX *strēnos*) has come into my ears'. It is the *arrogant power* which enabled the merchants of Rome and Asia Minor to grow fat at the expense of peasant and townsman.

**4**

*Come out of her, my people:* escape from doomed Babylon (Isa. 48²⁰, 52¹¹, Jer. 50⁸, 51⁶) becomes a figure for moral separation, as at II Cor. 6¹⁷ (the whole passage 6¹⁴–7¹ breathes the same spirit as Revelation). Moral co-existence and toleration of the Nicolaitans can only lead to complicity in sin which is about to recoil upon the sinners.

**5**

*heaped high as heaven:* cf. Jer. 51⁹. 'Let us build ourselves a city, a tower with its top in the heavens' said the men of Babel (Gen. 11⁴), but God came down and scattered them, as he came down to see about the sin of Sodom which 'had grown very great' (Gen. 18²⁰ᶠ·).

*God has remembered:* see 16¹⁹. To *remember* in the Bible is often to make present and operative what is latent – cf. I Kings 17¹⁸.

**6**

*Render to her . . . :* the imperative is a rhetorical expression of the divine sentence. If agents are in mind they are not *my people*, but angels or the 'ten horns' of 17¹⁶. As we said on 6⁹⁻¹¹, John is concerned not with private vengeance ('Render to no man evil for evil' said Paul, Rom. 12¹⁷) but public justice ('Vengeance is mine; I will repay, says the Lord', Rom. 12¹⁹).

*repay her double:* probably an echo of the treatment of Jerusalem, as we have said, but perhaps merely conventional for full requital (cf. Jer. 17¹⁸).

*the cup she mixed:* the wine of her idolatry is laced with the blood of those who opposed it.

**7**

*played the wanton: estrēniasen* – see on v. 3. Better 'flaunted her power'.

*torment and mourning: basanismos* (picking up 9⁵ and 14¹⁰ᶠ·) and *penthos* are key words in this chapter. The aim of the plagues is to pierce the blindness of affluence and power.

*in her heart she says 'A queen I sit':* cf. Isa. 47⁷⁻⁹, about Babylon: 'You said, "I shall be mistress for ever", . . . who say in your heart "I am, and there is no one besides me; I shall not sit as a widow, or know the loss of children." ' See also 3¹⁷, of Laodicea: 'You say, I am rich . . . I need nothing.'

**8**

*so shall her plagues come in a single day:* cf. Isa. 47⁹. Pestilence is *thanatos*, lit. 'death', as at 2²³, 6⁸.

*she shall be burned with fire:* the punishment of harlotry; as at 17¹⁶, the reference is to Ezek. 23²⁵ᶠᶠ·, about Jerusalem.

*for mighty is the Lord God who judges her:* better *has sentenced her*. This *mighty* city (cf. vv. 10, 18) is no match for the *might* of God.

⁹*And the kings of the earth, who committed fornication and were wanton with her, will weep and wail over her when they see the smoke of her burning;* ¹⁰*they will stand far off, in fear of her torment, and say,*

'*Alas! alas! thou great city, thou mighty city, Babylon!*

*In one hour has thy judgment come.*'

¹¹*And the merchants of the earth weep and mourn for her, since no one buys their cargo any more,* ¹²*cargo of gold, silver, jewels and pearls, fine linen, purple, silk and scarlet, all kinds of scented wood, all articles of ivory, all articles of costly wood, bronze, iron and marble,* ¹³*cinnamon, spice, incense, myrrh, frankincense, wine, oil, fine flour and wheat, cattle and sheep, horses and chariots, and slaves, that is, human souls.*

¹⁴'*The fruit for which thy soul longed has gone from thee,*

*and all thy dainties and thy splendour are lost to thee, never to be found again!*'

¹⁵*The merchants of these wares, who gained wealth from her, will stand far off, in fear of her torment, weeping and mourning aloud,*

¹⁶'*Alas, alas, for the great city that was clothed in fine linen, in purple and scarlet,*

*bedecked with gold, with jewels, and with pearls!*

¹⁷ *In one hour all this wealth has been laid waste.*'

*And all shipmasters and seafaring men, sailors and all whose trade is on the sea, stood far off* ¹⁸*and cried out as they saw the smoke of her burning,*

'*What city was like the great city?*'

¹⁹ *And they threw dust on their heads, as they wept and mourned, crying out,*

'*Alas, alas for the great city where all who had ships at sea grew rich by her wealth!*

*In one hour she has been laid waste.*'

The chief mourners are the *merchants* (vv. 11–17), flanked by *kings* (vv. 9, 10) and *shipmasters* (vv. 17–19), and Ezekiel's dirges over Tyre (26–28) are the model. If we ask why John for his dirge over Rome centres on trade, the answer may be partly that trade, with the foreign ties and wealth it brought, had in the eyes of the OT prophets destroyed the primitive simplicity of Israel's national life, partly that Christianity was rooted in the cities, which were centres of commerce – especially Thyatira and Laodicea –, but more deeply, perhaps, that wealth creates a false *security* (the root meaning of *mammon*) which prevents men seeing greed, cruelty, injustice, etc. in their true light – cf. the pattern of affluence, arrogance, infatuation, retribution in Greek tragedy.

Ezekiel's real admiration for Tyre's magnificence is echoed by John's for Rome, but neither was dazzled – as many of their contemporaries were. In the catalogue of vv. 11–13 all is good and precious in itself, but the sting is in the tail: the *slave*-trade reveals the mark of the beast in the whole set-up – 'the sacrifice of human life which recruited the huge *familiae* of the rich, filled the *lupanaria* (brothels) and ministered to the brutal pleasures of the amphitheatre' (Swete, p. 231).

But 'Babylon', like Vanity Fair, is infinitely more than any city which was its model.

೫೦೫

**9**

*the kings of the earth:* the tributaries of Rome (17²), not the *ten horns* (17¹², ¹⁶).

*were wanton with her: strēniasantes*; see on vv. 3, 7. They 'flaunted their power', like the Herodian princes of Judaea.

*weep and wail over her: wail over* is *kopsontai epi*, the words used at 1⁷. A dirge traditionally stated the virtues of the departed and the grief felt at his loss – in order to preserve the living from misfortune. These laments are openly self-regarding (vv. 10f., 19).

*the smoke of her burning:* cf. v. 18, 19³ and 14¹¹ – evoking the fate of Edom (Isa. 34¹⁰) and Sodom (Gen. 19²⁸).

10

*stand far off:* cf. vv. 15, 17 – an echo of the Passion (Matt. 26⁵⁸ par., 27⁵⁵ par.)?

*torment:* an echo of the scorpion's sting (9⁵), and the fire and brimstone of Sodom (14¹⁰). It is the destruction of a city, symbolized by a woman, not torture of a person.

*in one hour:* or 'moment' – see on 17¹²; cf. 18⁸, ¹⁷, ¹⁹.

11–13

The list of cargo breaks into the dirge like the similar list at Ezek. 27¹²⁻²⁴, but John as usual condenses and clarifies his model (see pp. 39ᶠ·). He leaves out the places of origin, and catalogues the goods according to kind: precious metals and jewels, costly materials for clothing and building, spices, foodstuffs, livestock – and slaves. *Slaves* came early in Ezekiel's list (27¹³). Here they come at the end of a list which is in descending order of value, *human souls* in the category of livestock. Slavery was taken for granted in the ancient world, including the church – this is an indictment of that world's values, the more telling for its restraint.

*slaves, that is, human souls:* lit. *bodies* (a regular term for slaves), *that is,*ᵇ *souls of men* (an OT term for slaves, as at Ezek 27¹³). *Soul* (*psuchē*) carries a double meaning: anything that is alive, and something for which even the whole world is no exchange (Matt. 16²⁶).

14

*for which thy soul longed:* an ironical contrast to the *souls* treated as merchandise without feelings in v. 13.

16

The items of the city's array come at the head of the list in v. 12, and echo 17⁴ – in contrast with 19⁸ and 21¹⁰ᶠᶠ· where the *fine linen*, and the *gold, jewels* and *pearls*, come into their own, but not the *purple* and *scarlet* which were too closely associated with the beast. The *jewels* also echo the dirge over the king of Tyre (Ezek. 28¹³).

b *that is:* Gk *kai*, taken 'epexegetically'. Normally it means 'and', which would give '. . . horses, chariots, slaves and the lives of men' (NEB), but it is hard to see in what sense 'lives of men' were part of the city's merchandise except as slaves.

**17–19**

*shipmasters:* kubernētēs is lit. 'steersman' but means 'captain'; cf. Acts 27¹¹. See Ezek 27²⁷⁻³⁴ for much of the phraseology.ᶜ

**18**

'*What city was like the great city?':* 'Who is there like Tyre?' (Ezek. 27³²). But the primary echo is of the acclamation of the beast (13⁴), in contrast with OT acclamations of God. Wealth leads men and nations to lord it as if they were divine. Ezekiel applied a version of the Eden story to the king of Tyre and identified his 'fall' thus: 'in the abundance of your trade you were filled with violence, and you sinned' (28¹⁶). John underlines this aspect of Rome's wealth – might, not right – in vv. 20 and 24.

18²⁰⁻²⁴ THE JUDGMENT OF BABYLON (2)

²⁰'*Rejoice over her, O heaven, O saints and apostles and prophets, for God has given judgment for you against her!'*
²¹ *Then a mighty angel took up a stone like a great millstone and threw it into the sea, saying*
'*So shall Babylon the great city be thrown down with violence,*
 *and shall be found no more;*
²² *and the sound of harpers and minstrels, of flute players and trumpeters,*
 *shall be heard in thee no more;*
 *and a craftsman of any craft*
 *shall be found in thee no more;*
 *and the sound of the millstone*
 *shall be heard in thee no more;*
²³ *and the light of a lamp shall shine in thee no more;*
 *and the voice of bridegroom and bride shall be heard in thee no more;*
 *for thy merchants were the great men of the earth,*
 *and all nations were deceived by thy sorcery.*

c Verses 11–19 perhaps show knowledge of the port of Ostia, where goods were unloaded for transport to Rome and traders congregated.

²⁴ *And in her was found the blood of prophets and of saints,*
*and of all who have been slain on earth.'*

Verse 21 gives perspective to the vengefulness of v. 20, which recurs
at 19²ᶠ· Another *mighty angel* carries out the acted parable which
Jeremiah had enjoined on Seraiah (51⁵⁹⁻⁶⁴). He was to read aloud the
sentence on Babylon which Jeremiah had written, tie a *stone* to the
book and *throw* it into the Euphrates, and say 'Thus shall Babylon
sink, to rise no more.' By adding *like a great millstone* and changing
Euphrates to *sea*, John deepens the sign and widens its application:
'Whoever causes one of these little ones to stumble (*skandalisei*), it
would be better for him to have a *great millstone* fastened round his
neck and to be drowned in the depth of the *sea*' (Matt. 18⁶). The
grudge against 'Babylon' is not just its wealth and power but the
threats and seductions by which it leads little ones into sin. And by the
same token it is a warning to the churches, in which influential
leaders are 'putting a stumbling block (*skandalon*) before Israel',
tripping them into idolatry and fornication (2¹⁴, ²⁰). 'If hand or foot
makes you stumble, cut it off and throw it from you; better to enter
into life maimed than be thrown whole into the eternal fire'
(Matt. 18⁸).

The *millstone* also makes a link with the lament of vv. 22f., based
on the threat to Jerusalem at Jer. 25¹⁰ (cf. Jer. 7³⁴, 16⁹), – it suggests a
return to the silence and darkness of primeval chaos (cf. Jer. 4²³⁻²⁶)
which must precede the new creation (see on 8¹), in which *bridegroom*
*and bride, music* and *light*, will be gloriously restored. Babylon's ruin
must be total because her influence was total, and lethal: *all nations*
*were deceived* by her, and the *blood* of every murder from the beginning is on her hands – cf. Matt. 23³⁴ᶠᶠ·, about Jerusalem; another
reminder that 'Babylon' is not simply Rome.

א

20
*Rejoice over her, O heaven:* just as the earth-dwellers *rejoiced*, or 'kept
festival' over the two witnesses, whose corpses lay in her *street* (11⁸, ¹⁰).
See on 12¹² and 13⁶: the blasphemies of the beast have been finally
silenced. Satan's apparent victory in court, in the condemnation of

Jesus and of his *saints, apostles* and *prophets*, had been secretly his defeat: now *judgment* has been openly given. The Greek is literally 'God has judged your judgment (*krima*) from her.' *Krima* here must mean not 'case' but 'sentence passed' – the sentence passed on Christians in Roman law-courts. The meaning then, as Caird argues (pp. 229f.), is that God has exacted from her the sentence she passed on you, in accordance with the law of malicious witness (Deut. 19¹⁶⁻¹⁹): 'if he has accused his brother falsely, then you shall do to him as he had meant to do to his brother.' On John's vindictiveness see pp. 49–51.

21

*a mighty angel:* cf. 5², 10¹. He proclaims the drowning of a corrupt earth, as by the flood, but *mighty* links him with the angel of the *rainbow* and little scroll (see on 4³): the final chapters show that what they signify has not been forgotten.

*Millstone* and *sea* are additions to Jer. 51⁶³ on which we have commented.

*With violence (hormēmati)* is an addition to Jer. 51⁶⁴; the word occurs only here in the NT, but the verb (*hōrmēsan*) is used for the Gadarene swine's rush down the cliff into the sea (Matt. 8³²). The verse signifies the sudden and total removal of the matrix of evil in the earth, like the binding of Satan in the abyss (20¹⁻³).

22f.

To the basic model of Jer. 25¹⁰ John adds the *musicians* (from Ezek. 26¹³ – Tyre also was to be thrown into the sea, 26¹² – cf. Isa. 14¹¹, 24⁸) and the *craftsman* – a link with the commercial and industrial picture of vv. 11–13. All the work and play, marrying and giving in marriage, of Babylon's world is suddenly stopped – as in the days of Noah and Lot, and of the Son of man (Luke 17²⁶⁻³⁰; cf. Matt. 24³⁷⁻³⁹). These words would have had added point after AD 79 when 'the lamps and gaiety of Pompeii and Herculaneum were extinguished for ever by a pall of volcanic ash' (Caird, p. 231).

*all nations were deceived by thy sorcery:* cf. II Kings 9²², about Jezebel (see on Rev. 2²⁰); Nahum 3⁴, about Nineveh; and Isa. 47¹², about Babylon. Practice of the black arts was common in John's world, but the reference here is wider: to Rome's apparent control of the world's powers and resources, which led men to accept her claims to divinity and eternity.

**24**

*in her was found the blood of prophets and of saints:* as Jesus had said of Jerusalem, the *great city* in one of its guises (11$^8$) – see Matt. 23$^{29-37}$, Luke 11$^{47-51}$. The *great city* represents all human arrogance, all suppression of witnesses to higher authority, from Cain to Nero. *Slain (esphagmenōn)* evokes the Lamb and the souls under the altar (5$^6$, 6$^9$).

19$^{1-10}$      THE VINDICATION OF THE SAINTS

**19** *After this I heard what seemed to be the mighty voice of a great multitude in heaven, crying, 'Hallelujah! Salvation and glory and power belong to our God,*
²*for his judgments are true and just; he has judged the great harlot who corrupted the earth with her fornication,*
*and he has avenged on her the blood of his servants.'*
³*Once more they cried,*
*'Hallelujah! The smoke from her goes up for ever and ever.'*
⁴*And the twenty-four elders and the four living creatures fell down and worshipped God who is seated on the throne, saying, 'Amen. Hallelujah!'*
⁵*And from the throne came a voice crying,*
*'Praise our God, all you his servants, you who fear him, small and great.'*
⁶*Then I heard what seemed to be the voice of a great multitude, like the sound of many waters and like the sound of mighty thunderpeals, crying,*
*'Hallelujah! For the Lord our God the Almighty reigns.*
⁷*Let us rejoice and exult and give him the glory,*
*for the marriage of the Lamb has come,*
*and his Bride has made herself ready;*
⁸*it was granted her to be clothed with fine linen, bright and pure'* –
*for the fine linen is the righteous deeds of the saints.*

⁹*And the angel said*\* *to me, 'Write this: Blessed are those who are invited to the marriage supper of the Lamb.' And he said to me, 'These are true words of God.'*

¹⁰*Then I fell down at his feet to worship him, but he said to me, 'You must not do that! I am a fellow servant with you and your brethren who hold the testimony of Jesus. Worship God.' For the testimony of Jesus is the spirit of prophecy.*

\*Greek *he said*

The call to heaven to rejoice, or keep festival, at 18²⁰, is taken up by the *great multitude in heaven*, and the repeated *Hallelujah!* – 'Praise Jah(veh)' – recalls the *Hallel* Psalms (113–118), with their 'Praise the Lord' refrain, which were used at the great pilgrim festivals, above all Passover. The liturgy is in two balancing parts:

(i) Verses 1–4 take up the theme stated at 18²⁰, the judgment of the *great harlot* and the vindication of the saints;

(ii) in vv. 5–10 the theme is God's kingdom or *reign*, of which the judgment of the harlot is but the negative aspect. The positive is God's *marriage* with his people, a theme of Passover when the Song of Songs was read as an allegory of God's betrothal to Israel in the wilderness. Now Jesus is the divine Bridegroom, who by his death as the Passover *Lamb* has ransomed a new Israel (5⁹), and has cleansed the church to be his glorious *Bride* (cf. Eph. 5²⁵⁻²⁷). Her *clothing* is the sanctified lives of her members who have washed their robes in the blood of the Lamb (7¹⁴). *Bride* and *marriage* belong to the future (21²ᶠᶠ.), but here, as in the church's liturgy on earth, the event is celebrated in advance; through the celebration, on the Jewish-Christian understanding of worship (p. 62), it begins to take effect.

The 'beatitude' of v. 9 introduces another staple of Jewish expectation, the messianic banquet, which Jesus in his parables had portrayed as a *wedding supper*, and which the Lord's Supper of the church pre-enacted. As in the parables, so here there is a latent warning. We must keep in mind the eucharistic setting of the letters, especially those to Thyatira and Laodicea. John is not simply reassuring the church, but calling it to self-examination, lest it be found naked and ashamed at the Lord's coming. *Worship God:* that is the nub. But worship can drift into idolatry; marital fidelity can be let slip. The coming of the Bridegroom will be diasaster for all who have been deceived into the ranks of the beast ($19^{20f.}$).

ℵℶ

**1**

*Salvation and glory and power:* the ascription recalls the acclamations of $4^{11}$ and $5^{12ff.}$, and the shout of the *great multitude* who had come out of the great tribulation ($7^{9ff.}$).

**2**

*his judgments are true and just:* cf. $15^3$, $16^7$. Contrast the slanders of the 'accuser of our brethren' ($2^9$, $12^{10}$), which bore fruit in the punishment of the Roman Christians for the fire of AD 64, and perhaps of Antipas ($2^{13}$). The continued triumph of the *corrupting* power of Rome and her unavenged murder of God's *servants* was a standing denial of his *justice*, which in the Bible is never merely abstract, but connotes putting right the wrong and delivering the oppressed. Carrying witness to the point of martyrdom must have seemed to most Christians useless.

*he has avenged on her the blood of his servants:* as Jehu was told to avenge the prophets on Jezebel (II Kings $9^7$). Was the Thyatiran Jezebel guilty of murder? Hardly, but by encouraging idolatry she was accessory to the murder it involved (see on $9^{21}$, $13^{15}$).

**3**

*The smoke from her goes up for ever and ever:* liturgical language like $14^{11}$ – a ghastly contrast with the incense of heaven ($5^8$, $8^4$). The destruction of the powers of destruction (cf. $11^{18}$, $19^{20}$, $20^{10}$) is celebrated in the traditional language of the destruction of Sodom. *For ever and ever* mocks the Roman claim to AETERNITAS ('eternity') which appeared on Flavian coins.

**4**

The *elders* and *living creatures*, who are nearest the *throne*, ratify these praises with their *Amen*, and introduce a second burst of praise with their *Hallelujah!*

**5**

*Praise our God:* = *Hallelujah* put into Greek, echoing the first of the

Hallel Psalms ($113^1$). *You who fear him, small and great* echoes Ps. $115^{13}$; contrast the 'small and great' who worshipped the beast ($13^{16}$).

## 6

*the voice of a great multitude:* God's *servants* respond. There is an echo again of $7^{9ff.}$ but the *sound of many waters* and *mighty thunderpeals* reminds us also of the 'new song' of the redeemed at $14^{2f.}$.

*the Lord ... reigns:* the verb is aorist as at $11^{17}$ – 'has entered on his reign'.

## 7

*rejoice and exult:* words which echo the last Hallel Psalm ($118^{24}$), and Jesus' words to the persecuted (Matt. $5^{12}$; cf. I Peter $4^{13}$).

*give him the glory:* man's proper response to God ($14^{6f.}$; cf. Rom. $1^{21}$, $4^{20}$) – an echo of Ps. $115^1$.

## 7

*the marriage of the Lamb:* 'The Kingdom of heaven may be compared to a king who gave a marriage feast for his son' (Matt. $22^2$). Jesus was very quickly identified as himself the Bridegroom, and the idea of Christians, not Israel, as the Bride can be seen at Rom. $7^{2-4}$; II Cor. $11^{2f.}$ (the new Adam's Eve), and is developed at Eph. $5^{25ff.}$; presumably it was a commonplace in Asia.[d]

## 7–8

*his Bride has made herself ready:* contrast the preparations of $16^{12}$, which come to fruition in the ghastly *supper* of the next section ($19^{17}$).

*it was granted to her:* her clothing is the lives of her members, but not by human achievement – see on $13^5$, $17^{17}$, and cf. Eph. $2^{10}$, $4^{11-16}$.

*fine linen, bright and pure:* cf. the armies of heaven (v. 14) and contrast the array of the harlot ($17^3$); note too the soiled garments at Sardis and nakedness at Laodicea ($3^{4,17f.}$).

d The ancient Near Eastern 'myth and ritual' pattern culminated in a 'sacred marriage' and the fixing of destinies ($20^{11-15}$); see Introduction, p. 41 note $k$, and p. 191 note $b$ on $11^{15-19}$.

*for the fine linen is the righteous deeds of the saints:* many regard this as a gloss, like 'the prayers of the saints' at 5$^8$. But such 'glosses' are part of John's style.

### 9

As RSV margin indicates, the *angel* is not in the text; he is supplied, no doubt correctly, from 17$^1$; cf. 21$^9$. Why is John told to *write* down this rather obvious 'beatitude'? Because as we said at 16$^{15}$, which is closely relevant to this passage, a beatitude is a call to self-examination, a threat as well as a promise. *Those who are invited* is perfect participle – 'those who are the invited guests'; not simply 'those who have received an invitation', like the busy men in Jesus' parable (Matt. 22$^{3ff\cdot}$, Luke 14$^{16ff\cdot}$), but those who have validated it by coming, properly dressed (cf. Matt. 22$^{11-14}$).

### 9-10

'*These are true words of God*': a paraphrase of *Amen*, confirming not just the preceding words but all that has gone before, as at 22$^6$. Again there is a warning: it balances the *Amen* of the elders and creatures at v. 4, but John's falling to worship the *angel* clashes with their falling to worship *God*. The repetition of this misplaced worship$^e$ at 22$^8$ suggests he is obliquely addressing a contemporary aberration, as in his misplaced marvelling at 17$^6$. An angel is a personified message from God, so it is as if John should put the revelation before God who gave it: was there a tendency, as in the Montanist 'new prophecy' in Phrygia in the next century,$^f$ to overvalue the Spirit who speaks now (e.g. in the prophetess at Thyatira), at the expense of the historical revelation which Jesus brought? He is the Amen, the faithful and true witness (3$^{14}$), and *all* God's servants, high and low, do no more than *hold* his *testimony* (see on 1$^2$), which is the inspiration of true *prophecy*. I John 4$^{1-6}$ may reflect a similar situation.

According to the Fourth Gospel total dependence on God is the heart of Jesus' testimony: 'the Son can do nothing of himself, but only what he sees the Father doing' (John 5$^{19}$). It was this that enabled him to say 'I and the Father are one' (John 10$^{30}$). In the next scene heaven is opened. Jesus appears as Faithful and True, the Word of God (19$^{11, 13}$): witness and principal are one; cf. I John 5$^{20-21}$.

*e* Cf. Dan. 2$^{46}$: Nebuchadnezzar fell on his face and worshipped Daniel, who had revealed the mystery.

*f* See p. 94 note *y* on 3$^{20}$.

*the spirit of prophecy:* this was the regular rabbinic term for the Holy Spirit; there is an implicit 'trinitarian' structure to the verse, as at 14[f.]. But the Spirit is given only through Jesus; the seven spirits of God are the seven eyes of the Lamb (5[6]).

19[11-16]      THE COMING OF CHRIST

[11]*Then I saw heaven opened, and behold, a white horse! He who sat upon it is called Faithful and True, and in righteousness he judges and makes war.* [12]*His eyes are like a flame of fire, and on his head are many diadems; and he has a name inscribed which no one knows but himself.* [13]*He is clad in a robe dipped in* blood, and the name by which he is called is The Word of God.* [14]*And the armies of heaven, arrayed in fine linen, white and pure, followed him on white horses.* [15]*From his mouth issues a sharp sword with which to smite the nations, and he will rule them with a rod of iron; he will tread the wine press of the fury of the wrath of God the Almighty.* [16]*On his robe and on his thigh he has a name inscribed, King of kings and Lord of lords.*

   * Other ancient authorities read *sprinkled with.*

We now reach what was the climax of the Lord's Apocalypse and of any Christian apocalypse. The heavenly worship, praising God for his victory and kingdom, dissolves into the reality it celebrates – just as the coming was celebrated, and experienced in anticipation, in the church's eucharistic worship on earth.

Verse 7 has prepared us to see the Coming One as the bridegroom, and this is confirmed by echoes of Ps. 45, the royal marriage psalm, and the letter to Laodicea. Verse 10 has prepared us to see the coming in terms of the testimony of Jesus, and this is confirmed by the *white horse*, the titles *Faithful and True* and *The Word of God*, and by the *sword* issuing from his *mouth*. The *sword* and the *eyes* like *fire* identify him as the 'one like a son of man' of the traditional picture, the Lord of the churches, whose coming will sort them out (1[12-16]).

That the *testimony* is the witness given on the cross is shown by the *robe dipped in blood* and (if we were right about 14²⁰) the *winepress*. But it is the cross now not as the world's judgment on Jesus, but Jesus' judgment of the world: his *eyes like a flame of fire* pierce those those who pierced him (1⁷); he himself tramples the *winepress*. The defendant is now the Judge, and all who suffered the same judgment are with him (v. 14). As in ch. 12 the 'battle' is forensic – the victory of truth over the lie (cf. John 19³⁶, ³⁷). 'For John, what the future will bring is the unveiling of the reality already created in the history of Jesus' (Rissi, *Future*, p. 30).

෨෧

### 11

*I saw heaven opened:* cf. Ezek. 1¹. Through the open door (4¹) he had seen the throne and him who sat upon it: now heaven is 'wide open' (perfect participle) and God breaks out into the world, in the form of a *white horse* and him who *sat upon it. White* is the colour of heaven and of Christ. It is the final victory of his witness on the cross, which was adumbrated by the rider on the white horse at the first unsealing – see on 6² and 19¹⁴.

*Faithful and True:* cf. 'the Amen, the faithful and true witness' who addressed the Laodiceans (3¹⁴).

*in righteousness he judges:* cf. Isa. 11⁴, and Ps. 96¹³ of God's coming to judge the earth; cf. too Ps. 45⁴ 'ride forth victoriously for the cause of truth' – the royal marriage psalm, in which the king is addressed as God (45⁶, Heb. 1⁸).

*and makes war:* on the beast and all his followers (16¹⁴, 17¹⁴), including those within the church (2¹⁶). Note the closeness of military and forensic terms – see on 'conquer' at 2⁷. Contrast the injustice of the beast's *war* (11⁷, 13⁷).

### 12

*his eyes are like a flame of fire:* cf. 1¹⁴, 2¹⁸ – searching mind and heart (2²³).

*many diadems:* contrast the dragon and beast (12³, 13¹).

*a name inscribed:* contrast the harlot ($17^5$), and cf. $2^{18}$, $3^{12}$ and the name inscribed on the foreheads of the 144,000 ($14^1$).

*which no one knows but himself:* it can hardly be the name given at v. 13 or 16. Is it a way of saying that the secret of his being, which is beyond men of this age, will then be disclosed (cf. I Cor. $13^{12}$)?

**13**

*a robe dipped in blood:* there is good support for the reading 'sprinkled', but it may be a scribal reminiscence of Isa. $63^3$, 'their lifeblood is sprinkled on my garments', in view of the *wine press* reference (v. 15). But if he comes to tread the wine press, his robe can hardly be sprinkled already with his enemies' blood, and *dipped* (*bebammenon*, from *baptō*, cognate with *baptizō*) has strong connotations of its own: (*a*) Gen. $49^{9-11}$ – 'Judah is a lion's whelp . . . he washes his vesture in the blood of grapes' – which was glossed in Jewish tradition by Isa. $63^{1-6}$ but reinterpreted by John in terms of Calvary ($5^{5f.}$, $14^{20}$); (*b*) the cross as a *baptism* (Mark $10^{38}$, Luke $12^{50}$).

*the Word of God:* the closest parallel is Wisd. $18^{14-16}$ – the personification of God's will suddenly made lethally present in the disobedient world. But the creative *Word* of the prologue to the Fourth Gospel is probably also in mind: see on $3^{14}$, 'the beginning of God's creation'.

**14**

*the armies of heaven:* not the angels, but the faithful of $17^{14}$, the 144,000 who *follow* the Lamb wherever he goes ($14^4$). Their clothing has been made *white* in the blood with which his is dyed (cf. $7^{14}$). The *fine linen* must be 'righteous deeds' as at v. 8 – specifically witness: their *white horses* link them with the first horseman at $6^2$. They have overcome the dragon 'by the blood of the Lamb and the word of their testimony' ($12^{11}$): this 'Last Battle' is not a bolt from the blue but the consummation of a long and costly struggle.

**15**

*a sharp sword to smite the nations:* see on $1^{16}$ and on $11^6$, the prophetic word by which God smites and heals (Hos. $6^{1-5}$); cf. again Isa. $11^4$.

*rule them with a rod of iron:* Ps. $2^9$ – see on $12^5$ and $2^{27}$, the promise to the faithful at Thyatira. *Rule* is *poimainein* – the result of this 'shepherding', severe though it be, is seen at $21^{24}-22^2$. The *nations* are the Son's heritage (Ps. 2$^8$); for the use of this Psalm see on 11$^{15-19}$ and note *b* there.

*he will tread the wine press: he* is emphatic, in contrast with the passive tense at 14$^{20}$: the victim becomes victor, the defendant becomes judge. But it is the same 'judgment': the principle of the cross which has been at work like leaven in the world through Christian witness, the Spirit of prophecy, comes suddenly into the open, like lightning in a clear sky.

*the wine press of the fury of the wrath of God the Almighty:* the cross represents the wrath of devil and men trampling out the blood of the righteous (cf. 11$^{2, 8}$), but recoils on them as the wrath of God; see on 1$^7$, 6$^{16}$; and on 14$^{20}$ for possible reinterpretation of Isa. 63$^{1-6}$.

**16**
*on his thigh:* 'Gird your sword upon your thigh, O mighty one' (Ps. 45$^3$): his 'sword' is what he *is*, King of kings and Lord of lords; cf. 17$^{14}$ and Deut. 10$^{17}$, Dan. 2$^{47}$.

19$^{17-21}$          THE DEFEAT OF THE BEASTS

$^{17}$*Then I saw an angel standing in the sun, and with a loud voice he called to all the birds that fly in midheaven, 'Come, gather for the great supper of God, $^{18}$to eat the flesh of kings, the flesh of captains, the flesh of mighty men, the flesh of horses and their riders, and the flesh of all men, both free and slave, both small and great.' $^{19}$And I saw the beast and the kings of the earth with their armies gathered to make war against him who sits upon the horse and against his army. $^{20}$And the beast was captured, and with it the false prophet who in its presence had worked the signs by which he deceived those who had received the mark of the beast and those who worshipped its image. These two were thrown alive into the lake of fire that burns with brimstone. $^{21}$And the rest were slain by the sword of him who sits upon the horse, the sword that issues from his mouth; and all the birds were gorged with their flesh.*

The last battle is framed by the *birds* which are summoned to gorge
on men's flesh. This revolting scene stems from Ezekiel's account of
the destruction of Gog's demonic army (39¹⁷⁻²⁰); it was John's aim
to shock – to alert Christians to the nature and destiny of the world
with which they were tempted to compromise. So the angel echoes
the eagle in *midheaven*, crying 'Woe' to the earth-dwellers (8¹³), and
there is the ghastly parody of the marriage supper of the Lamb: there
he gives his flesh; here their flesh is devoured.

No battle is described. The beasts are dethroned and their followers
killed simply by what the Lamb and his followers are, faithful and
true over against deceivers and deceived. This is not yet the Last
Judgment (see on 14⁷). The deceivers are thrown into the *lake of fire*,
signifying eternal destruction; the deceived are *slain* by the Word,
which is also the giver of life. Their *flesh* is destroyed, but what of the
spirit? It is the *second death* that matters, and the books are not yet
closed.

ᏚᎯ

**17**
*standing in the sun:* the direction from which the kings were gathered
for Armageddon (16¹²).

*the birds that fly in midheaven:* cf. the eagle flying in *midheaven* (8¹³) –
'Where the body is, there the eagles will be gathered' (Matt. 24²⁸) –
and contrast the angel with an eternal gospel (14⁶). To refuse the one is
to have the other.

*the great supper of God:* a traditional motif – God preparing a great
'sacrifice', a grisly parody of religious observances in which animals are
slaughtered to keep God quiet and let men feast. The primary reference
is to Ezek. 39⁴, ¹⁷⁻²⁰, though in Revelation Gog's invasion is not taken
up till 20⁸, but see also Isa. 34⁶, Jer. 46¹⁰, Zeph. 1⁷. The parody of the
New Testament 'sacrifice' is even more ghastly.

**18**
*the flesh of all men:* not just princes and all kinds of warriors, as at Ezek.
39¹⁸⁻²⁰, but all kinds of men – all who have been deceived by the
beasts; cf. 13¹⁶.

**19**

*the kings of the earth . . . gathered:* another echo of Ps. 2 – see on 11$^{15-19}$.

**20**

*the false prophet who . . . had worked the signs:* the second beast of 13$^{11ff.}$.. *These two* were thrown *alive,* like the rebels at Num. 16$^{30}$, into the *lake* of fire – *the* lake, as if a familiar concept like *the* beast at 11$^7$. *Brimstone* suggests the fate of Sodom and Gomorrah (Gen. 19$^{24}$); *lake* (*limnē*) was used of the Dead Sea. The image incorporates also the bonfire of Gehenna outside Jerusalem. See 14$^{10}$, 20$^{10, 14}$, 21$^8$.

**21**

*the rest were slain:* and wait as shivering ghosts till the resurrection for the fiery punishment which has already engulfed the beasts? (Farrer, p. 201). Or may death by the *sword* of his *mouth,* the word of God, be not simply punitive? Does destruction of the *flesh* leave open the fate of the spirit (cf. I Cor. 5$^5$, 3$^{15}$)? See on 6$^{12-17}$, 14$^{7, 20}$.

20$^{1-6}$                    THE MILLENNIUM

**20** *Then I saw an angel coming down from heaven, holding in his hand the key of the bottomless pit and a great chain.* $^2$*And he seized the dragon, that ancient serpent, who is the Devil and Satan, and bound him for a thousand years,* $^3$*and threw him into the pit, and shut it and sealed it over him, that he should deceive the nations no more, till the thousand years were ended. After that he must be loosed for a little while.*

$^4$*Then I saw thrones, and seated on them were those to whom judgment was committed. Also I saw the souls of those who had been beheaded for their testimony to Jesus and for the word of God, and who had not worshipped the beast or its image and had not received its mark on their foreheads or their hands. They came to life again, and reigned with Christ a thousand years.* $^5$*The rest of the dead did not come to life again until the thousand years were ended. This is the first resurrection.* $^6$*Blessed and holy is he who shares in the first resurrection! Over such the second death has no power, but they shall be priests of God and of Christ, and they shall reign with him a thousand years.*

After the agents of deception the deceiver himself is removed – but why only for *a thousand years*? An interim period was part of current Jewish expectation; it occurs nowhere else in the NT, but was held enthusiastically by Christians in Asia in the second century and probably earlier.

(i) It served as a bridge between the OT prophets' idea of a renewal of this world, centred on Palestine, and the apocalyptists' idea of a new transcendent heaven and earth; it could harbour the materialistic prophecies about the messianic age and the resurrection of the dead.

(ii) It could express the reward of the righteous in this world rather than in shadowy immortality, with marvellous enhancement of human life and natural fertility.

(iii) It could also symbolize the restoration of man – a *thousand years* was the intended age of Adam but for the Fall. This fitted in with the idea that the seven 'days' of creation were each a thousand years (Ps. 90⁴); the seventh would be the messianic age – the world-sabbath, followed by the eighth day of the new age.

The striking thing about John's treatment of the theme, in contrast with later interpreters, is its restraint. Of the ideas mentioned only the second is evident, the reward of the saints, but that is reserved for those who have been *beheaded for their testimony* (a tacit warning to those who take the joys of the millennium for granted?) The fulfilment of the creation story and the removal of the curse of the fall is kept for the New Jerusalem, which only 'those who wash their robes' may enter (22¹⁴). What John expresses is the unveiling of the royal and priestly nature of the church, which is hidden in the present (see Rissi's admirable discussion – *Future*, pp. 29–34).

გურ

1f.

*an angel coming down from heaven*: contrast the star fallen from heaven who was *given* the key of the pit, and let out Apollyon (9¹ᶠᶠ·). Like Michael at 12⁷⁻⁹ this angel puts into effect the victory of others. Christ *holds the keys* of Death and Hell by virtue of his death and resurrection (1¹⁸), and the *great wrath* in which Satan, defeated in heaven, came down to earth has been exhausted in his war against the saints (12¹¹ᶠ·).

*that ancient serpent:* see on 12⁹. The reference to Gen. 3 prepares for the removal of the curse and recovery of the tree of life which is the theme of the next chapters.

*bound him for a thousand years:* the period is symbolic – the seventh world-day, which is the Messiah's, after the sixth which was Antichrist's; see on 1¹⁰. This imprisonment is not for punishment, as at Isa. 24²¹⁻²³ or I Enoch 10, 18, but for the liberation of the victims; cf. Jubilees 48¹⁵ and the 'binding of the strong man' (Matt. 12²⁹).

**3**
*sealed it . . . that he should deceive the nations no more:* an echo of Matt. 27⁶³⁻⁶⁶? The Jews *sealed* the tomb to prevent 'that deceiver' escaping to cause further mischief.

*the nations:* see on vv. 6 and 7ff.

*he must be loosed for a little while:* cf. the *short time* of Satan's wrath (12¹²). *Must* expresses divine necessity; see on v. 7.

**4**
*Then I saw thrones:* in the heavenly court scene of Dan. 7⁹ᶠᶠ⁻ judgment is given by the 'Ancient of Days' *for* the one like a son of man, who represents the persecuted saints: he and they are given dominion over all peoples. Soon it came to be thought that the Son of man himself sat in judgment (NB the transference to him of the attributes of the 'Ancient of Days' at Rev. 1¹²ᶠᶠ⁻), with the saints as his assessors on the *thrones* of Dan. 7⁹; cf. I Cor. 6².

*Also I saw the souls . . .:* also (*kai*) is better taken as 'that is'. They occupy the *thrones*. Some take it that only actual martyrs are meant, because all who *had not worshipped the beast* had been killed (13¹⁵), but that is over-literal – see above on *him who conquers* (2⁷). Still, the main point is that the *souls* under the altar (6⁹⁻¹¹) at last have their reward.

*beheaded:* lit. 'axed' – the old Republican method of execution which, though replaced by the *sword*, still lingered in the memory of the provincials (Swete, p. 258).

*their testimony to Jesus:* better 'the testimony of Jesus', parallel with the *word of God* – Jesus' testimony to God which they 'held' (6⁹). See on 1², 12¹⁷, 19¹⁰.

For the *image* and *mark* of the *beast*, see on 13¹⁴⁻¹⁸.

*They came to life:* as Christ did (2⁸), and the two witnesses (11¹¹).

*reigned with Christ:* lit. *the* Christ, as at v. 6 and 11¹⁵, 12¹⁰ – perhaps in reference to Ps. 2²: the Lord's anointed, against whom the nations raged, is installed as king on Zion.

*a thousand years:* the length of the messianic kingdom was usually undefined (but 400 years in II Esd. 7²⁸). A *thousand* is unique to John, and clearly significant – the phrase occurs six times in vv. 2–7. This was the proper span of man's life, but Adam died at 930 because he disobediently ate of the tree of life, after which there was a gradual decline (Gen. 5⁵ᶠᶠ·). For the restoration cf. Jubilees 4³⁰, 23²⁷ and Isa. 65²², 'like the days of a *tree* shall the days of my people be', which is taken by LXX and Targum as the tree of life. But John reserves this theme for the New Jerusalem.

5f.

*the first resurrection:* most Jews followed the Pharisees in believing in a general resurrection followed by a second death, the final exclusion of the wicked from the Age to Come (see on v. 14), and the idea of two *resurrections* is peculiar to John. The *first* is a foretaste and guarantee, for the deserving, of the eternal priestly reign (22⁴ᶠ·).

*Blessed and holy:* again a veiled warning – see on 16¹⁵, 19⁹, 22¹¹, ¹⁴ᶠ· – as well as encouragement.

*priests of God:* through Christ's death Christians are already *kings* and *priests* (1⁶ and perhaps 5¹⁰). The two lamps of witness (11⁴) represent the royal Zerubbabel and priestly Joshua. So the millennial priestly reign may signify not only compensation for the miseries of their earthly life, but also the hidden powers and functions of that life now openly revealed, because Christ is revealed (cf. Col. 3¹⁻⁴). The resurrection of the two witnesses brought men to repentance (11¹³): these could be the subjects of the kingdom, the *nations* of v. 3, deceived no

more (Irenaeus saw the millennium as a time for men to be trained for
the vision of God, like astronauts for the moon; *Adversus Haer.* V.
31, 35f.). But John does not say so.

⁷*And when the thousand years are ended, Satan will be loosed from his
prison* ⁸*and will come out to deceive the nations which are at the four
corners of the earth, that is, Gog and Magog, to gather them for battle;
their number is like the sand of the sea.* ⁹*And they marched up over the
broad earth and surrounded the camp of the saints and the beloved city;
but fire came down from heaven*★ *and consumed them,* ¹⁰*and the devil who
had deceived them was thrown into the lake of fire and brimstone where
the beast and the false prophet were, and they will be tormented day and
night for ever and ever.*

★ Other ancient authorities read *from God, out of heaven,* or *out
of heaven from God.*

The release of Satan after being bound is peculiar to John. He is
following the order of Ezekiel: resurrection and messianic kingdom
(37), onslaught and destruction of Gog (38, 39) and New Jerusalem
(40–48). But why, theologically, must he be *loosed* to *deceive the
nations?* Why did he have to come down to earth with great wrath
(12¹²)? Why could he not have been liquidated from the beginning?
Because he represents man's free will, the capacity God has given for
sin, and the terrible reality of the consequences. *This* heaven and earth
cannot exist without him. He may be suppressed for a time, just as the
strong man was bound in Jesus' ministry, but dualism can only be
overcome in a new order of existence – where there is 'no more sea'!
(21¹; see above on 4⁶).

But who are the *nations* he *deceives?* Surely they have already been
gathered and destroyed (16¹²⁻¹⁶, 19¹⁷⁻²¹) and wait as ghosts for the
general resurrection? Ghosts, according to Rissi (*Future,* pp. 34–6),

is what they are, the demonic forces of Gog from the underworld. Like their fleshly counterparts in ch. 19 they are annihilated by the breath of heaven, and Satan joins the leaders of the earthly armies in the *lake of fire*: it is 'the final and total unveiling of his nature, of the defeat he had experienced long ago', just as 19$^{11ff.}$ unveils the nature of Christ and 20$^{4-6}$ the nature of the church.

But there was no suggestion at 20$^3$ that *the nations* were ghosts or demons. They are probably just 'the nations' who are always over against God's people, and the point is that even under 'millennial' conditions there can be no permanent security in this world – Caird points out that the forces of Gog come up against the people who, after war and devastation, 'dwell securely' at the centre of the earth; 'dwell securely' is emphasized (Ezek. 38$^8$, $^{11, 14}$, 39$^{26}$). Were Christians too sure of their immunity from Satan's attacks (2$^{24}$)? or relying on other means for his suppression than the *heavenly fire* (see on 13$^{13f.}$)?

ღღ

7

*Satan will be loosed*: his binding, release and renewed activity is a counterpart to the beast's death, healing and return (13$^3$, 17$^{8-11}$), and is followed by a counterpart to Armageddon (16$^{12-16}$, 19$^{21}$). Does the duplication reflect the conviction that life on this earth, however nearly perfected, is always precarious?

8

*the nations . . . at the four corners of the earth*: this may indicate the underworld, Satan's prison, whose entrances were thought to lie at the fringes of the earth; the *four corners* are the source of demonic attack at 7$^1$; cf. 9$^{14ff.}$. Gog leads the demonic 'foe from the north' (Ezek. 38$^{15}$), and two of his nations, Meshech and Tubal, are found among the slain in Sheol (Ezek. 32$^{26}$, 38$^2$), where presumably are the *slain* of 19$^{21}$. But the double reference to *deceiving the nations* (vv. 3, 8) suggests the residual turbulence of this earth even under the millennial kingdom.

*Gog and Magog*: Ezekiel has 'Gog of the land of Magog' (38$^2$), but in Jewish writings the two names are paired as enemies of the Messiah.

*the sand of the sea*: cf. the innumerable host at 9$^{16}$, in contrast with the promised descendants of Abraham (Gen. 22$^{17}$). Does their *number*, like the beast's, reveal their character? Satan *stood on the sand of the sea* (12$^{17}$) – over against the rock of Zion (14$^1$), the *beloved city*.

**9**

*the broad earth*: lit. 'the breadth of the earth', which may mean the *centre*, which Jerusalem was held to be (Ezek. 38$^{12}$). See also Hab. 1$^6$ and Isa. 8$^8$: the Assyrian flood which 'will fill the breadth of your land, O Immanuel', but will come to nothing because 'God is with us'.

*the camp of the saints and the beloved city*: evoking both Israel dependent on God's leading in the desert (Num. 9$^{23}$) and Zion where God chose to dwell (Pss. 87$^2$, 132$^{13}$).

*fire came down from heaven: from God* (RSV margin) is probably a gloss. The model is the fire which consumed those who came to arrest Elijah (II Kings 1$^{10}$), in the light of the fire of Pentecost – cf. the two witnesses (11$^5$), and the false prophet's parody (13$^{13}$). Cf. also the fate of Gog (Ezek. 38$^{22}$), and the contemporary II Esd. 13, where the *fire* is the law (13$^{10, 38}$).

**10**

*the devil who had deceived them*: rather who was 'their deceiver' (present participle).

*the lake of fire and brimstone*: see on 19$^{20}$, 20$^{14}$.

*tormented day and night for ever and ever*: the language is liturgical (cf. 4$^8$). Abstractions like the dragon and beasts can hardly be tortured, though those who build their lives on them may (14$^{10}$). If Satan symbolizes freedom to sin and its consequences, this may be to say that the human drama is not an episode in the divine plan which can be simply transcended. If the blood of the Lamb's victory is eternal, so must be the smoke of Satan's defeat.

$^{11}$*Then I saw a great white throne and him who sat upon it; from his presence earth and sky fled away, and no place was found for them.* $^{12}$*And I saw the dead, great and small, standing before the throne, and books were opened. Also another book was opened, which is the book of life. And the dead were judged by what was written in the books, by what they had done.* $^{13}$*And the sea gave up the dead in it, Death and Hades gave up the dead in them, and all were judged by what they had done.* $^{14}$*Then Death and Hades were thrown into the lake of fire. This is the second death, the lake of fire;* $^{15}$*and if any one's name was not found written in the book of life, he was thrown into the lake of fire.*

All the structures of this world are stripped away and nothing veils men from God's presence. The *dead* must be the earth-dwellers – all who 'had not worshipped the beast' have already risen (v. 4). They are judged on what they are – as determined by their *deeds* and by God's purpose for them in Christ, the *book of life* of the Lamb slain before the foundation of the world (see on 13$^8$). There is a tension here which can be resolved by simply taking their *deeds* as evil and the *book of life* as containing none of them: this then is the final unveiling of the earth-dwellers' nature, determined long ago, as of the church's nature (vv. 4–6) and Satan's (vv. 7–10). But what then of 'the nations' at 21$^{24-27}$, who *are* 'written in the Lamb's book of life'? It is perhaps better to see here not so much the 'who's who' of judgment as its criterion, which in the last resort is not 'works' but the Lamb's *book:* not to be found written there is to have sided finally with the beast.

Again what is striking about John's account is its restraint. It is worth remarking the proportions of his book: chs. 4 and 5 set out God's plan, 20–22 its fulfilment, and the whole of 6–19 the long-drawn-out overcoming of men's opposition and stripping away of the structures behind which they hide. Why could this not have been depicted (why could Satan not have been liquidated) in one comprehensive scene? Because John is concerned not primarily with the end but with the swaying conflict of free choice in the present – a present, however, which can only be seen truly in the light of the End and the Beginning, the final judgment and the sacrifice of the Lamb.

ღღ

**11**

*a great white throne:* The phrase echoes 19¹¹: *a white horse, and he who sat on it.* The *horse* symbolizes God's word going forth (cf. 6², Isa. 55¹¹); the *throne* symbolizes God in himself, source of royal and judicial power.

*earth and sky fled away:* cf. 6¹⁴, 16²⁰. The boundaries of the old order disappear: there is nothing between men and God.

**12**

*the dead, great and small:* Jewish belief was at first in a selective resurrection (Dan. 12²), the specially good and bad. This is total.

*the books were opened:* cf. Dan. 7¹⁰; these are the records, like those kept by Persian kings (Esther 2²³, 6¹), on which judgment is based.

*another book . . . the book of life:* cf. Dan. 12¹ and see on 13⁸. It is perhaps to be seen as the register of God's people, like the citizen list of a Greek town, which is scrutinized according to the *books* of *deeds* to see who shall be counted in or out (Farrer, pp. 209f.). If the *dead* are the 'nations', the 'earth-dwellers', this should mean that all are excluded, but 21²⁴-22³ implies that even those who have once served the beast may be found written in the Lamb's *book of life*. As in 'water of life', 'tree of life' (22¹ᶠ·), *life* suggests, 'life-giving': his *book* is not just a bare list, 'the roll of the living' (NEB), but embodies the redemptive intention of his sacrifice; cf. those 'written for life' in Jerusalem in Isa. 4³. John works with formally contradictory pictures – like Paul: e.g. the Jews in their resistance to God's will are under his wrath for good and all (I Thess. 2¹⁶), but as his people are beloved for good and all – and are finally all to be saved (Rom. 11²⁵⁻²⁹). Paul emphasizes one side or the other – human behaviour ('judgment by works') or God's intention ('justification by grace') according to the situation. John emphasizes 'judgment by works': like Paul in I Cor. he was writing to people many of whom were taking God's grace and their 'justification' for granted; cf. Rev. 14¹²ᶠ· and the scrutiny of 'works' in the letters. But the *book of life* has the last word.

**13-15**

These verses elaborate what was summarily stated in v. 12.

*the sea gave up the dead:* i.e. drowned sailors, or on another level all drowned in the floods of evil; cf. Ps. 18$^{4,\ 16}$. Likewise *Death and Hades* are on one level the repositories of the dead, on another the tyrants who have captured them.

**14**

*Death and Hades were thrown into the lake of fire:* where the satanic trinity already are (v. 10; see on 19$^{20}$); 'the last enemy to be destroyed is death' (I Cor. 15$^{28}$). Does Christ's completed victory over *Death and Hades* (cf. 1$^{18}$), the powers that held men captive, open the possibility of salvation even to those who were dupes of the beast and whose deeds were evil? The question reflects modern concern about the fairness of damnation. John is not giving advance information about the fate of x or y, but painting the end-term of present decisions; some of his readers may think the issue is already settled in their favour by the Lamb's *book*. His God does not lack concern for the healing of the nations he had allowed to be smitten (22$^2$), but it is expressed in a separate picture.

*the second death:* see on 2$^{11}$. In the Targums it can signify 'eternal torment', as at Isa. 65$^{5f.}$, or simply exclusion from the resurrection and from enjoyment of life in the New Creation (McNamara, pp. 117-25). Is the latter John's view, since *torment* is not mentioned here or at 21$^8$, as it is at v. 10 in reference to the devil? Perhaps it is better not to ask what John 'believed', but to recognize that he uses pictures, as Jesus used parables, and attend to the point: the utter disaster of not belonging to Christ (see on 13$^8$ and 14$^{11}$).

**21$^{1-8}$**     A NEW HEAVEN AND A NEW EARTH

21 *Then I saw a new heaven and a new earth; for the first heaven and the first earth had passed away, and the sea was no more.* $^2$*And I saw the holy city, new Jerusalem, coming down out of heaven from God, prepared as a*

*bride adorned for her husband;* ³*and I heard a great voice from the throne saying, 'Behold, the dwelling of God is with men. He will dwell with them, and they shall be his people,\* and God himself will be with them;† he will wipe away every tear from their eyes, and death shall be no more, neither shall there be mourning nor crying nor pain any more, for the former things have passed away.'*

⁵*And he who sat upon the throne said, 'Behold, I make all things new.' Also he said, 'Write this, for these words are trustworthy and true.'* ⁶*And he said to me, 'It is done! I am the Alpha and the Omega, the beginning and the end. To the thirsty I will give water without price from the fountain of the water of life.* ⁷*He who conquers shall have this heritage, and I will be his God and he shall be my son.* ⁸*But as for the cowardly, the faithless, the polluted, as for murderers, fornicators, sorcerers, idolaters, and all liars, their lot shall be in the lake that burns with fire and brimstone, which is the second death.'*

\* Other ancient authorities read *peoples.*

† Other ancient authorities add *and be their God.*

Why a new *heaven*? Because heaven and earth are correlative terms (see pp. 16, 113 above). The *first heaven* is not for John the eternal and perfect realm of which earthly life is a mere shadow: it is the inward and spiritual behind the outward and physical. It is God's dwelling, but Satan had a place there and the 'sea of glass' symbolized its ambivalences. Beyond this heaven and earth and their inherent dualism lies the New Age in which the *sea* is *no more* and God is all in all (I Cor. 15²⁸, 13¹²).

So the old order dominated by the *great city* is replaced by the *holy city*, which a voice interprets as *God dwelling with men:* Immanuel, 'God with us.' The frail 'tabernacle' of the incarnation (John 1¹⁴) has been left as the one remaining reality when all else has been shaken (Heb. 12²⁷). The new order is simply *God.* He is paradise regained, and this *heritage* of the conqueror (v. 7) is set out in what follows.

But before we can move on to that we must consider the 'inconsistencies' which have made some scholars follow Charles in rearranging the text. First a minor point: the angel seems to show John in vv. 9ff. what he has just seen (v. 2). But it is a common trait of biblical narration to state a theme, and then restate it in more detail as if recounting a subsequent event; $21^{1-8}$ can be seen as a text which is expounded in $21^{9ff.}$ almost verse by verse.

Secondly a point of substance: how can the new heaven and earth beyond space and time contain all the material and measurable elements of $21^{10ff.}$? Surely these belong to the millennial kingdom on earth and have been transposed. But the point may be that the consummation, though it lies beyond what eye can see or heart conceive, is yet compounded of the materials and choices of everyday life now. For John the 'eighth day' of eternity is already present and accessible because Jesus is, who is the first-born of the dead and the beginning of God's creation. In him the *water of life* (v. 6) is available now, to all who *desire* it $(22^{17})$.

Other 'inconsistencies' are dealt with in the notes. It is better if possible to listen to what the text is saying than to rearrange it according to our canons of consistency.

ঙঙ

1

*a new heaven and a new earth:* 'Behold, I create new heavens and a new earth; and the former things shall not be remembered . . . I create Jerusalem a rejoicing and her people a joy . . . no more the sound of weeping . . .' (Isa. $65^{17-19}$); cf. II Peter $3^{13}$. *New (kainos)* connotes 'new in kind' not just 'another', but as with the 'new convenant' we are not dealing here with the brand new but with radical renewal. 'A primitive Christian might think of the world what he thought of his own body; raised again and transformed, yet without loss of individual identity' (Farrer, p. 213).

On *heaven* see pp. 15f. above; see also Minear, *New Earth*, pp. 270–78, and 'Cosmology . . .' in *Current Issues in NT Interpretation*, pp. 23–37.

*the sea was no more:* removed like Death and Hades $(20^{13f.})$. Some find here a symbol of separation overcome (John was on an island), but see notes on the *sea of glass* in the first heaven: it represents the primeval waters of chaos with their potentiality for both creation and destruction.

**2**

*new Jerusalem:* the Lamb's *Bride* (19^{7f.}) becomes, like the harlot, the *city* she symbolizes. See notes on vv. 9ff. where the theme is expounded. The idea of a *new* Jerusalem goes back to the destruction of 587 BC and the prophecies of the second Isaiah. But disillusionment with the actual restoration led to the idea being spiritualized, like that of the Messiah. The new order is a society to which men may already belong by foretaste (see pp. 41f. above and comment on 2^7), and which is *prepared* and adorned by their lives.

**3**

*the dwelling of God is with men: dwelling* is *skēnē*, tabernacle, and has the same consonants as Hebrew *shekinah*, the bright cloud which symbolized God's presence; see on 7^{15}. The 'dwelling' (*eskēnōsen*) of John 1^{14} is completed, and the hopes of the great feast of Tabernacles are fulfilled – see John's exposition at 21^{22}–22^5.

*and they shall be his people: peoples* (RSV margin) has slightly better MS support than *people*, and is to be preferred as much the harder reading. *They shall be my people* is such a common OT phrase that a copyist could easily have changed plural to singular, but hardly singular to plural. The plural suggests that the *men* God is *with* are not simply 'Israel', but the diversity of *peoples* witnessed to by the church (10^{11}, 11^9) – and deceived by the beasts (13^6) – which is confirmed by the exposition at vv. 24ff.

*and God himself shall be with them:* picking up the Immanuel prophecy (Isa. 7^{14}, 8^8, ^{10}) and Ps. 46^{4-7}. Many ancient authorities read . . . *be with them, their God* – probably through the influence of OT phraseology on copyists, but John may have meant 'and God-with-them (= Immanuel) himself will be their God' (Farrer, p. 212).

**4**

*wipe away every tear:* see on 7^{16f.}. 'He will swallow up death for ever . . . and wipe away tears from all faces' – after removing 'the veil that is spread over all nations' (Isa. 25^8); cf. the *healing* of the nations in the exposition, 22^2.

*death shall be no more:* not merely a restatement of 20^{14}, but a reference to mortality as punishment for sin and the grief and pain that go with it (Gen. 3<sup>16-19</sup>); cf. again Isa. 65<sup>19</sup>, and 35<sup>10</sup>, 51<sup>11</sup>. The refrain *shall be no more* echoes the dirge over Babylon (18<sup>21-23</sup>).

*the former things:* lit. 'the first things', of the first heaven and earth. Cf. Isa. 65<sup>16f.</sup>, 43<sup>18f.</sup>, II Cor. 5<sup>17</sup>.

## 5

*The voice from the throne* (v. 3) is ratified by him *who sat on it.* For the first time God himself speaks – vocal proof of the abolition of distance between God and man.

*I make all things new:* Paul spoke of Isaiah's 'new creation' as present fact in Christ (II Cor. 5<sup>17</sup>, Gal. 6<sup>15</sup>); John describes the fulness of what Christians already enjoy in foretaste.

*these words are trustworthy and true:* in the exposition this is the subject of a new paragraph (22<sup>6ff.</sup>). The division here, then, should come after v. 5a, not before.

## 6

*It is done!: gegonan*, echoing the declaration of Babylon's ruin (16<sup>17</sup>); this is the other side of the coin. In both cases there is an echo of Jesus' cry 'It is finished!' on the cross (John 19<sup>30</sup>): that was the beginning of the new creation.

*To the thirsty . . . .:* the Alpha and Omega ratifies the promise which his Son, who is also Alpha and Omega (22<sup>13</sup>) has already made and honoured in the eucharist; see on 7<sup>16f.</sup>; cf. John 4<sup>10</sup>, 7<sup>37</sup>. Again there are echoes of Isaiah (43<sup>19f.</sup>, 55<sup>1ff.</sup>). The promise is to him who knows his need – contrast Laodicea (3<sup>17</sup>).

## 7

*He who conquers:* cf. the promises at the end of the letters. Again there is a warning – that the fulness of which the sacraments give a foretaste is only for those who maintain the Son's 'works' to the end; cf. the letter to Thyatira (2<sup>18, 26-28</sup>): power over the nations is the Son's heritage in Ps. 2<sup>8</sup>. *This heritage* here refers to all that follows.

*I will be his God, and he shall be my son:* the prophecy about the Christ, 'I will be his father and he shall be my son' (II Sam. 7<sup>14</sup>), is applied to the Christian, with the significant change of 'father' to *God*. Nowhere in Revelation is he called the father of Christians. This relationship was felt to belong peculiarly to Christ (cf. 1⁶, 2¹⁸, John 20¹⁷), who communicated it to them.

**8**

*But as for the cowardly . . . :* their mention after 20¹²⁻¹⁵ is not 'inconsistent'. John's stance varies often from the future he sees to the present in which he sees it; in vv. 5–8 God is himself ratifying what John has seen.

The list belongs, like similar lists in the epistles, to the context of baptism, the putting off of the 'old man' and putting on of the new; cf. Col. 3⁵ᶠᶠ·. The *cowardly* are placed first, in contrast with the *conqueror*: fear leads to compromise (2¹⁰, ¹³ᶠᶠ·). *Liars* are equally significantly placed last, as summing up the whole list; cf. 22¹⁵. *Pseudēs* means more than 'liar': one who has no standing in the truth, and hates it; thence springs *murder*; cf. John 8³⁹⁻⁴⁴ and I John 3¹², referring to Cain and Abel (Gen. 4). For *murderers, fornicators, sorcerers and idolaters* cf. 9²⁰ᶠ·, 18²³–19². The warning is not to the world but to the church (see on 2¹⁴, ²⁰), the community of those who have 'put off' these things.

For the *lake*, see on 19²⁰: for the *second death*, see on 20¹⁴.

21⁹⁻²¹     THE NEW JERUSALEM

⁹*Then came one of the seven angels who had the seven bowls full of the seven last plagues, and spoke to me, saying, 'Come, I will show you the Bride, the wife of the Lamb.'* ¹⁰*And in the Spirit he carried me away to a great, high mountain, and showed me the holy city Jerusalem coming down out of heaven from God,* ¹¹*having the glory of God, its radiance like a most rare jewel, like a jasper, clear as crystal.* ¹²*It had a great, high wall, with twelve gates, and at the gates twelve angels, and on the gates the names of the twelve tribes of the sons of Israel were inscribed:* ¹³*on the east three gates, on the north three gates, on the south three gates, and on the west three gates.* ¹⁴*And the wall of the city had twelve foundations, and on them the twelve names of the twelve apostles of the Lamb.*

$^{15}$*And he who talked to me had a measuring rod of gold to measure the city and its gates and walls.* $^{16}$*The city lies foursquare, its length the same as its breadth; and he measured the city with his rod, twelve thousand stadia;* * *its length and breadth and height are equal.* $^{17}$*He also measured its wall, a hundred and forty-four cubits by a man's measure, that is, an angel's.* $^{18}$*The wall was built of jasper, while the city was pure gold, clear as glass.* $^{19}$*The foundations of the wall of the city were adorned with every jewel; the first was jasper, the second sapphire, the third agate, the fourth emerald,* $^{20}$*the fifth onyx, the sixth carnelian, the seventh chrysolite, the eighth beryl, the ninth topaz, the tenth chrysoprase, the eleventh jacinth, the twelfth amethyst.* $^{21}$*And the twelve gates were twelve pearls, each of the gates made of a single pearl, and the street of the city was pure gold, transparent as glass.*

\* About fifteen hundred miles.

John's concern is the church and the world. The description of the interpreting angel links this passage with the seven bowls of wrath and the destruction of the harlot Babylon (16–18; see p. 237). Here now is the glorious new city for which that slum-clearance made room. What is the relation between the two? The hinge of the transition was the coming of the Son of man – the climax of the Lord's Apocalypse, in which it was associated with the gathering of the elect. Just as the first 'son of man' vision (1$^{13ff.}$) was followed by the letters to the churches, so the second (19$^{11ff.}$) is followed by the vision of the *new Jerusalem*, which picks up the themes of the letters. John is expounding 21$^{1-8}$: the angel of the bowls of wrath reminds us not only of the destruction of the harlot but also of the warning of v. 8, addressed to the churches in which the harlot had her foothold. So it is not a simple replacement of the bad (the world) by the good (the church, the elect).

The image of the *Bride* also tells against complete discontinuity between church and world. The idea of the 'sacred marriage' (see p. 279 note *d*). of the god and his land had been taken over from the Canaanite fertility cults and spiritualized by the prophets in polemic against them: God betrothed Israel to himself at the exodus; in the promised land she 'played the harlot'; but after discipline costly to both parties (Hos. 1–3) God would bring her back to himself. So the second Isaiah intepreted the Babylonian exile and restoration; so the Jews looked forward to a new exodus, reading as part of their Passover celebrations the Song of Songs. Christians very soon saw Jesus as the Bridegroom, and his death at Passover as the sacrifice which bought a new people for God out of the world, or cleansed the church to be a spotless Bride (Eph. $5^{25-27}$).

The two cities, then, are not radically different entities, but the same entity under radically different aspects, like the 'harlot Jerusalem' of Isa. $1^{21}$ and the glorious Zion of Isa. $62^{1-5}$; they are travesty and reality. For Isaiah the link between them was the faithful remnant, the shoot from Jesse's stump, the suffering servant; so for John it is the faithful witness and his witnesses ($11^{1-13}$): the *holy city*, trampled then, is now *measured* ($21^{15}$), a symbol of the sanctity which has absorbed the entire outside world.

Each city's clothing and adornment is the lives of its citizens. In contrast with the harlot's purple and scarlet, mourned by the merchants of the earth ($18^{11ff.}$), the fine linen of the Bride is the righteous deeds of the saints, who have made their robes white in the blood of the Lamb. Likewise the gold and precious stones of the Bride may represent the works and witness of her members, built on the foundation of Christ's sacrifice (see on $14^{13}$). The measurements – 12,000 and 144 (vv. 15–17) – remind us of the number of the elect ($7^{4-8}$), who are spotless ($14^{1-5}$).

In the background also perhaps are ancient astrological ideas of the 'city of the Gods' – 'suggested by the heaven with the sun and moon and the twelve signs of the Zodiac and the twelve gates through which they were conceived to pass . . . also the great Milky Way which was conceived as the great street of the heavenly city' (Charles, *Rev*. II, p. 158). As with the glorious woman of $12^{1ff.}$, which is closely related to this passage, magical or astrological reference is probable – the signs of the Zodiac, for example, were linked with jewels – but the primary echoes are biblical:

(*a*) Isaiah's Zion: 'O afflicted one, storm-tossed, not comforted . . . I will lay your foundations with sapphires . . . I will make your gates of carbuncles and all your wall of precious stones' ($54^{11f.}$);

(*b*) the twelve jewels on the high priest's breatplate, which were engraved with the *names of the twelve tribes of the sons of Israel* (Ex. 28¹⁵⁻²¹);

(*c*) the jewels which covered the king of Tyre in paradise (Ezek. 28¹³). In the next section the city is identified with 'paradise regained', as in contemporary Jewish texts;

(*d*) the beauty of the Bride in the Song of Songs (6⁴, ¹⁰, 7¹): it is John's purpose and method to show the ugliness of the false and the beauty of the true (see p. 70);

(*e*) the story of Babel: men said 'Come let us build ourselves a city, and a tower with its top in the heavens' (Gen. 11⁴). The city *comes down out of heaven from God*, and the old earth and heaven are absorbed into it.

ໜ

**9**

*one of the seven angels . . .:* see 15¹, ⁶ᶠ·. He shows him the Bride and her adornment as he had showed him the harlot and hers (17¹⁻⁶). Threat and promise, plague and blessing, are two sides of one coin throughout Revelation.

**10**

*in the Spirit:* see on 17³ – another link with that vision.

*a great high mountain:* contrast the *wilderness* of 17³ – another echo of Jesus' temptations (Matt. 4⁸⁻¹⁰): Satan's counterfeit offer of the kingdoms of the world is fulfilled, through refusal to worship and serve him; cf. 22³⁻⁵. But the primary reference is to Ezek. 40² and his vision of Jerusalem, cleansed and rebuilt.

*the holy city Jerusalem:* his concern is now not her newness but her holiness. This exposition of v. 2 is not further prediction of the end, but exhortation for the present, as the links with the letters confirm.

*coming down out of heaven:* the idea of a heavenly Jerusalem was a familiar one (cf. Gal. 4²⁶ᶠᶠ·, Phil. 3²⁰, Heb. 12²², II Baruch 4³ and the long allegory II Esd. 10²⁷ᶠᶠ·), but there is no parallel to its *coming down* from heaven. This, like the millennium, is a bridge between this-worldly and other-worldly pictures of the end, and it is more than mere spatial metaphor: it is something given, *from God*, not achieved by man – contrast Babel.

**11**

*having the glory of God:* i.e. the brightness of the *Shekinah*, which in Ezekiel's vision left the old temple ($10^{18}$) and returned to the new ($43^4$). This city is all temple (vv. 16, 22).

*its radiance:* the Greek *phōstēr* normally means 'luminary'; cf. Dan. $12^3$, Phil. $2^{15}$, referring to the saints. The city which is made up of their lives fulfils the OT prophecies that she should be a beacon; see on vv. 22ff. Totally purified, she totally reflects God: *jasper* is the appearance of the enthroned one ($4^3$), who was above 'the terrible *crystal*' (Ezek. $1^{22}$).

**12**

*on the gates the names of the twelve tribes:* the twelve portals of the Zodiac in the city of the heavens are brought under the control of the Bible: Israel is the nucleus of the divine society. The *twelve tribes* and *twelve apostles* (v. 14) are brought together by the jewels of vv. 19f. The *twelve angels* perhaps represent the watchmen of Isa. $62^6$.

**13**

The order east-north-south-west is puzzling. At Num. $2^{3ff.}$ the square in which the twelve *tribes* are marshalled is described in the order east-south-west-north, and at Ezek. $48^{31-34}$ the *gates* which bear their *names* in the order north-east-south-west. For a brilliant but complicated explanation, linked with the square of the twelve tribes at $7^{4-8}$, see Farrer, pp. 215f., 105–8. *On the east* etc. is literally *from* (*apo*): had John in mind the picture of many coming from the four points of the compass (Isa. $49^{12}$, Luke $13^{29}$)? See on v. 24.

**14**

*twelve foundations:* cf. Eph. $2^{20}$: *apostles* and prophets form the foundation of God's house, Jesus being the chief corner-stone (see on v. 19). To the NT writers Jesus' disciples were the patriarchs of God's renewed Israel (Matt. $19^{28}$, Luke $22^{30}$) – not as individuals but as the twelve.

**15**

*a measuring rod of gold:* cf. Ezek. $40^{3ff.}$, Zech. $2^{1ff.}$. John with his natural reed had been told *not* to *measure* the 'court outside'; the *holy city* was to be trampled by the nations. Now the angel with his reed of *gold,* the city's material (vv. 18, 21), *measures* it to signify its inviolable sanctity.

**16**

*The city lies foursquare:* a feature of Ezekiel's city and temple (41²¹, 43¹⁶, 45¹, 48²⁰) – a natural symbol of perfection; it was applied by the Greeks to the good man. But John goes further: it is a cube, an even more 'perfect' figure – in Solomon's temple it was the shape of the Holy of Holies, which is 'fulfilled' in the new Jerusalem (v. 22).

*Twelve thousand stadia:* about 1500 miles, as RSV notes; but that destroys the point, which as with all John's numbers is symbolical (see pp. 14f.). Historical Babylon was a square of 120 stadia (Herodotus I. 178): the new Jerusalem is a square of the twelve thousands of the tribes of Israel (7⁴⁻⁸); which together make up 144,000 – echoed in the *hundred and fotry-four cubits* of the *wall*. Jewish writers saw restored Jerusalem extending to Joppa or Damascus, and up to the clouds; ancient temple-cities were seen as linking heaven and earth. Here the link has absorbed both poles.

**17**

*its wall, 144 cubits:* or 216 feet, on the literal level. If this were breadth it would not be out of proportion; if height, ludicrously small – perhaps intentionally: the wall is meant not for defence, but delimitation (v. 27, 22¹⁵); cf. Zech. 2⁴ᶠ.: God will be to her a wall of fire round about, and the glory within her.

*a man's measure, that is an angel's:* Babylon's wall was measured in 'royal' cubits (Herodotus), equivalent to the 'long' cubit of the reed in the *man's* hand at Ezek. 40⁵. Is it a way of saying that these human measurements are 'angelic', or spiritual (cf. 11⁸)? Or since angels are twice said to be fellow servants with men (19¹⁰, 22⁹), and men are to be 'equal to angels' (Luke 20³⁶), is it a way of saying that the human is taken up into the divine? (In either case the *human number* of 13¹⁸ is not parallel.)

**18**

This summary statement of the city's materials is expanded in vv. 19–21. *Jasper* is the jewel of God himself (v. 11).

**19**

*The foundations were adorned with every jewel:* i.e. with every kind of jewel, lit. 'costly stone'. The metaphor of the bride *adorned* for her husband has passed into that of a city built, like Solomon's temple, on foundations of 'great costly stones' (I Kings 5$^{17}$) – the whole city is temple (v. 16b).

19f.
The high priest's breastpiece was *square*, and held *twelve* jewels in four rows of three, each bearing the name of a tribe (Ex. 28$^{16ff.}$). The king of Tyre was covered with 'every precious stone' (Ezek. 28$^{13}$; nine in the Hebrew, but the LXX has the same twelve as Exodus). John's list is close to the LXX's but not identical in names or order. We cannot tell if this is significant: the Hebrew names did not have firm Greek equivalents and John on Patmos was presumably working from memory. In any case his use of scripture is not verbatim but creative: *jasper* is no doubt put first for the same reason that *Judah* headed the list of tribes at 7$^5$, as the tribe of the Messiah. Jesus is the 'chief cornerstone' (Eph. 2$^{20}$); the Messiah is one both with his Father (*jasper* is the jewel of God) and with his brethren (cf. Rom. 8$^{29}$).

The overall arrangement is probably for euphony (Farrer, p. 219). The individual jewels may have astrological significance,[g] but their function here is to express the priestly character of Christ and his church as the foundation of the renewed world (cf. Wisd. 18$^{20-25}$, where Aaron the high priest brings the wrath of God to an end by the symbolic power of his vestments), and to contribute, like the euphony of their arrangement, to the beauty which John sets over against the harlot's obscenity (cf. pp. 14, 70).

*the twelve gates were twelve pearls:* here too is the contrast of the true beauty with the false; cf. 17$^4$, 18$^{12,\ 16}$. The Jews took the 'carbuncles' of Isa. 54$^{12}$ to be *pearls*, and Jesus had compared entrance to the kingdom with finding one *pearl* of great value (Matt. 13$^{46}$).

g Charles believed that in antiquity each jewel was linked with a particular sign of the Zodiac, in opposite order to John's, which represents a deliberate reversal, to dissociate himself from pagan astrology (*Rev.* II, pp. 167f.). But the evidence he relied on is worthless (T. F. Glasson, 'The Order of Jewels in Rev. xxi. 19–20: A Theory Eliminated', *JTS* 26, 1975, pp. 95–100). Philo (*Special Laws* I. 87) and Josephus (*Ant.* III. 186) link the jewels with the Zodiac, but only as part of the cosmic symbolism which they claim for the high priest's vestments; cf. Wisd. 18$^{24}$. John's aim is similar. Any direct astrological reference is destroyed by his linking them not with the twelve *gates* of the heavenly city but with the foundations.

*the street . . . was pure gold, transparent as glass:* it replaces the *street* of the great *city* ($11^8$) and the heavenly sea of *glass* ($4^6$) – see on $22^{1f\cdot}$.

$21^{22}-22^5$   THE HEALING OF THE NATIONS:
PARADISE REGAINED

$^{22}$*And I saw no temple in the city, for its temple is the Lord God the Almighty and the Lamb. $^{23}$And the city has no need of sun or moon to shine upon it, for the glory of God is its light, and its lamp is the Lamb. $^{24}$By its light shall the nations walk; and the kings of the earth shall bring their glory into it, $^{25}$and its gates shall never be shut by day – and there shall be no night there; $^{26}$they shall bring into it the glory and the honour of the nations. $^{27}$But nothing unclean shall enter it, nor any one who practises abomination or falsehood, but only those who are written in the Lamb's book of life.*

22   *Then he showed me the river of the water of life, bright as crystal, flowing from the throne of God and of the Lamb $^2$through the middle of the street of the city; also on either side of the river, the tree of life\* with its twelve kinds of fruit, yielding its fruit each month; and the leaves of the tree were for the healing of the nations. $^3$There shall no more be anything accursed, but the throne of God and of the Lamb shall be in it, and his servants shall worship him; $^4$they shall see his face, and his name shall be on their foreheads. $^5$And night shall be no more; they need no light of lamp or sun, for the Lord God will be their light, and they shall reign for ever and ever.*

\* Or *the Lamb. In the midst of the street of the city, and on either side of the river, was the tree of life,* etc.

The commentary on $21^{1-8}$continues; vv. 22–27 take up v. 3. Just as the angel showed John first the adornment of the harlot, then her destruction in internecine strife, amid the self-regarding lamentations of kings and merchants, so he shows now, after the Bride's adornment, her marriage spiritualized as the union of God with his people, or *peoples* (v. 3), their meretricious *glory* cleansed to contribute to the divine *glory* which is the one abiding reality. There is no need of a *temple*, a place of atonement: the whole city is At-one-ment, 'God-with-them' (v. 3); its *temple* is God and the Lamb. The terrible splendour which brought destruction to Babylon (18¹) now replaces *sun* and *moon*. The *nations* and their *kings*, who had grown rich on the harlot's arrogant power, now bring their wealth into the holy city; their *abominations* they leave outside.

22¹⁻⁵ take up 21⁴. The new Jerusalem as paradise regained was a theme of the prophets, nobly stated at Ezek. 47 where the *river* flowing from the restored temple brings *life* wherever it goes, the *trees* by its bank bearing *fruit* every month, their fruit for food and their *leaves* for *healing*. Healing *of the nations* is John's addition. The centre of Ezekiel's conception of the world-become-paradise is personal relationship with God; the name of his city is simply 'The Lord is there' (48³⁵). Ezekiel's scope is universal, but he barely mentions the nations, because his focus is on the chosen people, through whom universal knowledge of God is to be achieved. As before, John condenses and clarifies his model (see pp. 39f. above).

But who are these *nations*? What relation have they to the nations deceived by the beasts and slain by the Word? Some say none. They are merely scriptural 'colour', drawn from the last chapters of Isaiah, to enhance the city's splendour. But that is not how John uses scripture, and his own touches at 21³ and 22² suggest otherwise. Or some say that John has reinterpreted Isaiah as pointing to the inclusion of Gentiles within the Jewish church: these are Gentile Christians. But, once converted, men cease to be Gentiles (*ethnē*); they become part of God's Israel (see on 3⁹, 7⁴, ⁹).

It seems best to regard these as *the nations* in the same biblical sense as in the rest of the book, and see *the kings of the earth* as in the same category as those who dallied with the harlot (17²) and hid from God's face (6¹⁶): John works with pictures which are formally contradictory and does not explicitly resolve the enigma. Just as in the Psalms which he cites the nations, in that they are arrogant and rebellious, are to be put down (Ps. 2⁴⁻⁹), but in that they are God's creatures, are to be included in his city (Pss. 86⁹, 87⁴⁻⁶), so in his vision the nations who bear the beast's mark and are not written in the Lamb's book are destroyed, but God the Creator and Redeemer gathers *all the nations* ($15^4$) into his renewed creation (and not as serfs to Israel, as in Isaiah). Both pictures are all embracing. See also on $6^{12-17}$.

John sees fulfilled the prophet's hope: purified Zion is a beacon to draw in all nations; the curse of Genesis is healed ($22^{2f.}$). To resolve the enigma we can only point to other pictures: sacrifice expiating sin ($5^{6-10}$); the Accuser expelled, the woman's seed bruising the serpent's head (ch. 12); the first fruits and the wine press (ch. 14). None can share in the *tree of life* or *enter the city* except those who *wash their robes* ($22^{14}$), and though these words are addressed to Christians in danger of dirtying them, they must mean that the *nations* will have been in some sense *washed*, even if from another point of view they were being trampled in the winepress of the wrath of God. But this was not a question John addressed himself to: his concern was the purity of the beacon, and his aim was to depict the end term of two opposing courses which lay before Christians then. These chapters, like the letters, are not prediction so much as exhortation.

$22^{3-5}$ expound $21^5$, *I make all things new:* all men are united and fulfilled in the vision of God, the goal of man's quest to the Greek as to the Jew. The sensual satisfactions of the new creation, and their sacramental anticipations here and now, are only metaphors of the reality, which is God. For Paul too 'new creation' meant reconciliation and a new kind of knowing (II Cor. $5^{14-19}$, I Cor. $13^{12}$).

ꙮ

**22**
*I saw no temple:* there is no need of a place for meeting and sacrificial cleansing – *God* dwells with men (v. 3); the *Lamb* is the removal of sin. The city is one great holy of holies (v. 16) to which all have access all the year round; see on $11^{19}$.

**23–26**
John condenses and adapts Isa. 60:

> The sun shall be no more your light by day,
> nor for brightness shall the moon give you light by night;
> but the Lord will be your everlasting light,
> and your God will be your glory (v. 19).

**23**

*Its lamp is the Lamb:* he is God's glory (John $1^{14, 18}$).

> Nations shall come to your light,
> and kings to the brightness of your rising (v. 3).

**24**

*By its light shall the nations walk:* the light is for their benefit, not simply to glorify Israel (cf. Luke $2^{32}$); and the *kings of the earth* freely ~~bring~~ in *their glory.* Contrast $6^{16}$, where they hide from God's face.

> Your gates shall be open continually;
> day and night they shall not be shut (v. 11);

**25**

*There shall be no night there,* the normal time for shutting gates. Continuous day is a feature of Zechariah's prophecy ($14^7$), which lies behind $22^{1\mathrm{ff}}$.

> that men may bring to you the wealth of nations,
> with their kings led in procession (v. 11).

**26**

*They shall bring into it the glory and honour of the nations:* but not as captives or second-class citizens 'bowing down at your feet' (cf. Isa. $60^{10-16}$). Contrast the kings of the old earth bringing their glory into Babylon (Rev. $18^{9-19}$).

The generosity of John's picture is remarkable when it is compared with its source, and with I Enoch 48, 50: there the earth-dwellers repent (there is a striking parallel with Rev. $11^{13}$) and are saved, but 'without honour'; for the earth-possessors, the kings and the mighty, there is no hope at all. The closest parallel to Rev. is Test. Levi 18 (about 100 BC?), which looked forward to a 'new priest' under whom the Gentiles would be enlightened, sin come to an end and paradise be reopened.

**27**

*nothing unclean shall enter it: unclean* is *koinon* = 'common'. There is no distinction between sacred and profane in the city; cf. Zech. $14^{20\mathrm{f}}$. But there is still an 'outside' (as at $22^{15}$): the perspective is that of the letters, in which commerce with the heavenly Jerusalem as with the harlot Babylon is a present possibility; see on $3^{13}$, $22^{14\mathrm{f}}$.

*Abomination* refers to the pollutions of idolatry, which stems from rejection of truth (cf. Rom. $1^{18ff.}$): again the *lie* appears as the root of evil; see on $21^8$, $22^{15}$.

*the Lamb's book of life:* see on $13^8$, $20^{12-15}$.

$22^1$
*the river of the water of life:* cf. $7^{17}$. Drawing on Ezek. $47^{1-12}$ and Zech. $14^{8, 11}$, John depicts paradise regained: the river of Gen. $2^{10}$ becomes a river of life-giving water; the *curse* of Gen. $3^{15ff.}$ is *no more* (like the sea, and death and pain, $21^{1, 3}$); the *tree of life* is restored (cf. $2^7$).[h] Ezekiel's river flowed from the temple, which in this City is *the throne of God and the Lamb* ($21^{22}$). *Bright as crystal* recalls the *sea of glass* in the old heaven ($4^6$), its potentiality for good fulfilled, and the *street* recalls the great city's street, where the *dead* witnesses lay ($11^8$): water of *life* flows from them as from their Master; cf. John $4^{10-14}$, $7^{38}$: 'Out of his heart shall flow rivers of living water.' This promise was made at the feast of Tabernacles (see on $21^3$ and $7^{15-17}$), whose themes were *water* and *light*. It was the harvest feast of 'ingathering' – here the ingathering of the nations as at Zech. $14^{16}$ – looking forward to the fulfilment of God's dwelling in tabernacles with his people in the wilderness.

As RSV margin indicates, the text could be punctuated differently. In either case the single *tree of life* in the middle of the garden (Gen. $2^9$) has become, after Ezek. $47^{12}$, a line of 'tree of life', as we might say a line of cedar of Lebanon, on *either side of the river*.

*with its twelve kinds of fruit:* lit. 'making twelve fruitings or harvests', which fits better what follows. In the city there is no time either of darkness ($21^{25}$) or of unfruitfulness.

*the healing of the nations:* in memory of the carnage of $19^{17-21}$, or the smiting of $11^{5f.}$ (cf. Hos. $6^{1, 5}$)? cf. $21^4$, $7^{17}$.

3
*There shall no more be anything accursed:* lit. 'no kind of curse (*katathema*)'. This could mean what RSV says; cf. $21^{27}$. But Zech. $14^{10}$, referring to

h *Tree* is *xūlon*, a word often used for the cross, in reference to the 'curse' of Deut. $21^{23}$, which Christians saw as Jesus as having borne (Gal. $3^{13}$). There is no overt indication here of the theme of the tree of Calvary healing the hurt caused by the tree of Eden, but it could have been in mind; see note *o* on $2^7$.

the 'ban', suggests the absence not of things destroyed but of the power of destruction, leading the mind back to Gen. 3. RSV's full stop after *nations* should be put after *accursed*, and the following *but* removed; it is not in the Greek.

### 3–5

The rest of vv. 3–5 continues the Tabernacles theme of 21³, and echoes 7¹⁵ almost verbatim, except for the addition of the *Lamb* as enthroned with God. Yet for all his associating the Lamb wholly and equally with God, John's final picture, like Paul's in I Cor. 15²⁸, is of God alone. All the pronouns are singular. The *lamp* of the City is the Lamb, (21²³), but our eyes pass finally to the source of *light* himself.

*his servants shall worship him:* lit. 'his slaves shall serve him' (*latreuein* = carry out religious duties). Like Paul, John did not shrink from the word *slave* to describe himself and his fellows (1²). This is the true basis of man's kingship – see on 21¹⁰.

### 4

*they shall see his face:* like a king's ministers. Moses was not allowed to see God's face (Ex. 33²⁰ff.), but see Ps. 17¹⁵ for the hope, and Matt. 5⁸, I Cor. 13¹², I John 3². For the Greeks also it was the sum of human happiness, which they joined the church to secure. 'The church undertook the amazing task of transforming this self-centred cult of the divine into an ideal of disinterested worship and service.'[i]

### 4f.

*his name shall be on their foreheads:* the *seal* of 7³ff. was probably the last letter of the Hebrew alphabet, *tau*, which stood for the divine name, but the thought here is perhaps of the high priest's frontlet, which according to Philo (*Life of Moses* II. 114f.) and Josephus (*Ant.* III. 187) was inscribed with the Name itself (YHWH). They are priestly through and through, and they *reign for ever and ever*: the Lamb's work (5¹⁰) is completed, and the Lord God alone fills the eye.

*will be their light:* lit. 'will shed light upon them', evoking the priestly blessing by which Aaron and his sons were to put God's name upon Israel (Num. 6²³⁻²⁷).

i K. E. Kirk, *The Vision of God*, Longmans 1931, p. 54.

<sup>6</sup>*And he said to me, 'These words are trustworthy and true. And the Lord, the God of the spirits of the prophets, has sent his angel to show his servants what must soon take place.* <sup>7</sup>*And behold, I am coming soon.'*

*Blessed is he who keeps the words of the prophecy of this book.*

<sup>8</sup>*I John am he who heard and saw these things. And when I heard and saw them, I fell down to worship at the feet of the angel who showed them to me;* <sup>9</sup>*but he said to me, 'You must not do that! I am a fellow servant with you and your brethren the prophets, and with those who keep the words of this book. Worship God.'*

<sup>10</sup>*And he said to me, 'Do not seal up the words of the prophecy of this book, for the time is near.* <sup>11</sup>*Let the evildoer still do evil, and the filthy still be filthy, and the righteous still do right, and the holy still be holy.*

<sup>12</sup>*Behold, I am coming soon, bringing my recompense, to repay every one for what he has done,* <sup>13</sup>*I am the Alpha and the Omega, the first and the last, the beginning and the end.'*

<sup>14</sup>*Blessed are those who wash their robes,* that they may have the right to the tree of life and that they may enter the city by the gates.* <sup>15</sup>*Outside are the dogs and sorcerers and fornicators and murderers and idolaters, and every one who loves and practises falsehood.*

<sup>16</sup>*I Jesus have sent my angel to you with this testimony for the churches. I am the root and the offspring of David, the bright morning star.'*

<sup>17</sup>*The Spirit and the Bride say. 'Come.' And let him who hears say, 'Come.' And let him who is thirsty come, let him who desires take the water of life without price.*

<sup>18</sup>*I warn every one who hears the words of the prophecy of this book: if any one adds to them, God will add to him the plagues described in this book,* <sup>19</sup>*and if any one takes away from the words of the book of this prophecy, God will take away his share in the tree of life and in the holy city, which are described in this book.*

<sup>20</sup>*He who testifies to these things says, 'Surely I am coming soon.' Amen. Come, Lord Jesus!*

<sup>21</sup>*The grace of the Lord Jesus be with all the saints.† Amen.*

\* Other ancient authorities read *do his commandments.*

† Other ancient authorities omit *all;* others omit *the saints.*

The exposition of 21¹⁻⁸ continues: these verses take up the themes of 21⁵ᵇ⁻⁸ – the reliability of the message, promises to the faithful and warnings to the careless. They can also be seen as the ending of the *letter* (14ᶠᶠ·) of which the visions are a part. Paul ended his letters with personal news, exhortations which underlined the main points he had been making, and warnings and greetings with a liturgical ring, as if his letter was to be read out at the meeting for the eucharist. Here John refers to his own role and authority; he echoes motifs from the first three chapters which confirm what we have identified as his main concerns; and there is a strong eucharistic ring.

As early Christians understood the eucharist, the Christ who died and rose again comes in a tangible foretaste of his final coming, which will mean total blessing to those who are ready, total disaster to those who are not. This foretaste is powerful now, for good or ill. So their liturgies included a sorting out of the worshippers, with exclusion of the unfit in order that they might repent and become fit; cf. I Cor. 11²⁶⁻³². This scrutiny is built into the structure of the seven letters (see pp. 41, 78 above). But in this closing chapter we stand beyond the scrutiny, on the brink of the Bridegroom's final coming, when the door will be shut and knocking vain (Matt. 25¹⁰). There is a last call to the hearer to choose, and a final prayer to Christ to *come*, and bring with him the Holy Communion of eternity.

ᴙᴙ

**6–9**

*And he said to me:* as at 19⁹ᶠ·, which vv. 6–9 echo, and throughout this passage, it is not clear who is speaking. *I am coming soon* (v. 7) might suggest that it is Jesus here, but probably it is the interpreting angel, who like the OT prophets both reports the words of his principal and speaks in his person. As at 19⁹ he reasserts the *trustworthiness* of the message, in the words used by God himself (21⁵), with a blessing on those who respond; again John falls to worship him, is rebuked in similar terms and is again told to *worship God*. What lies behind these repetitions?

*the God of the spirits of the prophets:* John can talk of the spirit of prophecy (19¹⁰) or of the prophets' spirits; cf. I Cor. 14³², 'the spirits of prophets are subject to prophets', paraphrased by NEB: 'it is for prophets to control prophetic inspiration.' Control or testing of these *spirits* was a delicate matter in view of Jesus' words about blasphemy against the Holy Spirit – see on $2^{20}$, 'Jezebel, who calls herself a prophetess'. The centrality of the letter to Thyatira justifies us in suspecting this issue here, as at $19^{10}$. The spirits of the prophets (are not autonomous but) belong to God, who has revealed himself in *the words of this book*. In contrast with Jezebel, John nowhere calls himself a *prophet* (though the angel implies it, v. 9) but emphasizes the source of his revelation.

*to show his servants what must soon take place:* see on $1^1$. Some take *his servants* to be Christian prophets (cf. $10^7$), who are to transmit the revelation to the seven churches; *you* (plural) at v. 16 would then refer to these prophets too. But, as at $1^{1-3}$, surely all Christians are meant.

**7**

*Blessed is he . . .:* cf. $1^3$. Again there is warning as well as promise: there would be many who would not be inclined to keep *the words of the prophecy of this book*; cf. vv. 18f. Its status as *prophecy* is underlined.

**8**

*I John:* likewise John's own experience is emphasized; cf. $1^9$. *These things* are surely the whole series of visions, and the next sentence should be translated 'And when I *had* heard and seen them'.

*I fell down to worship:* as at $19^{10}$ an oblique reference to a contemporary error? The repetition underlines the significance of the issue – perhaps the overvaluing of contemporary revelation, at the expense of the historical revelation of Jesus (the point at $19^{10}$) and testimony to that revelation (the point here). John's falling to worship the angel expresses his overwhelming conviction of the divine authority of his message, and the angel's rebuke emphasizes the personal insignificance of any vehicle of revelation. Even the highest angel is but a *fellow slave* with John and his *brethren*, who are not only the *prophets* (as RSV punctuates) but all faithful Christians; cf. $1^9$, $10^{10}$. Read . . . *the prophets and those . . .*

*Worship God:* the positive theme of the whole book (see on $22^{3-5}$), just as negatively the theme is ideolatry and its results. True worship is the locus of the divine victory (as in Jesus' temptations) (see pp. 62, 200). At $19^{10}$ the sequel was the coming of the Word himself; so here there is the repeated promise *I am coming soon* (vv. 7, 12, 20).

**10**

*Do not seal up the words of the prophecy:* as Daniel was told to, for a time centuries ahead (Dan. 12⁴; cf. Isa. 8¹⁶).

**11**

*Let the evildoer still do evil:* Daniel was told that many would purify themselves and make themselves white, but the wicked would do wickedly until the final crisis (12¹⁰). For John *the time is near*, and he seems to acquiesce in this polarization, as if it were already too late for change. But the 'beatitude' at v. 14 shows that it is *not* too late; no one can be smugly secure. That is why Jesus has sent his angel (v. 16).

**12**

*to repay everyone for what he has done:* the words pick up the warning to those at Thyatira who side with Jezebel (2²³). Contrast the blessing on those who 'die in the Lord' (14¹³). On 'judgment by works' see on 20¹²⁻¹⁵. There is no clash with 'justification by faith' – see on 12⁷⁻¹². John is at one with Paul: cf. Rom. 2⁶, 14¹², I Cor. 3¹²⁻¹⁵, II Cor. 5¹⁰. The more gifted and successful the Christians (cf. 2¹⁹, 3¹⁷, I Cor. 14⁻⁷, 4⁸), the greater the danger of their taking their 'justification' for granted.

**13**

*I am the Alpha and the Omega:* see on 1⁸. The end is not an event but a person, from whom the world devolves and to whom it moves; he has shared his throne and his title with Jesus. For *beginning and end* see 21⁶, where God is speaking. *First and last* is used of God at Isa. 44⁶, 48¹², but in Rev. only of Jesus, at 1¹⁷ and 2⁸ where it is linked with his resurrection. He is the first-born of the dead (1⁵), the beginning of God's creation (3¹⁴), in contrast to all transitory claimants of ultimacy and purveyors of life – see on 13¹⁸.

**14**

*Blessed are those who wash their robes:* see on 16¹⁵; again the warning is clear. *Do his commandments* is very similar in Greek to *wash their robes;*ʲ the latter is less obvious but more pointed, and almost certainly original. *Wash* is present participle, an ongoing thing, which confirms that

---

ʲ *wash their robes* is *plunontes tas stolas autōn; do his commandments* is *poiountes tas entolas autou.*

'washing robes in the blood of the Lamb' (7$^{14}$) does not refer necessarily to physical martyrdom but to maintaining the once-for-all washing of baptism to the end. Contrast the *soiled* garments at Sardis (3$^4$).

*that they may have:* 'so that they shall have'. Through baptism and eucharist Christians already enjoyed in foretaste a share in the *tree of life* and the heavenly *city*, but the fulness is only for the *conqueror* – cf. the promises to Ephesus, commended for hating the works of the Nicolaitans (2$^{6f.}$), and to Philadelphia, the victim of Jewish polemic (3$^{9, 12}$). That these things (not Rome and emperor worship) were John's main concerns is confirmed by the imagery of the following verses.

## 15

*Outside:* where the unquenchable fire burns up the rubbish (Isa. 66$^{24}$, quoted at Mark 9$^{48}$); see on *the lake of fire* (19$^{20}$). For the catalogue, see on 21$^8$; it is a reminder of baptismal commitment. The collocation with the beatitude of v. 14 suggests the invitation to the worthy and exclusion of the unworthy at the eucharist.$^k$

*the dogs:* heading the list they must be significant, like the *cowardly* heading the otherwise almost identical list at 21$^8$. It was a traditional term among Jews, to whom *dogs* were unclean, for non-Jews; cf. Matt. 7$^6$, 15$^{26}$. Paul used it for men he regarded as false Jews (Phil. 3$^2$), which is probably John's meaning here, in view of the reference to Philadelphia above – see on vv. 16 and 19.

*who loves and practises falsehood:* an expansion of *all liars* which sums up the list at 21$^8$ – see commentary there. The regular occurrence of *sorcerers* in these lists reflects another aspect of the local situation.

## 16

*I Jesus have sent my angel to you: you* is plural, the hearers (but see v. 6). This *testimony* or warning (cf. v. 18) is not only for them but all *the churches*, which the seven represent; see on 1$^{11}$. Jesus' titles illuminate the situation for which John was writing. *Root and offspring of David*

---

$^k$ Likewise at celebrations of the mystery religions. G. Bornkamm quotes the formula in the second-century sophist Lucian (*Alexander*, 38): 'If there be any atheist or Christian or Epicurean here spying upon our rites, let him depart in haste; and let all such as have faith in God be initiated and all blessing attend them' (*Early Christian Experience*, p. 178, note 5).

takes up the messianic title of 5$^5$ and Isa. 11, and *star* takes up an equally popular messianic prophecy, Num. 24$^{17}$ – the *star* seen by Balaam; see on 2$^{28}$. The linking of Balaam, the ancestor of magic, with the Nicolaitans (2$^{14}$), the connection of Jezebel (2$^{20}$) with sorcery as well as fornication and idolatry (II Kings 9$^{22}$), the promise of the *morning star* to the faithful at Thyatira – all this fits with the emphasis on *sorcery* (9$^{21}$, 18$^{23}$, 21$^8$, 22$^{15}$) to confirm that the local issue is not the emperor cult but general compromise with pagan religion and morals. The letter to Thyatira is both the central letter and the longest.

But why *David*? the 'false Jews' of Smyrna and Philadelphia (2$^9$, 3$^9$ – the *dogs* of v. 15?) were perhaps an equal danger, as Ignatius' letters to Magnesia and Philadelphia suggest; see pp. 28ff. But it is Jesus who holds the key of David and assures the Philadelphian Christians that they are his chosen people (3$^{7-9}$). He is the Root of David who has opened the scriptures (5$^5$).

17

*The Spirit and the Bride say, 'Come'*: the invitation is not to the *thirsty* but to Jesus. The Spirit who speaks in the prophets; the church as its true self, roused from Sardian slumber and cleansed from Nicolaitan impurity; and everyone who *hears* what the Spirit is saying to the churches: all respond to *I am coming* with the liturgical invocation *Come!* (see on v. 20).

*let him who is thirsty come*: this was Jesus' own invitation at John 7$^{37}$, echoing Isa. 55$^1$ – see on 21$^6$, where it is God who speaks. He is the fulfilment of all God's promises.

18f.

*I warn*: lit. *testify*, as at vv. 16, 20 and 1$^2$. This warning seems so out of keeping with the sublimity of the passage that some think it was interpolated at a time when Revelation had become 'scripture': similar warnings to future copyists are common. But such warnings are also found in ancient authors, and John no doubt had Deut. 4$^{2ff.}$ in mind: 'You shall not add to the word I command you, nor take from it'; the next verse refers to the syncretism of Baal-peor (instigated by Balaam; see on Rev. 2$^{14}$); cf. the warning against syncretism and complacency at Deut. 29$^{16-20}$: 'the curses written in this book would settle upon him, and the Lord would blot out his name from under heaven.' John is convinced that his message is not his but God's.

The strength of the language is explicable if the message was likely to be unpopular ('Jezebel' clearly had great prestige), and its details confirm what we gathered from vv. 14 and 16. The *plagues described in this book* were the punishment of idolatry, including the *death* with which Jezebel's children were threatened at Thyatira ($2^{23}$). The *tree of life* was promised to the conqueror at Ephesus, commended for its opposition to the Nicolaitans ($2^{6f.}$), and the *holy city* was promised to the Philadelphian victims of Jewish slander ($3^{12}$).

**20**

*He who testifies: ho marturōn* – the 'faithful witness' (*martus*), who is *coming soon* to back up his words. *Surely* is *nai* = 'yes' or 'even so' as at $1^7$, 'Behold he comes with the clouds . . . Yes. Amen': divine affirmation and human response; cf. II Cor. $1^{20}$.

*Come, Lord Jesus!*: this echoes the Aramaic invocation *marana tha* ('Come Lord'), which occurs at I Cor. $16^{22}$ and in a eucharistic dialogue in the collection of very ancient materials called the *Didache* ($10^6$, *ECW*, p. 232):

Let grace (i.e. Jesus) come, and let this world pass away.
*Hosanna to the God of David.*
Whoever is holy, let him come; whoever is not, let him repent.
*Marana tha. Amen.*

The eucharist, as the anticipation of the Lord's final coming as judge, demands self-examination (I Cor. $11^{26-32}$), and a demand for self-examination may therefore be made in eucharistic terms,[l] just as a demand for commitment may be phrased to remind the hearers of their baptismal dedication. Such baptismal and eucharistic reference can be seen in the letters to the churches (see pp. 41f. and commentary on chs. 2–3), and in other NT Epistles. The ending of I Cor. suggests it was intended to be read at the eucharistic gathering.[m] Revelation was in literary form a letter ($1^{4ff.}$), no doubt to be read aloud ($1^3$) in the same context.

---

l *Marana tha* could be used simply to support a curse or ban: 'Lord, come – as witness, and judge!' See C. F. D. Moule, 'A Reconsideration of the Context of *Maranatha*', NTS 8, 1962, pp. 307–10.

m See J. A. T. Robinson, 'The Earliest Christian Liturgical Sequence?', in his *Twelve New Testament Studies*, SCM Press and Allenson 1962, pp. 154–7; cf. G. Bornkamm, *Early Christian Experience*, pp. 147–52, 169–76.

21

Like Paul's letters John's ends with *the grace*. The original text was probably the shortest. *The grace of the Lord Jesus be with all*; cf. the last verses of I and II Thess. This could have been expanded at different times by the addition of *saints* (= *holy*) and *Amen*; cf. *Didache* 10⁶. If the words were original, why were they ever dropped?

*Grace* meant God's favour, embodied in Jesus for man's salvation (cf. II Cor. 8⁹). *God* was at the centre at the end of John's vision (22⁵): at the end of the letter whose aim is to make that vision effective the centre is *Jesus*.

# Index of References

## THE BIBLE
### Old Testament

**GENESIS**

| | |
|---|---|
| 1 | 68, 116, 121, 218 |
| $1^2$ | 164 |
| $1^3$ | 159 |
| $1^{6f.}$ | 167 |
| $1^7$ | 119 |
| $1^{14-18}$ | 164 |
| $1^{21}$ | 215 |
| $2^9$ | 83, 311 |
| $2^{10}$ | 311 |
| 3 | 9, 11, 83, 201, 288 |
| $3^{1-5}$ | 215 |
| $3^{15}$ | 173, 196, 205, 210, 258 |
| $3^{15-20}$ | 194, 203 |
| $3^{16}$ | 196 |
| $3^{16-19}$ | 299 |
| $3^{20}$ | 195 |
| 4 | 300 |
| $4^{10}$ | 141 |
| $5^{5ff.}$ | 289 |
| $7^{11}$ | 119 |
| 9 | 116 |
| $9^{13}$ | 117 |
| 11 | 187 |
| $11^{3-5}$ | 211 |
| $11^4$ | 268, 303 |
| $14^{15}$ | 15 |
| $14^{22}$ | 178 |
| $14^{24}$ | 15 |
| $18^{20f.}$ | 268 |
| 19 | 253 |
| $19^1$ | 187 |
| $19^{24}$ | 173, 227, 286 |
| $19^{28}$ | 168, 173, 227, 271 |
| $22^{17}$ | 291 |
| $32^{25}$ | 200 |
| $32^{28}$ | 91 |
| $37^9$ | 195 |
| 49 | 232 |
| $49^{9ff.}$ | 96, 127, 283 |
| $49^{10}$ | 149 |
| $49^{11f.}$ | 153, 232 |
| $49^{17}$ | 149 |

**EXODUS**

| | |
|---|---|
| $1^{15}-2^{10}$ | 197 |
| $1^{22}$ | 203 |
| $3^{14}$ | 61, 65 |
| $7^{14-25}$ | 186 |
| $7^{17ff.}$ | 163, 244 |
| 8–12 | 161 |
| $8^{2ff.}$ | 248 |
| $8^{22ff.}$ | 168 |
| $9^{4ff.}$ | 168 |
| $9^{8f.}$ | 168 |
| $9^{19ff.}$ | 251 |
| $9^{18, 24}$ | 250 |
| $9^{23f.}$ | 162 |
| $9^{25}$ | 163 |
| $10^{12-20}$ | 168 |
| $10^{21-29}$ | 164, 166 |
| $10^{23}$ | 168 |
| 12 | 148 |
| $13^{21}$ | 154, 177 |
| $14^{5-8}$ | 175 |
| $14^8$ | 204 |
| $14^{21ff.}$ | 203, 248 |
| 15 | 131 |
| $15^{1-18}$ | 240 |
| $15^{11}$ | 210 |
| $15^{12}$ | 205 |
| 16 | 90 |
| $16^{32-34}$ | 90 |
| $19^4$ | 203f. |
| $19^{4-6}$ | 61 |
| $19^{5f.}$ | 176 |
| $19^6$ | 66, 130 |
| $19^{16ff.}$ | 118, 159, 176, 250 |
| $24^{10, 17}$ | 117 |
| $25^{9, 16}$ | 241 |
| $25^{31}$ | 71 |
| $28^4$ | 71 |
| $28^{15-21}$ | 303 |
| $28^{16ff.}$ | 306 |
| $30^{11-16}$ | 30 |
| $32^8$ | 212 |
| $32^{15}$ | 123 |
| $32^{32}$ | 100 |
| $32^{32f.}$ | 212 |
| $33^{20ff.}$ | 312 |
| $34^{29}$ | 241 |
| $39^{37}$ | 74 |
| $40^4$ | 74 |
| $40^{34}$ | 154 |
| $40^{35}$ | 241 |

| LEVITICUS | |
|---|---|
| $15^{18}$ | 222 |
| $16^{2ff.}$ | 193 |
| $21^9$ | 262 |
| $26^{18-28}$ | 15, 135 |
| $26^{26}$ | 140 |

| NUMBERS | |
|---|---|
| $2^{3ff.}$ | 304 |
| $6^{23-27}$ | 312 |
| $9^{23}$ | 292 |
| $16^{10}$ | 286 |
| $16^{21}$ | 239 |
| $16^{30}$ | 205 |
| $22^{1ff.}$ | 89 |
| $24^{17}$ | 89, 96f., 318 |
| $25^{1-9}$ | 89 |
| $31^{16}$ | 89 |

| DEUTERONOMY | |
|---|---|
| $4^{2ff.}$ | 318 |
| $7^{13}$ | 140 |
| $10^{17}$ | 284 |
| $13^{1ff.}$ | 216 |
| $19^{15}$ | 14, 184 |
| $19^{16-19}$ | 275 |
| $23^{9-14}$ | 222 |
| $29^{16-20}$ | 318 |
| $32$ | 224 |
| $32^{1-43}$ | 240 |
| $32^4$ | 240 |
| $32^{8f.}$ | 201 |
| $32^{11}$ | 203f. |
| $32^{16-21}$ | 173 |
| $32^{32f.}$ | 224, 230 |
| $32^{33}$ | 241 |
| $32^{40}$ | 178 |
| $32^{44}$ | 240 |
| $34^{5f.}$ | 188 |

| JOSHUA | |
|---|---|
| $4^{23}$ | 248 |
| $6^{1-20}$ | 193 |
| $6^{4ff.}$ | 159 |

| JUDGES | |
|---|---|
| $5^{19f.}$ | 250 |

| I SAMUEL | |
|---|---|
| $4^8$ | 186 |
| $6^{5-8}$ | 189 |

| II SAMUEL | |
|---|---|
| $7^{14}$ | 299 |

| I KINGS | |
|---|---|
| $5^{17}$ | 305 |
| $7^{23-26}$ | 119, 239 |
| $8^{10}$ | 154 |
| $8^{11}$ | 241 |
| $16^{31}$ | 242, 255 |
| $17^1$ | 185, 216 |
| $17^{2-4, 8f.}$ | 198 |
| $17^{18}$ | 268 |
| $18$ | 252 |
| $18^4$ | 242 |
| $18^{13}$ | 94 |
| $18^{17}$ | 188 |
| $18^{19ff.}$ | 250 |
| $18^{38}$ | 216 |
| $21$ | 252 |
| $21^{20}$ | 188 |
| $22$ | 250 |
| $22^{19}$ | 118 |
| $22^{20-22}$ | 249 |

| II KINGS | |
|---|---|
| $1^8$ | 184 |
| $1^{10ff.}$ | 185, 292 |
| $2^{11}$ | 188 |
| $9^7$ | 278 |
| $9^{22}$ | 92, 94, 226, 237, 275, 318 |
| $18^4$ | 255 |
| $19^{28}$ | 268 |
| $22^{19}$ | 116n. |
| $23^{29}$ | 250 |

| I CHRONICLES | |
|---|---|
| $21^1$ | 199 |

| | |
|---|---|
| $24^{4-6}$ | 118 |
| $29^{11}$ | 121 |

| II CHRONICLES | |
|---|---|
| $3-5$ | 115 |
| $4^6$ | 119, 239 |
| $16^9$ | 129 |
| $35^{20-25}$ | 250 |

| ESTHER | |
|---|---|
| $2^{23}$ | 294 |
| $6^1$ | 294 |
| $9^{19, 22}$ | 187f. |

| JOB | |
|---|---|
| 1, 2 | 85, 144n., 199 |
| $2^7$ | 168 |
| $3^{21}$ | 169 |
| $39^{30}$ | 165n. |
| $40^{15}$ | 173, 215 |
| $41^{1ff.}$ | 215 |
| $41^{19-21}$ | 173 |
| $41^{33}$ | 173 |

| PSALMS | |
|---|---|
| $1^{1f.}$ | 60 |
| 2 | 191f., 197n., 284, 286 |
| $2^1$ | 193 |
| $2^{1-6}$ | 221 |
| $2^2$ | 249, 261, 289 |
| $2^4$ | 192 |
| $2^{4-9}$ | 308 |
| $2^5$ | 193 |
| $2^{6-9}$ | 93, 194 |
| $2^8$ | 284 |
| $2^9$ | 9, 93, 96f., 196f., 283 |
| $3^8$ | 152 |
| $13^{1f.}$ | 142 |
| $16^5$ | 227 |
| $17^{15}$ | 312 |
| $18^4$ | 204, 295 |
| $18^{16}$ | 295 |

| | | | |
|---|---|---|---|
| $19^{10}$ | 180 | $137^1$ | 252 |
| 23 | 154 | $141^2$ | 129 |
| $23^4$ | 96 | | |
| $23^5$ | 227 | **PROVERBS** | |
| 29 | 178 | 3 | 108 |
| $33^3$ | 129 | $3^{11f.}$ | 108 |
| $40^3$ | 129 | $30^{27}$ | 170 |
| 45 | 281 | | |
| $45^3$ | 284 | **ECCLESIASTES** | |
| $45^{4f.}$ | 139n., 282 | $9^8$ | 100 |
| $45^6$ | 282 | | |
| $46^{4-7}$ | 298 | **SONG OF SONGS** | |
| $51^4$ | 199 | $5^2$ | 109 |
| $68^{17f.}$ | 131, 172 | $6^{4, 10}$ | 303 |
| $69^{24}$ | 243 | $7^1$ | 303 |
| $69^{28}$ | 100 | $8^{6f.}$ | 108, 126 |
| $74^{14}$ | 196 | $8^{10}$ | 70 |
| $75^8$ | 224, 227 | | |
| $79^{2f.}$ | 187 | **ISAIAH** | |
| $86^{8f.}$ | 240 | $1^1$ | 57 |
| $86^9$ | 308 | $1^{10}$ | 187 |
| 87 | 196 | $1^{18}$ | 153 |
| $87^2$ | 292 | $1^{21}$ | 253, 302 |
| $87^{4-6}$ | 308 | $2^{12ff.}$ | 145 |
| 89 | 61 | $2^{19}$ | 145 |
| $89^6$ | 210 | $3^9$ | 187 |
| $89^{27}$ | 65f. | $4^3$ | 294 |
| $89^{37}$ | 65 | $4^{5f.}$ | 154 |
| $90^4$ | 67, 218, 287 | 6 | 115, 120 |
| $91^{13}$ | 173 | $6^1$ | 118 |
| $95^{7ff.}$ | 212 | $6^3$ | 120 |
| $96^{13}$ | 282 | $6^4$ | 160 |
| $98^1$ | 129 | $6^{11}$ | 142 |
| $104^2$ | 70, 117 | $6^{13}$ | 205 |
| $109^6$ | 85 | $7^{14}$ | 196, 298 |
| $111^{2, 9}$ | 240 | $8^8$ | 292, 298 |
| 113–118 | 277 | $8^{10}$ | 298 |
| $113^1$ | 193, 279 | $8^{16}$ | 316 |
| $115^1$ | 279 | $8^{22ff.}$ | 248 |
| $115^{13}$ | 193, 279 | 11 | 129, 318 |
| 118 | 153 | $11^{1-4}$ | 96f. |
| $118^{24}$ | 279 | $11^{1-10}$ | 128 |
| $118^{25}$ | 153 | $11^{2f.}$ | 72 |
| $121^6$ | 154 | $11^4$ | 72, 186, 282f. |
| $132^{13}$ | 292 | $13^{21}$ | 267 |
| | | $14^{11}$ | 275 |

| | |
|---|---|
| $14^{12}$ | 81, 119, 163 |
| $14^{12-14}$ | 215 |
| $14^{13f.}$ | 200, 250 |
| $14^{14}$ | 164 |
| $21^{1ff.}$ | 262 |
| $21^{2ff.}$ | 254 |
| $21^5$ | 222 |
| $21^9$ | 226 |
| $22^{15ff.}$ | 101 |
| $22^{15-25}$ | 103 |
| $22^{17, 21}$ | 104 |
| $22^{22}$ | 102n. |
| $22^{23}$ | 104 |
| $24^8$ | 275 |
| $24^{19-23}$ | 145 |
| $24^{21-23}$ | 288 |
| $24^{23}$ | 118 |
| $25^6$ | 154 |
| $25^8$ | 154, 298 |
| $26^{17}$ | 196 |
| $27^1$ | 196, 201, 216 |
| $27^{13}$ | 159 |
| $29^{11, 18}$ | 123 |
| $30^7$ | 196 |
| $34^{2-4}$ | 145 |
| $34^6$ | 285 |
| $34^{10}$ | 271 |
| $34^{11-14}$ | 267 |
| $35^{10}$ | 299 |
| 40–66 | 62 |
| $40^2$ | 267 |
| $40^3$ | 248 |
| $42^{9f.}$ | 129 |
| $43^{8-12}$ | 59 |
| $43^{16-17}$ | 132 |
| $43^{18f.}$ | 299 |
| $43^{19f.}$ | 299 |
| $44^3$ | 217 |
| $44^6$ | 72, 316 |
| $44^{27}$ | 248 |
| $45^{1ff.}$ | 103 |
| $45^7$ | 144n. |
| $45^{14}$ | 103 |
| $47^{7ff.}$ | 267, 269 |
| $47^9$ | 269 |

ISAIAH – *contd*

| | |
|---|---|
| 47$^{12}$ | 275 |
| 48$^{12}$ | 72, 316 |
| 48$^{20}$ | 268 |
| 49$^2$ | 72 |
| 49$^{10}$ | 154 |
| 49$^{12}$ | 304 |
| 49$^{13}$ | 202 |
| 49$^{16-19}$ | 21 |
| 49$^{23}$ | 103 |
| 50$^2$ | 248 |
| 50$^3$ | 145 |
| 51$^{9ff.}$ | 119, 132, 196 |
| 51$^{10}$ | 248 |
| 51$^{11}$ | 299 |
| 51$^{17-23}$ | 224, 241 |
| 52$^{7-12}$ | 224, 226 |
| 52$^{11}$ | 268 |
| 52$^{13}$–53$^{12}$ | 226 |
| 53$^7$ | 124 |
| 53$^9$ | 124, 223 |
| 53$^{10-12}$ | 124 |
| 53$^{12}$ | 221 |
| 54$^{11-14}$ | 21, 302 |
| 54$^{12}$ | 306 |
| 55$^{1ff.}$ | 299, 318 |
| 55$^4$ | 65 |
| 55$^{10f.}$ | 59 |
| 55$^{11}$ | 294 |
| 55$^{12}$ | 70 |
| 60$^3$ | 310 |
| 60$^{10-16}$ | 310 |
| 60$^{11}$ | 310 |
| 60$^{14}$ | 103 |
| 60$^{19}$ | 309 |
| 61$^7$ | 267 |
| 62$^{1-5}$ | 302 |
| 62$^2$ | 91, 105 |
| 62$^6$ | 304 |
| 63 | 232 |
| 63$^{1-6}$ | 128, 230, 283f. |
| 63$^3$ | 232, 283 |
| 63$^6$ | 232 |
| 64 | 241 |
| 65$^{5f.}$ | 295 |

| | |
|---|---|
| 65$^{15ff.}$ | 91, 107 |
| 65$^{16f.}$ | 299 |
| 65$^{17ff.}$ | 196, 297 |
| 65$^{19}$ | 299 |
| 65$^{22}$ | 289 |
| 66$^6$ | 243 |
| 66$^{7f.}$ | 196f. |
| 66$^{22}$ | 196 |
| 66$^{24}$ | 317 |

JEREMIAH

| | |
|---|---|
| 2$^2$ | 198 |
| 4$^{23-26}$ | 274 |
| 4$^{24}$ | 145 |
| 4$^{30}$ | 254 |
| 7$^{34}$ | 274 |
| 9$^{15}$ | 164 |
| 10$^{6f.}$ | 240 |
| 10$^{25}$ | 243 |
| 11$^{19}$ | 124 |
| 14$^{12}$ | 140 |
| 15$^2$ | 212f. |
| 15$^{16-18}$ | 180 |
| 16$^9$ | 274 |
| 16$^{18}$ | 267 |
| 16$^{21}$ | 240 |
| 17$^{5-18}$ | 95 |
| 17$^{18}$ | 269 |
| 23$^{15}$ | 164 |
| 23$^{18}$ | 59 |
| 25$^{1ff.}$ | 224 |
| 25$^{10}$ | 274f. |
| 25$^{30}$ | 178 |
| 31$^{35f.}$ | 164 |
| 32$^{9-14}$ | 123 |
| 43$^{11}$ | 212 |
| 46$^{10}$ | 285 |
| 50$^8$ | 268 |
| 50$^{38}$ | 248 |
| 50 | 267 |
| 51 | 26, 163, 224 |
| 51$^6$ | 268 |
| 51$^{6-10}$ | 224 |
| 51$^7$ | 224, 226f., 252, 254 |
| 51$^8$ | 226 |

| | |
|---|---|
| 51$^9$ | 268 |
| 51$^{13}$ | 252 |
| 51$^{25}$ | 163, 193 |
| 51$^{34}$ | 196 |
| 51$^{36}$ | 196, 248 |
| 51$^{37}$ | 267 |
| 51$^{59-64}$ | 274 |
| 51$^{63f.}$ | 275 |

LAMENTATIONS

| | |
|---|---|
| 4$^7$ | 153 |

EZEKIEL

| | |
|---|---|
| 1 | 42, 115n., 116f. |
| 1$^1$ | 282 |
| 1$^{4, 7}$ | 72 |
| 1$^{10}$ | 120 |
| 1$^{22}$ | 117 |
| 1$^{24}$ | 72 |
| 1$^{24-26}$ | 222 |
| 1$^{27}$ | 72, 117 |
| 1$^{28}$ | 117 |
| 2$^8$–3$^3$ | 176 |
| 2$^8$–3$^{11}$ | 180 |
| 2$^{10ff.}$ | 122, 127 |
| 3$^3$ | 123 |
| 4$^{16}$ | 140 |
| 5$^{16f.}$ | 138, 140 |
| 8$^2$ | 72 |
| 9$^1$–10$^2$ | 241 |
| 9$^{4ff.}$ | 148, 160 |
| 10$^2$ | 160 |
| 10$^{12}$ | 120 |
| 10$^{18}$ | 304 |
| 14$^{21}$ | 140 |
| 16$^{11-13}$ | 254 |
| 16$^{37-41}$ | 262 |
| 20$^{28}$ | 251 |
| 23$^{25-29}$ | 262, 269 |
| 26, 27 | 26, 253 |
| 26–28 | 271 |
| 26$^{12}$ | 275 |
| 26$^{13}$ | 275 |
| 27 | 252 |
| 27$^{12-24}$ | 272 |

$27^{27-34}$ 273
$28^{13}$ 119, 241, 272, 306
$28^{16}$ 273
$29^3$ 196
$32^{26}$ 291
$33^3$ 159
$34^{23}$ 154
37 216, 290
$37^{10f.}$ 188
38–39 170, 290
$38^2$ 291
$38^{4ff.}$ 171f.
$38^{8, 11}$ 291
$38^{12}$ 292
$38^{14f.}$ 291
$38^{22}$ 292
$39^{4, 17-20}$ 285
40–48 266, 290
$40^2$ 303
$40^{3ff.}$ 182f., 304
$40^5$ 305
$41^{21}$ 305
$43^{2ff.}$ 72, 266f.
$43^4$ 304
$43^{16}$ 305
$45^1$ 305
47 308
$47^{1-2}$ 311
$48^{20}$ 305
$48^{31-34}$ 304
$48^{35}$ 308

DANIEL
1–6 78
$1^{12-15}$ 86
$2^{19ff.}$ 248
$2^{22, 27ff.}$ 73
$2^{29f.}$ 254
$2^{35}$ 200
$2^{44}$ 248
$2^{46}$ 280n.
$2^{47}$ 284
3 18, 72, 214, 216
$3^4$ 180
$3^{4-6}$ 216

$3^{22}$ 245
$3^{25}$ 80, 93
$3^{27}$ 245
$3^{28}$ 245
4 63
$4^{19}$ 261
$4^{28-32}$ 226
$4^{34-37}$ 120, 189
$5^{23}$ 174
$6^{25}$ 180
7 9, 18, 129, 206, 261
$7^{2ff.}$ 147, 196, 209
$7^{7, 20}$ 196
$7^8$ 210
$7^9$ 69, 72, 100
$7^{9ff.}$ 115, 288
$7^{9-14}$ 126
$7^{10}$ 131, 172, 294
$7^{11}$ 210
$7^{13}$ 62, 69, 129, 229, 231
$7^{14ff.}$ 180, 259
$7^{20}$ 210
$7^{21}$ 184
$7^{24}$ 260
$7^{25}$ 15, 182, 184, 204, 210
$8^{9-12}$ 211
$8^{10}$ 196
$8^{12f.}$ 207
$8^{13}$ 18, 184
$8^{16}$ 177
$9^{21}$ 177
$9^{27}$ 18
$10^5$ 71, 177
$10^6$ 72
$10^{7ff.}$ 72
$10^{12ff.}$ 73
$10^{13ff.}$ 201
$10^{13-21}$ 18, 200
$11^{1-39}$ 18
$11^{30-35}$ 18
$11^{30-36}$ 205, 207ff., 211
$11^{31}$ 18, 152, 216
$11^{32-36}$ 215

$11^{40f.}$ 18
12 17
$12^1$ 153, 200, 250, 294
$12^2$ 294
$12^3$ 74, 304
$12^4$ 127, 316
$12^7$ 178f., 182, 204
$12^{7ff.}$ 177ff.
$12^{10}$ 153, 316
$12^{11}$ 18, 182

HOSEA
1–3 302
$2^{14ff.}$ 109
$6^{1-5}$ 186, 283, 311
$8^1$ 165
$10^8$ 145
$11^{10}$ 178
$13^{14}$ 169

JOEL
2 166, 168
$2^1$ 159, 166
$2^2$ 250
$2^{11}$ 146, 149
$2^{15}$ 159, 166
$2^{31}$ 145, 149
3 10
$3^{9ff.}$ 249
$3^{12}$ 221
$3^{13}$ 229, 232
$3^{16}$ 178

AMOS
$1^1$ 68
$1^2$ 178
$1^4$ 162
$2^4$ 166
$3^{4-8}$ 178
$3^6$ 144n., 159, 161
$3^7$ 59, 179
$3^8$ 179
$5^6$ 164
$5^{18ff.}$ 164
$6^{12}$ 164

AMOS – *contd*

| | |
|---|---|
| $7_1$ff. | 166, 168, 170, 172 |
| $7^4$ | 162f. |
| $8^9$ | 164 |

JONAH

| | |
|---|---|
| 2 | 129 |
| $3^{6, 8}$ | 184 |

MICAH

| | |
|---|---|
| $5^{2-4}$ | 197 |
| $5^{2-6}$ | 96 |
| $7^{14}$ | 96 |

NAHUM

| | |
|---|---|
| $1^6$ | 146 |
| $3^{1-4}$ | 26 |
| $3^4$ | 253, 275 |

HABAKKUK

| | |
|---|---|
| $1^6$ | 292 |

| | |
|---|---|
| $2^3$ | 179 |
| $3^2$ | 178 |
| $3^{5-9}$ | 139n. |

ZEPHANIAH

| | |
|---|---|
| $1^7$ | 285 |
| $1^{14}$ff. | 249 |
| $2^{14}$f. | 267 |
| $3^8$ | 243 |
| $3^{13}$ | 223 |

ZECHARIAH

| | |
|---|---|
| $1^8$ | 139 |
| $1^{8-15}$ | 137 |
| $1^{12}$ | 142 |
| 2 | 182 |
| $2^1$ff. | 304 |
| $2^4$f. | 305 |
| 3 | 85 |
| $3^1$ff. | 199 |
| $3^{8-10}$ | 129 |

| | |
|---|---|
| $4^2$ | 65, 118 |
| $4^{2-10}$ | 71, 98, 129 |
| $4^3$ | 130n. |
| $4^6$ | 129n., 185 |
| $4^7$ | 186 |
| $4^{10}$ | 65, 118 |
| $4^{11}$ff. | 130n. |
| $6^{1-8}$ | 137 |
| $6^2$f. | 139 |
| $12^{10}$ff. | 63, 67, 188 |
| $12^{10}-13^4$ | 250 |
| $12^{11}$ | 250 |
| $12^{12}$ff. | 66 |
| $14^2$ff. | 249 |
| $14^4$f. | 250 |
| $14^7$f. | 154n. |
| $14^8$, 10f., 16 | 311 |
| $14^{20}$f. | 310 |

MALACHI

| | |
|---|---|
| $3^2$ | 181 |
| $4^{4-6}$ | 146 |

## Apocrypha

**II ESDRAS**

| | |
|---|---|
| $4^{33-37}$ | 142 |
| $6^{39}$ | 159 |
| $7^{28}$ | 289 |
| $7^{29ff.}$ | 159 |
| $7^{75ff.}$ | 230n. |
| $7^{79-87}$ | 227 |
| $9^{38}-10^{55}$ | 195 |
| $10^{27ff.}$ | 303 |
| $11-12$ | 257n. |
| $12^{22-28}$ | 25 |
| $13^{5-11}$ | 221 |
| $13^{10}$ | 292 |
| $13^{34-38}$ | 221 |
| $13^{38}$ | 292 |

**TOBIT**

| | |
|---|---|
| $12^{15}$ | 160 |

**WISDOM OF SOLOMON**

| | |
|---|---|
| $1^{13-16}$ | 205 |

| | |
|---|---|
| $2^{23f.}$ | 205 |
| $5^{1-14}$ | 189 |
| $5^{17}$ | 243, 250 |
| $11-19$ | 161, 169, 245 |
| $11^{5}$ | 248 |
| $11^{15f.}$ | 166 |
| $11^{16}$ | 243f. |
| $11^{20}$ | 172 |
| $12^{10,\ 19f.}$ | 173 |
| $12^{23ff.}$ | 166, 169 |
| $14^{12}$ | 166, 174 |
| $14^{22}$ | 166 |
| $14^{24-27}$ | 174 |
| $16^{9}$ | 245 |
| $16^{17}$ | 186 |
| $16^{24}$ | 186, 248 |
| $17$ | 168, 246 |
| $17^{3ff.}$ | 166 |
| $17^{11-15}$ | 164 |
| $17^{11-21}$ | 248 |
| $18^{1}$ | 168 |
| $18^{4f.}$ | 186 |

| | |
|---|---|
| $18^{14-16}$ | 159, 283 |
| $18^{20-25}$ | 306 |
| $18^{24}$ | 71, 306 |
| $19^{1-6}$ | 186 |
| $19^{14ff.}$ | 168, 187 |

**SIRACH**

| | |
|---|---|
| $39^{10}$ | 168, 173 |
| $39^{24-31}$ | 162 |
| $48^{1}$ | 185 |
| $50^{7}$ | 118 |

**I MACCABEES**

| | |
|---|---|
| $4^{54-59}$ | 152 |
| $13^{51}$ | 152 |

**II MACCABEES**

| | |
|---|---|
| $7^{1-19,\ 30-38}$ | 126 |
| $10^{6f.}$ | 152 |
| $11^{8}$ | 100 |

# INDEX OF REFERENCES

## New Testament

**MATTHEW**

| Reference | Pages |
|---|---|
| $2^{1\text{ff.}}$ | 148, 195, 248 |
| $2^{2\text{ff.}}$ | 192 |
| $2^{6}$ | 197 |
| $3^{12}$ | 232 |
| $4^{1}$ | 253 |
| $4^{8-10}$ | 303 |
| $5^{2}$ | 85 |
| $5^{3}$ | 130 |
| $5^{3-11}$ | 60 |
| $5^{8}$ | 312 |
| $5^{12}$ | 279 |
| $5^{14-16}$ | 71, 96, 185n. |
| $5^{15}$ | 71 |
| $6^{9\text{f.}}$ | 192 |
| $7^{6}$ | 317 |
| $7^{15\text{ff.}}$ | 81, 214 |
| $7^{24-27}$ | 205 |
| $8^{12}$ | 184, 248 |
| $8^{32}$ | 275 |
| $9^{37}-10^{42}$ | 183 |
| $9^{38}$ | 184 |
| $10$ | 180 |
| $10^{17\text{f.}}$ | 184 |
| $10^{17-21}$ | 53 |
| $10^{18}$ | 180 |
| $10^{20}$ | 185 |
| $10^{23}$ | 186 |
| $10^{28}$ | 142 |
| $10^{28-33}$ | 85 |
| $10^{32}$ | 98, 100 |
| $10^{33}$ | 99 |
| $10^{34}$ | 140 |
| $10^{42}$ | 107 |
| $11^{22}$ | 184 |
| $11^{29}$ | 120 |
| $12^{29}$ | 288 |
| $12^{31}$ | 94 |
| $12^{43-45}$ | 166 |
| $13^{9}$ | 82 |
| $13^{30}$ | 232 |
| $13^{46}$ | 306 |
| $15^{26}$ | 317 |
| $16^{18}$ | 205 |
| $16^{26}$ | 272 |
| $16^{38\text{f.}}$ | 102 |
| $17^{2}$ | 100 |
| $18^{6,\,8}$ | 274 |
| $18^{22}$ | 15 |
| $18^{32-34}$ | 228 |
| $19^{10-12}$ | 222 |
| $19^{28}$ | 110, 304 |
| $20^{16}$ | 261 |
| $21^{8\text{f.}}$ | 153 |
| $21^{18-21}$ | 145 |
| $21^{21}$ | 163 |
| $21^{39}$ | 184 |
| $22^{2}$ | 279 |
| $22^{3\text{ff.}}$ | 280 |
| $22^{11-14}$ | 280 |
| $22^{14}$ | 261 |
| $22^{20}$ | 216 |
| $23^{13}$ | 102 |
| $23^{29-38}$ | 26, 276 |
| $23^{34-36}$ | 141, 165, 274 |
| $23^{34-39}$ | 186 |
| $24$ | 19, 58, 114, 135n. |
| $24^{4\text{f.}}$ | 52 |
| $24^{5}$ | 94, 137 |
| $24^{6-8}$ | 53 |
| $24^{8}$ | 157, 196n. |
| $24^{9}$ | 142 |
| $24^{9-12}$ | 52 |
| $24^{9-14}$ | 184 |
| $24^{11}$ | 94 |
| $24^{11\text{f.}}$ | 79 |
| $24^{12}$ | 81 |
| $24^{13-14}$ | 53 |
| $24^{14}$ | 137, 179, 186-8, 231 |
| $24^{14-15}$ | 53 |
| $24^{15}$ | 53, 79, 152, 254 |
| $24^{15\text{f.}}$ | 217 |
| $24^{15-24}$ | 157 |
| $24^{16-20}$ | 53 |
| $24^{21}$ | 153, 250 |
| $24^{21-22}$ | 53 |
| $24^{22}$ | 86, 178 |
| $24^{23-26}$ | 53 |
| $24^{24}$ | 81, 94, 207, 216, 249, 259 |
| $24^{27}$ | 158 |
| $24^{28}$ | 165, 187, 285 |
| $24^{29}$ | 53, 54, 153 |
| $24^{29-30}$ | 53 |
| $24^{30}$ | 54, 63 |
| $24^{30\text{f.}}$ | 54, 230 |
| $24^{31}$ | 53, 159 |
| $24^{36}$ | 231 |
| $24^{37-40}$ | 54, 275 |
| $24^{42-51}$ | 100 |
| $24^{43\text{f.}}$ | 98, 249 |
| $24^{49-51}$ | 98 |
| $25^{1-13}$ | 54, 109 |
| $25^{6}$ | 109 |
| $25^{10}$ | 106, 314 |
| $25^{34,\,41}$ | 212 |
| $26^{39}$ | 213 |
| $26^{40}$ | 259 |
| $26^{41}$ | 98, 109 |
| $26^{51-56}$ | 213 |
| $26^{52}$ | 208 |
| $26^{58}$ | 272 |
| $26^{64}$ | 201 |
| $27^{51\text{f.}}$ | 193 |
| $27^{51-54}$ | 188, 251 |
| $27^{54}$ | 145 |
| $27^{55}$ | 272 |
| $27^{63-66}$ | 288 |
| $28^{2}$ | 145, 188, 251 |
| $28^{4}$ | 188 |
| $28^{18-20}$ | 96 |

**MARK**

| Reference | Pages |
|---|---|
| $1^{3}$ | 248 |

| | | | | | |
|---|---|---|---|---|---|
| $1^6$ | 184 | $9^{54}$ | 22 | $24^5$ | 189 |
| $1^{24}$ | 103 | 10 | 180 | $24^{37}$ | 189 |
| $3^{17}$ | 37 | $10^1$ | 184 | $24^{45-49}$ | 176 |
| $4^{28f.}$ | 229 | $10^{1-20}$ | 183 | | |
| $8^{35}$ | 202 | $10^2$ | 184 | **JOHN** | |
| $9^{48}$ | 317 | $10^{10-12}$ | 187 | $1^{12-16}$ | 99 |
| $10^{18}$ | 177 | $10^{18f.}$ | 86, 164, | $1^{14}$ | 154, 159, 241, |
| $10^{37-39}$ | 185n. | | 169, 201 | | 296, 298, 310 |
| $10^{38}$ | 37, 239, 283 | $10^{19}$ | 173, 185 | $1^{18}$ | 310 |
| $10^{42-45}$ | 50 | $11^{27f.}$ | 60 | $1^{29}$ | 124, 212 |
| $12^8$ | 184 | $11^{33-36}$ | 185n. | $2^{19ff.}$ | 182, 184, 187 |
| $12^{17}$ | 33 | $11^{47-51}$ | 276 | $3^{16}$ | 212 |
| 13 | 19f., 135n. | $12^{4-8}$ | 85 | $3^{16-19}$ | 126n., 144 |
| $13^{3-8}$ | 7 | $12^6$ | 109 | $3^{16-21}$ | 106 |
| $13^9$ | 66 | $12^8$ | 98, 100 | $3^{19}$ | 103 |
| $13^{9-13}$ | 53 | $12^{35ff.}$ | 109 | $3^{19-21}$ | 226 |
| $13^{14}$ | 20, 216 | $12^{39}$ | 98 | $3^{36}$ | 144 |
| $13^{21-24}$ | 20 | $12^{39-46}$ | 100 | $4^{10ff.}$ | 154, 299 |
| $13^{28-37}$ | 21 | $12^{45f.}$ | 98 | $4^{10-14}$ | 311 |
| $13^{29}$ | 109 | $12^{49f.}$ | 22, 239 | $4^{21-24}$ | 182 |
| $13^{36}$ | 247 | $12^{49-51}$ | 160 | $4^{22}$ | 150 |
| $14^{37ff.}$ | 247 | $12^{49-53}$ | 177 | $4^{35-38}$ | 230f. |
| $14^{62}$ | 20 | $12^{50}$ | 283 | $5^{19}$ | 280 |
| $15^{38-39}$ | 46 | $13^{29}$ | 304 | $5^{27}$ | 231 |
| | | $14^{13-16}$ | 184 | $6^{27}$ | 148 |
| | | $14^{16ff.}$ | 280 | $6^{31-35}$ | 90 |
| **LUKE** | | $17^{26-30}$ | 275 | $6^{35}$ | 154 |
| $1^6$ | 240 | $17^{37}$ | 165 | $6^{53-63}$ | 177 |
| $1^{10}$ | 129, 159 | $18^{1-8}$ | 129, 141, 160 | $6^{66}$ | 100 |
| $1^{32ff.}$ | 192 | $18^8$ | 163 | $6^{69}$ | 103 |
| $1^{78}$ | 148 | $20^{15}$ | 184 | $7^{37}$ | 299, 318 |
| 2 | 129 | $20^{36}$ | 305 | $7^{37-39}$ | 154 |
| $2^{11ff.}$ | 192 | 21 | 19, 135n. | $7^{38}$ | 311 |
| $2^{32}$ | 310 | $21^9$ | 58 | $8^{12}$ | 154n. |
| $2^{35}$ | 203 | $21^{12}$ | 58, 137 | $8^{17}$ | 184 |
| $2^{51}$ | 60 | $21^{20}$ | 262 | $8^{31ff.}$ | 80 |
| $3^{17}$ | 22 | $21^{24}$ | 182 | $8^{37}$ | 85 |
| $4^{5-8}$ | 201 | $21^{26, 34-36}$ | 104, 146 | $8^{39-44}$ | 300 |
| $4^6$ | 192 | $22^{18-34}$ | 86 | $8^{44}$ | 80, 85 |
| $4^{25}$ | 185 | $22^{24ff.}$ | 109n. | $9^6$ | 108 |
| $4^{29}$ | 184 | $22^{28-34}$ | 99 | $9^{34}$ | 184 |
| $6^{24ff.}$ | 108 | $22^{30}$ | 110, 304 | $9^{39-41}$ | 108 |
| $8^{31}$ | 167 | $22^{33}$ | 212 | 10 | 106 |
| $9^{31, 51}$ | 197 | $22^{40-46}$ | 86 | $10^{2f.}$ | 109 |
| $9^{53-55}$ | 185 | $23^{28-31}$ | 144f. | $10^3$ | 99 |

JOHN – *contd*

| | |
|---|---|
| $10^{7-9}$ | 103 |
| $10^{10f.}$ | 154 |
| $10^{27f.}$ | 99 |
| $10^{30}$ | 280 |
| $11^{36}$ | 108 |
| $12^{12f.}$ | 153 |
| $12^{19}$ | 210 |
| $12^{23}$ | 152 |
| $12^{25}$ | 202 |
| $12^{31-33}$ | 138, 197, 201, 225f. |
| $13^1$ | 61 |
| $13^{2ff.}$ | 109 |
| $13^{36-38}$ | 223 |
| $14^{2f.}$ | 198 |
| $14^3$ | 160 |
| $14^{26}$ | 118 |
| $15^{7f.}$ | 177 |
| $15^{20}$ | 187 |
| $15^{26}$ | 118 |
| $16^{1-4}$ | 85 |
| $16^{8ff.}$ | 138, 186, 188 |
| $16^{12-14}$ | 82 |
| $16^{20}$ | 188 |
| $16^{23}$ | 160 |
| $16^{33}$ | 80 |
| $17^{14-19}$ | 177 |
| $18^{11}$ | 177, 208, 213, 227 |
| $18^{37}$ | 59, 80, 99, 109, 130 |
| $19^5$ | 231 |
| $19^{11}$ | 124 |
| $19^{26f.}$ | 195, 203 |
| $19^{30}$ | 250, 299 |
| $19^{34-37}$ | 64 |
| $19^{35}$ | 66 |
| $19^{36f.}$ | 282 |
| $19^{39}$ | 84 |
| $20^{14ff.}$ | 125 |
| $20^{17}$ | 99, 300 |
| $20^{21-23}$ | 102, 129 |
| $20^{25ff.}$ | 128 |
| $21^{11}$ | 219 |
| $21^{15}$ | 128 |
| $21^{15-17}$ | 108 |

ACTS

| | |
|---|---|
| $1^{6-8}$ | 185 |
| $1^8$ | 88 |
| $1^9$ | 188 |
| $1^{11}$ | 188 |
| $2^{3f.}$ | 216 |
| $2^{5ff.}$ | 216 |
| $2^{19}$ | 216 |
| $2^{33}$ | 131 |
| $4^{25}$ | 193 |
| $6^5$ | 90 |
| $6^{10}$ | 185 |
| $7^{41}$ | 173 |
| $7^{56}$ | 117 |
| $7^{58}$ | 184 |
| $8^{9ff.}$ | 249 |
| $8^{9-24}$ | 89 |
| $8^{30}$ | 60 |
| $9^4$ | 72 |
| $10^{15}$ | 46 |
| $13^2$ | 184 |
| $13^{6ff.}$ | 216 |
| $13^{15}$ | 60 |
| $13^{33}$ | 197 |
| 15 | 33 |
| $15^{20}$ | 89 |
| $15^{28f.}$ | 95 |
| $15^{29}$ | 89 |
| $15^{39f.}$ | 184 |
| $16^{14}$ | 92 |
| $16^{25}$ | 129 |
| $17^{29-31}$ | 225 |
| $17^{30f.}$ | 216 |
| $18^{19}$ | 39n. |
| $18^{19}-19^{10}$ | 79 |
| $18^{25}$ | 107 |
| 19 | 197 |
| $19^{13ff.}$ | 79 |
| $19^{18f.}$ | 174 |
| $19^{34}$ | 31 |
| 20 | 88 |
| $20^7$ | 67 |

ROMANS

| | |
|---|---|
| $1^4$ | 197 |
| $1^{16-18}$ | 123n., 161, 175 |
| $1^{18ff.}$ | 243, 311 |
| $1^{18-32}$ | 174, 119 |
| $1^{21}$ | 279 |
| $1^{21-23}$ | 200 |
| $1^{24ff.}$ | 166 |
| $1^{24-28}$ | 144 |
| $2^{4-5}$ | 173 |
| $2^6$ | 316 |
| $2^{16}$ | 138, 225 |
| $2^{28f.}$ | 46, 103 |
| $3^4$ | 82, 128, 199 |
| $3^{24}$ | 202 |
| $4^{11}$ | 148 |
| $4^{20}$ | 279 |
| $4^{20-22}$ | 200 |
| $5^{9f.}$ | 72 |
| $5^{11}$ | 201 |
| $5^{11ff.}$ | 124 |
| $5^{18}$ | 240 |
| $6^{3ff.}$ | 239 |
| $7^{2-4}$ | 279 |
| $8^1$ | 199, 201 |
| $8^{19-21}$ | 132 |
| $8^{28-30}$ | 212 |
| $8^{29}$ | 199, 203, 306 |
| $8^{30}$ | 100 |
| $8^{31ff.}$ | 102 |
| $8^{37-39}$ | 39 |
| 9–11 | 51n. |
| $9^{13}$ | 103 |
| $9^{27-29}$ | 205 |
| 11 | 46 |
| $11^{13-24}$ | 31 |
| $11^{22-32}$ | 126n. |

| | | | | | |
|---|---|---|---|---|---|
| $11^{25-29}$ | 294 | $8^{1-10}$ | 33 | $4^{17}$ | 225 |
| $11^{32}$ | 5ın. | $8^4$ | 34, 92, 173 | $5^{10}$ | 316 |
| $11^{32-36}$ | 166 | $10^1$ff. | 239 | $5^{14-19}$ | 309 |
| $12^{16}$ | 107 | $10^{1-13}$ | 49, 205 | $5^{17}$ | 49, 91, 299 |
| $12^{17,\,19}$ | 269 | $10^3$ | 90 | $6^{14}-7^1$ | 268 |
| $12^{19-21}$ | 160 | $10^{10}$ | 170 | $6^{17}$ | 268 |
| $12^{21}$ | 80 | $10^{14}$ff. | 92 | $7^{8-10}$ | 180 |
| $13^1$ff. | 33, 163, 201 | $10^{14-22}$ | 33, 173 | $8^9$ | 320 |
| $13^{1-7}$ | 4, 215 | $10^{25-29}$ | 33 | $11^2$f. | 279 |
| $13^4$ | 88 | $11^{10}$ | 95 | $11^{4-15}$ | 81 |
| $14^1$ff. | 33 | $11^{20}$ | 109 | $11^{14}$ | 81, 119 |
| $14^{12}$ | 316 | $11^{23-32}$ | 106 | $12^3$ | 178 |
| $15^1$ | 81 | $11^{25}$ | 109 | | |
| $15^6$ | 99, 130 | $11^{26}$ | 12 | **GALATIANS** | |
| $15^{8-12}$ | 150 | $11^{26-32}$ | 65, 314, 319 | $2^9$ | 37, 104 |
| $16^{25}$ | 179 | $11^{27-32}$ | 78, 80, 82 | $3^{13}$ | 83n., 311n. |
| | | $11^{32}$ | 95, 108 | $3^{16,\,29}$ | 151 |
| **I CORINTHIANS** | | $12^{28}$ | 81 | $3^{27}$ | 100 |
| $1^{4-7}$ | 316 | 13 | 80 | $4^{26}$ff. | 303 |
| $1^{18}$f. | 170 | $13^{12}$ | 283, 296, 309, | $5^{20}$ | 174 |
| $1^{23}$f. | 125, 128 | | 312 | $6^1$f. | 81 |
| $2^{6-8}$ | 85, 187 | $14^{24}$ | 186 | $6^{15}$ | 299 |
| $2^{6-10}$ | 222, 254 | $14^{32}$ | 314 | $6^{16}$ | 150, 203 |
| $2^{6-16}$ | 187 | $15^{5-9}$ | 81 | $6^{17}$ | 217 |
| $2^7$ | 258 | $15^{15}$ | 258 | | |
| $2^{10}$ | 95 | $15^{17}$ | 103 | | |
| $3^8$f., 10-16 | 231 | $15^{20}$ | 65, 84 | **EPHESIANS** | |
| $3^{12-15}$ | 316 | $15^{20}$ff. | 223 | $1^{14}$ | 148 |
| $3^{15}$ | 286 | $15^{24-26}$ | 201 | $2^2$ | 250 |
| $3^{16}$ | 183 | $15^{24-28}$ | 166 | $2^{10}$ | 279 |
| $4^5$ | 80 | $15^{25}$ | 96, 139 | $2^{19}$ | 150 |
| $4^7$f. | 107 | $15^{28}$ | 295, 296, 312 | $2^{20}$ | 304, 306 |
| $4^8$ | 49, 316 | $15^{45}$ff. | 223 | $2^{21}$ | 183 |
| $4^{8-13}$ | 130 | $15^{52}$ | 159 | $3^{2-10}$ | 179 |
| 5-6 | 89 | $15^{56}$ | 169 | $4^{8-11}$ | 131 |
| $5^5$ | 286 | $16^2$ | 67 | $4^{11-16}$ | 279 |
| $5^7$ | 124 | $16^5$ | 223 | $4^{18}$ | 248 |
| $6^2$ | 288 | $16^9$ | 102 | $4^{30}$ | 148 |
| $6^{9-11}$ | 100 | $16^{22}$ | 319 | $5^{25}$ff. | 66, 277, 279, 302 |
| $6^{12-19}$ | 32 | | | $6^{12-17}$ | 201 |
| $6^{13}$ | 33 | **II CORINTHIANS** | | $6^{17}$ | 72 |
| $6^{20}$ | 108, 130 | $1^{20}$ | 67, 107, 319 | | |
| $7^{32-35}$ | 222 | $1^{22}$ | 148 | **PHILIPPIANS** | |
| 8-10 | 89 | $2^{12}$ | 102 | $2^{5-11}$ | 126 |
| $8^{1-4}$ | 95f., 215 | $3^{14}$ff. | 123 | $2^{15}$ | 304 |

PHILIPPIANS – *contd*
$3^{20}$ 303
$4^3$ 100

COLOSSIANS
$1^{15-20}$ 66, 107
$1^{18}$ 65
$1^{24}$ 142, 200
$2^{12}$ 239
$2^{15}$ 66
$2^{20-23}$ 32
$3^1$ 49
$3^{1-4}$ 289
$3^{5ff.}$ 300
$3^{11}$ 125
$4^3$ 102, 179
$4^{16}$ 107n.

I THESSALONIANS
$1^{9f.}$ 225
$2^{16}$ 294
$4^{16}$ 159
$4^{17}$ 188
$5^{1ff.}$ 249
$5^{2-6}$ 99
$5^3$ 215
$5^{21}$ 81
$5^{28}$ 320

II THESSALONIANS
$2^{3ff.}$ 259
$2^{3-7}$ 4, 207
$2^{6f.}$ 215
$2^7$ 254
$2^{8-12}$ 202, 211
$2^9$ 216
$2^{9ff.}$ 201, 214, 224, 244, 249
$3^5$ 104
$3^{14f.}$ 81
$3^{17}$ 320

I TIMOTHY 37, 94n.
$1^{3ff.}$ 79
$1^{3-7}$ 94n.

$1^{17}$ 240
$2^{1f.}$ 33
$2^8-3^{13}$ 94n.
$4^1$ 81
$4^{13}$ 60
$5^{1-22}$ 94n.
$6^{12-14}$ 200
$6^{13}$ 59, 205

II TIMOTHY 37, 94n.
$2^{24-26}$ 81
$4^{7f.}$ 86

TITUS 37, 94n.
$3^1$ 34

HEBREWS
$1^{1-4}$ 123
$1^8$ 282
$2^{14}$ 73
$3^7-4^{13}$ 205
$4^{12}$ 51, 70, 88
$4^{12f.}$ 72
$5^{7ff.}$ 104
$9^{3ff.}$ 193
$9^{22}$ 153
$10^{20}$ 193
$10^{34}$ 85
$10^{37}$ 179
$11^2$ 118
$12^{1ff.}$ 104
$12^{5f.}$ 108
$12^{18ff.}$ 118, 176
$12^{18-24}$ 118n.
$12^{18-29}$ 250
$12^{19}$ 178
$12^{22}$ 303
$12^{22-24}$ 221
$12^{24}$ 142, 232
$12^{27}$ 296
$13^{11-14}$ 184
$13^{12-14}$ 230

JAMES
$1^1$ 150

$1^{12}$ 86
$2^5$ 108
$5^{1ff.}$ 108
$5^9$ 109

I PETER
$1^1$ 150
$1^7$ 108
$1^{18f.}$ 66, 124
$1^{18-20}$ 128
$1^{20}$ 212
$2^9$ 66, 150, 176
$2^{13-17}$ 33, 215
$2^{21-25}$ 124
$3^{1f.}$ 96
$3^{1-4}$ 237
$3^{19-22}$ 167
$3^{20}$ 119
$4^{12-16}$ 85
$4^{13}$ 279
$5^{8f.}$ 201
$5^{13}$ 226

II PETER
$2^4$ 167
$2^{15}$ 89n.
$2^{19}$ 95
$3^{11-13}$ 58
$3^{13}$ 297
$3^{15}$ 173

I JOHN
$1^5$ 44
$1^7$ 153
$1^7-2^2$ 66
$1^{8f.}$ 96
$1^{29}$ 66
$2^{1ff.}$ 200
$2^2$ 199, 212
$2^{18ff.}$ 81, 207
$3^2$ 312
$3^{8-20}$ 80
$3^9$ 96
$3^{12}$ 300
$4^{1-6}$ 81, 280

| | | |
|---|---|---|
| $4^3$ | 207 | |
| $4^{10}$ | 66, 82 | |
| $4^{20}$ | 80 | |
| $5^{20}$f. | 280 | |

**II JOHN**

| | |
|---|---|
| 7 | 207 |

**JUDE**

| | |
|---|---|
| 8ff. | 211 |
| 9 | 200 |
| 11 | 89n. |

**REVELATION**

| | |
|---|---|
| 1 | 5, 44 |
| 1–3 | 13, 158 |
| $1^1$ | 115, 315 |
| $1^1$f. | 179 |
| $1^{1-3}$ | 12, 73, 115, 315 |
| $1^2$ | 142, 205, 289, 314 |
| $1^3$ | 17, 38, 99, 319 |
| $1^4$ | 5, 68, 98, 258 |
| $1^4$f. | 14, 192, 201, 281 |
| $1^4$ff. | 57, 118, 319 |
| $1^5$ | 59, 63, 88, 107, 118, 130, 149, 153, 261, 316 |
| $1^5$f. | 129, 257 |
| $1^6$ | 64, 99, 130, 185, 222, 249, 289, 300 |
| $1^7$ | 58, 69, 93, 145, 188f., 230f., 243, 250, 261, 271, 284, 319 |
| $1^8$ | 58, 120, 192, 193, 249, 255, 316 |
| $1^9$ | 37, 59, 80, 84, 117, 130, 142, 315 |
| $1^{10}$ | 80, 115, 117, 254, 288 |
| $1^{11}$ | 123, ?17 |
| $1^{12}$ff. | 288 |
| $1^{12-16}$ | 281 |
| $1^{12-20}$ | 14, 80 |
| $1^{13}$ | 229 |

| | |
|---|---|
| $1^{13}$ff. | 301 |
| $1^{14}$ | 90, 282 |
| $1^{15}$ | 222 |
| $1^{15}$f. | 177 |
| $1^{16}$ | 14, 51, 68, 88, 204, 283 |
| $1^{17}$ | 85, 316 |
| $1^{17}$f. | 84, 257 |
| $1^{18}$ | 101, 130, 117, 140, 166, 167, 287, 295 |
| $1^{19}$ | 57 |
| $1^{20}$ | 81, 99, 129, 168, 254 |
| $1^{20-25}$ | 164 |
| $1^{26}$ | 117 |
| 2 | 11, 65 |
| 2–3 | 5, 319 |
| $2^1$ | 129 |
| $2^{1-7}$ | 231 |
| $2^2$ | 85, 94 |
| $2^{2-19}$ | 231 |
| $2^2$f. | 67 |
| $2^4$ | 198, 201 |
| $2^5$ | 90, 95, 99, 104, 108f., 258 |
| $2^6$ | 32, 88 |
| $2^6$f. | 317, 319 |
| $2^7$ | 90, 110, 128, 151, 186, 202, 212, 239, 258, 282, 288, 311 |
| $2^8$ | 103, 216, 289, 316 |
| $2^{8-10}$ | 30 |
| $2^9$ | 28, 47n., 147, 164, 278, 318 |
| $2^9$f. | 104 |
| $2^{10}$ | 82f., 104, 118, 139, 151, 153f., 169, 202, 213, 300 |
| $2^{11}$ | 30, 295 |
| $2^{12}$ | 51, 139, 208 |
| $2^{12-17}$ | 208 |
| $2^{13}$ | 65, 103, 157, 183, 197, 208f., 247, 258, 278 |
| $2^{13}$ff. | 300 |

| | |
|---|---|
| $2^{14}$ | 4, 33, 49, 82, 92, 164, 237, 253, 274, 300, 318 |
| $2^{14}$f. | 32 |
| $2^{15}$ | 222 |
| $2^{16}$ | 82, 92n., 104, 109, 185f., 208, 282 |
| $2^{17}$ | 105, 129, 139, 222 |
| $2^{18}$ | 72, 282f., 299f. |
| $2^{19}$ | 67, 99, 316 |
| $2^{20}$ | 4, 32f., 49, 92, 164, 222, 224, 237, 252, 274f., 280n., 300, 315, 318 |
| $2^{20}$ff. | 266 |
| $2^{20-23}$ | 226 |
| $2^{22}$ | 140 |
| $2^{22}$f. | 267 |
| $2^{23}$ | 93, 296, 282, 316, 319 |
| $2^{24}$ | 167, 237, 291 |
| $2^{24}$f. | 33, 89 |
| $2^{24-27}$ | 197 |
| $2^{25}$ | 81 |
| $2^{26}$ | 35, 65, 238 |
| $2^{26}$f. | 130, 139 |
| $2^{26-28}$ | 299 |
| $2^{27}$ | 110, 144, 154, 197, 283 |
| $2^{28}$ | 73, 89, 93, 238, 318 |
| 3 | 65 |
| $3^1$ | 65, 118, 129 |
| $3^2$ff. | 104 |
| $3^3$ | 60, 82, 108, 109, 231, 246, 249 |
| $3^4$ | 222, 245, 249 |
| $3^4$f. | 254 |
| $3^5$ | 103, 108, 118, 139, 142, 211f., 227 |
| $3^7$ | 30, 142 |
| $3^{7-9}$ | 128, 318 |
| $3^8$ | 88, 115, 117 |
| $3^9$ | 28, 47n., 85, 117, 147, 184, 308, 317f. |

REVELATION – *contd*

3¹⁰  67, 84, 86, 142,
    153, 165
3¹¹  49, 82, 86,
    118, 139
3¹²  62n., 90, 105n.,
    107, 148, 184,
    186, 222, 254,
    283, 317, 319
3¹³  310
3¹⁴  40n., 65f., 88,
    157, 280, 282f.,
    316
3¹⁷  262, 267, 269,
    299, 316
3¹⁷ᶠ.  85, 252, 254, 279
3¹⁸  71, 118, 249
3¹⁹  99
3²⁰  45, 99, 115, 117
3²¹  82, 93, 128, 197
    209
3²⁶  107
4  13, 41, 42, 46,
    51, 192, 265
4–5  6, 126, 151, 167,
    190, 194, 293
4–7  45
4–11  46
4¹  103, 123, 188, 282
4²  185, 254
4³  177, 185, 275, 304
4⁴  153
4⁵  65, 72, 98, 160
    178, 185,193,
    222, 247
4⁶  16, 167, 239, 290,
    307, 311
4⁶ᶠᶠ.  204n.
4⁶⁻¹⁰  153
4⁸  67, 151, 153,
    202, 228, 292
4⁹  178
4⁹ᶠ.  241
4¹¹  118, 130f.,
    178, 278

4¹⁴  127, 185
5  13, 41, 43, 51,
    135, 157, 176f.,
    192
5¹  180
5¹ᶠᶠ.  177
5²  176f.
5³  82
5⁴  278
5⁵  30, 96, 97n., 102,
    118, 138, 149,
    153, 318
5⁵ᶠ.  66, 93, 144,
    198f., 211, 230,
    232, 240, 283
5⁶  63n., 65, 72, 82,
    93, 98, 117f., 120,
    126, 142, 159, 209,
    221, 276, 281
5⁶⁻¹⁰  17, 309
5⁷  179
5⁸  114, 160, 239, 280
5⁸⁻¹⁰  222
5⁹  102, 108, 118f.,
    151n., 180, 202,
    222, 245, 277
5⁹ᶠ.  176, 221
5¹⁰  66, 96, 118f., 139
    185, 222, 241, 312
5¹¹  172, 222
5¹¹ᶠ.  153
5¹²ᶠᶠ.  278
6  6, 43, 58, 189
6–7  114
6–19  293
6¹  178
6¹ᶠᶠ.  115, 123
6¹⁻⁷  120
6¹⁻⁸  20, 241
6¹⁻¹¹  147
6²  82, 130, 172, 175,
    282f., 294
6⁴  88
6⁵⁻⁸  173
6⁶⁻²⁰  47, 49, 126

6⁸  73, 95, 162, 269
6⁹  128, 159f., 245,
    276, 289
6⁹⁻¹¹  24, 165, 213, 228,
    243, 269, 288
6¹⁰  49, 103, 104, 114,
    117, 129, 160, 179
6¹¹  118, 120, 231
6¹²  189, 250
6¹²⁻¹⁷  114, 164, 192,
    286, 309
6¹³  123, 147
6¹⁴ᶠᶠ.  251
6¹⁶  43, 104, 124, 200,
    227f., 241, 249,
    251, 284, 308, 310
6¹⁶ᶠ.  152
7  6, 125, 158, 190
7¹  14, 172, 244, 291
7¹ᶠᶠ.  166
7¹⁻⁸  162, 182, 184
7²ᶠᶠ.  104f.
7³  86, 160, 168, 266
7³ᶠᶠ.  175, 222, 312
7⁴  15, 125n., 172, 186,
    198, 223, 308
7⁴⁻⁸  302, 304f.
7⁵  306
7⁹  117f., 125n., 142,
    146, 198, 223, 308
7⁹ᶠᶠ.  86, 100, 221, 278f.
7⁹⁻¹⁴  114
7⁹⁻¹⁷  193
7¹³  118, 142
7¹⁴  66, 83f., 95, 100,
    117, 128, 202, 232,
    277, 283, 317
7¹⁵  105, 120, 202, 312
7¹⁵⁻¹⁷  114, 311
7¹⁶  245
7¹⁶ᶠ.  298f.
7¹⁷  96, 128, 154n., 311
8  24, 46
8–9  7f., 86, 178, 189
8–10  161

| | |
|---|---|
| 8–14 | 237 |
| $8^{1}$ | 274 |
| $8^{1}$ff. | 68 |
| $8^{1}$–$14^{20}$ | 88 |
| $8^{3}$ | 117 |
| $8^{3-5}$ | 129, 142, 159, 171, 190, 230, 241f. 245, 266 |
| $8^{4}$ | 278 |
| $8^{5}$ | 118, 145, 166, 178, 189, 193, 247 |
| $8^{6}$ff. | 147 |
| $6^{6-13}$ | 242 |
| $8^{7}$ | 168, 244, 249 |
| $8^{7}$f | 160 |
| $8^{7}$ff. | 140, 147, 219 |
| $8^{7-12}$ | 196, 226, 242 |
| $8^{8}$ | 145, 166, 193, 259 |
| $8^{8}$f. | 186 |
| $8^{8-11}$ | 242 |
| $8^{8-12}$ | 226 |
| $8^{8}$–$9^{1}$ | 201 |
| $8^{9}$ | 201 |
| $8^{10}$ | 81, 160, 167f., 259 |
| $8^{10}$f. | 244 |
| $8^{11}$ | 180 |
| $8^{12}$ | 168 |
| $8^{13}$ | 104, 157, 170, 187, 190, 202, 224f., 285 |
| 9 | 24, 46, 165n. |
| $9^{1}$ | 16, 73, 81, 119, 164, 170, 177, 186, 210, 258, 259 |
| $9^{1}$ff. | 199, 287 |
| $9^{1-11}$ | 206 |
| $9^{1-12}$ | 171 |
| $9^{2}$ | 160, 244–6 |
| $9^{2}$ | 160 |
| $9^{2}$ff. | 164 |
| $9^{3}$ | 210 |
| $9^{3-5}$ | 205 |
| $9^{4}$ | 147, 172, 208, 244 |
| $9^{5}$ | 210, 269, 272 |
| $9^{5}$f. | 208 |
| $9^{5}$ff. | 188, 247 |
| $9^{7}$ | 166 |
| $9^{10}$ | 205 |
| $9^{11}$ | 164, 194, 258 |
| $9^{12}$ | 157, 162 |
| $9^{13}$ | 142, 245 |
| $9^{14}$ | 147, 246, 248 |
| $9^{14}$ff. | 291 |
| $9^{15}$ | 245 |
| $9^{16}$ | 149, 291 |
| $9^{16-19}$ | 206 |
| $9^{17}$ | 160, 227 |
| $9^{17-19}$ | 166 |
| $9^{19-21}$ | 205 |
| $9^{20}$ | 144, 210, 226 |
| $9^{20}$f. | 104, 157, 159, 166, 175, 181, 238, 240, 248, 300 |
| $9^{21}$ | 278, 318 |
| 10 | 159, 181, 192 |
| 10–11 | 8 |
| 10–12 | 45 |
| $10^{1}$ | 118, 148, 167, 197, 267 |
| $10^{1}$–$11^{13}$ | 147, 157, 220, 243, 251 |
| $10^{2}$ | 123 |
| $10^{2}$ff. | 127 |
| $10^{6}$ | 182, 241 |
| $10^{7}$ | 59, 186, 190ff., 239, 254, 262, 315 |
| $10^{10}$ | 315 |
| $10^{11}$ | 184, 225, 262, 298 |
| 11 | 22, 46, 175, 178 |
| 11–13 | 46, 179 |
| $11^{1}$ | 266 |
| $11^{1}$f. | 203f., 207, 211 |
| $11^{1-4}$ | 130 |
| $11^{1-13}$ | 23, 140, 169, 302 |
| $11^{2}$ | 211, 230f., 284 |
| $11^{2}$f. | 46, 198 |
| $11^{2}$ff. | 266 |
| $11^{3}$ | 4, 14, 177 |
| $11^{3}$ff. | 71, 129 |
| $11^{3-7}$ | 210 |
| $11^{3-13}$ | 96, 138, 214, 255 |
| $11^{4}$ | 216, 289 |
| $11^{5}$ | 216, 249, 292 |
| $11^{5}$f. | 96n., 311 |
| $11^{5}$ff. | 168 |
| $11^{5-10}$ | 138 |
| $11^{6}$ | 193, 198, 204, 210 |
| $11^{6-10}$ | 180, 211 |
| $11^{7}$ | 80, 82, 167, 179, 202, 205, 209, 231, 282, 286 |
| $11^{7}$ff. | 142, 244, 261 |
| $11^{8}$ | 8, 15, 26, 34, 46, 168, 204, 226, 233, 251, 266f., 276, 284, 305, 307, 311 |
| $11^{9}$ | 15, 46, 152, 177, 211, 262, 298 |
| $11^{9}$f. | 225 |
| $11^{10}$ | 104, 169, 186, 202, 241, 274 |
| $11^{11}$ | 46, 216, 289 |
| $11^{11-13}$ | 220, 261 |
| $11^{12}$ | 117, 229, 231 |
| $11^{13}$ | 63, 67, 100, 145, 157, 169, 175, 180, 183, 193, 225, 230, 240, 243–5, 248, 250f., 289, 310 |
| $11^{14}$ | 162, 170, 175, 190 |
| $11^{14}$f. | 157, 202 |
| $11^{15}$ | 160, 201, 289 |
| $11^{15-19}$ | 279n., 284, 286 |
| $11^{16}$ff. | 118 |
| $11^{17}$ | 67, 240, 244, 279 |
| $11^{18}$ | 59, 93, 168, 194, 197, 205, 221, 251, 278 |
| $11^{19}$ | 118, 160, 178, 189, 240, 247, 309 |
| 12 | 14, 41n., 44, 157, 167, 175, 208, 210, 230, 282, 309 |
| 12–13 | 8ff. |

REVELATION – *contd*

| | |
|---|---|
| 12–14 | 190 |
| 12–20 | 46 |
| $12^{1}$ | 239 |
| $12^{1}$ff. | 192, 252, 302 |
| $12^{1-6}$ | 204 |
| $12^{1-11}$ | 240f. |
| $12^{1-12}$ | 164 |
| $12^{3}$ | 15, 140, 209, 239, 258, 282 |
| $12^{4}$ | 81 |
| $12^{5}$ | 96, 97, 117, 191, 240, 283 |
| $12^{6}$ | 46, 182, 254, 266 |
| $12^{7}$ | 148n. |
| $12^{7}$ff. | 113, 119 |
| $12^{7-11}$ | 197 |
| $12^{7-12}$ | 16, 85, 190, 192, 211, 225, 250, 316 |
| $12^{9}$ | 81, 166, 288 |
| $12^{9}$f. | 80 |
| $12^{10}$ | 152, 164, 192, 231, 278, 289 |
| $12^{10}$f. | 82, 128 |
| $12^{10-12}$ | 49 |
| $12^{11}$ | 80, 83, 151, 153, 177, 211, 261, 283 |
| $12^{11}$f. | 287 |
| $12^{12}$ | 15, 157, 162, 166, 171, 188, 189f., 206, 211, 225, 227, 241, 259, 268, 274 |
| $12^{12}$ff. | 170 |
| $12^{12}$–$13^{18}$ | 46, 183 |
| $12^{13}$ | 34 |
| $12^{13-17}$ | 34 |
| $12^{13}$–$13^{18}$ | 190 |
| $12^{14}$ | 46, 182, 198, 254, 266 |
| $12^{15}$f. | 249 |
| $12^{16}$ | 214 |
| $12^{17}$ | 60, 142, 173, 182, |
| $12^{17}$ | 60, 142, 173, 182f., 186, 206, 208, 210, 221, 228, 237, 241, 258, 262, 289, 292 |
| $12^{17}$–$13^{18}$ | 49, 266 |
| 13 | 45, 58, 68, 84, 88, 93, 138, 157, 163, 165n., 166, 171, 173, 186, 220, 255f. |
| 13–14 | 184 |
| $13^{1}$ | 14f., 119, 128, 167, 186, 196, 205, 243, 245, 260, 282 |
| $13^{1}$ff. | 147, 157, 166, 190, 202, 258 |
| $13^{1-8}$ | 157 |
| $13^{2}$ | 173, 208, 247, 260, 267 |
| $13^{2}$ff. | 67 |
| $13^{3}$ | 21, 23, 194, 205, 255–9 |
| $13^{3}$ff. | 166, 202, 258 |
| $13^{4}$ | 273 |
| $13^{4}$f. | 66 |
| $13^{5}$ | 15, 46, 167, 198, 243, 245, 279 |
| $13^{5}$ff. | 139, 182f. |
| $13^{6}$ | 15, 85, 113, 274, 298 |
| $13^{7}$ | 80, 82, 129, 184, 186f., 202, 205, 208, 211, 244, 261f., 282 |
| $13^{8}$ | 100, 113, 123, 128, 132, 259, 293f., 295, 311 |
| $13^{9}$f. | 10f., 82, 228, 247 |
| $13^{10}$ | 67, 88, 183, 208, 223, 227f., 255 |
| $13^{11}$ | 51, 125, 164 |
| $13^{11}$ff. | 157, 208, 286 |
| $13^{12}$ | 88, 104 |
| $13^{13}$ | 185, 292 |
| $13^{13}$f. | 291 |
| $13^{13}$ff. | 249 |
| $13^{14}$ | 23, 88, 104, 167, 248, 257–9 |
| $13^{14-18}$ | 157, 239, 289 |
| $13^{15}$ | 72, 186, 208, 244, 278, 288 |
| $13^{15-17}$ | 243 |
| $13^{16}$ | 168, 285 |
| $13^{16}$f. | 88, 221, 254 |
| $13^{16}$ff. | 166 |
| $13^{17}$ | 222 |
| $13^{18}$ | 11, 15, 82, 183, 233n., 247, 256, 259, 316 |
| 14 | 10, 105, 148, 149n., 158, 179, 186, 191, 205, 219, 237, 239, 254, 283, 292 |
| $14^{1}$ff. | 190, 210 |
| $14^{1-5}$ | 149, 151, 203, 302 |
| $14^{1-7}$ | 239 |
| $14^{2}$ | 239, 284 |
| $14^{2}$f. | 129, 279 |
| $14^{3}$ | 117 |
| $14^{3}$f. | 108 |
| $14^{4}$ | 46, 49, 148n., 149, 151n., 223n., 239, 283 |
| $14^{5}$ | 66, 124 |
| $14^{6}$ | 165, 178, 180, 187, 240, 262, 285 |
| $14^{6}$f. | 179, 244, 279 |
| $14^{6-11}$ | 138 |
| $14^{7}$ | 189, 243f., 285f. |
| $14^{8}$ | 241, 251, 253f., 268 |
| $14^{8-11}$ | 200, 244 |
| $14^{9-11}$ | 145f., 151, 166, 169, 171, 189, 202, 208, 243 |
| $14^{10}$ | 173, 213, 241, 251, 254, 272, 286, 292 |
| $14^{10}$f. | 188, 202, 269 |
| $14^{11}$ | 49, 120, 153, 160, 240f., 271, 295 |

| | |
|---|---|
| 14¹² | 67, 82, 183, 213 |
| 14¹²f. | 10f., 247 |
| 14¹³ | 99, 120, 142, 188, 201, 254, 302, 316 |
| 14¹⁴ | 169 |
| 14¹⁴ff. | 69, 188, 211 |
| 14¹⁸ | 142, 244f. |
| 14²⁰ | 49, 63, 128, 153, 184, 240, 243, 282–4, 286 |
| 15–16 | 10 |
| 15–22 | 21 |
| 15¹ | 190, 243, 262, 303 |
| 15¹–22⁵ | 45, 93 |
| 15² | 167, 222 |
| 15²f. | 119, 129 |
| 15²⁻⁴ | 222 |
| 15³ | 67, 278 |
| 15³f. | 220f., 225, 243f., 251 |
| 15⁴ | 102, 189, 225, 230, 244, 309 |
| 15⁵ | 251 |
| 15⁶f. | 303 |
| 15⁷ | 120, 224, 243 |
| 15⁸ | 160, 243, 250, 262 |
| 16 | 140, 162, 178 |
| 16–18 | 301 |
| 16¹ | 159 |
| 16²⁻⁸ | 226 |
| 16⁴⁻⁷ | 160, 255 |
| 16⁴⁻⁹ | 154 |
| 16⁵ | 11, 108, 142, 230 |
| 16⁷ | 67, 142, 240, 278 |
| 16⁹ | 104, 189, 225, 238, 240, 244, 263 |
| 16⁹ff. | 144 |
| 16¹⁰⁻²¹ | 239 |
| 16¹¹ | 104, 168, 189, 238, 240, 263 |
| 16¹² | 148, 279, 285 |
| 16¹²ff. | 260 |
| 16¹²⁻¹⁶ | 172, 290f. |
| 16¹²⁻¹⁷ | 24 |
| 16¹³ | 14, 63, 204, 214, 267 |
| 16¹⁴ | 67, 191, 201, 253, 261, 282 |
| 16¹⁵ | 60, 82, 99, 104, 183, 251, 259, 266, 280, 289, 316 |
| 16¹⁵⁻²⁴ | 162 |
| 16¹⁷ | 117, 299 |
| 16¹⁷⁻²¹ | 193 |
| 16¹⁸ | 118, 145, 160, 189 |
| 16¹⁹ | 187, 189, 243, 268 |
| 16¹⁹⁻¹⁹⁵ | 237 |
| 16²¹ | 104, 238, 240, 263 |
| 17 | 22, 24, 39, 93, 166, 265 |
| 17–18 | 11, 187, 232, 237 |
| 17–22 | 222 |
| 17¹ | 280 |
| 17¹ff. | 237 |
| 17¹⁻⁶ | 303 |
| 17¹⁻¹⁹² | 141 |
| 17² | 104, 226, 268, 271, 308 |
| 17²⁻⁵ | 266 |
| 17³ | 128, 196, 198, 204, 243, 245, 303 |
| 17⁴ | 195, 241, 268, 272, 306 |
| 17⁴f. | 14 |
| 17⁵ | 283 |
| 17⁶ | 24, 26, 88, 226, 232, 244, 266, 280 |
| 17⁷ | 73 |
| 17⁸ | 100, 104, 167, 212 |
| 17⁸⁻¹¹ | 23, 27, 28n., 291 |
| 17⁹ | 11, 82 |
| 17⁹ff. | 209 |
| 17⁹⁻¹⁷ | 207, 256 |
| 17¹⁰ | 266 |
| 17¹⁰f. | 60, 216 |
| 17¹¹ | 15, 219 |
| 17¹² | 259, 271f. |
| 17¹²⁻¹⁴ | 15, 253 |
| 17¹²⁻¹⁷ | 23 |
| 17¹⁴ | 82, 124, 210, 282f. |
| 17¹⁶ | 23, 227, 251, 266, 269, 271 |
| 17¹⁶f. | 169, 247 |
| 17¹⁷ | 279 |
| 17¹⁸ | 191 |
| 18 | 22, 39, 252 |
| 18¹ | 308 |
| 18² | 163 |
| 18²ff. | 266 |
| 18³ | 253 |
| 18⁴ | 11, 183, 204, 224, 247, 251 |
| 18⁶ | 227 |
| 18⁷ | 195 |
| 18⁸ | 272 |
| 18⁸f. | 23, 163 |
| 18⁸ff. | 263 |
| 18⁹ | 262f. |
| 18⁹ff. | 253 |
| 18⁹⁻¹⁹ | 163, 310 |
| 18¹¹ff. | 302 |
| 18¹² | 306 |
| 18¹⁶ | 195, 241, 254, 306 |
| 18¹⁷, ¹⁹ | 272 |
| 18²⁰ | 49, 142, 188, 202, 211, 277 |
| 18²⁰ | 24 |
| 18²¹ff. | 266 |
| 18²¹⁻²³ | 299 |
| 18²³ | 174, 237, 318 |
| 18²³f. | 94, 237 |
| 18²³⁻¹⁹² | 399 |
| 18²⁴ | 24, 128, 244, 266 |
| 19 | 188, 291 |
| 19–20 | 170, 173, 193 |
| 19¹ | 152 |
| 19¹ff. | 153 |
| 19¹⁻⁸ | 159 |
| 19¹⁻²²⁵ | 11f. |
| 19² | 24, 142, 192, 244 |
| 19²f. | 227, 274 |
| 19³ | 228, 271 |
| 19⁴ | 118 |
| 19⁵ | 117, 193 |

REVELATION – *contd*

| | |
|---|---|
| $19^6$ | 67 |
| $19^{7f.}$ | 298 |
| $19^8$ | 12, 96, 108, 118, 237, 240f., 249, 254, 272 |
| $19^9$ | 109, 247, 289 |
| $19^{9f.}$ | 59, 314 |
| $19^{10}$ | 59, 82, 289, 305, 315 |
| $19^{11}$ | 90, 142, 186, 232, 280, 294 |
| $19^{11ff.}$ | 21, 58, 69, 72, 124, 137, 158, 210, 229, 237, 240, 261, 291, 301 |
| $19^{11-15}$ | 90 |
| $19^{11-16}$ | 138, 139n. |
| $19^{11-21}$ | 220 |
| $19^{12}$ | 72, 90, 105, 222 |
| $19^{13}$ | 280 |
| $19^{13-15}$ | 232, 243 |
| $19^{14}$ | 100, 232, 241, 282 |
| $19^{15}$ | 51, 64, 67, 90, 96, 128, 154, 185f., 191, 197, 230, 232 |
| $19^{15-21}$ | 193 |
| $19^{17}$ | 165, 225, 279 |
| $19^{17-21}$ | 63, 262, 290, 311 |
| $19^{19}$ | 191 |
| $19^{20}$ | 63, 173, 214, 227f., 248, 258, 278, 292, 295, 317 |
| $19^{20f.}$ | 278 |
| $19^{21}$ | 189, 208, 291 |
| 20 | 59, 130, 191, 251 |
| 20–22 | 293 |
| $20^1$ | 73, 167 |
| $20^{1ff.}$ | 68, 275 |
| $20^2$ | 65 |
| $20^3$ | 201, 291 |
| $20^4$ | 24, 59, 118, 142, 201 |
| $20^{4-6}$ | 66, 110, 193, 291 |
| $20^6$ | 86, 130, 201 |
| $20^8$ | 147, 201, 285 |
| $20^9$ | 63 |
| $20^{9f.}$ | 193 |
| $20^{10}$ | 173, 214, 227, 228, 258, 278, 286 |
| $20^{10-15}$ | 189 |
| $20^{11}$ | 117, 200, 251 |
| $20^{11ff.}$ | 145, 193, 226 |
| $20^{11-15}$ | 279n. |
| $20^{12}$ | 95, 100, 212 |
| $20^{12-15}$ | 311, 316 |
| $20^{13f.}$ | 140, 297 |
| $20^{14}$ | 73, 86, 166, 258, 286, 292, 298, 300 |
| $20^{15}$ | 100, 259 |
| 21 | 13, 113 |
| 21–22 | 86, 91, 100, 126, 192 |
| $21^1$ | 16, 116, 119, 130, 167, 251, 290, 311 |
| $21^{1-8}$ | 107, 297, 301, 307, 314 |
| $21^{1-22^5}$ | 51, 167 |
| $21^{2ff.}$ | 277 |
| $21^3$ | 117, 153f., 193, 266, 307f., 311f. |
| $21^{3-6}$ | 151 |
| $21^4$ | 308, 311 |
| $21^5$ | 132, 232, 309, 314 |
| $21^{5-8}$ | 314 |
| $21^6$ | 154, 250, 316, 318 |
| $21^{7f.}$ | 83 |
| $21^8$ | 92, 166, 173f., 189, 227, 286, 295, 317f. |
| $21^9$ | 12, 251, 280 |
| $21^{9ff.}$ | 237, 297 |
| $21^{9-22^5}$ | 232 |
| $21^{10}$ | 195, 254, 312 |
| $21^{10ff.}$ | 266, 272, 297 |
| $21^{11}$ | 119 |
| $21^{11ff.}$ | 254 |
| $21^{11-21}$ | 14 |
| $21^{12-14}$ | 15, 118 |
| $21^{14}$ | 37, 81 |
| $21^{15}$ | 182, 184 |
| $21^{15ff.}$ | 183, 231 |
| $21^{16}$ | 15 |
| $21^{17}$ | 217 |
| $21^{18}$ | 108, 119 |
| $21^{19-21}$ | 241 |
| $21^{21}$ | 108, 119 |
| $21^{22}$ | 67, 93, 311 |
| $21^{22ff.}$ | 103, 145 |
| $21^{22-22^5}$ | 66, 298 |
| $21^{24}$ | 189, 263 |
| $21^{24f.}$ | 264 |
| $21^{24ff.}$ | 221, 230, 243 |
| $21^{24-27}$ | 211 |
| $21^{24-22^2}$ | 283 |
| $21^{24-22^3}$ | 63, 126, 142, 154n., 294 |
| $21^{24-22^5}$ | 151 |
| $21^{25}$ | 311 |
| $21^{26}$ | 189n. |
| $21^{27}$ | 100, 311 |
| 22 | 13, 41 |
| $22^1$ | 117, 119, 128, 154, 232 |
| $22^{1f.}$ | 294, 307 |
| $22^{1-3}$ | 63, 310 |
| $22^{1-5}$ | 151 |
| $22^2$ | 186, 295, 298 |
| $22^{2f.}$ | 83n. |
| $22^3$ | 93, 117, 128, 153 |
| $22^{3-5}$ | 110, 153, 193, 303, 315 |
| $22^4$ | 105, 120, 148 |
| $22^{4f.}$ | 289 |
| $22^5$ | 130, 320 |
| $22^6$ | 59, 280 |
| $22^{6ff.}$ | 59, 115, 299 |
| $22^{6-9}$ | 38, 57 |
| $22^{6-21}$ | 12f., 44 |
| $22^7$ | 21, 104 |
| $22^{8f.}$ | 59 |
| $22^9$ | 38, 179, 305 |

| | |
|---|---|
| $22^{10}$ | 17, 60 |
| $22^{11}$ | 289 |
| $22^{12}$ | 21, 95, 104, 193 |
| $22^{13}$ | 70, 299 |
| $22^{13f.}$ | 105 |
| $22^{14}$ | 83, 100, 151, 153, 202, 287, 309f. |
| $22^{14f.}$ | 289 |
| $22^{15}$ | 92, 174, 189, 300, 305, 310, 318 |
| $22^{16}$ | 30, 93, 96n., 97, 128, 148, 164, 238 |
| $22^{17}$ | 106, 110, 137, 139, 151, 154, 297 |
| $22^{18}$ | 59 |
| $22^{18f.}$ | 16, 60, 68 |
| $22^{18-20}$ | 38 |
| $22^{20}$ | 12, 21, 59, 67, 104, 106, 110, 137, 139 |

# NON-BIBLICAL JEWISH WRITINGS

**II BARUCH**

| | |
|---|---|
| $3^7$ | 159 |
| $4^3$ | 303 |
| $6^4$ | 148 |
| $29^8$ | 90 |

**EIGHTEEN BENEDICTIONS**

| | |
|---|---|
| 12 | 100n. |

**I ENOCH**

| | |
|---|---|
| $6^6$ | 148 |
| 10 | 288 |
| $14^{15}$ | 117 |
| 18 | 288 |
| $18^{13ff.}$ | 163 |
| 19 | 168 |
| 20 | 160 |
| $21^{3ff.}$ | 163 |
| $24^{4ff.}$ | 83 |
| $39^{12}$ | 120 |
| $40^{7ff.}$ | 201 |
| $46^1$ | 72 |
| 48, 50 | 310 |
| $66^2$ | 244 |
| $69^{4ff.}$ | 201 |
| 76 | 147 |
| 81 | 123 |
| $89^{45f.}$ | 124 |
| $90^{9-16}$ | 124 |
| 93 | 123 |
| $100^{1-3}$ | 232 |

**II ENOCH**

| | |
|---|---|
| $21^1$ | 120 |

**JOSEPHUS**
*Antiquities*

| | |
|---|---|
| III. 186 | 306n. |
| III. 187 | 312 |
| XX. 97f. | 20 |
| XX. 169–72 | 20 |

**JUBILEES**

| | |
|---|---|
| $1^{20}$ | 201 |
| $2^2$ | 118 |
| $4^{30}$ | 289 |
| $10^{2-5}$ | 201 |
| $16^{30}$ | 86 |
| $23^{27}$ | 289 |
| $48^{15}$ | 288 |
| $48^{25ff.}$ | 201 |

**MIDRASH**
*Shemoth R.*

| | |
|---|---|
| 23 | 120 |

**MISHNAH**
*Tamid*

| | |
|---|---|
| | 159 |

**PHILO**
*Cherubim*

| | |
|---|---|
| $49^f.$ | 223 |

*Life of Moses*

| | |
|---|---|
| II. 114f. | 312 |

*Special Laws*

| | |
|---|---|
| I. 87 | 306n. |

**PSALMS OF SOLOMON**

| | |
|---|---|
| $2^{29}$ | 196 |

**QUMRAN**
*War Rule*

| | |
|---|---|
| XVII. 7f. | 200n. |

**SIBYLLINE ORACLES**

| | |
|---|---|
| I. 324ff. | 218 |
| IV and V | 209 |
| V. 1–50 | 257n. |
| VII. 65ff. | 218n. |

**TALMUD**
*Hagigah*

| | |
|---|---|
| 12b. | 159 |

**TESTAMENTS OF THE TWELVE PATRIARCHS**
*Dan*

| | |
|---|---|
| $5^6$ | 149 |

*Joseph*

| | |
|---|---|
| $19^8$ | 124 |

*Levi*

| | |
|---|---|
| $5^1$ | 117 |
| 18 | 83, 310 |

# EARLY CHRISTIAN WRITINGS

ASCENSION OF
ISAIAH
4$^{1}$ff.    218n.

I CLEMENT
34$^{6}$    120

DIDACHE
10$^{6}$    319f.
11    81
11–13    94
11$^{7}$f.    94
16$^{6}$    63n.

EPISTLE OF
BARNABAS,
4$^{4}$    257n.
12$^{2-4}$    63n.

EUSEBIUS
*Historia Ecclesiastica*
III. 5    203

IGNATIUS
*Ephesians*
10    81
13    62
13$^{1}$    200
19    97
*Magnesians*
8$^{2}$    159

*Philadelphians*
6$^{1}$    105n.
9$^{1}$    103, 105n.
*Polycarp*
1f.    81

IRENAEUS
*Adversus Haereses*
I. 26.3    90
III. 11.7    90
V. 30.3    21
V. 31, 35f.    290

JOHN OF DAMASCUS
*De Fide Orthodoxa*
II. 29    144n.

## OTHER ANCIENT WRITINGS

**CICERO**
*Pro Flacco*
31.5                     86n.

**HERODOTUS**
I. 178                   305
I. 191                   248

**JUVENAL**
VII. 122ff.              254

**LUCIAN**
*Alexander*
38                      317n.

**PLINY**
*Letters*
X. 96.7                  130
X. 96f.                   29

**SUETONIUS**
*Nero*
39.2                     217

**TACITUS**
*Annals*
XV. 29                   121
XV. 44               23, 210
*Histories*
II. 8                    209

**QURAN**
XXVII                    119

# Index of Authors

Aland, K., 37n.
Arvedson, T., 129n.

Balfour, M. L. G. and Frisby, J., 209n.
Barclay, W., 77n.
Barnes, T. D., 29
Bauckham, R. J., 109n., 145n., 189
Beasley-Murray, G. R., xii, 169, 194, 257
Beckwith, I., xii, 15n., 130, 202, 257, 259
Blake, W., 3
Bornkamm, G., xii, 41n., 78, 123n., 162n., 317n.
Bruce, F. F., 196n.
Boman, T., 14n., 70
Bowman, J. W., 45n.
Brewer, R. R., 45n., 116n.
Brown, C., 90n.
Brown, S., 104n.
Bultmann, R., 32n., 39n.

Caird, G. B., xiif., 16n., 65, 71, 113, 116, 118, 119, 121, 125f., 141, 144, 164, 168, 172, 178, 189, 195, 204, 226, 232, 233n., 244, 245, 264f., 273, 275
Calder, W. M., 94n.
Charles, R. H., xiif., 16n., 135n., 159, 167, 181, 210, 213, 229, 249, 296, 302, 306n.,
Cicero, 86n.
Chadwick, H., 81n.

Daniélou, J., xiii, 41n., 90n., 97n., 105, 148, 151n., 152n.
Davies, W. D., and Daube, D., 82n.
de Ste Croix, G. E. M., 29

Deeks, D. G., 38n.
Deissmann, A., 68n.
Dionysius of Alexandria, 36f., 38

Eliot, T. S., 51n.
Eusebius, 203

Farrer, A. M., xiif., 39, 42n., 44, 51n., 52, 67, 73, 78n., 119, 149n., 165, 168, 169n., 172, 176–9, 183, 185f., 193, 195n., 204, 217f., 231, 239, 250, 258, 286, 294, 297f., 304, 306
Feuillet, A., xiii, 46n., 138n., 182
Fiorenza, E. S., 40n., 85n., 90n.
Ford, J. M., 36, 94, 223n.
Frend, W. H. C., 25n., 26n., 28n., 30n.

Giet, S., 181, 256
Glasson, T. F., 306n.
Guthrie, D. S., 37n.

Hanson, A. T., xii, 144n., 214, 227
Harrington, W. J., 46n.
Heaton, E. W., 17n.
Hemer, C. J., xiii, 30n., 39, 72, 77, 83n., 87, 90n., 94n., 100n., 105n., 140n.
Hennecke, E., xiii, 218n.
Hill, D., 38n., 59
Hooke, S. H., 41n., 191n., 196n.
Hort, F. J. A., 67
Houlden, J. L., 94n., 97

Ignatius of Antioch, 62, 73, 81, 85n., 97, 102ff., 105n., 159, 200, 318

Irenaeus, 21, 27, 36, 90, 217, 218n., 256

John of Damascus, 144n.
Josephus, 20, 306n., 312
Jung, C. G., 38, 42–44, 50, 70n.
Justin Martyr, 36
Juvenal, 24, 254

Kirk, K. E., 312n.
Kraft, H., xii
Kuhn, G., 162n.

Lampe, G. W. H., 148n.
Lawrence, D. H., 3, 15n., 48–51
Lindblom, J., 42n., 127
Lohmeyer, E., xii, 125, 207, 214, 249
Lohse, E., 32n., 39n.
Lucian, 317n.

McNamara, M., 40n., 74, 119, 205n., 295
Magie, D., 25n.
Melito of Sardis, 24, 36
Millar, F., 26n.
Minear, P. S., xiii, 15n., 94, 95, 207, 247, 249, 297
Morris, L., xiif., 184
Morrison, C. D., 208n.
Moule, C. F. D., 49, 82n., 319
Mowry, L., 116n.
Munck, J., 185n.
Mussies, G., 16n.

Niles, D. T., xiii, 15n.

Ozanne, C. G., 16n.

Papias, 38
Philo, 223, 306n., 312
Pleket, H. W., 25n.
Pliny, 29, 130, 217
Polycarp, 21
Preston, R. H., xii, 214
Prigent, P., xiii, 26n., 41f., 78, 83n., 116, 122, 129, 131, 151

von Rad, G., 40n., 162n.
Ramsay, Sir William, xii, 38f., 77, 82, 83n., 92, 93, 102, 131
Reicke, B., 210n., 218n.
Rissi, M., xiii, 137n., 139, 158, 210, 207, 223, 256, 259, 261ff., 282, 287, 291
Roberts, R., 83n.
Robinson, J. A. T., 22f., 257n., 319n.
Roller, O., 123n., 127
Rordorf, W., 68
Roszak, T., 3
Rowley, H. H., xiii, 17n.
Rudwick, M. J. S. and Green, E. M. B., 107n.
Rupp, E. G., 42n.
Russell, D. S., xiii, 37n.

Sanders, J. N., 64n.
Scott, E. F., xii
Sherwin-White, A. N., 29, 79n.
Staniforth, M., ix, 62n.
Stauffer, E., xiii, 71, 78, 116n., 136, 158, 163n., 218n., 253
Stevenson, J., xi, 23n., 25n., 29n., 38n., 39n, 94n, 203
Strack, H. L. and Billerbeck, P., x, 225
Suetonius, 30, 217
Swete, H. B., xii, 15n., 71, 239, 268, 271, 288

Tacitus, 121, 209, 210
Taylor, L. R., 26n.
Tertullian, 36n., 64n.
Touilleux, P., 194n., 223n.

van Unnik, W. C., 73, 261n.

Vanhoye, A., 40n.
Vermes, G., xi, 89n., 200n.

Whiteley, D. E. H., 144n.

# Index of Subjects

Aaron, 187, 306, 312

Abaddon, 170

Abel, 142, 165, 300

Abomination of desolation, 18, 20, 58, 182, 254

Abominations, 14, 22, 254, 262, 266, 308, 311

Abraham, 150, 291

Abyss, bottomless pit, 8, 11f., 16, 119, 167f., 170, 186, 205, 209, 258, 275, 288

Accuser, 9, 80, 199, 201, 225, 278, 309

Adam, 146, 287, 289; new Adam, 83, 199, 279

Adversary, 85, 198f.

Age to come, 19, 68, 72, 86, 105, 147, 218, 225, 289; see also New Age

Ahab, 249f., 252

Alexander the Great, 18, 209, 261

Allegory, 187, 206f., 253, 255, 277

Alpha and Omega, 48, 67, 70, 193, 299, 316

Altar, 7, 115, 142, 159f., 183, 245; incense-altar, 171f.

Amen, 62, 106f., 278, 280, 282, 319

Anath, 232

Ancient of Days, 18, 62, 69, 72, 126, 288

Angels, 2, 7–10, 59, 118, 167f., 231; of the churches, 5, 73, 77, 80, 168; evil, fallen, angels, 2, 9, 16, 85, 164, 167f., 170, 172, 177, 200f.

Anger, 144, 205, 227, 268

Antichrist, false Christs, 4, 9, 14f., 20, 68, 137f., 147, 149, 157, 190, 207f., 214f., 218f., 256, 259, 288

Anti-Semitism, 47n.

Antinomianism, 89n.

Antioch, 90

Antiochus Epiphanes, 17f., 26, 34, 99, 152, 207, 209, 216, 257

Antipas, 27, 65, 87f., 106f., 183, 208, 258, 278

Apocalypse, synoptic, 17, 19f., 41, 44, 58, 63, 78, 94, 104, 114, 136, 141, 143, 157f., 182, 190, 207, 220, 243, 281, 301; apocalyptic, 1–5, 18f., 26, 35, 37, 40n., 42f., 50, 57, 127, 162n., 177f., 191n. apocalyptic Christianity, ff.

Apollo, 170, 194

Apollos, 79, 170

Apollyon, 170, 287

Apostasy, 29, 79, 86, 186

Apostles, 15, 81, 104, 118; false, 5, 44, 80f. apostolic authorship, 37, 47

Aramaic, 16, 40, 241, 261

Archangels, 18, 159f., 171, 200

Ark of the covenant, 90, 186, 189, 192f., 241

Armageddon, 249f., 285, 291

Artemis, 79, 83n.

Ascetism, 32

Asclepius, 87

Asia, 5, 9, 21, 29f., 38f., 48, 62n., 65, 68, 79, 94n., 136, 145, 223n., 258, 268, 279

Astrology, 39, 45, 89, 92, 99, 194, 204, 302, 306

Atheism, 31, 186

Atonement, 66, 124n., 193, 212, 245, 308; Day of, 159, 192

Attis, 223n.

Augustus, 25, 225, 256

Authority, 19, 66, 96, 128, 192, 210f., 215, 266f., 276, 315
Authorship, 21, 35–43, 47, 257; pseudonymous, 36–8, 257

Baal, 89, 216
Baal-peor, 318
Babel, Tower of, 17, 105, 187, 211, 268, 303
Babylon, 10f., 15, 17, 21ff., 26, 39, 45f., 49, 62, 93f., 106, 121, 131, 154, 158, 163, 186ff., 193, 196, 224, 225ff., 232, 244, 248, 250–4, 257, 266–76, 299, 301, 305, 308, 310
Balaam, 33, 92, 97, 164, 251, 318; Balak and, 5, 45, 89, 157, 203, 208
Baptism, 41, 83, 86, 88, 91, 98, 102, 105, 131, 147ff., 151, 153, 177, 239, 283, 300, 317, 319
Beast, 9f., 23, 45f., 51, 147f., 166f., 213ff., 221, 253–63; authority of, 182, 210f.; city of, 158, 190, 237, 243; mark of, 148, 151, 217; death and resurrection of, 9, 214, 291; defeat of, 284–6; with seven heads, 11, 15, 21, 37, 196, 206ff., 258; see also Number
Beatitudes, 59, 249, 277, 280, 316f.
Beginning, 107; and End, 40, 215, 294, 316
Behemoth, 173, 215
Belial, 204
Belshazzar, 174
Bithynia, 29, 130, 217
Black Death, 140
Blasphemy, 10, 31, 207, 211, 243, 245, 247f., 255, 274; against Holy Spirit, 94, 315
Blessedness, 59f., 230ff., 249, 289, 314
Blindness, 43, 108, 144, 240, 269
Blood, 66, 142, 148, 162f., 232, 243f.; of the Lamb, 7, 153, 199, 232, 277, 283; of the saints, 11, 226f., 232, 255, 275, 284; -offering, 159
Bolshevism, 215

Book, 68; of life, 100, 211, 259, 293ff., 308, 311; of Destiny, 123; opened, 294; sealed, 30, 123
Bowls, the seven, 190, 224, 241ff.
Bride, 11f., 45, 93, 96, 109, 141, 158, 194f., 220, 222, 232, 237, 241, 252f., 264, 274, 277, 279, 298, 301ff., 318
Bridegroom, 106, 109, 158, 237, 253, 274, 277ff., 281, 301, 314

Caesar, 2, 20, 33, 66, 153, 208, 240
Caiaphas, 187
Cain, 276, 300
Caligula, 218n., 256
Calvary, 144, 199, 213, 283, 311n.
Canon of the NT, 47
Cayster, River, 82
Cerinthus, 90
Chaos, 13, 47, 113, 119, 143, 159, 164, 166f., 215, 261, 274, 297
Chastity, 222
Cherubim, 120
Child, 44, 195–7; see also Offspring
Christ, birth and death of, 9n., 96f., 121, 192; death of, 12, 28, 43, 45, 48, 50, 62, 64, 66, 81f., 93, 124, 128, 142, 151, 187, 193, 197, 207, 223, 231, 239, 241, 272, 277, 289; death and resurrection, 19, 35, 58, 82, 84, 102, 117, 145, 183, 188f., 208, 218, 225, 287; denial of Christ, 86, 100f., 103, 211f., 217; dying with Christ, 148n., 153; divinity of, 48, 99, 127, 130; as Divine Wisdom, 40n., 106ff.; as Judge, 99, 282, 288, 319; presence, nearness of, 69, 104; victory of, 6, 10, 125, 198ff., 261; see also Coming of Christ, Word of God
Christians, passim; Alexandrian, 47; Asian, 41, 287; false, 209; Gentile, 150, 308; Jewish, 31, 150, 218, 249, 277, 308; Judaizing, 28n., 85n.
Church, 45f., 79, 149n., 184f., 195,

197, 203, 207–9, 253, 277, 312; and Jews, 28f., 46; priestly nature of, 287, 306

Circumcision, 28, 148

City of God, holy city, 11, 83n., 96, 100, 184, 190, 266f., 296, 302–8; great, 184, 186f., 198, 208, 266f., 276, 296; see also Babylon, Rome

Cleansing, 12, 63, 153, 277

Cleopatra, 253

Clouds, 4, 10, 18, 20, 62, 66, 115, 154, 176f., 188, 220, 229, 231, 298

Coinage, 25, 30f., 61, 71, 194f., 211, 214, 216, 278

Colossae, 40, 66

Colossians, epistle to, 40, 48

Colours, 13, 70, 90, 139f., 153, 173

Coming of Christ, 4, 17, 19f., 32, 34f., 42, 48, 63–6, 69, 78, 82, 106, 109, 115, 137, 139, 141, 158, 185n., 188, 211, 226, 229–32, 247, 258f., 277, 281–4, 314, 319 coming of Son of Man, 58f., 62f., 69–72, 143, 186, 188, 237, 301; conditional, 82, 99

Completeness, completion, 14, 65, 99, 124, 141f., 177, 179, 215, 250, 262, 312

Compromise, 6, 11, 26, 28, 31, 34, 45, 88, 93, 96, 98, 100, 157, 208f., 213, 221, 285, 300, 318

Conquest, conqueror, 35, 80, 82f., 88, 90, 96, 99, 109, 128, 137ff., 164, 186, 199, 222, 238f., 288, 296, 299, 317, 319

Corinth, Corinthians, 31, 33, 40, 49, 89

Covenant, 124, 129, 176; ark of the, 90, 186, 189, 192f., 241; everlasting, 117; see also New, 129, 148, 297

Crassus, 24, 172

Creation, 6, 41, 51, 119, 132f., 143; new, 12, 113, 131, 218, 250, 295, 299, 309; and redemption, 51, 126 fulfilment of, 287

Creator, 4, 6, 13, 47, 113, 116, 121f., 137, 143, 178, 192, 223, 309

Creatures, the four living, 6f., 17, 120, 136f., 139f., 153, 204n., 227, 241, 278, 280

Croesus, 98

Cross, crucified, crucifixion, 63n., 126, 128, 144, 131, 148n., 177, 183, 188, 195, 200f., 203, 211, 227, 230, 282ff., 299, 311n. see also Christ, death of, victory of

Crowns, 49, 82, 84, 104, 118, 137ff., 169; of life, 86

Cult, Emperor, 9, 25f., 31, 34, 79, 84, 86f., 207f., 214, 216f., 225, 317; fertility, 31, 33, 79, 301; local, 194; mystery, 86; Pacific Cargo cults, 42; see also Paganism

Cup, 10f., 37, 177, 208, 224, 226f., 232, 252, 254

Curse, 11, 16, 63, 83, 89, 288, 309, 311f.; curse Christ, 29; see also Blasphemy; cursing of opponents, 50; of heretics, 100n.

Cybele, 194, 217, 223n.

Cyrus, 99, 248f.

Damascus, 305

Darkness, 20, 44, 58f., 164, 166, 168, 171, 208, 246, 248, 274, 311

Date of Revelation, 21–7, 36, 255–8

David, 30, 63, 65, 124, 128, 185f., 317f.; see also Key

Day, Emperor's, 68; New Year's, 159; of Atonement, 159, 192; of judgment, 226; of the Lord, 5, 64, 67f., 80, 143, 159, 216, 222, 231

Dead, 64, 72, 95, 98, 293ff.; judgment of, 191, 193

Death, 6, 9, 19, 61, 80, 83, 96, 98, 101, 110, 121, 125f., 128, 135, 140, 142, 151, 157, 166, 169, 171, 183, 199, 211f., 227f., 230n., 266, 269, 286, 298f., 311, 319; second death, 30, 86, 100, 166, 174, 284, 295, 300;

Death (*contd*), gnostic idea of, 32; and Hades, 139f., 295, 297

Deceiver, 9, 199, 201, 225

Dedication, feast of, 152f.

Delay, 8f., 27, 135, 142, 146f., 172, 175, 177–80

Demons, 16, 147, 168, 171, 173, 254, 258, 290f.

Demythologizing, 208

Desert, 49, 90, 109, 151f., 266, 292

Determinism, 2, 204

Devil, 9, 50, 65, 73, 85, 113, 201f., 284, 292; *see also* Satan

Diana, 79

Docetism, 72f.

Domitia, 71

Domitian, 21, 23–8, 30, 39n., 64n., 67, 87n., 121, 140n., 170, 216, 218n., 256ff.

Door, open, 102f., 106, 109, 282; of the sheep, 103

Dragon, 9, 11, 49, 51, 67, 113, 119, 125, 167, 182, 190, 191n., 193–8, 202–5, 207, 209f., 214, 241, 248, 267, 282f., 292

Drink-offering, 159, 162

Dualism, 2, 113, 144n., 290, 296


Eagle, 8, 10, 120, 162, 165, 203f., 224, 285

Earthquake, 8, 20, 24, 31, 104, 107, 145, 188, 193, 247, 250ff.

Easter, 67

Ecstasy, 42, 117, 136

Eden, 17, 258, 273

Edom, 267, 271

Egypt, Egyptians, 6, 8, 10, 15, 17, 46, 61f., 121, 124, 130ff., 148, 159, 163, 168, 192, 194, 196, 198, 205n., 248, 251, 267; flight to, 195; *see also* Plague

Elders, 115f., 118, 127f., 131, 151, 153, 191–3, 222, 278, 280

Elect, 20, 50, 63n., 81, 104, 141, 178, 216, 229ff., 237, 242, 249, 252, 301f.

Eliakim, 42n., 101

Elijah, 5, 17, 31, 92, 181, 183ff., 188, 197f., 216, 224, 250, 292

End, 1f., 10, 18, 20, 24, 35, 59, 65, 83f., 96, 131, 141, 143, 166, 179, 186, 188, 190, 293f., 303; *see also* Beginning

Endurance, 64, 67, 114, 130, 135, 157, 213, 231

Enoch, 1, 5, 40, 189n.

Ephesus, 5, 38, 39n., 40f., 44f., 62n., 64, 78, 92, 94, 98f., 107f., 163, 174, 225, 317, 319

Ephraim, 149

Eucharist, 35, 41f., 68, 78, 82f., 86, 88, 90, 92, 106, 116, 131, 154, 192, 277, 281, 299, 314, 317, 319; eucharistic presence, 42, 68; *see also* Supper

Euphrates, 8, 172, 246, 248, 274

Eve, 9, 195f., 203, 279

Evil, 14, 19, 80n., 81, 88, 119, 141, 172, 201, 204, 218, 230, 261, 275, 295, 311, 316; punished by evil, 169; reservoir of, 167, 172; self-destruction of, 260, 262f.

Exile, Babylonian, 17, 91, 257, 267, 302; return from, 21, 62

Exodus (event), 6, 17, 62, 109, 116, 118, 130, 132, 162, 168, 175ff., 194f., 203, 205, 240, 301; new, 131, 239, 302

Ezekiel, 6, 8, 11, 39, 42, 69f., 135, 148, 160

Ezra, 40n.


Faith, 118, 163, 205; *see also* Justification

Faithfulness, fidelity, 12f., 19, 80, 83ff., 93, 98, 124, 151, 205, 208, 261, 278; *see also* Remnant, Witness

Falsehood, 64, 70, 81, 85, 94, 103, 189, 227, 300, 317

Famine, 20, 31, 135–8, 140, 185f.

Father, God as, 6, 9, 61, 93, 116, 209, 300, 306

Felix, 138, 189

Feasts, festivals, 115; see Dedication, Passover, Pentecost, Tabernacles

Fire, 23f., 117f., 129, 160, 162f., 173, 176f., 185f., 197, 227, 230, 239, 241, 248, 272, 292; from heaven, 12, 63, 214, 216, 291f.; of Rome, 22, 28, 136, 278; see also Lake of

First and last, 70, 72, 84, 257, 316; first-born, 61, 63, 65, 157, 203, 257, 297, 316; first (eighth) day, 67f., 118, 218; first-fruits, 65, 149, 221, 223, 226, 230f., 237, 239, 309

Flavians, 23, 25, 258

Flood, 116, 119, 143, 177, 203f., 250, 260, 262, 275

Forehead, 10, 148, 151, 168, 217, 221, 252, 254, 283, 312

Fornication, 5, 32ff., 45, 49, 89, 92, 95f., 226, 237, 252f., 274, 300, 318

Forty-two years, 198, 203; months, see Three and a half years

Free-will, 192, 212, 290, 292f.; see also Predestination

Furnace, 80, 93, 168, 216, 245

Gabriel, 18, 160, 177

Galba, 23, 256

Galilee, 23

Gadarene swine, 275

Games, 31, 79, 82, 86, 116n., 158

Gehenna, 286

Genesis, 6, 118, 132

Gentiles, 30, 46, 102f., 169, 184, 225, 310; converts, 28, 33, 308

Geography, John's, 8, 15f., 78, 119, 167, 187, 204, 257

Gethsemane, 78, 98f., 212, 247, 259

Ghosts, 286, 290f.

Glory of God, 66, 70, 240, 304

Gnosticism, 31f., 34f., 89f., 92, 95f., 107, 113, 116; gnostic Christianity, 48

God, passim; activity of, 65, 239; Almighty, 67, 249; as Creator, 6, 13, 47, 113, 116, 122, 132, 137, 143, 177f., 192, 205, 309; as Judge, 178, 237; as Redeemer, 13, 131, 192, 309; Christ's dependence on, 280; Israel's dependence on, 292; face of, 146, 310, 312; permissive will of, 144n., 167, 183, 192, 204, 210f., 227, 245, 263, 288, 290; plan of, 47, 57–9, 85, 114, 123, 141, 172, 177, 212, 262, 292; presence of, 61, 66, 99, 151, 153f., 160, 178, 193, 216, 251, 266, 292, 298; purpose of, 19, 124, 176, 179, 247, 260, 293; 'God with us', 292, 296, 298; union with his people, 47, 228, 307; will of, 148, 165, 176ff., 247, 283, 294; see also Kingdom, Word

Gods, 61, 73, 120; false, 241, 258

Gog, 170ff., 285, 290ff.; and Magog, 291

Gold, 108, 174, 231, 254, 272, 302, 304, 307; golden calf, 157, 173, 212

Gospel, 10, 20, 123, 135, 137ff., 175ff., 179ff., 190, 220, 223–8, 267; eternal, 165, 244, 285; synoptic, 19, 40, 58, 106, 152, 207, 248; triumph of, 220–33

Grace, 61f., 96, 320

Grammar, John's, 16, 65

Greeks, 19, 32, 39, 70

Greek tragedy, 116n., 118, 227, 265, 271

Guernica, 15, 42

Guilt, 108, 123

Hades, 139f., 295, 297; see also Key

Hail, 162, 193, 247, 251

Half an hour, 7, 158, 259

Hallel, 153, 277, 279

Haman, 187

Hardening of hearts, 157, 162, 175, 189, 240, 251

'Harder reading', 36, 130, 241

Harlot, 11f., 14, 34, 89, 141, 264, 279, 283, 298, 301ff., 306ff.; stripping of, 21, 45, 237, 252; judgment of, 12, 35, 237, 260–3, 277, 301, 307

Harvest, 10, 151, 223, 311; and vintage, 228–33

Hasidim, 34

Healing, 51, 63, 126, 199, 291, 298

Hearing and seeing, 17, 42, 125–32, 139, 149ff., 171f., 198, 215, 222, 231, 255, 262, 315; see also Imagery

Heaven, 2, 6f., 9, 113, 118f., 123, 167; and earth, 12, 16, 107, 116, 137, 251, 287, 303, 305; new, 295ff.; armies of, 241, 279, 283; 'heaven dwellers', 15, 47n., 49; host of, 116, 145, 211; opened, 11, 117, 143, 280, 282; war in, 198ff.; see also Kingdom

Hell, 2, 16; see also Hades, Abyss

Hellenism, 39, 102

Herculaneum, 24

Herod, 187, 195, 197

Herod, 187, 195, 197; Herodian princes, 271

High Priest, 20, 63, 71, 185, 302; vestments of, 306, 312

Hitler, 27, 34, 209, 215

Holiness, holy, in OT, 222; of God, 102, 240, 244; of men, 249, 289, 320; Holy, Holy, Holy, 116, 120, 228; of Holies, 193, 305, 309

Horn, little, 18, 206, 209ff., 215; seven, 70n., 128; two, 215; ten, 14, 15, 196, 209, 258, 260f., 263, 269, 271

Horses, 6, 166, 171f., 173, 232, 294

Horsemen, four, 6, 20, 136–40, 162, 241, 282f.; lion-headed, 8, 173, 206

Hour, 260f., 272

Humanity, 19, 203; Christ's, 72;

hatred of, 22, 31; true, 169, 203, 208, 231

Hundred and forty-four, 301, 305; hundred and forty-four thousand, 7, 10, 15, 46, 124f., 147ff., 150–2, 184, 186, 221ff., 230, 254, 283, 305

Hymns, 6, 8, 11, 13, 41, 120, 126, 129ff., 152, 222, 265

Idolatry, 10, 32–4, 89, 92, 173ff., 208

Idols, 95, 173, 225, 267; food offered to idols, 32f., 89

Imagery, 21, 50, 70, 86, 127, 138, 143, 151, 159, 187, 194, 230ff.; auditory rather than visual, 14, 17, 70, 125, 164; see Hearing and Seeing; Hebrew, 13–17; kaleidoscopic quality of, 14, 118, 239; rebirth of, 43, 230, 240

Immanuel, 196, 292, 298; see also 'God with us'

Imminent end, 1, 4, 19, 27; did John expect one? 58f.

Immorality, 4, 8, 12, 89, 93, 174, 208, 210, 226

Incense, 115, 129, 142, 160, 217, 278; = prayer of saints, 245

Incense-altar, 171f., 241; -liturgy, 7, 162; -offering, 159

Infidelity, 89, 95, 222, 253

Inscriptions, 25, 33, 90n., 208, 211, 225

Inspiration, 42, 94, 115, 253f., 280

Interpolations, 35, 207, 229, 256, 318

Irony, 93, 96, 108, 140, 144, 187, 192, 197, 272

Islam, 102n.

Israel, redeemed, 61, 124, 248; persecuted, 62f.; disobedient, 46, 186, 208; church as true, 28, 30, 34, 68, 114, 149f., 184, 203, 277, 279, 304; Jesus as true, 59; God's choice of, 109, 125, 301, 312; new, 277

Jacob, 91

James, 37, 185

Jasper, 117, 304ff.

Jehu, 278; and Joram, 92

Jeremiah, 8, 90, 140, 164, 177, 180, 213, 243; and Seraiah, 274

Jericho, fall of, 193

Jerusalem, 15, 22, 26, 148, 184, 186f., 189, 221, 250f., 276, 286; church in, 37, 203; triumphal entry into, 152; fall, punishment of, 23, 46, 182, 184, 207, 262, 266ff., 298; new, 12, 14, 45f., 63, 102, 105, 298, 300–8

Jesus, passim; exaltation of, 97, 197; God's self-revelation in, 118; teachings of, 2, 80n., 100, 160; see also Christ, Parables, Temptations, Testimony

Jews, Judaism, 1, 4, 8, 17f., 34, 39, 81, 89, 102ff., 107, 116, 125f., 130, 148, 151, 159, 183, 187, 196, 200, 209, 218, 222, 266, 288, 302, 306; false, 6, 46f., 84, 101, 103, 317f.; and Christians, 28ff., 46; and Gnosticism, 32; beliefs of, 19, 201, 261, 289, 294; conversion of, 46; in Asia, 79, 84; and war with Rome, 20, 23, 28, 181, 203; see also Slander

Jewels, 11f., 14, 118, 231, 241, 251, 254, 272, 282, 302, 304ff.

Jezebel, 5, 11, 17, 26, 31, 38, 45, 81, 92, 94, 106, 164, 195, 197f., 222, 224, 226, 237, 242, 250–3, 255, 267, 275, 278, 315f., 318f.

JHVH, 67, 312

Job, 168ff., 173

Joel, 171ff., 216, 230, 232

Johannine epistles, 36, 38, 43, 48

John, 5f., 8, 12, 16f., 19, 20, 27, 50, 264 and passim; as a prophet, 41, 82, 217, 315; message, 194, 314f., 318f.; restraint, 287, 293, 310; role and authority, 314; theology of, 128, 261; use of OT, 63, 118, 125f.,

230, 306, 308; see also Geography, Grammar, Language of Rev.

John, the apostle, 5, 36–8, 39n., 79, 90

John the Baptist, 36n., 79, 183f.

John the elder, 38

John's Gospel, 5, 40n., 42, 48, 79, 93, 197, 226, 280; prologue of, 107, 283

Jonah, 189

Joppa, 305

Jordan, river, 248

Joseph, 149, 195

Joshua the high priest, 130n., 185, 289

Joshua, son of Nun, 240

Josiah, 250

Judaea, 19f., 22

Judah, 149, 306; see also Lion

Judaism, see Jews

Judas Iscariot, 48, 50

Judgment, 28, 32, 46, 64, 69, 80, 82, 106, 108, 136ff., 145, 158ff., 165, 178, 225f., 229–32, 240, 244f., 247, 251, 282, 284, 293–5; of the harlot (= Babylon), 12, 141, 237, 264–9, 273–6; of the dead, 191, 193

Julius Caesar, 256

Jupiter Capitolinus, 30

Justice of God, 58, 160, 199, 243, 269, 278

Justification, 90, 98, 100, 108, 118, 151, 202, 294; by faith 199, 316

Key, of bottomless pit, 166f., 287; of David, 30, 101, 103, 318; of Death and Hades, 73, 101, 166, 287

King, God as, 191, 240, 261, 284; King Messiah, 191n.

Kingdom of God, 8, 19, 102, 277, 279, 281; millennial, 289f., 297; of heaven, 123, 279

Kingship, 50, 312; of Christ, 61, 93, 130

Knowledge, see Gnosticism

Lake of fire, 11f., 258, 285f., 291f., 295, 317

Lamb, 6, 10, 12, 17, 70n., 122–6, 128f., 131f., 160, 227, 240, 245, 281, 308–12; death of, slain, 35, 48, 50, 63n., 113, 124–6, 128, 137, 151, 176, 212, 283; victory of, 58, 138, 186, 192; marriage of, 11, 109, 276f., 279, 285, 298; followers of, 35, 46f., 48, 124, 149n., 205, 211, 220–3, 260ff., 283, 285; light of heavenly city, 126, 310, 312; name of, 148, 254; countefeit, 51, 213ff.; see also Book of life; Moses, song of; Wrath of

Lament for Babylon, 163, 262–4, 270–4, 307; see also Mourning

Lamp, 126, 310, 312; lampstands, 184f.; seven, 5, 34, 65, 69, 71, 74, 80, 82, 100, 118, 129, 159, 185

Language of Rev., 16, 35f., 38, 40, 58, 181, 187, 226, 229, 266, 319; violence of, 22, 44, 49f., 244; liturgical, 62, 278, 292; see also Grammar

Laodicea, 38, 40, 65f., 70, 85, 210, 252, 271

Last Supper, 78, 109f.

Law, 28, 31, 41, 115f., 122f., 176, 178, 180, 209, 245, 248

Lawlessness, 79, 207, 254

Leopard, 209

Letters, form of, 41, 57, 61, 319

Leviathan, 173, 196, 210, 215

Lies, 221, 223f., 249, 251, 311; liars, 300, 317; see also Falsehood

Life, eternal, 19, 98

Living creatures, see Creatures

Light, 70, 154, 185n., 194, 245, 274, 310ff.; eternal, 116; hatred of, 208;

Lightning, 116, 118, 162, 193, 247, 284

Lion, 120, 139, 144, 178, 209; of tribe of Judah, 50, 124f., 127f., 149, 199; lion-headed horses, 8, 173, 206

Literal interpretation, 58; to be avoided, 13, 16, 97, 182

Liturgy, 12, 41f., 45, 60, 78, 120, 137, 151f., 200, 227, 292, 314, 318; heavenly, 190–3, 277f.; Jewish, 109, 116, 120, 122, 131, 162, 166, 231, 243; of John's own church, 131; see also Eucharist, Incense, Worship

Locusts, 8, 166, 168ff., 171f., 206

Lord's day, 61, 67, 80, 120

Lot, 266, 275

Love of God, 102f., 126, 145; of Christ, 50, 61, 66, 106, 108; of Israel for Yahweh, 198; of Christians for Christ, 79–82, 94

Loyalty, see Faithfulness

Lucifer, 215, 250; see also Satan, Devil

Luke, 19

Lydia, 84, 92, 98, 102

Maccabees, cleansing of Temple, 152; revolt of, 17ff.

Magi, 89

Magic, 14, 39, 67, 79, 89, 92f., 97, 99, 216, 238, 248f., 302, 318

Man, 120, 177; gnostic theory of, 32; true, 124, 196, 208, 231; see also Humanity, Child

Manasseh, 149

Manicheanism, 264

Manna, 90, 198

Marcion, 31

Marie Antoinette, 31

Marriage, 222f., 275, 277; sacred, 191n., 279n., 301; see also Lamb

Martyrdom, 19, 34, 37, 66, 151, 278, 317; of Ignatius, 30, 62

Martyrs, 7, 48, 83, 88, 126, 141–3, 147, 188, 255, 258, 288; see also Saints, Witness

Mary, 9, 195, 203

Mary Magdalene, 125

Materialism, 34, 264, 268; see also Paganism

Matthew, 19

Measuring the temple, 8, 183f., 266; the city, 302, 304f.

Meditation, 60; on events, 42, 136

Megiddo, 250

Meshech, 291

Mesopotamian world view, 167; *see also* Mythology

Messenger, 59, 73; *see also* Angels

Messiah, 9, 34, 46, 61, 63, 65, 68, 89, 109, 124, 148, 173, 191, 195f., 201, 203, 218, 221, 232, 248, 288, 291, 298, 306; messianic age, 86, 129, 151, 287; claimants, 20; community, 104

Michael, 9, 18, 198–201, 207

Millennium, 12, 68, 130, 218, 286–90, 303; millennial kingdom, 59, 289, 297

Millstone, great, 274f.

Mission of Jesus, 129, 178; Gentile, 80, 184

Moab, 89

Montanism, 94n., 280

Morning Star, 96f., 148, 164, 238, 318

Moses, 61, 135, 181, 183, 185–8, 196f., 200, 216, 222, 312; law of, 28; song of, 178, 224; song of Moses and the Lamb, 238–41, 244

Mother, *see* Mary, Eve, Cybele

Mountain, 143, 145, 163, 186, 193, 303

Mount Carmel, 250

Mount of Olives, 2, 7, 58, 135

Mount of Assembly, 250

Mount Olympus, 200

Mount Sinai, 17, 160

Mount Zion, *see* Zion

Mourning, 63, 145, 180, 189, 250, 269; *see also* Lament

Murder, 25n., 28, 165, 174, 300

Music, 13, 60, 274; musicians, 275

Myrrh, 84

Mystery, 43, 73, 179, 239, 254ff., 258; mystery religions, 32, 90, 317n.

'Myth and ritual', 41n., 191n., 279n.

Mythology, 9, 194, 196; imperial, 70f.

Naked, nakedness, 108, 249, 262, 277

Name, divine, 65, 67, 105, 148; used by emperors, 209, 211; of Christ, 88, 283, 312; kept, feared, by Christians, 88, 103, 193; given to Christians, 90, 148; their names 'in the book', 18, 259; given to the harlot, 252ff.

Nations, 180, 182, 184, 189, 201; deceived, 141, 237, 273ff., 290f., 308; hostile to God, 192f., 201, 221, 289; smitten, 283, 311; power over, 92f., 96f., 164, 196f., 238, 299; healing of, 126, 145, 186f., 295, 298, 307–12; coming to worship, 221, 239; bringing glory to the New Jerusalem, 12, 46, 63, 308ff.

Nazareth, 184f.; Nazarenes, 100n.

Nebuchadnezzar, 63, 189, 280n.; image set up by him, 18, 72, 214, 216, 245

Neocaesarea, 105

Nero, 11, 21–8, 136, 142, 152, 207, 210, 216–18, 244, 255ff., 276; image of, 121

Nerva, 30, 256

New Age, 19, 91, 129, 135, 196, 231, 287, 296; *see also* Age to come

New Year, 159, 191f.

New Testament, 30, 40f., 50, 61, 90, 100, 102, 126, 143f., 201, 226f., 275, 287

Nicolaitans, 5f., 32, 45, 48n., 79, 81ff., 88ff., 91f., 130, 208, 213ff., 268, 317ff.

Nicolaus, 90

Nile, the, 163

Nineveh, 26, 253, 267, 275

Noah, 118, 177, 275; Noah's ark, 70, 148

North, foe from the, 166, 291

Numbers, number symbolism, 13ff., 67, 147, 149, 172, 182ff., 195, 198, 210, 217–19, 221, 233, 288, 305f.; of the beast, 9f., 15n., 215, 217n., 256–8

Oath-taking, 177f.

Obedience, 17, 130, 205; of Jesus, 93, 210

Offspring, 197, 199, 203, 205f., 262; see also Child

Oil and wine, 140; boiling oil, 39n., 67

Old Testament, 2, 24, 26, 30f., 39f., 50, 59f., 100, 102, 138f., 142f., 145, 172, 188f., 222, 230, 232, 250, 252, 272f.; see also John; Prophets

Opisthograph, 122

Ostia, 273

Orthodoxy, 80f., 92

Otho, 23, 256

Paganism, 29, 31–4, 71, 97, 148, 171, 186, 208, 214, 217, 318; pagan dinner-parties, 33, 88f.; see also Idolatry

Palestine, 28, 233, 248, 287

Parables of Jesus, 50, 109, 163, 166, 228f., 277, 280; acted, 274

Paradise regained, 2, 80f., 83, 90, 296, 303, 307–12

Paradox, 93, 125, 144f.

Parataxis, 82

Parody, 9, 11, 14, 51, 70, 138, 169, 185, 192, 205, 207, 209f., 214, 216, 252, 255, 257f., 285, 292

Parthians, Parthia, 24, 121, 136ff., 139, 173, 209, 248

Passover, 6, 42, 109, 277, 302; lamb, 61, 66, 124, 130, 148, 277

Patmos, 5, 36, 64, 67, 78, 306

Patriotism, 25, 31, 215.

Paul, 5, 31, 33, 35, 37, 40f., 46, 49f., 51n., 61, 64, 72f., 79ff., 80, 89, 92, 99, 102, 107, 128, 148, 150, 160f.,

166, 170, 173, 178, 183, 185, 189f., 215, 225, 231, 239, 243, 268, 294, 299, 309, 312, 314, 316f., 320

Peace, 61

Pella, 203

Pentecost, 216; pentecostal fire, 185, 292

Penultimacy, 14f., 215, 218f., 257

Pergamum, 30, 79, 84, 87–91, 197f., 208ff., 247

Persecution, 19–29, 48, 69, 85, 103, 126, 128, 140, 160, 187, 204, 207, 244, 246, 279, 288

Persia, Persians, 18, 24n., 89, 194, 294

Pestilence, 6, 95, 138–40, 269; see Plague

Peter, 23, 33, 37, 102, 110, 183, 185, 212, 215, 223

Pharisees, 26, 50, 102, 289

Pharaoh, 26, 132, 157, 162, 175, 196f., 203f., 251

Philadelphia, 30, 84, 100–5, 140n., 317ff.

Philistines, 186, 189, 193

Phoenicia, 34

Phrygia, 94n., 102, 108, 280

Picasso, 42

Pit, see Abyss

Pius IX, 218n.

Plague(s), 139n., 140, 160–71, 186, 190, 237–51; of Egypt, 7, 10, 17, 44, 148, 157, 186, 190

Platonism, 113, 125

Polycarp, 62n., 85

Pompeii, 24, 217

Pompey, 196

Pontius Pilate, 22, 59, 84f., 187

Power of love, 50, 124ff.

Powers, demonic, 147, 210, 260, 267

Praise, 78, 84, 122, 127, 131, 159, 202, 277f.; weakens Satan's power, 62, 129; see Liturgy, Worship

Prayer, 41, 61, 98; see also Saints

Predestination, 100, 212, 259

Prediction, 2, 18, 58, 60, 73, 102, 226, 257, 303, 309

Priene, 225

Priests, 66, 126, 222f., 289, 310, 312

Prophecy, 2f., 19f., 60, 280f., 314f.

Prophet, 32, 38, 42, 94, 216; Christian, 59, 216, 315; murder of, 25n., 26; OT, 46, 57ff., 192, 271, 287; false, 20, 63, 193, 207f., 214, 428ff., 280, 292; see also Balaam

Prophetess, 11, 38, 94, 280

Purple and scarlet, 11, 195, 254, 272, 302;

Qumran, 34, 68, 222

Rahab, 196

Rainbow, 116f., 176, 275

Ramoth-Gilead, 249

Ransom, 6f., 102, 126, 130, 151, 245, 277

Reading aloud, 12f., 41, 60, 107n., 274, 319

Reality, 237; spiritual, divine, 2, 70, 115f., 125, 130, 166f., 281f., 296, 308; earthly, 80, 129, 150, 230; of Christ's death, 73, 128

Rebirth, regeneration, 4, 119

Red, 140, 153, 173, 196

Red Sea, 116, 119, 122, 124, 131, 157, 203, 205n., 239, 248

Redeemer, 13, 47, 137, 192, 194, 309

Redemption, 47, 51, 64, 109, 113, 116, 119, 121, 126, 129f., 177, 221f., 225, 230, 239, 243; in the OT, 41, 115, 122, 124, 131, 192; see Passover, Exodus

Reign, see Kingdom

Rejoicing, 9, 187f., 202, 274, 277, 279

Remnant, faithful, 46, 149n., 151, 203, 205, 302

Remorse, contrasted with penitence, 67, 189

Repent, repentance, 6, 10, 82, 90, 95, 108, 166, 171, 175, 181, 189

Repetition, 13f., 58, 82, 147, 280, 314f.

Rest, 68, 120, 142, 153, 228, 231

Restoration, 90, 182, 205, 267, 287, 302

Resurrection, 4, 12, 17, 19, 32, 61, 65, 84, 126, 152, 197n., 216, 245, 286f., 289f.; selective or total, 294f.; two resurrections, 289

Retribution, 144, 227, 243; see also Vengeance

Reuben, 149

Revealer, Gnostic, 32, 35

Revelation (= making effective), 123

Right hand, 71f., 148, 197, 201, 217

Righteous, reward of, 287; righteous deeds, see Saints; righteousness, 74, 100, 123, 160, 240, 249, 282

Rigorism, 92

Rivers, 203f., 242, 246, 248; see also Waters

Ritual, 32, 39, 119, 159

Robes, dipped in blood, 232, 282f.; washed, 100, 277, 287, 309, 316f.; see also White

Rock, 221

Rod, 138; of iron, 9, 93, 96f., 144, 154, 197, 283; measuring, 304

Roma (the Goddess), 194f.

Rome, 11, 15, 19, 20, 22-7, 30, 34, 39, 46, 62, 85, 88, 131, 136, 163, 172, 185, 187, 195f., 203, 207-10, 215, 254-9, 261, 267ff., 271, 273ff., 278, 317; divine pretensions of, 208ff.; see also Cult, Emperor

Roman Empire, 4, 8, 10, 12, 100, 207ff., 224, 247f., 255, 260, 268

Sackcloth, 4, 145, 184

Sacraments, 35, 151, 214, 299, 309; see Eucharist

Sacrifice, 129n., 141f., 153, 159f., 223, 245, 309; of Christ, 6, 48, 64, 123-6, 131, 151, 197, 199, 221, 294, 302; parody of, 285

Sacrilege, *see* Abomination of Desolation

Saints, 18, 129, 261, 287; prayers of, 141f., 158–60; righteous deeds of, 12, 96, 254, 302; vindication of, 276–81; *see also* Blood

Salvation, 10, 28, 32, 48ff., 123, 152f; history of, 131; through the emperor, 25, 152; through *gnosis*, 32, 34f.

*Sanctus, see* Holy, Holy, Holy

Sand, 260; contrasted with rock, 205, 221, 291f.

Sardis, 6, 97–101, 106, 249, 279, 317

Satan, 9f., 12, 85f., 88, 119, 167–70, 199, 204ff., 249ff., 260, 274, 290–4; binding and release of, 12, 275, 287f., 290f.; *see also* Beast, Devil, Dragon, Trinity; fall of, 164, 166f., 201; as public prosecutor, 85; synagogue of, 30, 47n., 103; throne of, 30, 45, 208, 247

Saviour, of pagan gods, 87; as Imperial title, 25, 27, 209

Scarlet, *see* Purple

Scorpions, 168, 173, 204n., 206, 208

Scriptures, 30f., 39ff.; *see also* Old Testament

Scroll with seven seals, 6, 121–3, 157ff.; unsealing of the, 127, 135–54; scroll, little, 8, 139, 175–80; Ezekiel's, 123, 180

Sea, 113, 167; brazen, 115, 239; beast from the, 206–13; of glass, 119, 239, 296f., 307, 311; absent from New Age, 296f.; *see also* Waters

Seal, 148; *see also* Scroll

Sealing of God's servants, 125, 146–9; 184; as protection, 48, 135; which sinners lack, 168, 172, 208; in their foreheads, 312; = sign of the cross, 177, 183

See, 68, 73, 108, 188; *see* Hearing and Seeing

Seed, of Abraham, 150; of the woman, 9, 194; *see* Offspring

Septuagint, 16, 40, 65, 128, 139n., 306

Seraphim, 120

Serpent, 9, 17, 80, 113, 194, 196f., 203, 208, 215; symbol of Asclepius, 87, 90n.

Servants of God, 59, 312; *see* sealing of

Shadrach, Meshach and Abed-nego, 216

Shebna, 101, 104

*Sheol*, 73, 170, 291

Shepherd, 93; of the Lamb, 154

Signs, 63n., 81, 137; deceitful, 20, 249

Silence, 7, 158f., 274

Simeon and Anna, 129

Simon Magus, 89

Sin, 32, 61, 124n., 143f., 199, 227; sinlessness, 43, 96

Sinai, 116ff., 124, 176ff., 250

Slander, Jewish, 6, 28, 45, 114, 128, 147, 319

Slanderer, of Satan, 85, 201

Slave, 59, 312, 315

Slavery, 130, 272

Smyrna, 47n., 79, 83–6, 100n., 101f., 105n., 318

Sodom, 8, 15, 46, 168, 187, 230, 251, 266ff., 271f., 278; and Gomorrah, 173, 227, 253, 286

Solomon, and queen of Sheba, 119; temple of, 41n., 70, 115, 119, 239, 305f.

Son, 71

Son of God, 25, 35, 59, 80, 93, 191n., 196f., 209

Sons of God, 201

Son of man, 18–21, 69–73, 78n., 80, 84, 88, 126, 129, 158, 169, 177, 188, 204, 220, 222, 228–33, 241, 243, 249, 275, 281, 288, 301

Song of Songs, 106, 109, 277, 302f.; new, 6, 17, 129, 131, 221f., 239, 279; *see also* Moses, song of

Sorcery, 92, 174, 237, 275, 300, 317f.

Soul, 32, 272; souls under the altar, 135, 243, 276, 288

Sovereignty, 18, 64, 117, 192f., 197

Spain, 23

Spirit, Holy Spirit, 9, 32, 42, 58, 64f., 68, 82, 88, 98, 118, 138, 148n., 186, 214, 216, 253, 280f., 315, 318; seven spirits of God, 61, 65, 68, 98, 118, 120, 129, 281; gifts of the, 131; power of the, 185; of prophecy, 281, 284, 314f., 318; of Truth, 204; unclean spirits, 63, 248-50, 267

Star, 81, 92f., 163f., 318; Morning, 96f., 148, 164, 238, 318; stars, fallen, 81, 145, 166f., 200, 244, 287; seven, 69, 74, 80, 98f., 170

Stephen, 88, 183f., 204

Stoicism, 67

Structure, of Rev., 42, 44-7, 51; of the seven letters, 65

Suffering, before the End, 141; of Christians, 102, 130; of martyrs, 22ff., 87; of Jesus, 84; servant, 226, 302; basis of sovereignty, 64, 93, 128; vicarious, 125, 213n.

Sun, 148, 164, 242, 245, 285, 308; Christ as the, 68; darkening of, 58, 168; sun, moon and stars, 145, 195;

Sunday, 64, 67f., 72

Supper, Lord's, 64, 78, 106, 109, 277; see also Eucharist; great supper of God, 49, 277, 279, 285

Sword, 6, 64, 87f., 138f., 216, 283f.; from the mouth of the Lamb, 11, 72, 88, 281, 286

Symbolism, symbol, 13ff., 41, 73, 81, 83n., 119, 176, 187, 203; see Astrology, Number

Synagogue, 40, 60, 68, 100, 115f., 123, 217; of Satan, 30, 47n., 103

Syncretism, 89, 318

Syria, 17

Tabernacles, feast of, 42, 86, 151-4, 298, 311f.

Targum, 40, 74, 119, 128, 173, 205, 210, 215, 232, 241, 289, 295

Tartarus, 167

Tau (Hebrew Letter), 105, 148, 312

Temple, earthly, 8, 18, 30, 109, 118f., 154, 159, 181f., 304ff.; destroyed, 20, 28, 90; heavenly, 114-21, 142, 193, 240-44; of the church, 20, 104, 182, 207, 209; pagan temples 31, 33, 79, 87, 89, 216; see also Solomon, temple of

Temptation, test, trial, 86, 104, 110; temptations of Jesus, 253f., 303, 315; see peirasmos, Testing

Testimony of Jesus, 59, 205, 210, 241, 251, 280ff.; see also Witness

Three and a half, 46, 179, 187, 204, 231; days 183; years, 8f., 19, 44, 182, 185, 198, 210, 218n.

Throne of God, 6f., 12, 115ff., 128, 294; and of the Lamb, 311f.; of Satan and the beast, 87, 157, 208f., 246, 250; of the saints, 126, 288

Thunder, 118, 139, 178

Thyatira, 72, 91f., 252, 271

Tiamat, 196

Tiberius, 22

Time, 57f., 73, 132, 201; see also Three and a half

Timothy, epistles to, 37, 94n.

Tiridates, 121

Titus, 23, 256

Torah, 122f., 131

Trade-guilds, 33, 92

Trajan, 21, 29, 256, 258

Transfiguration, the, 72

Tree of life, 12, 289f., 307ff., 311, 317, 319

Trinity, 118, 281; Satanic, 9, 214, 248, 295

Trumpets, 7f., 157, 161, 179

Truth and falsehood, 79f., 300, 303, 306

Tubal, 291
Turkey, 5, 29, 57
Twelve, significance of, 15, 302–6; the, 118; 183f., 304; *see also* Apostles
Tyre, 11, 26, 224, 252ff., 267, 270–74; king of, 303, 306

Ugarit, 196n., 232
Unconscious mind, 42f., 169
Universe, number of, 14
Uriel, 160, 170

Vengeance, 49f., 141f., 144; *see also* Retribution, Vindication
Venus, 96
Vespasian, 23, 25, 30, 256
Vesuvius, 24, 136, 163n.
Victory, 198ff., 281f.
Vindication, 102, 141f., 229f.
Vindictiveness, 22, 24, 26, 43, 49
Vitellius, 23, 256
Vulture, 162, 165

Wakefulness, 98f., 120, 266
War, 136f., 222; in heaven, 9, 198ff.
Washing, 66, 100, 119, 151, 153, 239; *see* Robes
Waters, 119, 167, 186, 252f.; waters of chaos, 167, 196, 209, 297; angels of the, 148; water of life, 154, 294, 311
White, 18, 70, 90, 231f., 282f., 316; robes, 100, 108, 118, 151ff., 232, 283; throne, 294

Wilderness, 62, 197f., 203f.
Winepress, 227ff., 282ff.
Witness, 20f., 71, 88; faithful, 65, 80, 138; of Jesus, 59, 107, 266, 282, 319; two witnesses, 180ff., 210f.
Woman, the, 9, 252, 254, 262, 266, 272, 302; opposed by the Dragon, 193ff., 202–5; giving birth to Child, 196ff.; *see* Seed; Offspring; in purple and scarlet, 11, 252ff.; *see* Harlot
Word of God, 59; of Christ, 72, 123, 137, 281, 283
Works, 80, 230f., 294
Wormwood, 164, 224
Worship, 41f., 120, 130ff., 153, 200, 280, 315; *see also* Cult
Wrath, 43, 123f., 143ff., 181, 192, 199f., 205, 226f., 230, 239, 268, 284, 287; of the gods, 163n.; of God, 10, 12, 19, 24, 31, 49, 120, 162, 175, 190, 199f., 224, 227, 230, 232, 284, 294, 306; of the Lamb, 7, 43, 50, 143–6; of Satan, 200, 288, 290

Yahweh, 67, 222, 230; Israel's bridegroom, 109, 194, 198

Zealots, 181, 213
Zerubbabel, 129, 130n., 185, 289
Zeus, 18, 87, 216
Zion, 10, 205, 221, 289, 292, 309; personified, 194, 196, 302
Zodiac, symbols of, 15, 36, 168, 169n., 204, 302, 304, 206n.

# Index of Hebrew, Greek
# and Latin Words

adikein, 86
aeternitas, 61, 278
agapō, 108
aiōn, 225, 240
aiōnios, 225
akathartos, 248, 267
amnos, 128
anathema, 78
anatolē, 148
angelos, 73
aparchē, 223
ap'arti, 231
aparti, 231
apestalmenos, 129
apokalupsis, 57
apōleia, 170, 258
apostolos, 81
apsinthos, 164
arnion, 124f., 128
atē, 227
axios, 245

bala'am, 89
baptō, -izō, 283
basanismos, 269
basileia, 192
bdelugmata, 14
biblaridion, 177
biblion, 122f., 177
blasphēmia, 85
bussinon, 241

chalkolibanos 72
charagma, 217
chlōros, 140

christos, 201
chronisei, 179
chronos, 179

dbr, 139n.
deipnein, 109
diabolos, 85, 201
dikaiōma, 240
dies solis, 68, 72
diplōma, 123
divi filius, 25
divus, 25
drakōn, 196

ecclēsia, 68
echein, 142
edothē, 210, 211n.
ekbale, 183f.
ekdikein, 141
erēmōmenēn, 262
ergon, 231
eskēnōsen, 154
esphagmenon, 124, 128, 142, 209, 276
estrēniasen, 269
ethnos, 240, 308
euangelion, 225
exōthen, 184
ezēsen, 216

fisci Judaici calumnia sublata, 30

Gaios Kaisar, 218n.
gegonan, 299
gēmatria, 15n., 217
Geullah, 131

*ginou*, 86
*gnōsis*, 32, 39

*har mo'ed*, 250
*hōde*, 228
*honestiores*, 64
*hōrmēsan*, 275
*hormēmati*, 275
*Hosanna*, 153
*hubris*, 227, 268
*hupagein*, 223

IAO, 67
*Iēsous*, 217
*isopsēphia*, 15n., 217
*ius gladii*, 87

*kainos*, 91, 297
*katathema*, 311
*kekopiakas*, 81
*klinē*, 95
*koinē*, 16n.
*koinon*, 310
*kopos*, 81, 231
*kopsontai epi*, 67, 271
*koros*, 227
*kosmos*, 104
*krima*, 275
*krisis*, 226
*kubernētēs*, 273
*kuriakē*, 68

*latreuein*, 153, 312
*limnē*, 286
*linon*, 241
*lithon* 241
*lousanti*, 66
*lusanti*, 66

*machaira*, 88
*mammon*, 271
*marana tha*, 319
*martus*, 88, 319
*marturōn*, 319
*marturia*, 19

*martures*, 255
*mellein*, 85
*minim*, 100n.
*mustērion*, 254

*nai*, 67, 319
*naos*, 142, 183
*nemesis*, 144, 227
*nikan*, 80, 82, 128, 199
*nikolaos*, 89

*orgē*, 193
*orgisthē*, 205
*ōrgisthēsan*, 192

*pantokratōr*, 67, 249
*parestai*, 259
*parousia*, 17, 82, 109, 137, 259
*parthenos*, 222
*peirasmos*, 104, 110
*peirazein*, 86
*penthos*, 269
*pepōkan*, 268
*peptōkan*, 268
*phialai*, 241
*philō*, 108
*phōstēr*, 304
*piyilē*, 241
*planan*, 94
*plēgē*, 210
*poiein*, 211
*poimainein*, 96, 197, 283
*presbuteros*, 38
*presbuteroi*, 118
*pseudēs*, 300
*pseudos*, 138
*psuchē*, 272

*qinah*, 108

*redivivus*, see Nero
*relegatio ad insulam*, 64
*religio licita*, 26n.
*rhabdos*, 97
*rhomphaia*, 88

*sardius,* 117
*Sebastē,* 68
*sebaoth,* 67, 249
*shakan,* 154n.
*shebet,* 97
*shakinah,* 154, 298, 304
*skandalon,* 274
*skandalisei,* 274
*skēnē,* 154, 298
*skēnoun,* 153, 154n., 298
*sōteria,* 152
*sperma,* 205
*sphragis,* 148
*strēnos,* 268

*strēniasantes,* 271
*stēlai,* 105n.
*stuloi,* 105n.

*tērein,* 60, 99
*thanatos,* 95, 140, 269
*theion,* 173
*thlipsis,* 153
*thumos,* 226f., 268

*xulon,* 83n., 311n

*Yotser,* 41, 116, 131